Property of:
El Camino College
Social Justice Center
Please Check Book Out At Information Desk

Civil
Rights
in Peril:

The Targeting of Arabs and Muslims

Property of
El Camino College
Social Justice Center

DISCARDED

Civil
Rights
in Peril:

The Targeting of
Arabs and Muslims

Edited by Elaine C. Hagopian

Haymarket
Books

Chicago, Illinois

PLUTO PRESS

London
Ann Arbor, Michigan

© 2004 Trans-Arab Research Institute

First published 2004 by Haymarket Books and Pluto Press

Haymarket Books
P.O. Box 180165, Chicago, IL 60618
www.haymarketbooks.org

Pluto Press
345 Archway Road, London N6 5AA
and 839 Greene St., Ann Arbor, MI 48104
www.plutobooks.com

The right of the individual contributors to be identified as the authors
of this work has been asserted by them in accordance with the
Copyright, Designs and Patents Act 1988.

Library of Congress Cataloging-in-Publication Data

Civil rights in peril : the targeting of Arabs and Muslims / by Elaine C.
Hagopian, editor.
      p. cm.
Includes bibliographical references.
  ISBN 0-7453-2265-4 (hardcover) — ISBN 0-7453-2264-6 (pbk.)
  1. Arab Americans—Civil rights. 2. Muslims—Civil rights—United
States. 3. Arab Americans—Legal status, laws, etc. 4. Muslims—Legal
status, laws, etc.—United States. 5. War on Terrorism, 2001—Social
aspects. 6. War on Terrorism, 2001—Political aspects. 7. Racism—
United States. 8. United States—Race relations. 9. United States—
Politics and government—2001- 10. United States—Foreign relations—
2001- I. Hagopian, Elaine Catherine, 1933-
E184.A65C585 2004
323.1192'7073'090511—dc22
                                        2003026559

British Library Cataloguing-in-Publication Data
A catalogue record for this book is available from the British Library.

ISBN: 0-7453-2265-4 (hardcover)
ISBN: 0-7453-2264-6 (paperback)

10 09 08 07 06 05 04 1 2 3 4 5 6 7

Designed and produced by Eric Ruder, redrhinodesign.com

Printed in Canada

CONTENTS

ACKNOWLEDGMENTS

Any editor of a multi-authored book is first and foremost indebted to the individual authors. M. Cherif Bassiouni, who authored the introduction, Susan M. Akram and Kevin R. Johnson, Nancy Murray, Robert Morlino, Will Youmans, Samih Farsoun, and Naseer Aruri produced their chapters in a timely fashion and with a moral commitment that stemmed from their sense of human rights and just laws. In each step of the process, their cooperation was outstanding.

I owe a special debt of gratitude to Drs. Nancy Murray and Naseer Aruri. Their critical expertise in reviewing and evaluating each of the chapters is what has made this book an important and comprehensive analysis of the violation of American constitutional principles, and specifically the Bill of Rights, involved in the targeting of Arabs and Muslims. I am also indebted to Dr. Naseer Aruri, who, as president of the Trans-Arab Research Institute, commissioned this book as a resource for civil rights and antidiscrimination workers.

Finally, I express my deep appreciation for the informed and patient staff at Haymarket Books: Anthony Arnove, Ahmed Shawki, and Julie Fain. Ahmed Shawki's critical review of the chapters added clarity and value to the completed work. Anthony Arnove extended himself to accommodate the concerns authors had regarding various technical issues of production. His extraordinary patience and expertise resolved all concerns expeditiously. Copy editor Mikki Smith gallantly reconciled the differences of authors' preferred styles to a consistent and readable one.

PREFACE

The emergence of the United States as the sole superpower after the demise of the Soviet Union in the early 1990s coincided with the rise and solidification of the new radical Right, which brought together neoconservatives, Christian Evangelicals, and the pro-Israel lobby. The ascendancy of George W. Bush to the presidency ushered into government the coherent set of neoconservatives whose decades-long strategic planning for the US role in the post–cold war world was in full vigor. Buttressed by the Christian Right and the pro-Israel lobby, along with a wide array of institutes, forums, and organizations, the neoconservatives favored an American global expansion secured through exemplary, unilateral, preventive war unrestrained by international law. The oil-rich and strategically located central Asian and Middle Eastern regions were seen as the trigger areas for this bold enterprise. More specifically, and for all sorts of propaganda, political, economic, geographic, and military reasons, Afghanistan and Iraq were the first candidates for preventive war. Iraq, however, was the priority target.

The abhorrent events of September 11, 2001, provided a mobilizing banner under which the new strategy and goal of global reach could be pursued. The pre–September 11 "war on terrorism," which had singled out Arabs and Muslims, was given vigorous new life. The post–September 11 focus on terrorism allowed the Bush administration to pursue its quest for control in the Middle Eastern and central Asian areas as well as to enact laws and regulations in rapid succession that abridged human and civil rights. Arabs and Muslims in the United States were targeted for investigation and prosecution under these laws. The demonization of Arabs and Muslims as terrorists served to "justify" war on Afghanistan and Iraq as well as the intimidation of other regional countries. It also fed prejudice and accelerated "legal" discrimination against Arabs and Muslims in the United States.

This book analyzes the way that the demonization of Arab and Muslim communities facilitates the legal, political, and social diminution of their civil and human rights. Although the process began earlier, it gathered speed as a result of the climate following September 11, 2001. The targeting of Arabs and Muslims as the "enemy within" and the creation of new legislation, regulations, data banks, and technologies that potentially affect every citizen and noncitizen bring particular urgency to the subject. The intention of this volume is to lay bare the interplay of domestic and foreign policy that must be understood if we are to reverse the dangerous course on which the nation is embarked and restore rights guaranteed under the US Constitution.

The book is divided into three parts. Part 1 focuses on the legislation and regulations affecting civil liberties before and after September 11, 2001, and includes specific case studies. Law professors Susan M. Akram and Kevin R. Johnson cover the pre–September 11 period, demonstrating how ideological exclusion and secret evidence frameworks were manipulated negatively against Arabs and Muslims. Nancy Murray, director of the American Civil Liberties Union of Massachusetts' Bill of Rights Education Project, documents the post–September 11 measures that have subverted constitutional rights and protections in the name of the domestic "war against terrorism."

Part 2 examines how the demonization of Arabs and Muslims is sustained through the manufacturing of racist images. Media play a key role in keeping public fear and dislike of Arabs and Muslims activated to support the most egregious violation of their rights here and aggression abroad. Media specialist and researcher Robert Morlino presents his review of the portrayal of Arabs and Muslims in politically diverse and varied media vehicles. Will Youmans, graduate of the Boalt Hall School of Law at the University of California, Berkeley, exposes select pro-Israel institutional networks that feed anti-Arab and anti-Muslim images into public circles. The incessant barrage of negative images against Arabs and Muslims from what appear to be scholarly and expert sources perpetuates the phobia against Arabs and Muslims and prepares the way for repressive governmental measures.

Part 3 examines the convergence of the domestic shift in the United States to the Far Right and the Bush Doctrine, leading to the criminalization of Arab and Muslim communities as communities. Sociology professor Samih Farsoun traces the roots of the present American antiterrorism campaign to the resurgence of the right wing in this country after the liberalizing period of the 1960s. Political science professor Naseer Aruri reviews current American foreign policy and analyzes how Bush's antiterrorism crusade hinges on creation of fear among the American public, providing the president majority support for aggression in and control of central Asia and the Middle East. Sociology professor Elaine Hagopian focuses on how US political actors work to shape images of Arabs and Muslims in the Middle East by promoting "good and friendly" exile leaders, committed to recognizing Israel and developing secular governments, in contrast to existing "evil and hostile" Arab and Muslim leaders, who are portrayed negatively for particular political goals.

Elaine C. Hagopian
Boston, July 2003

DON'T TREAD ON ME: IS THE WAR ON TERROR REALLY A WAR ON RIGHTS?*

M. Cherif Bassiouni

The Declaration of Independence heralded the values of freedom, justice, and equality in a country whose government was accountable to the people. The Constitution and the Bill of Rights enshrined these and other principles, which became the hallmark of this country. We extolled the virtues of our legal system and held it as a model to others.

Across 200 years, the progress has been steady in affirming constitutional rights and embedding the rule of law in our society.

Among the memorable road hazards of that historic trip are Lincoln's suspension of habeas corpus during the Civil War, Roosevelt's internment of Japanese Americans, and Senator Joseph McCarthy's witch-hunt for Communists or their sympathizers among Americans of all walks of life but particularly among intellectuals and the movie industry.

But the nation has never before seen a more systematic erosion of civil rights than after 9/11. This has taken the form of undermining the legal system, coupled with egregious governmental abuses of power, all in the name of combating terrorism.

The targets of these measures have been Arabs and Muslims, but the effects extend to everyone.

---

*©2003, *Chicago Tribune*. Originally published in the *Chicago Tribune* on August 24, 2003. Reprinted with permission.

The erosion actually started in 1996 with antiterrorism and immigration legislation. Permanent residents who were recognized by the Constitution's equal-protection clause as having most of the rights enjoyed by citizens were stripped of them. Noncitizens could be arrested and deported on "secret evidence," which revoked the constitutional right to confront and cross-examine evidence presented against them.

This was precisely the practice used by dictatorial regimes the US has repeatedly denounced since the cold war.

After September 11, 2001, the administration embarked on a series of measures that started with a wave of arrests of aliens whose status was irregular. But the administration's campaign only focused on people of Arab origin and others who were Muslims. Their numbers were not confirmed, their status undisclosed, and their cases' outcomes have not been revealed.

The Justice Department's inspector general reported that many cases were unjustified and many individuals were harshly treated, something heretofore deemed shocking by our legal standards.

Two years later the US Circuit Court of Appeals for the District of Columbia, in a 2–1 decision, reversed an earlier federal court ruling ordering the government to release the names of hundreds of people detained after September 11. One of the concurring judges wrote, "America faces an enemy just as real as its former Cold War foes, with capabilities beyond the capacity of the judiciary to explore."

The government contended that the disclosure of even one name would compromise national security. In a courageous dissent, however, Judge David Tatel wrote that the majority's "uncritical deference" to the government's vague assertions not only contravened the purpose of the Freedom of Information Act but prevented the American people from discovering whether the present administration "is violating the constitutional rights of hundreds of persons whom it has detained in connection with the terrorism investigation."

The war in Afghanistan brought about another type of violation, the placing of enemy war prisoners in Guantánamo Bay, Cuba. Their detention without due process is in clear violation of our international legal obligation under the Third Geneva Convention.

The convention requires the US to properly adjudicate their

status as prisoners of war and to treat them well. It also provides for their release after the conflict ends. The conflict is over, but they are still detained. Moreover, they were treated in a manner that may fall in the category of torture: sensory deprivation, prolonged hooding and solitary confinement, degrading and humiliating treatment.

All of that was glossed over and no one from the US media or human rights organizations was allowed to go inside, view the conditions of detention, and talk to the detainees.

Among the detainees were people ages 15 to 95, including some who were sick. Secretly, some of them were released to avoid embarrassment, and soon the remaining ones will be released or tried by military commission before which their rights to a fair and impartial defense will not be guaranteed.

US courts have shockingly refused to review this situation on the fictitious grounds that Guantánamo Bay, a territory leased from Cuba by the US, is not part of the United States. Our courts found that they are not competent to examine what our troops are doing to their prisoners.

That is simply absurd, and judges with moral courage must reverse this position.

The arrests and indictments under the USA PATRIOT Act, which Attorney General John Ashcroft has defended in a series of appearances around the nation, turned out in some cases to be media blitzes. At his October 2002 appearance in Chicago, Ashcroft claimed that contributions of a Chicago-area Muslim charity had been converted into "terrorist blood money."

The proceedings did not prove what had been proclaimed. Nevertheless, the funds were seized. Its president, Enaam Arnaout, had no choice but to plead guilty to a single count of "racketeering conspiracy," totally unrelated to funding terrorism. The charge arose out of the fact that he provided legitimate humanitarian assistance to the Afghan rebels who fought the Soviet Union's occupation of Afghanistan, this at a time when the rebels were also being supported by the United States.

He also provided legitimate assistance to the Bosnians fighting for their independence—a cause that the US also supported.

But because he did not disclose that assistance to the corporate directors and funders of the charity, the behavior was deemed a crime. Before and during his trial, Arnaout was kept in solitary confinement twenty-three hours a day, with one hour a day to view sunlight from the rooftop of a federal detention center.

In another case of abuse of power, University of South Florida professor Sami al-Arian is being held on charges of conspiracy to provide "material support" to the Palestinian Islamic Jihad.

According to the 50-count indictment, al-Arian is also charged with conspiracy to commit racketeering, conspiracy to murder and maim persons abroad, conspiracy to violate a 1995 executive order forbidding transactions with organizations the government deems "specially designated terrorists," and obstruction of justice.

For now, he is held in solitary confinement, and, in order to see his wife and children under guard supervision and through a glass partition, he must submit to a strip search before and after the visit. This is clearly abuse of power designed to degrade and humiliate a person, a violation of the Constitution.

In another case, a Detroit jury acquitted two of four defendants on charges that they provided "material support" to terrorists. The four men, Arab immigrants, were alleged to have been part of a sleeper cell that aided terrorists by fundraising and manufacturing false documents.

Then there is the case of the so-called Lackawanna Six, who were said to be a sleeper terrorist cell. This too proved false, but the defendants had no choice but to plead guilty to lesser charges. Last but not least are the cases of two US citizens, Jose Padilla and Yaser Esam Hamdi, who are held without charges, without visitation rights, and without access to counsel for an indefinite period of time.

Both are held under a controversial presidential order declaring them "unlawful enemy combatants."

No one knows exactly what it means, but it places them outside the protection of the Constitution. There is no constitutional basis for the president to suspend the rights of US citizens.

While the ACLU and other organizations have opposed these unconstitutional measures, the organized bar has been circumspect. The media has occasionally discussed these cases, but in a guarded manner, seldom denouncing them.

What is at issue is not only the specifics of these and other cases of violations of the Constitution and abuses of power, but the broader issue of the rule of law's fate in this country. For sure, throughout our history, there have been many miscarriages of justice against individuals and classes of people, particularly people of color, but never before has there been such an insidious and systematic undermining of the rule of law and due process of law.

This is what we must be concerned about.

Now we learn that some 5,000 Iraqis have been held as prisoners without any legal process.

What has the notion of laws come to?

After the Nazi regime, a story spread throughout the world about a Protestant pastor by the name of Martin Niemoller, who said, "At first they came for the Jews and I did not speak out—because I was not a Jew. Then they came for the Communists, and I did not speak out—because I was not a Communist. Then they came for the Catholics, and I did not speak out—because I was a Protestant. And then they came for me, and by that time there was no one left to speak out."

PART I

PRE– AND POST–SEPTEMBER 11, 2001, LEGISLATION AND REGULATIONS AFFECTING CIVIL LIBERTIES

CHAPTER 1

RACE AND CIVIL RIGHTS
PRE–SEPTEMBER 11, 2001:
THE TARGETING OF ARABS AND MUSLIMS*

Susan M. Akram and Kevin R. Johnson

The federal government's response to the tragedy of September 11, 2001, demonstrates the close relationship between immigration law and civil rights in the United States. Noncitizens historically have been vulnerable to civil rights deprivations, in no small part because the law permits, and arguably encourages, extreme governmental conduct with minimal protections for the rights of noncitizens. Unfortunately, the current backlash against Arabs and Muslims fits comfortably into a long history of US government efforts to stifle political dissent.[1] This backlash is especially troubling because of the possibility—exemplified by the internment of persons of Japanese ancestry during World War II—that racial, religious, and other differences have fueled the animosity toward Arabs and Muslims.

It is in the context of a particular historical and legal environment that the post–September 11 targeting of Arabs and Muslims must be understood, as this context both explains Arab and Muslim fears in time of crisis and permits such targeting to be acceptable in the public eye. Such government, public, and private acts as the unjustified FBI investigations of Arab- or Muslim-owned

---

*Originally published as part of a longer article, "Race, Civil Rights, and Immigration Law After September 11, 2001: The Targeting of Arabs and Muslims," in the *NYU Annual Survey of American Law* 58, no. 3 (2002): 295–356 [58 N.Y.U. Ann. Surv. Am. L. 295 (2002)].

businesses, or the closing of Muslim and Arab bank accounts, or the shutting down of Muslim charities, or FBI visits to mosques and Muslim/Arab academics, or "special registration" and other targeted monitoring of persons only of Arab origin or Muslim faith have become quite an accepted part of the "war on terrorism." Yet, should either the government or others target white Irish Catholics or Jews or another racial/ethnic minority in such a sustained manner, they would doubtless face significant and vociferous challenge for racial or religious profiling.

Commentators have observed how popular perceptions of racial and other minorities influence their treatment under the law.[2] As with other minority groups, this seems true for Arabs and Muslims. As Professor Natsu Saito summarizes,

> Arab Americans and Muslims have been "raced" as "terrorists": foreign, disloyal, and imminently threatening. Although Arabs trace their roots to the Middle East and claim many different religious backgrounds, and Muslims come from all over the world ..., these distinctions are blurred and negative images about either Arabs or Muslims are often attributed to both. As Ibrahim Hooper of the Council on American-Islamic Relations notes, "The common stereotypes are that we're all Arabs, we're all violent and we're all conducting a holy war."[3]

The demonization of Arabs and Muslims in the United States, accompanied by harsh legal measures directed at them, began well before the tragedy of September 11, 2001.[4] It can be traced to popular stereotypes,[5] years of mythmaking by film and media,[6] racism during times of national crisis,[7] and a campaign to build political support for US foreign policy in the Middle East.[8] Since at least the 1970s, US laws and policies have been founded on the assumption that Arab and Muslim noncitizens are potential terrorists and have targeted this group for special treatment under the law.[9] The post–September 11 targeting of Muslims and Arabs is simply the latest chapter in this history.[10]

The stereotyping of Arabs as terrorists and religious fanatics

Similar to the animus toward other racial minorities, anti-Arab, anti-Muslim animus can be viewed as part of a dynamic process of "racialization."[11] Racialization, as used here, views "race" as "an unstable and 'de-centered' complex of social meanings constantly being transformed by political struggle."[12]

This understanding of race breaks with the traditional view that race is fixed by biology; it instead considers "racial formation" to explain how race operates in the United States.[13]

Defining race as a process in which racial difference is socially, not biologically, constructed assists in examining the treatment of Arabs and Muslims in the United States; their experiences show the severe damage that racialization can do and offer hope that the process can be reversed.[14] Recognizing that race is the product of social construction, the US Supreme Court held that different groups may be racialized and that Arabs can be discriminated against as members of a different "race" in violation of the civil rights laws.[15]

Through the process of racialization, Arabs and Muslims have been considered racially different from whites and other racial minorities. Professor Nabeel Abraham, a leading commentator on racism against Arabs and Muslims in the United States, identifies three distinct ways in which Arabs and Muslims have been racialized: (1) through political violence by extremist groups based on the Arab-Israeli conflict in the Middle East, (2) by xenophobic violence targeting Arabs and Muslims at the local level, and (3) through the hostility arising from international crises affecting the United States and its citizens.[16] The law and its enforcement also have contributed to hostility toward Arabs and Muslims in the United States.[17]

The silencing of Arabs through politically motivated violence and intimidation

Conflict in the Middle East provokes violence against Arabs and Muslims in the United States, as well as the lesser-known intimidation tactics followed by some mainstream activist organizations. A Rand Corporation study conducted for the US Department of Energy concludes that the Jewish Defense League (JDL) was, for more than a decade, one of the most active terrorist groups, as classified by the FBI, in the United States.[18] The study reviews the violence known to have been committed by the JDL, as well as incidents in which the JDL's involvement was suspected, all of which was described as part of a strategy "to eliminate perceived enemies of the Jewish people and Israel."[19] The violence included bombings of Arab foreign offices and planting bombs in American-Arab Anti-Discrimination Committee offices across the country.[20] According to the FBI, Jewish extremist organizations were responsible for twenty terrorist incidents in the 1980s.[21]

Despite the many incidents of anti-Arab violence at the hands of Jewish extremist groups, influential hate-crime studies fail to include these groups as perpetrators of these crimes.[22] According to Professor Abraham, "Jewish extremist groups constitute an undeniable source of anti-Arab hate violence not discussed in conventional accounts of racist violence in the United States."[23]

Even less publicized than the anti-Arab violence of extremist groups is the campaign by mainstream organizations, such as the Anti-Defamation League of B'nai B'rith (ADL), to intimidate and silence Arabs and Muslims. Established in the early 1900s as an organization with the mission of fighting anti-Semitism, the ADL gained a reputation as a leading antidiscrimination organization in the United States. Unfortunately, after the creation of Israel in 1948, the ADL added a new mission: to discredit or silence critics of Israel or defenders of Palestinian human rights.[24] The ADL has aggressively engaged in efforts to intimidate Arabs, Muslims, and others with similar views on the Middle East conflict, discouraging them from participating in political debate. In 1983, for example, the ADL released a handbook entitled *Pro-Arab Propaganda in America: Vehicles and Voices.*[25] It lists as "anti-Israel propagandists" some of the most prominent scholars on Middle East issues, including Columbia University's Edward Said and Harvard University's Walid Khalidi, as well as humanitarian organizations dealing with the Middle East or Palestine. Alfred Lilienthal, an influential commentator on Middle East issues, himself on the ADL's blacklist, claims, "Many ADL charges against critics of Israel are totally inaccurate, questionable, or based upon half-truths," and the ADL often characterizes groups or individuals who criticize Israel or Zionism as "extremists" intent on eradicating Israel or inciting anti-Semitism in America.[26] The ADL handbook was widely distributed throughout the United States to, according to critics, challenge, harass, and silence groups and individuals on the list.

The ADL is not the only mainstream organization to distribute lists of Arab American individuals and groups and those working with them. The American Israel Public Affairs Committee (AIPAC) issued two similar lists.[27] Through a campaign, primarily on college campuses, organized against groups and individuals on these lists, AIPAC and the ADL have harassed and intimidated academics and activists for years.[28]

Aside from its campaign to discredit and silence academics on university campuses, the ADL has also sought to silence pro-Muslim and pro-Arab speakers from engaging in public debate concerning the Middle East. Most recently, the Florida ADL unsuccessfully lobbied the Florida Commission on Human Relations to exclude a Muslim representative from a panel at a civil rights conference.[29] Similarly, the American Jewish Committee sought to exclude Ghazi Khankan, executive director of the New York chapter of the Council on American-Islamic Relations (CAIR), from participating in a public forum on multicultural understanding because he was "anti-Israel."[30] The ADL demanded that CAIR's Northern California director be prevented from testifying about hate crimes before the California Select Committee on Hate Crimes.[31]

The full extent of the ADL's activities against Arabs did not come to light until January 1993, when the results of an FBI investigation of a veteran San Francisco Police Department officer and an ADL-paid undercover agent became public. Law enforcement authorities uncovered computerized files on thousands of Arab Americans and information on Arab organizations, as well as many other mainstream organizations.[32] These files reflected surveillance of organizations and leaders, including the NAACP, Greenpeace, the ACLU, the Asian Law Caucus, the National Lawyers Guild, the Rainbow Coalition, Jews for Jesus, and three current or past members of the US Congress.[33] The information included confidential law enforcement files and information from the Department of Motor Vehicles.[34] The FBI confirmed that the ADL provided information from the surveillance activities to the South African government.[35] The ADL's attorney admitted that the ADL had passed surveillance information to Israel.[36] At least one US citizen of Arab descent who had been the subject of surveillance was arrested in Israel when he visited the Israeli-occupied Palestinian territories.[37] When the spying became public, an array of civil rights lawsuits was filed.[38] As part of the settlement of a class action, the ADL was permanently enjoined from illegal spying on Arab American and other civil rights groups.[39]

Despite the settlement and the permanent injunction, the

damage to the civil liberties of Arabs in the United States from
the ADL's surveillance activities has been done. The discovery of
espionage has contributed to the climate of fear for Arab and
Muslim Americans. US intelligence agencies may have obtained
information from the ADL that could potentially place politically
active Arab groups and individuals under heightened government
scrutiny.[40] Consequently, Arab Americans may perceive that the
US government is in collusion with Israeli and anti-Arab organizations. Such perceptions have been reinforced by the revelation
that information provided by the ADL triggered the FBI investigation and arrest of the "LA Eight," a group of noncitizens, for
alleged technical violations of the Immigration and Nationality
Act (INA).[41] Furthermore, "no ... major American Jewish organization has condemned the ADL for its political excesses or its
documented association with Israeli intelligence organizations."[42]
Our research has not discovered any publication in which the
ADL admitted culpability or disavowed these activities.

In sum, the ADL has engaged in surveillance of Arab and
Muslim groups in an apparent effort to intimidate and silence
those voices it deems "anti-Semitic."[43] As Professor Abraham
summarizes: "The overall effect of the ADL's practices is to reinforce the image of Arabs as terrorists and security threats,
thereby creating a climate of fear, suspicion, and hostility towards Arab-Americans and others who espouse critical views of
Israel, possibly leading to death threats and bodily harm."[44]

The impact of anti-Arab images in popular culture

Racism against Arabs is not all the work of political activists.
Importantly, media and film, feeding on existing stereotypes in
US society about Arabs and Muslims, have found a ready audience for dangerous and one-dimensional images. Such depictions
contribute to the racialization of Arabs and Muslims. In addition, in a study on anti-Arab racism, Professor Abraham documents a range of racial epithets, intolerant speech, and violence
directed at Arabs by private citizens and public officials.[45]

Jack Shaheen's review of US films offers convincing evidence
of the vilification of Arabs and Muslims by the movie industry.
Shaheen catalogs hundreds of Hollywood movies in which
Arabs or Muslims are portrayed as terrorists or otherwise placed
in a negative, often nonhuman, light. Muslims are shown as hos-

tile invaders or "lecherous, oily sheikhs intent on using nuclear weapons."[46] A far-too-common scene shows a mosque with Arabs at prayer, then cuts away to show civilians being gunned down.

These movies show Westerners hurling such epithets at Arabs as "assholes," "bastards," "camel-dicks," "pigs," "devil-worshipers," "jackals," "rats," "rag-heads," "towel-heads," "scum-buckets," "sons-of-dogs," "buzzards of the jungle," "sons-of-whores," "sons-of-unnamed goats," and "sons-of-she-camels."[47] Arab women are often portrayed as weak and mute, covered in black, or as scantily clad belly dancers.

The US Department of Defense has cooperated with Hollywood in making more than a dozen films showing US soldiers killing Arabs and Muslims. Audiences apparently embrace the demonization in these movies. As Shaheen notes,

> To my knowledge, no Hollywood WWI, WWII, or Korean War movie has ever shown America's fighting forces slaughtering children. Yet, near the conclusion of [the movie] Rules of Engagement, US marines open fire on the Yemenis, shooting 83 men, women, and children. During the scene, viewers rose to their feet, clapped and cheered. Boasts director Friedkin, "I've seen audiences stand up and applaud the film throughout the United States."[48]

One-sided film portrayals omit images of Arabs and Muslims as ordinary people with families and friends or as outstanding members of communities, scholars, writers, or scientists. Few US movies have depicted Arabs or Muslims in a favorable light and even fewer have included them in leading roles. Commentators rarely criticize the unbalanced depiction of Arabs and Muslims.[49] The stereotyping and demonization of Arabs and Muslims by American films may well have gone largely unnoticed because these characterizations are entirely consistent with widespread attitudes in US society.

Reinforcing the anti-Arab, anti-Muslim stereotypes in film, public officials have openly used intolerant speech toward Arabs and Muslims—speech that would be clearly unacceptable if directed at other minority groups.[50] For example, a mayoral candidate in Dearborn, Michigan, a suburb of Detroit, distributed a campaign brochure in which he claimed the city's Arab Americans "threaten our neighborhoods, the value of our property and a darned good way of life."[51] In 1981, the governor of

Michigan proclaimed that Michigan's economic woes were due to the "damn Arabs."[52] Such statements by public officials fuel the perception that prejudice and animosity directed at Arabs and Muslims are socially acceptable.

Moreover, prominent politicians have returned financial contributions from Arab American and American Muslim groups, fearing the political risks of the acceptance of such monies. For example, in the 1984 presidential campaign, Walter Mondale returned five thousand dollars in contributions made by US citizens of Arab ancestry.[53] Philadelphia mayoral candidate Wilson Goode returned more than two thousand dollars in campaign contributions from Arab Americans.[54] In his first congressional race, Joe Kennedy returned one hundred dollars to James Abourezk, a former US senator who is Arab American.[55] New York senator Hillary Clinton returned fifty thousand dollars to Muslim organizations.[56] Although several of these politicians stated that they returned the funds because of the contributors' anti-Semitic remarks, the perception remains that Arabs and Muslims cannot participate in the body politic. For similar reasons, New York City mayor Rudolph Giuliani returned ten million dollars donated by a Saudi Arabian prince for the victims of the World Trade Center destruction due to a public outcry caused by the contributor's criticism of US foreign policy in the Middle East.[57]

Racism in times of national crisis

Hostility toward minorities often accompanies times of crisis in the United States. For Arabs and Muslims, this may be even more problematic. Perpetrators of hate crimes against Arabs and Muslims frequently fail to differentiate among persons based on religion or ethnic origin, from Pakistanis, Indians, Iranians, and Japanese to Muslims, Sikhs, and Christian Arabs.[58] The widespread perception in the United States is that Arabs and Muslims are identical and eager to wage a holy war against the United States. In fact, according to a 1993 report, only 12 percent of the Muslims in the United States are Arab,[59] and Arab Muslims at that time were even a minority in the Arab American community.[60] Although there are Muslim extremists, the majority of Muslims are "decent, law-abiding, productive citizens."[61]

Because of the lack of differentiation between different types of

Arabs and Muslims, terrorist acts by small groups of Arabs and Muslims often have been followed by generalized hostility toward entire communities of Arabs and Muslims in the United States. For example, after Lebanese Shiite gunmen in 1985 hijacked TWA Flight 847 to Beirut, beat an American on the plane to death, and held the remaining passengers hostage for more than two weeks,[62] violent attacks against persons of Arab and Muslim origin occurred across the United States. Islamic centers and Arab American organizations were vandalized and threatened. A Houston mosque was firebombed. A bomb exploded in the American-Arab Anti-Discrimination Committee office in Boston, severely injuring two police officers.[63] Later that same year, after terrorists hijacked the *Achille Lauro* cruise liner and murdered a passenger, a wave of anti-Arab violence swept the country, including the bombing of an American-Arab Anti-Discrimination Committee office that killed its regional executive director.[64]

In 1986, in apparent response to the Reagan administration's "war on terrorism" directed at Libya, another episode of anti-Arab harassment and violence broke out. The same night as a US bombing raid on Libya, the American-Arab Anti-Discrimination Committee national office in Washington received threats. Shortly thereafter, the Detroit American-Arab Anti-Discrimination Committee office, the Dearborn Arab Community Center, and the Detroit Arab American newspaper received bomb threats.[65] Threats, beatings, and other violent attacks on Arabs were reported across the United States. At this time, someone broke into a Palestinian family's home, set off a smoke bomb inside the house, and painted slogans such as "Go Back to Libya" on the walls.[66]

The first Gulf War intensified anti-Arab hostility in the United States. The American-Arab Anti-Discrimination Committee reported four anti-Arab hate crimes for 1990 before the invasion of Kuwait in August of that year. Between the invasion and February 1991, the committee reported 175 incidents.[67] When US intervention commenced in January 1991, Arab and Muslim businesses and community organizations were bombed, vandalized, and subjected to harassment.[68]

The US government and the role of law

Institutional racism through the law and its enforcement has contributed to the racialization and targeting of Arabs and Muslims. The federal government's actions taken in the name of fighting terrorism have been followed by indiscriminate threats and violence against Arabs and Muslims in the United States. This frightening pattern has repeated itself in the wake of September 11.[69]

The Nixon administration's "Operation Boulder" was an early effort of the US government to target Arabs in the United States for special investigation and discourage their political activism on Middle Eastern issues.[70] Ostensibly designed to confront the threat posed by terrorists who took hostages and murdered athletes at the 1972 Munich Olympics, the president's directives authorized the FBI to investigate people of "Arabic origin" to determine their potential relationship with "terrorist" activities related to the Arab-Israeli conflict.[71] The FBI admittedly wiretapped prominent Detroit lawyer Abdeen Jabara, then president of the Association of Arab-American University Graduates.[72]

Later in the 1970s, President Carter took numerous steps against Iranians and Iran in response to the crisis in which US citizens were held hostage in Tehran. In the 1980s, the Reagan administration's foreign policy also involved combating "terrorism." President Reagan in 1986 announced that the US government had evidence that Libyan leader Muammar Qaddafi was responsible for terrorist attacks, such as those at the Rome and Vienna airports, and was planning further attacks in the United States.[73] The US Navy later that year shot down two Libyan planes off the coast of Libya. President Reagan announced that "we have the evidence" that Qaddafi was sending hit teams to assassinate the US president.[74] Despite official responses from the Austrian, Italian, and Israeli governments that there was no evidence of Libyan involvement in the Rome and Vienna attacks or that any Libyan "hit squads" had been sent to the United States,[75] the United States bombed Libya. Violence against US residents of Arab or Middle Eastern origin and vandalism of their community centers, mosques, businesses, and homes followed the public announcements.

In the 1990s, after the US invasion of Kuwait, the US government's "war on terrorism" shifted focus to Iraq and its leader, Saddam Hussein. The Bush administration accused Iraqi forces of atrocities against Kuwaitis. The administration then launched a surveillance program directed at Arab Americans. The FBI interrogated Arab and Muslim leaders, activists, and antiwar demonstrators across the country.[76] The Department of Justice instituted fingerprinting of all residents and immigrants of Arab origin in the United States; the Federal Aviation Administration commenced a system of airline profiling of persons from the Arab world.[77] Private harassment and violence against Arab and Muslim communities followed.

Foreign policy has played a large role in immigration measures directed at Arabs and Muslims in the United States. The Immigration and Naturalization Service (INS)[78] sought to deport noncitizens of Palestinian ancestry[79] at the same time that the federal government attempted to shut down Palestine Liberation Organization (PLO) offices in the United States and at the United Nations.[80] In the 1980s, President Reagan issued a secret National Security Decision Directive that authorized the creation of a network of agencies designed to prevent "terrorists" from entering or remaining in the United States. Under one proposal, intelligence agencies would provide the INS with "names, nationalities and other identifying data and evidence relating to *alien undesirables and suspected terrorists* believed to be in ... the U.S."[81] The Alien Border Control Committee also considered an INS-created strategy outlined in a document entitled "Alien Terrorists and Undesirables: A Contingency Plan." The strategy called for mass arrests and detentions of noncitizens from Arab nations and Iran, and suggested using ideological exclusion grounds in the immigration laws to remove noncitizens from Arab countries and Iran already in the United States.[82]

Efforts to stifle political dissent: The case of the LA Eight

Critics long have pointed out that the United States has discriminated against Arabs and Muslims in applying the terrorist exclusion provisions of the INA, the comprehensive US immigration law.[83] Arabs, particularly Palestinians, are the primary groups subject to many of the terrorism provisions. During the first Gulf War crisis, for example, government officials fingerprinted and photographed all entrants to the US who held Iraqi or Kuwaiti passports without regard to evidence of past terrorist activities or sympathies.[84]

Related to the terrorist provisions in the immigration laws are those permitting exclusion of noncitizens based on political beliefs or associations, passed during the anticommunist fervor of the McCarthy era.[85] The courts generally upheld application of the ideological exclusions, which provoked sharp academic criticism. In 1977, Congress enacted the McGovern Amendment, which permitted the attorney general to waive the exclusion of any noncitizen affiliated with an organization proscribed by the United States.[86] In 1979, Congress created a single exception to the McGovern Amendment that denied the exclusion waiver for only one group: PLO officials or representatives.[87] In any event, through a variety of means, consular officers could continue to exclude a person based on ideology.

The federal government's efforts to remove the LA Eight illustrate the extremes to which it will resort in order to deport political dissidents from the country.[88] The case began before dawn on January 26, 1987, when officers of the FBI, INS, and Los Angeles Police Department descended on the home of Khader Hamide, a US lawful permanent resident, and his Kenyan-born wife, Julie Mungai. They were handcuffed, told they were being arrested for "terrorism," and taken into custody while police blocked the street and an FBI helicopter hovered overhead.[89] Six other individuals were arrested that morning.

The INS sought to remove the LA Eight from the United States based on political ideology. Both the director of the FBI and the regional counsel of the INS testified before Congress that the sole basis of the government's efforts to deport the LA Eight was their political affiliations. In the words of FBI director William Webster, "All of them were arrested because they are alleged to be members of a world-wide Communist organization which under the [INA] makes them eligible for deportation ... *If these individuals had been United States citizens, there would not have been a basis for their arrest.*"[90] The evidence underlying the government's charges amounted to a claim that the LA Eight read or distributed literature linked to the Popular Front for the Liberation of Palestine (PFLP), which the district court found was engaged in a wide range of lawful activities from providing education, health care, social services, and day care to cultural and political activities.[91] The district court ruled that the ideological exclusion grounds violated the First Amendment.[92]

In 1990, while the LA Eight case was pending, Congress repealed the ideological exclusion grounds from the immigration laws. The INS then instituted new proceedings against the LA

Eight based on charges of terrorism, as well as other grounds. The INA permits removal of noncitizens who have "engaged in terrorist activity," which is defined as having committed "in an individual capacity or as a member of an organization, an act of terrorist activity or an act which the actor knows, or reasonably should know, *affords material support to any individual, organization, or government in conducting a terrorist activity at any time.*"[93] This broad language authorizes the INS to deport or exclude an individual who has donated money to an organization for its legal, social, or charitable activities, if any part of that organization also has engaged in terrorism, as broadly defined.[94]

The thrust of the INS case was based on the LA Eight's affiliation with the PFLP. Because this provision previously had never been used by the INS to seek to deport a noncitizen from the United States, the LA Eight claimed that the federal government selectively enforced the immigration laws against them for exercising their First Amendment rights. In the end, the Supreme Court ruled that the 1996 amendments to the immigration laws barred judicial review of their claim.[95]

Following the court's decision, the case was remanded to the immigration court. In 2001, the court dismissed the primary removal charges on the grounds that they were not meant to apply retroactively. Nonetheless, the federal government continues its efforts to deport the LA Eight, even relying on secret evidence in seeking removal of two of the eight.[96]

The secret evidence cases

The INS also has selectively targeted Arabs and Muslims through the use of secret evidence—evidence that it refuses to disclose to the noncitizen or his or her counsel—to charge, detain, and deny bond or release in removal proceedings. By 1999, twenty-five secret evidence cases were pending.[97]

In *Rafeedie v. INS*,[98] Fouad Rafeedie, a twenty-year lawful permanent resident of Palestinian origin, was arrested upon returning to the United States after a two-week trip to a conference in Syria sponsored by the Palestine Youth Organization. He was placed in summary exclusion proceedings based on ideological grounds. The INS claimed that disclosing its evidence against Rafeedie would be "prejudicial to the public interest, safety, or security of the United States."[99] The court of appeals rejected the

INS position and required application of the ordinary due process analysis in deciding whether the federal government's national security interests outweighed Rafeedie's First Amendment rights. The court observed that the only way Rafeedie could have prevailed over the secret evidence proceeding would have been to "rebut the undisclosed evidence against him ... It is difficult to imagine how even someone innocent of all wrongdoing could meet such a burden."[100]

Since repeal of the ideological exclusion provisions of the INA in 1990, the INS has relied on secret evidence to detain and deport Arabs and Muslims. Moreover, in response to the 1995 Oklahoma City bombing, Congress enacted antiterrorism legislation that has facilitated the targeting of Arab and Muslim noncitizens: the Antiterrorism and Effective Death Penalty Act (AEDPA)[101] and the Illegal Immigration Reform and Individual Responsibility Act (IIRIRA).[102] Both brought about radical changes to the immigration laws and effectively allowed for the possibility of ideological exclusion and removal through secret evidence proceedings.

Bolstered by the 1996 reforms curtailing the rights of noncitizens, the INS brought approximately two dozen deportation actions based on secret evidence, claiming that disclosing the evidence would compromise the security of the United States.[103] Although the INS denies that it selectively uses secret evidence against Arabs and Muslims, our research has not uncovered a single secret evidence case not involving an Arab or Muslim noncitizen.[104]

AEDPA established a special procedure for detaining and deporting "alien terrorists" that permits the use of secret evidence with certain procedural and constitutional safeguards designed to protect constitutional rights. The federal government, however, has not yet used the new procedure; instead, it has relied on preexisting regulations that it claims authorize the use of secret evidence in the immigration courts. By so doing, the government has avoided complying with AEDPA's safeguards, including requiring the production of an unclassified summary of the secret evidence to the noncitizen and having a federal court assess the constitutionality of the use of secret evidence. This strategy has allowed the US government to avoid charging the noncitizen under a substantive "terrorism" provision of the INA, which would require the government to prove such a charge.[105]

The cases of the "Iraqi Seven" arose out of the US government's resettlement of Iraqi Kurds after the Gulf War.[106] The Iraqi men, who had all worked for a CIA-funded Iraqi opposition group, were evacuated from Iraq by the United States. The INS commenced exclusion proceedings against them based on alleged visa violations. Fearing persecution if returned to Iraq, the seven sought asylum in the United States. Relying primarily on secret evidence, the immigration judge found them to be national security risks.

As a result of the litigation, the INS released five hundred pages of evidence used against the Iraqi Seven. James Woolsey, the former head of the CIA who directed the US government's efforts to organize the overthrow of Saddam Hussein, was one of the lawyers representing the Iraqis. Besides concluding that hundreds of pages had been erroneously classified, Woolsey found that the evidence was based on serious errors in Arabic-English translations; ethnic and religious stereotyping by the FBI; and reliance on unreliable information, including rumors and innuendo. He claimed that that the US government made material misrepresentations to the immigration judge.[107] Despite the weakness of the government's case, the case was only concluded when five of the Iraqis entered into a settlement agreement, withdrawing their asylum claims in exchange for release from detention.

Mazen al-Najjar and Anwar Haddam experienced the longest detentions connected with secret evidence proceedings: Al-Najjar was detained for more than four years[108] and Haddam was jailed for four years,[109] both on allegations of association with terrorism. Al-Najjar, a stateless Palestinian, was editor of the journal of the World and Islam Studies Enterprise (WISE), a think tank based at the University of South Florida devoted to promoting discussion of Middle East issues. The INS arrested al-Najjar and placed him in removal proceedings as part of an FBI investigation against a former WISE administrator who became head of the Islamic Jihad. The arrest and detention was based on secret evidence.[110] Al-Najjar was held in custody for three years and seven months before his release in December 2000. He was then rearrested in November 2001, and remained in custody until his deportation in August 2002.[111] No terrorism charges were ever brought, but he was detained and his removal was sought on the basis of visa violations and on evidence the INS refused to disclose.[112]

Anwar Haddam was an elected member of the Algerian Parliament. A professor of physics at the University of Algiers, he ran for election as a member of the Islamic Salvation Front (FIS), a moderate Islamic party that swept the 1991 elections with 80 percent of the vote. The Algerian military staged a coup d'état, arrested the president of the FIS, and rounded up thousands of its members. Top FIS officials were killed or imprisoned, while thousands of FIS supporters were imprisoned, tortured, and executed. A civil war followed with tens of thousands of deaths. One of the few elected FIS officials who managed to escape Algeria, Haddam entered the United States on a valid nonimmigrant visa in 1992, and later filed an asylum claim. The INS took Haddam into custody and detained him based on secret evidence.[113]

In both the al-Najjar and Haddam cases, as the secret evidence was either unclassified or disclosed, it was demonstrated that the government's "terrorist" claims were based on unreliable evidence and apparently unfounded. Yet, the inability to challenge the secret evidence cost al-Najjar and Haddam years of their lives in custody.

Nasser Ahmed, a father of US-citizen children, was held in custody and denied bond for three-and-a-half years based on secret evidence.[114] Charged in April 1995 with overstaying his visa, he had been released on fifteen thousand dollars bond while he pursued a claim for political asylum. In 1996, while his own deportation proceedings were ongoing, Ahmed became the court-appointed translator for the attorneys representing Sheik Omar Abdel Rahman, later convicted in the 1993 World Trade Center bombing attempt. As Ahmed was going to immigration court for his asylum hearing, the INS arrested him and opposed his release on bond. On remand, the immigration court dismissed the evidence of the government's remaining contentions on the grounds that it was based on an informant who had personal reasons for seeking Ahmed's deportation.

As the secret evidence cases have slowly moved toward conclusion, the government's claims in all of the cases have evaporated. No case has included sufficient evidence of terrorism-related charges necessary to justify the years of detention. Besides the individual loss of liberty, the cases have chilled Arab and Muslim political speech.

Conclusion

Stereotypes about Arabs and Muslims have influenced immigration law and its enforcement, as well as the civil rights of Arab and Muslim noncitizens in the United States. This discussion is by no means comprehensive. Other examples of the US government's response to perceived fears of Arab and Muslim terrorism are plentiful. For example, in the 1990s, the much-publicized case of asylum-seeker Sheik Omar Abdel Rahman[115] by itself resulted in changes to the immigration laws that narrowed the rights of all asylum applicants.[116] An episode of the popular television show *60 Minutes*,[117] focusing on his alleged abuse of the asylum system, triggered a chain reaction that culminated in 1996 asylum reforms. These reforms included a summary exclusion procedure by which a noncitizen could be excluded from the country without a hearing on an asylum or other claim to relief.[118]

As shown above, demonization of Arabs and Muslims has had an impact on the evolution of the law and encouraged harsh governmental efforts to remove Arabs and Muslims from the United States. The same stereotypes have affected the civil rights of all persons of Arab and Muslim ancestry in the United States since September 11, 2001. Importantly, the aftermath of the security measures taken since then threatens to have enduring impacts on the civil rights of all immigrants, and on US citizens as well.

CHAPTER 2

PROFILED: ARABS, MUSLIMS, AND THE POST–9/11 HUNT FOR THE "ENEMY WITHIN"

Nancy Murray

"To those who pit Americans against immigrants and citizens against non-citizens ...," Attorney General John Ashcroft intoned before the Senate Judiciary Committee on December 6, 2001, "my message is this: Your tactics only aid terrorists, for they erode our national unity and diminish our resolve."[1]

Speaking two months after the attacks of 9/11, the attorney general's words already had a disingenuous ring. For his Justice Department had demonstrated little patience with US Supreme Court rulings, going back more than a century, that established noncitizens as "persons" under the Fifth and Fourteenth Amendments, entitled to freedom of expression and rights of association, equal protection, and due process under the law.[2] With the legal path eased by the anti-immigration legislation of 1996 and dozens of Immigration and Naturalization Service (INS) "secret evidence" cases in the late 1990s, Ashcroft's antiterrorism offensive made the nation's security contingent on the insecurity of its noncitizens, especially Muslims and those with Middle Eastern backgrounds. The unchecked anti-Arab racism of the 1980s and 1990s contributed to a sharp reversal of American attitudes toward racial, ethnic, and religious profiling immediately after 9/11, making the attorney general's resort to profiling in the hunt for "suspects" to interview, detain, and deport acceptable to the broad community.[3]

Noncitizens who are Muslim, primarily from the Middle East and South Asia, have been the chief targets of the repression,[4] but its impact is felt by all immigrants, as citizens are pitted against immigrants in the manner the attorney general says he deplores.[5] Among those against whom the Justice Department filed "terrorism" charges in the opening months of 2003 were twenty-eight Latinos accused of possessing fabricated Social Security numbers and working illegally at the Austin, Texas, airport.[6] Now that the local and state police can enforce immigration law and the slightest infraction of the rules can be grounds for arrest and deportation, the self-proclaimed "Nation of Immigrants" is a potential minefield for both documented and undocumented noncitizens.[7]

Shortly before Ashcroft made his appeal for "national unity" in the Senate, Congress, in the pages of the Uniting and Strengthening America by Providing Appropriate Tools Required to Intercept and Obstruct Terrorism (USA PATRIOT) Act, urged all citizens to stand together. "Arab Americans, Muslim Americans, and Americans from South Asia play a vital role in our Nation," states section 102, "and are entitled to nothing less than the full rights of every American."[8] Expressing its sense that their civil rights and civil liberties must be protected, Congress called upon the nation "to recognize the patriotism of fellow citizens from all ethnic, racial and religious backgrounds."

Few Americans who are Muslim or Arab have much reason today to take these words at face value. Their sense of vulnerability has been heightened by ethnic and religious profiling engaged in by law enforcement, airlines, and the general public; the resurrection of the kind of "guilt by association" that was discredited after the McCarthy period[9]; the government's watch lists and data-mining programs; the training of citizen spies to look for suspicious activity; and the chilling of their First Amendment and due process rights, as many Americans and noncitizens alike fear taking part in meetings or other events that might be seen as "controversial." The "patriotism" commended by Congress offers Muslim citizens little protection from the January 27, 2003, FBI directive that all field supervisors should count the number of mosques and Muslims in their areas and use this information to establish a yardstick for the number of terrorism investigations they are expected to carry out.[10] The FBI's executive assistant director Wilson Lowery Jr. explained to congressional staffers that mosque tallies would be used to help set investigative goals. "There were a lot of eyebrows that went up," said one of those present.[11] The approach raised concerns that the FBI was engag-

ing in a new form of religious profiling. Five months later, acting
on a directive from the president, the Justice Department issued
policy guidelines that barred federal law enforcement agents
from engaging in racial or ethnic profiling, except "in terrorist
identification" when "federal law enforcement personnel must
use every legitimate tool to prevent future attacks."[12] The last
time the US government profiled the "enemy within" the way it
is profiling Muslims and Middle Easterners today, it ended up
forcing more than 110,000 Japanese Americans and noncitizens
of Japanese descent into internment camps.

This chapter will outline the post–9/11 actions by the three
branches of federal government that have targeted Arabs and
Muslims, citizen and noncitizen, and draw some conclusions
about their effectiveness in the domestic "war against terrorism." Beyond its scope is the way government measures have
also undermined the "full rights of every American" and the system of checks and balances that is the hallmark of our constitutional system.

Executive actions

"Let the terrorists among us be warned: If you overstay your
visa—even by one day—we will arrest you. If you violate a local
law, you will be put in jail and kept in custody as long as possible. We will use every available statute. We will seek every prose-
cutorial advantage. We will use all our weapons within the law
and under the Constitution to protect life and enhance security
for America."[13]

True to his word, John Ashcroft's antiterrorism offensive has
been heavy on arrests and swift to use all available weapons
"within the law"—but not the law as commonly understood.
This is the law in which every loophole is exploited and every nu-
ance teased out and pressed into service by a Justice Department
that does its work behind a wall of secrecy and routinely invokes
"national security" to fend off the requirements of accountability.
Where suspected terrorists are concerned, the attorney general has
been prepared to dispense with the most basic constitutional
rights. He has been prepared to detain and deport not just the
"terrorists among us" who have overstayed their visas by one day,
but thousands of otherwise law-abiding noncitizens.

There is one line he will not cross. Ashcroft refused to permit the FBI to consult the National Instant Check System to see if any of 1,200 people detained in the wake of 9/11 had recently bought guns. He told the Senate Judiciary Committee that "the only permissible use for the National Instant Check System is to audit the maintenance of that system" and that by refusing to allow these background checks he was simply following the law.[14]

As head of the Department of Justice, Ashcroft has authority over the FBI and wide jurisdiction to run the INS, which on March 1, 2003, was folded along with twenty-one other federal agencies into the giant Department of Homeland Security.[15] The attorney general appoints the chief immigration judge and can modify detention and other rules by administrative order.

A change in the way a rule is enforced can give the department tremendous power over the lives of millions of people. For instance, on July 22, 2002, the Justice Department announced that it would start enforcing a fifty-year-old regulation requiring noncitizens to report any change of address to the INS within ten days of moving or face a two-hundred-dollar fine or up to thirty days in prison. Failure to report a change of address—or failure of the government to process that change of address form in a timely fashion[16]—results in a status violation that makes the offender subject to deportation. According to the INS, the rule applies to some eleven million people, including all nonimmigrant aliens (the official term for foreign nationals who enter the United States on temporary visas, including students), green card holders, asylum seekers, and refugees.[17] Even before the new interpretation of the old rule went into effect, the attorney general had used it to justify the secret detention of at least two of the "special interest" detainees who were arrested in the wake of 9/11.[18] The INS had used it in a deportation proceeding involving a legal Palestinian immigrant, Thar Abdeljaber, who had been pulled over in Raleigh, North Carolina, for driving four miles over the speed limit.[19]

A change of practice that makes the lives of millions of innocent people so much less secure may give the attorney general a new weapon in the "war against terrorism," but it is wholly at odds with his December 7, 2001, statement to the Senate Judiciary Committee: "Each action taken by the Department of Justice is carefully drawn to target a narrow class of individuals—terrorists."

To date, that "narrow class of individuals" has largely eluded the government, which has been unable to tie any of those apprehended since 9/11 with the attacks on the World Trade Center and Pentagon, although it maintains that it is tracking down "sleeper" operatives.[20] Justice Department actions targeting Muslims, Arabs, and South Asians since 9/11 have had a sweeping impact on individuals and their families who are in no way connected to terrorism. To understand just how insecure their lives have become, the cumulative weight of the following measures must be taken into consideration.

"Special interest" arrests

In the immediate aftermath of 9/11, some twelve hundred people, most of them Arab, South Asian, and Muslim citizens and noncitizens, were arrested and questioned by the FBI, INS, and state and local law enforcement as part of the FBI-led PENTT-BOM (Pentagon/Twin Towers Bombings) investigation.[21] Of this number, 762 noncitizens were placed on the "INS Custody List" because the FBI thought "they may have had a connection to the September 11 attacks or terrorism in general, or because the FBI was unable, at least initially, to determine whether they were connected to terrorism."[22] Those detained were held at first in conditions of complete secrecy, often in solitary confinement, for varying periods of time. Not one of these "special interest" detainees held in connection with the PENTTBOM investigation has been linked to the September 11 attacks.[23]

One case involving what the government termed a "sleeper operational combat cell" was concluded in early June 2003. On June 3, the jury convicted two Moroccans, Abdel-Ilah Elmardoudi and Karim Koubriti, in Detroit, Michigan, of providing material support to terrorists. It acquitted of terrorism charges another Moroccan, Ahmed Hannan, but found him guilty of one count of document fraud. An Algerian, Farouk al-Haimoud, was acquitted of all charges and released after more than a year and a half in prison.

Three of the men had been arrested on September 17, 2001, by law enforcement agents who raided their apartment looking for someone else and found a stack of forged passports and a videotape of Disneyland. Youssef Hmimssa, a Moroccan who originally also was charged, testified against the others and, in exchange, received forty-six months for ten unrelated felonies that could have resulted in eighty-one years in prison.[24] During the course of the trial, evidence was presented that revealed Hmimssa to be a liar who wanted revenge.[25] There was a widespread feeling in the Detroit-area Arab American community that "this is a case of railroading these guys to get P.R."[26] The jury's action in acquitting two of the men of terrorism charges suggests that they did not view the case as an example of a "terrorist cell" being dismantled by the government, as Ashcroft claimed when the verdict was announced.[27]

To date, this is the sole instance of "special interest" detainees being publicly identified with that "narrow class of individuals—terrorists." The government's insistence on secrecy in all national security matters has made this information—as well as information about all other immigration detainees—difficult to obtain. On September 21, 2001, Chief Immigration Judge Michael Creppy issued an internal memo stating that "special immigration" hearings should be held behind closed doors without disclosing to the public that these cases were even taking place. The INS then issued a rule stating, "No person, including any state or local government entity or any privately operated detention facility, that houses, maintains, provides services to, or otherwise holds any detainee on behalf of the Service ... shall disclose or otherwise permit to be made public the name of, or other information relating to, such detainee."[28] The Bush administration has repeatedly refused to release the names and numbers of all the "special interest" detainees who were being held in connection with terrorism investigations and has appealed all court orders that it make this information public.

Human Rights Watch, Amnesty International, the Lawyers Committee for Human Rights, the American Civil Liberties Union, and support groups such as the Blue Triangle Network collected the information that found its way into the public domain and carried out interviews with detainees after their deportations.[29] Their reports depicted a Kafkaesque world of the "disappeared," where people are guilty until proven innocent and due process is what the attorney general says it is. The presumption of innocence in individual cases is trumped by the government's "mosaic" theory, requiring individuals to be detained as possible pieces of a broad pattern of terrorist activity.[30]

On June 2, 2003, the veil of secrecy was lifted by the publication of a report on the September 11 detainees by Department of Justice Inspector General Glenn Fine, a Clinton appointee.[31] The report had been delayed for nearly a year because of internal disputes within the Justice Department about liability issues and who would take the blame for the many abuses documented. While names of detainees and other identifying information are either absent or redacted, the report gives a detailed account of the arrests, processing, charging, and "clearance" of detainees, and the Justice Department's "no bond" policy and long removal delays. It also describes the extremely harsh conditions of confinement in the Metropolitan Detention Center in Brooklyn, where those deemed "of high interest" were sent, and the somewhat better conditions in the Passaic County Jail in Paterson, New Jersey, the destination of detainees classified as "of interest" or "of undetermined interest" or "no longer of interest."[32]

Most of the 762 "special interest" detainees were picked up in the chaotic aftermath of 9/11. By September 18, 2001, the FBI had received more than ninety-six thousand tips from the public,[33] and "PENTTBOM leads that resulted in the arrest of a September 11 detainee were often quite general in nature, such as a landlord reporting suspicious activity by an Arab tenant."[34] An example cited in the report is that of "a Muslim man in his 40s" who was arrested "after an acquaintance wrote a letter to law enforcement officers stating that the man had made anti-American statements. The statements, as reported in the letter, were very general and did not involve threats of violence or suggest any direct connection to terrorism. Nonetheless, the lead was assigned ... and resulted in the man's arrest for overstaying his visa. Because he had been arrested on a PENTTBOM lead, he automatically was placed in the FBI New York's 'special interest' category." Cleared by the New York FBI field office by mid-November, he "was not cleared by FBI Headquarters until late February 2002 due to an administrative oversight."[35]

Most of the detainees were charged with civil violations of immigration law, such as overstaying a visa or entering without inspection or with invalid documents, which enabled the Justice Department to dispense entirely with criminal justice safeguards. The inspector general's report confirms the department's statement to the Senate and House Judiciary Committees that it was not making use of the USA PATRIOT Act to hold detainees.[36] Instead, it was relying on a new rule issued by the INS on September 20, 2001, and made retroactive to September 17, that extended the time that noncitizens could be held without charges from twenty-four to forty-eight hours, and provided for the forty-eight-hour limit to be extended "in the event of an emergency or other extraordinary circumstances" for an "additional reasonable period of time."[37] The government has interpreted "reasonable" to mean weeks or even months.

Likewise, it has changed the rules to enable a noncitizen to be kept behind bars even if an immigration judge orders that person to be released for lack of evidence. The noncitizen could be held indefinitely as a danger to the community or a "flight risk."[38] Indeed, the INS "tried to hold without bond any alien arrested on immigration charges in whom the FBI expressed an interest, or any alien in whom the FBI's interest was undetermined."[39] It blocked the departures of many detainees who were ordered to be deported, while the FBI and CIA conducted lengthy background checks to "clear" them.[40] The Justice Department inspector general found that the average time to clear a detainee was eighty days.

The Justice Department has claimed that it cannot release the names of detainees for national security reasons and to protect their privacy. It has similarly claimed that it cannot release the names or exact numbers of those being held as "material witnesses" in connection with terrorism investigations, although it says that "each of the detained material witnesses is free to identify himself publicly. The fact that few have elected to do so suggests they wish their detention to remain nonpublic."[41] The 1984 material witness statute was intended, according to Harvard University law professor Phil Heymann, to ensure testimony, not to hold people indefinitely.[42]

According to Human Rights Watch, many material witnesses endured long periods in solitary confinement in maximum security conditions with the lights on twenty-four hours a day and were rarely allowed out of their cells to exercise or shower. Many were released without ever testifying before a grand jury; others were eventually charged with crimes or visa violations.

One case detailed in Human Rights Watch's *Presumption of Guilt: Human Rights Abuses of Post–September 11 Detainees* gives an insight into the nightmare world of the post–9/11 "special interest" detainees. Eyad Mustafa Alrababah, a Palestinian with a Jordanian passport, voluntarily went to the FBI office in Bridgeport, Connecticut, after recognizing four of the alleged hijackers on TV as people who had attended his mosque, visited his home, and driven with him from Virginia to Connecticut. He was promptly arrested and placed for four months in total isolation as a "protected witness" in Hartford, and then in two different prisons in New York. He claims to have been beaten, interrogated without an attorney present, and threatened with being thrown out a window. He was assigned an attorney the day before he was supposed to appear before a grand jury, but he never did testify. He then was moved to Virginia, where he was charged with conspiracy and document fraud for giving false information on another man's application for a driver's license. He eventually pleaded guilty to document fraud and was sentenced to time served. At the time the Human Rights Watch report was written, some eight months after he went to talk to the FBI, Alrababah was still in prison awaiting deportation.[43]

Just how broad Ashcroft's "narrow class of individuals—terrorists" had become in the months after 9/11 was spelled out by Mike Johns, a spokesperson for the US Attorneys' office in Phoenix, Arizona. Johns was talking about the case of Malek Mohamed Seif, who had flown from Marseilles, France, to Phoenix because he heard the FBI wanted to interview him about two alleged hijackers who had attended his mosque. Arrested by the FBI for providing false information to the Social Security Administration in 1999 and to the Federal Aviation Administration, he went on a six-week hunger strike in a Phoenix cell. "The terrorist investigation has generated additional cases that we may not have run across in the normal course of events," Johns stated. "The Attorney General's policy is that we locate and detain people who have violated federal laws. We spend a substantial amount of time doing that."[44]

Attack on lawyer-client privilege

What kind of legal assistance will be available to people suspected of terrorism?

On October 31, 2001, Ashcroft issued an order permitting the monitoring of communications between lawyers and federal detainees, including those being held as material witnesses, if the attorney general has "reasonable suspicion" to "believe that a particular inmate may use communications with attorneys or their agents to further or facilitate acts of violence or terrorism."[45] Five months later, on April 9, 2002, Ashcroft announced the indictment of New York defense attorney Lynne Stewart on charges of providing material support to terrorists and stated that her case lay behind the new monitoring rules. Ashcroft claimed that Stewart had helped her imprisoned client, Sheik Omar Abdel Rahman, pass messages to the Islamic organization he once led.[46] On July 23, 2003, federal district court judge John Koeltl dropped charges that she had provided material support to terrorists, leaving her to face lesser charges of conspiring to defraud the United States and making false statements that could put her in prison for ten years. The attorney general then brought new charges against Stewart and her codefendants, accusing them of conspiring with Sheik Rahman to kill and kidnap people in a foreign country.

Whatever the outcome of her trial, the government's new surveillance powers, in Stanford law professor Deborah Rhode's words, erode "longstanding Fourth Amendment privacy protections and Sixth Amendment guarantees of effective assistance of counsel." The indictment of Stewart "could affect lawyers' willingness to defend despised groups, like suspected terrorists."[47]

Absconder Apprehension Initiative

In addition to the twelve hundred or more "special interest" cases arrested in the months after 9/11, well over a thousand people were arrested by May 2003 as part of another phase of the domestic war on terrorism.[48] A January 25, 2002, memo from the Office of the Deputy Attorney General to the commissioner of the INS, the director of the FBI, the director of the US Marshals Service, and US Attorneys ordered these agencies to apprehend and interview "priority absconders" from a list of 314,000 "alien fugitives" from Middle Eastern nations who had overstayed their visas and either had failed to comply with removal orders or had never received a final removal order.[49] Working together, the FBI and INS were to arrest absconders and interview them about their knowledge of "terrorist activity." An antiterrorism coordinator would then decide whether these absconders would be prosecuted for failure to depart or simply be deported by the INS. By February 2002, the names of six thousand people from countries where al-Qaeda was believed to operate were being entered into the National Crime Information Center (NCIC) database, and INS and FBI agents began to round those people up.

Many of those hunted down joined the "special interest" detainees in secret detention. Some, such as the blind Palestinian Munir Lami, were put on planes to destinations where they knew no one.[50] They left behind jobs, homes, and families, including American-born children.

Project Lookout

In mid-September 2001, a "watch list" was compiled of people whom the FBI wanted to question in connection with the September 11 attacks. It was circulated to banks, travel reservation firms, consumer-data businesses, casino operators, car rental and trucking companies, power plants, companies providing security guards, and the International Security Management Association, among other organizations.

In his report on the September 11 detainees, the Justice Department inspector general contrasts the way the FBI managed its watch list with the inefficient "clearance" process for "special interest" detainees. As the list grew to as many as 450 names, its coordinator, the FBI Inspection Division section chief Kevin Perkins, became concerned "that individuals were being placed on the list who had no connection to terrorists. For example, because the airlines use a 'soundex' system to retrieve like-sounding names, this resulted in names ending up on the list as soundex matches to names that were entirely different. Perkins also gave an example where a group of entries on the list all had the same first initial and a common last name, with no additional information."[51] The Department of Justice inspector general claimed that Perkins then acted rapidly to reduce the list to approximately twenty to thirty names.

But, according to the *Wall Street Journal,* "A year later, the list has taken on a life of its own, with multiplying—and error-filled—versions being passed around like bootleg music. Some companies fed a version of the list into their own database and now use it to screen job applicants and customers ... The list included many people the FBI didn't suspect but just wanted to talk to ... Yet a version on SeguRed.com, a South American security-oriented Web site that got a copy from a Venezuelan bank's security officer, is headed: 'list of suspected terrorists sent by the FBI to financial institutions.'"[52]

The article goes on to describe how some apparent "hits" turned out to be the wrong person. "Few companies had the skills to detect whether Middle Eastern names had errors or to check for common alternative spellings." At least fifty different versions of the list were in circulation, all marred by instances of misidentification, problems of "multipart Middle Eastern names ... degraded by typos," and the fact that the FBI had "cleared" many people on the list but then stopped updating it. Since many of the names were included without identifying addresses or Social Security numbers, people with the surname Atta are "still trying to chase their names off copies of the list posted on Internet sites in at least five countries."

The experience with Project Lookout has not stopped the FBI-run Terrorist Screening Center from seeking to create a giant database of "known and suspected terrorists" around the world. The database will be used for "one-stop shopping" by airport workers, consular officials, border agents, local police, and private industries.[53] Its starting point is the State Department's suspected terrorist list, which contains 112,000 names. According to the *New York Times*, "Officials insist they're not interested in tracking political activists, only those engaged in or supporting terrorism. Still, after the lists are weeded to eliminate duplication, they expect the final, secret, master list to include at least 100,000 people."[54]

FBI interviews

On November 9, 2001, the Justice Department announced that it was circulating to the newly created terrorism task forces at the ninety-four US Attorneys' offices a list of five thousand foreign men to be located and interviewed. Five months later, it added an additional three thousand names to the list. The men, aged eighteen to thirty-three, had entered the US on nonimmigrant visas from specific (unnamed) countries after January 1, 2000.

This initiative was immediately criticized by some police chiefs and former FBI officials. Police chiefs in Detroit, Michigan; Tucson, Arizona; and Portland, Oregon said they would not participate, as their departments had strict guidelines against any form of racial profiling, and these men were being targeted simply because of their country of origin, not because they were suspected of wrongdoing.[55]

The Justice Department has termed the interview project a public relations success, stating that it has strengthened its ties with the Arab and Muslim communities in the United States.[56] But on May 9, 2003, a General Accounting Office (GAO) report was made public that questions government claims that the FBI interviews helped to forward the war on terrorism. *Homeland Security: Justice Department's Project to Interview Aliens after September 11, 2001* describes how the interview project was developed as a kind of pilot data-mining study. It was implemented by the Foreign Terrorist Tracking Task Force, the INS, the Executive Office for US Attorneys, US Attorneys' offices, the Anti-Terrorism Task Force, the FBI, and the Justice Management Division, among other entities. Of the 7,602 names compiled after searching databases for people from fifteen different countries whose backgrounds were similar to those of the hijackers, only 42 percent, or 3,216 people, were actually located and interviewed. Of this number, fewer than twenty were arrested on immigration charges, three on criminal charges, and none with any links to terrorism.

The GAO found that there were problems with the databases. It also concluded that, although interviews "were conducted in a respectful and professional manner, and interviewees were not coerced to participate," those interviewed did not feel the interviews to be truly voluntary "because they worried about repercussions, such as future INS denials for visa extensions or permanent residency if they refused" to be questioned.[57] The report quoted attorneys who had sat in on the interviews and "expressed the view that the project had a chilling effect on relations between the Arab community and law enforcement."[58] Moreover, more than half of the law enforcement officers who participated in the interviews expressed concern about "the quality of questions asked and the value of the responses obtained." People were asked why they are in the United States and whether they have knowledge of the attacks of 9/11 or any other terrorist activities, know anyone "capable or willing to carry out acts of terrorism," have any ideas "as to how future terrorism can be prevented," know of people raising money or receiving training for terrorist activity, know anyone who has sympathy for the hijackers or is urging people to engage in violent acts against the United States, know any other individuals who might have this sort of information, or are "aware of any criminal activity whatsoever, regardless of whether it is related to terrorism."[59]

The Justice Department has been largely silent on the findings of the report, taking issue only with its focus on data limitations. It has stated that "some of the details that would demonstrate the efficacy of the program are too sensitive to release."[60]

Operation Green Quest

In its official interagency brochure, Operation Green Quest is promoted as "Finding the Missing Piece of the Terrorist Puzzle"—the money trail. Established by the Treasury Department in October 2001, the program involved representatives from a broad range of organizations (including Customs; the IRS; the Secret Service; the Bureau of Alcohol, Tobacco, and Firearms; the Office of Foreign Assets Control; the Financial Crimes Enhancement Network; the FBI; the Postal Inspection Service; the Naval Criminal Investigative Service; and the Department of Justice) in the attempt to cut "a cunning, devious enemy" off from its sources of funding. According to the brochure, "Green Quest is in constant contact with law enforcement, intelligence, and financial establishments worldwide, as it coordinates with its member agencies, while redirecting resources to meet national-security objectives."[61] Its investigative efforts have focused on charity or relief organizations; "front companies" for legitimate businesses that generate funds for terrorism; types of business and financial transactions that serve as "red flags," calling for further scrutiny by banking and trade communities; and illicit enterprises such as identity theft; credit-card, welfare, and food-stamp fraud; interstate cigarette smuggling; counterfeit merchandise schemes; and unlicensed currency remitters.

Clearly, this is a major growth area for agencies such as the Customs Service, which has opened nearly six hundred terror-financing investigations and set up a directorate of intelligence to find out how Islamic *hawalas* (informal money exchanges) may be used to funnel money to terrorists. FBI officials have grumbled that the Customs Service expansion represents a power grab.[62] In combination with the "material support" provisions of the 1996 Antiterrorism and Effective Death Penalty Act, it has the potential to destroy the lives of people who have nothing to do with terrorism.[63]

Operation Green Quest has been coordinating raids on homes and businesses around the country without any accountability or redress. In March 2002, an Arab American woman in Herndon, Virginia, described men breaking through her door and pointing a gun at her 19-year-old daughter as she tried to call 911 for help. She and her daughter were then handcuffed for three hours as raiders looked through contents of her drawers and took computer, credit card, passport, and bank information.[64] Simultaneous raids by armed agents were carried out at various organizations in Virginia, Georgia, and Washington, DC, including a charity, the Success Foundation, the Muslim World League, and various Muslim-owned businesses.[65] A few months later, in June and July 2002, raids took place in jewelry stores in New York, Pennsylvania, Florida, California, Alabama, Georgia, North Carolina, Texas, and Massachusetts. More than thirty foreign nationals were arrested as authorities seized computer disks and other material to see if the Intrigue Jewelers chain of kiosks funneled money to terrorists abroad.[66] Attention was focused on some five hundred businesses, mostly convenience stores, that authorities believe "are generating tens of millions of dollars a year for militant groups." The *Washington Post* reported that data-mining software was being used "to discern subtle patterns in the habits of financial scammers ... that could indicate surreptitious money movement." The report explains that the FBI "does not think the domestic schemes under investigation were used to finance the Sept. 11 attacks,"[67] but rather that funds were being channeled to groups such as Hamas and Hizbollah, which appear on the "Comprehensive List of Terrorists and Groups Identified Under Executive Order 13224."[68]

In late March 2003, raids were mounted in Los Angeles, New York City, Minneapolis, Newark, and Detroit as part of the "ongoing effort by Operation Green Quest to close down illegal financial systems in the US that have been exploited by terrorist groups in the past," according to the Web site of the Bureau of Immigration and Customs Enforcement. Targets included efforts to send money orders and private express parcels to Jordan, Lebanon, and Yemen in a manner that evaded foreign reporting requirements.[69]

Under the USA PATRIOT Act, any noncitizen who gives material support to even the lawful activities of a group designated as a foreign terrorist organization by the secretary of state, in consultation with the attorney general and secretary of the treasury, or who supports a group that is not on the list, but that at some point had engaged in the sort of violent activity that *could* have made it eligible for inclusion, can be arrested and deported.[70] As David Cole points out, under USA PATRIOT a "terrorist organization" is defined as "any group of two or more persons that has used or threatened to use a weapon, literally encompassing every organization that has ever been involved in a civil war or a crime of violence, from a pro-life group that once threatened workers at an abortion clinic to the African National Congress (ANC) ... Under this law, the thousands of noncitizens who supported the ANC's lawful, nonviolent antiapartheid activity could now be deported as terrorists."[71] Any American who gives material support or resources can be fined or sentenced to ten years in jail. Once an organization is "flagged" as having some kind of tie to terrorism, no matter how tenuous, the investigation proceeds entirely in secret, giving the organization no opportunity to clear its name.[72]

According to the Justice Department, by mid-2003 the federal government had frozen more than six hundred bank accounts and $124 million in assets around the world and conducted seventy investigations into terrorist financing.[73] The assets of seventeen Islamic charities have been frozen, including three in the US, which the Justice Department describes as "two Illinois-based charities suspected of being associated with al-Qaeda (Benevolence International Foundation and Global Relief Foundation), and a Texas entity believed to be a Hamas front (Holy Land Foundation for Relief Development)."[74] These US-based organizations with American board members are among the largest Arab American charities. They receive donations from Muslims across the country for whom giving to charity, known as *zakat*, is one of the five pillars of Islam. Under the USA PATRIOT Act, all these donors could now be at risk, and many Muslims are afraid to make further donations to any charity. The Treasury Department has suggested they consult its guidelines for giving, which advise obtaining information about the names and legal status of all staff members and groups abroad who administer the funds before making any donation.[75]

US foreign policy is a vital part of the financial crackdown. On February 26, 2003, as preparations were being made to launch the war against Iraq, the government arrested three men in Syracuse who ran Help the Needy, an unregistered Islamic charity based in New York. They were charged with conspiring to transfer funds to Iraq in violation of US law. Help the Needy provides food, clothes, lodging for families, and medicine for hospitals.[76]

In the early morning hours of the same day, more than one hundred FBI and INS agents staged a raid on the campus of the University of Idaho in Moscow, Idaho. Sami Omar al-Hussayyen, a computer-science graduate student and the popular former president of the Muslim Student Association, was arrested. Al-Hussayyen had organized a blood drive in the days following 9/11 and given talks about Islam to the university and town. After his arrest, agents went door to door, rounding up at least twenty other foreign students who had the misfortune to either know the suspect or have some minor immigration irregularities. They were interrogated for up to five hours, and copies of their computer hard drives were seized.[77] The main target of the raid, who lived in student housing with his wife Maha and three children, was taken to an isolation cell and charged with helping to establish Web sites that promoted violence against the United States, including one that was used by Help the Needy. The current president of the university's Muslim Student Association claimed that he searched for the specific article about suicide attacks mentioned in the indictment but could only find articles critical of US policy and its intention to invade Iraq.[78]

In April 2003, a federal immigration judge found al-Hussayyen guilty of visa fraud and ordered him to be deported to Saudi Arabia. By early October 2003, he was still in a US prison, although a magistrate had recommended that he be placed under house arrest. He was awaiting trial on criminal charges of maintaining a Web site used by radical terrorist groups while his wife and children faced their own deportation hearings.

Other people who have been arrested for giving "material support" to terrorists include Jesse Maali, a wealthy Palestinian American entrepreneur in Florida, who had contributed twenty-five thousand dollars to help finance a hospital wing in the West Bank and donated to humanitarian organizations, such as the Society of Ina'ash El-Usra in Ramallah, that provide day-care services and help distressed families. He was detained for what Assistant US Attorney Cynthia Hawkins Collazo called his "financial ties to Middle Eastern organizations who advocate violence."[79]

Global Relief Foundation's founding member Rabih Haddad, a well-known imam in Ann Arbor, Michigan, was taken into secret detention on December 14, 2001. On the same day, the foundation's assets were frozen and its headquarters in Bridgeview, Illinois, were raided by fifteen FBI agents. Its field offices in Albania and Kosovo were also raided, and two employees were beaten and arrested, but no charges have been filed against them. At the time of his arrest, Haddad was in the process of applying for permanent resident status. After being held for months in high-security solitary confinement on a minor visa irregularity, with his appeal for political asylum denied, he was deported to Lebanon on July 14, 2003. Neither his wife nor his attorney had been notified before he was removed from the country.

Both Global Relief and the Holy Land Foundation fought the freezing of their funds in federal court but found it impossible to bring a successful challenge given the government's use of secret evidence, which left defense attorneys "working in the dark."[80]

Special Registration

The National Security Entry-Exit Registration System (NSEERS) was called for by the immigration acts of 1996 and 2000 and amended by the USA PATRIOT Act before it was formally announced by the attorney general on June 6, 2002. The Department of Justice added to this system a special "call in" registration, which it began to implement in November 2002. Special Registration required male visitors (including foreign students, valid visa holders, and those with visa petitions pending), aged sixteen years and older from twenty-five Muslim and Middle Eastern countries as well as North Korea to come to INS offices to be fingerprinted, photographed, interviewed, and have their financial information copied, or to register when they enter the country, then re-register after thirty days.

These men also have to register again each time they leave the country, a requirement that has trapped, among many others, Yahya Jalil, a graduate student at the University of Pennsylvania Wharton School of Business, who was not permitted to enter the United States on his return from a four-day spring break trip to London because he had failed to register with the INS the day he left the country.[81] Dr. Shahid Mahmood, a Pakistani citizen, was not permitted to return to his North Carolina patients after a visit abroad.[82] Failure to submit themselves for inspection at the time of their departure is considered "unlawful activity," which could make them inadmissible to the United States unless they "can demonstrate good cause for the violation."[83]

Little outreach was done to publicize the program's requirements, which were presented in an ambiguous and confusing manner. Targeted males were expected to meet a series of poorly publicized rolling deadlines or face arrest, detention, fines, and deportation. Any future application for permanent residence status or citizenship could be barred by a failure to register by a specific date. Those who had failed to register opened themselves up for arrest in simple traffic stops, as the INS database was merged with the NCIC.

Around the country, different INS offices brought their own demands and approaches to the special registration process. People were asked which mosque they attended and what extracurricular activities they participated in at university. Some were asked to hand over their address books. In California, up to seven hundred men were arrested on the spot at the close of the deadline for visitors from Iran, Iraq, Libya, Sudan, and Syria. Among those detained were overstayers, others whose visas had some irregularities, people who had applied for green cards and were waiting to hear from the INS, and a sixteen-year-old who had entered the country lawfully on a student visa and was applying for permanent residency.[84] In Colorado, six foreign students were arrested and faced deportation for taking too few courses, even though they had permission from their universities to do so. In Minnesota, an electrical engineer was placed under arrest before his passport and paperwork were even checked. When he asked the special agent, "How can I be out of status when I have already filed change of status to J2 with the INS and have the INS receipt with the LIN number dated December 16th?" he was told, "It doesn't matter; rules are changing daily."[85]

Thousands of people who feared arrest because of irregularities in their status have sought asylum in Canada.[86] Thirteen thousand others who went to register now have court dates and face deportation. In at least one case, that of a teenage orphan from Pakistan who was raised in New York by his uncle and has four siblings who are naturalized citizens, the attention of the press and the efforts of his member of Congress have paid off. Mohammad Sarfaraz Hussain has been permitted to stay in the United States after he had been told he would be deported.[87]

The Justice Department claimed Special Registration as a major success, stating on April 25, 2003, that it had registered 133,000 temporary visitors and apprehended eleven "suspected terrorists," eight hundred criminal suspects, and nine thousand illegal aliens.[88] But many members of Congress and religious and advocacy groups around the country have denounced Special Registration as a blatantly discriminatory measure. In February 2003, Congress reluctantly agreed to fund the program in the Omnibus Appropriations Act but demanded a detailed report about its origins, how it was being implemented, and how it advanced the war on terrorism.[89] There was no sign of that report by the March 1 deadline Congress gave to the Department of Justice.

On December 1, 2003, the Department of Homeland Security announced that is was suspending those parts of the Special Registration program that required targeted males to re-register at local immigration offices within a week of the anniversary of their first registration. But they still have to notify immigration officials at airports before they leave the country and could be called in for special interviews at any time. According to Asa Hutchinson, US Undersecretary for Border and Transportation Security, the Special Registration program yielded no "national security gains" and none of the 143 criminals in custody as a result of registration were suspected terrorists.[90]

SEVIS

The Student and Exchange Visitor Information System (SEVIS) was launched in February 2003 to keep track of the more than a million foreign students enrolled in US colleges and universities. Under the USA PATRIOT Act, SEVIS is exempted from the Family Education Rights and Privacy Act of 1974, which bars the release of most student information without student approval. SEVIS links campuses electronically to the Department of Homeland Security, and information about foreign students—such as when they drop a course, change their major, move house, are disciplined, or take a part-time job—is transmitted instantly to immigration officials. Students are unable to access their files and see if the information contained in them is accurate. Once information has been entered into the system, it cannot be modified. The data in SEVIS on student visa violators is being shared with federal, state, and local law enforcement agencies.

In August 2003, immigration officials began looking through the SEVIS database to locate students who have violated their immigration status, as well as "suspected risks to national security."[91] Chris Bentley of the Bureau of Immigration and Customs Enforcement gave as a "hypothetical example" officials looking for "any large groups of students from a predominantly Muslim country who are involved in sensitive scientific research at a single university."

Expansion of FBI and police powers

On May 30, 2002, the attorney general announced a change in FBI guidelines to permit the bureau to carry out surveillance on lawful domestic religious, civic, and political activity without suspicion of wrongdoing. The previous guidelines had been issued in 1980 in response to the FBI's excesses of the COINTELPRO era.

In making the change, the attorney general declared that the old guidelines are too reactive at a time when we need "to detect and neutralize terrorists before they attack" and give agents "no clear authority to visit public places that are open to all Americans."[92] The new guidelines permit the FBI to freely infiltrate mosques, churches, and other meeting places; listen to online chat rooms, trawl for information on the Internet, and obtain information from data-mining companies; and conduct full investigations for one year with no evidence that a crime has been committed and no oversight from headquarters.

In its report to the House and Senate Judiciary Committees, the Justice Department stated that fewer than ten of the forty-five FBI field offices "have conducted investigative activities at mosques since September 11, 2001." However, the department has no statistics about how many times the FBI has visited mosques and other public places and events, since it "may not retain any information unless it relates to terrorism or other criminal activity" and an active investigation is going on.[93]

The reach of the FBI and law enforcement is being further extended by the merging of the databases of police departments, intelligence agencies, and the State Department. Tying them into one computer system gives police and the FBI (some one hundred thousand people) access to the database of fifty million overseas applications for US visas, including photographs— information that the State Department had previously only shared with the INS.[94] According to the Justice Department, some classified intelligence databases "are currently being used for data-mining and pattern recognition."[95]

On February 28, 2003, a Justice Department order went into effect that gives all eleven thousand FBI agents and several thousand US marshals the authority to arrest people on immigration violations. Before this time, only INS agents, some Customs agents, and a handful of police officers in South Florida had this authority.[96] The power was immediately used to detain "several dozen" Iraqis who were seen as wartime threats as part of the so-called Iraqi Initiative (see below).

On April 14, 2003, the American Civil Liberties Union filed a lawsuit seeking information about new powers given to local police to enforce noncriminal immigration laws. The organization cited its concerns about the secrecy surrounding the attorney general's rumored reversal of longstanding federal policy that had kept state and local police out of immigration law enforcement. In its report to Congress, the Justice Department played down the changes while stating that it is within the "inherent authority of the states" to permit state and local police to arrest aliens "who have violated criminal provisions of the Immigration and Nationality Act or civil provisions that render an alien deportable, and who are listed on the NCIC."[97] This authority, the Justice Department stated, "is crucial to the success of the absconder initiative."

How many state and local police jurisdictions are now enforcing immigration law? This information is not readily available. Only occasionally is the matter given the kind of publicity it received in a newspaper article about Alabama state troopers having the power to arrest illegal aliens and learning how to use the national computer database to find out whether an immigrant is a legal resident of the United States. Senator Jeff Sessions (R-AL) asked for the training in order "to reduce the number of illegal aliens in the state."[98]

Iraqi Initiative

In the months before the United States attacked Iraq and during the weeks of the war, the FBI searched for thousands of illegal Iraqi immigrants and conducted interviews with up to eleven thousand of the estimated fifty thousand Iraqis who are in the country legally, including thousands of students. The FBI was ordered to arrest people on immigration charges if they were believed to be a wartime threat.[99] Several dozen people were arrested under new FBI powers to enforce immigration law. Some American citizens were among those interviewed, including M.J. Alhabeeb, an economics professor at the University of Massachusetts, Amherst, who was questioned about the "un-American" comments he had reportedly made.[100]

Operation Liberty Shield

Based at the US Department of Homeland Security, Operation Liberty Shield "is a comprehensive *national* plan designed to increase protections for America's citizens and infrastructure while maintaining the free flow of goods and people across our border." As part of that national security effort, on March 18, 2003, the government announced that "asylum applicants from nations where al-Qaeda, al-Qaeda sympathizers, and other terrorist groups are known to have operated will be detained for the duration of their processing period."[101] The Department of Homeland Security did not specify exactly which countries are covered by the new rule, which has been condemned by Amnesty International and other human rights organizations. The department also refused to provide any information to the joint Judiciary Committee when asked, most recently in March 2003, about the three Operation Liberty Shield FBI sweeps of young Arab and Muslim males that had taken place in the months following September 11, 2001, stating that this information was classified.

"No fly" lists and CAPPS II

Many of the same problems that have bedeviled the Project Lookout "watch list" are associated with the "no fly" lists being implemented at airports by the Transportation Security Administration, which is part of the Department of Homeland Security. Are the names gathered from intelligence and law enforcement sources those of legitimate flight risks? Why are there so many "false positives" as innocent passengers are repeatedly flagged, searched, and in some cases detained? According to Ann Davis, writing in the *Wall Street Journal*, the "name matching" system simply doesn't work very well with Middle Eastern names.[102]

The Transportation Security Administration is intending to replace its current "no fly" lists with the Computer Assisted Passenger Pre-Screening System II (CAPPS II), being developed by Lockheed Martin. This data-mining system will match passenger names with material available in government, financial, criminal, and public databases and seek suspicious patterns. Each passenger will be assigned a "code" based on his or her security rating.

What can a passenger do to challenge a classification? With the merging of so many huge governmental and public databases now underway, accountability does not appear to be a major concern of the Bush administration. When asked about the problem of errors in the data that is being purchased by the FBI under its new guidelines and will be used to ferret out "suspicious activity," the Justice Department stated, "Persons listed in those data collections should seek to correct errors or inaccuracies with source agencies."[103] In response to a particular question about how the government can ensure that the information contained by the CAPPS II system is accurate and "does not constitute inappropriate profiling," the department stated that those questions should be directed to the Transportation Security Administration.[104] After the Senate Appropriations Committee withheld funding for CAPPS II pending a report from the General Accounting Office about its impact on privacy, however, the Department of Homeland Security announced that it would delete personal information from the CAPPS II database soon after a person completes his or her travel.

Operation TIPS

Although the attorney general's citizen-spy Terrorism Information and Prevention System program (Operation TIPS) was not funded by Congress, the idea of training people to participate in "terrorism prevention" is being pushed through various state efforts and entrepreneurial initiatives, such as the Community Anti-Terrorism Training Institute ("CAT Eyes"). Originating with two military men in New Jersey, CAT Eyes is training police and neighborhood watch groups in several states and hopes eventually to enlist one hundred million recruits.[105] It asks people to log any "terrorist indicators" they may have spotted into the FBI Web site, thereby giving the bureau a steady flow of information about "suspicious activity" around the country.

In Massachusetts, state troopers must respond to every call on the state's TIPS line, including an anonymous complaint alerting them to an article written by a University of Massachusetts, Boston, professor in *Sojourner* magazine.[106] In a single month, police, fire trucks, and the bomb squad rushed to BJ's Wholesale Club in Stoughton, Massachusetts, after four Muslim men were seen praying at sunset.[107] Brookline police and school officials held an emergency news conference to reassure panicked parents after reports that men of Middle Eastern appearance were seen with maps at neighborhood schools. The three men, of Turkish origin, had been speaking with school administrators in Brookline and Newton, Massachusetts, in order to decide where to move with their families.[108]

US Congress

Congressional oversight committees have been frustrated in their constitutional efforts to exercise a "check" on the executive by the secrecy of the Bush administration. Before 9/11, the General Accounting Office was prepared to sue Vice President Dick Cheney to obtain the names of people who served on his secret energy task force, so frustrated had it become by the vice president's refusal to part with this information. In February 2002, the GAO finally, for the first time in its history, filed a lawsuit against the executive branch. Cheney continued to stonewall, and the GAO's case was rejected by a federal court on December 9, 2002. Representative Henry Waxman (D-CA) said, "It is a convoluted decision by a Republican judge that gives Bush and Cheney near total immunity from scrutiny."[109]

That "immunity from scrutiny" has plagued Judiciary Committee efforts to know what use the executive branch is making of the powers given it under the USA PATRIOT Act, which has been the main contribution of Congress to the domestic "war on terrorism." Representative F. James Sensenbrenner (R-WI), head of the House Judiciary Committee, has repeatedly expressed his frustration at the Justice Department's refusal to report to the committee in a timely manner, and at its claim that much of the information sought by the committee is "classified." The leaking on February 7, 2003, of an 87-page secret Justice Department draft, "Domestic Security Enhancement Act of 2003" (often referred to as "PATRIOT II"), alerted Congress to the attorney general's wish list for a further expansion of executive branch power. This would include the provision for the summary deportation without evidence of crime or criminal intent of lawful permanent residents and others the attorney general says are a threat to national security (section 503) and the power to strip of their citizenship Americans who provide support for even the lawful activities of a group designated as "terrorist" (section 501).[110]

Thanks in large part to a growing grassroots movement demanding that the government respect the Constitution and roll back provisions of the USA PATRIOT Act that undermine constitutional rights and protections, members of Congress are increasingly attempting to act as a brake on the steady expansion of executive branch powers.[111] They refused to fund Operation TIPS and the Terrorism Information Awareness system, and they blocked (at least temporarily, at a closed hearing of the Senate Intelligence Committee) an administration proposal to permit the CIA and the military to use a little-known device called "national security letters" to force Internet providers, credit card companies, libraries, and other organizations and businesses to turn over their records. At present, only the FBI can use national security letters, which can be drafted by Ashcroft himself and need not be approved by any court. Congress defeated the administration's attempts to reclassify the nearly 900-page secret report compiled by the joint Congressional Committee on Intelligence on the government's failure to prevent the attacks of 9/11. Presidential lawyers had threatened to invoke executive privilege to keep the public from knowing about the long list of intelligence shortcomings and mistakes that paved the way for the attacks. The report, dated December 2002, was finally made public on July 24, 2003.[112]

USA PATRIOT Act

Congress has also blocked the attempt of Senator Orrin Hatch (R-UT) to make permanent those parts of the USA PATRIOT Act that are due to sunset at the end of 2005. Some members of Congress appear to be having second thoughts about the wisdom of passing such a massive piece of legislation without its being properly read and debated. On July 22, 2003, 113 Republicans joined the majority in a landslide 309–118 vote against section 213 of the USA PATRIOT Act permitting "sneak and peek" searches. Several other substantive challenges to the USA PATRIOT Act were put on the legislative agenda over the following months.

The USA PATRIOT Act was signed into law on October 26, 2001,[113] after John Ashcroft personally intervened to keep in the bill provisions that the House was prepared to drop in deference to civil liberties concerns. It is beyond the scope of this chapter to summarize this far-ranging law, which gives sweeping powers of detention and surveillance to the executive branch and law enforcement agencies and deprives the courts of meaningful judicial oversight to ensure that the new powers are not being abused. Everyone in the country is potentially affected by the broad new powers to search and share information given to a variety of government agencies and the erosion of privacy protections. Certain provisions are of special significance to noncitizens: Title II's expanded surveillance powers under the Foreign Intelligence Surveillance Act (FISA)[114]; Title III's focus on financial crimes (giving the government the power to freeze all assets of an organization and to defend its action on the basis of secret evidence) and on enlisting the services of banks in anti-terrorist activity[115]; the immigration provisions of Title IV, including the mandatory detention of suspected terrorists; Title VII's strengthening of criminal laws against terrorism.

Under the USA PATRIOT Act, a broad definition of "terrorist activity" permits noncitizens to be deported for the kind of wholly nonviolent associational activity protected by the First Amendment or to be locked up indefinitely—possibly for life— on mere suspicion, without charges or trial. Noncitizens can be arrested and held until deported if they are members of or have raised funds or provided some kind of material support for even the lawful activities of an organization designated as "terrorist" by the secretary of state or an organization that has not been so designated but might appear on the list in the future. No organization can challenge its designation as "terrorist" by the secretary of state. Noncitizens can continue to be detained if they have never been convicted of a crime but the attorney general "certifies" that he has "reasonable grounds to believe" that their release will endanger "the national security of the United States or the safety of the community or any person." After they are charged within seven days with either an immigration or criminal offense, noncitizens can be held indefinitely, with the attorney general reviewing their certification every six months. If they are ordered to be deported but no country will take them, they can be imprisoned for life in the United States.

How important is the USA PATRIOT Act to the administration's offensive against terrorism? The Justice Department informed Congress that it has not been using PATRIOT Act powers to detain suspects, because it could do this under other administrative rules. It was making good use, however, of new electronic and financial provisions, "sneak and peek" searches, and the sharing of information among various government agencies. "In our judgment," the Justice Department told the Senate and House Judiciary Committees, "the Government's success in preventing another catastrophic attack on the American homeland in the twenty months since September 11, 2001, would have been much more difficult, if not impossibly so, without the USA PATRIOT Act."[116] As evidence for this statement, it referred to the way "section 218 of the Act facilitated the terrorism investigation of Sami Al-Arian and other members of a Palestinian Islamic Jihad cell"—the second mention of Sami al-Arian in a report that referred to few other cases by name. "The USA PATRIOT Act was critical to the Department's ability to safeguard the Nation's security by bringing criminal charges against Al-Arian."[117]

Sami al-Arian is a former computer-engineering professor at the University of South Florida who had campaigned for George W. Bush during his 2000 presidential bid and had obtained Secret Service clearance for a June 22, 2001, visit to the White House as part of a delegation from the American Muslim Council.[118] An outspoken advocate of the Palestinian cause, his office and home had been raided eight years before by the FBI, but no charges were ever brought against him. His university later cleared him of any wrongdoing, and in 2000, a judge declared there was no evidence that he supported terrorism.

In February 2003, he and seven other people were indicted on racketeering charges, accused of helping to finance a Palestinian terrorist group, Islamic Jihad. What this group had to do with the "Nation's security" was not entirely clear. The government's evidence, based on telephone surveillance, had been collected in the mid-1990s by intelligence agents using a FISA warrant. Thanks to the USA PATRIOT Act's section 218, that evidence could now be used in criminal proceedings, enabling the government to make an end run around the Fourth Amendment.[119] The Justice Department stated that it is now sharing with criminal prosecutors forty-five hundred intelligence files with an eye to bringing additional cases. The implications are grave for people associated with organizations or causes that the government does not like.[120]

The courts

The first priority of the judicial branch must be to ensure that our government always operates within the statutory and constitutional constraints which distinguish a democracy from a dictatorship.

—Judge Gladys Kessler, *Center for National Security Studies, et al. v. US Department of Justice*

Executive branch secrecy

In some jurisdictions, the lower federal courts have attempted to restore constitutional balance and to "check" the excessive powers asserted by the executive branch in the domestic "war against terrorism." The refusal of the Justice Department to abide by these rulings has limited the impact of statements such as the one made by Judge Kessler. In her August 2, 2002, decision in *Center for National Security Studies, et al. v. US Department of Justice,*[121] Judge Kessler ordered the Justice Department to release the names of the more than one thousand people detained in the aftermath of 9/11. However, Judge Kessler did not rule that the names had to be made public immediately, and she then gave the department more time to make the case for why the names should be kept secret. On August 15, 2002, she issued a stay of her original order while waiting for the Court of Appeals for the District of Columbia Circuit to rule on the matter. On June 27, 2003, the Court of Appeals, by a 2–1 vote, upheld the government's refusal to release the names.[122] While Judges David Sentelle and Karen Henderson claimed that the judiciary was in no position to "second-guess" the government on national security, the dissenting judge David Tatel argued that "by accepting the government's vague, poorly explained allegations ... this court has converted deference into acquiescence."[123]

On March 27, 2002, New Jersey Superior Court judge Arthur D'Italia called secret arrests "odious to a democracy" and ordered the names of all INS detainees held in Hudson and Passaic County jails in New Jersey to be made public.[124] The government was granted a stay of the ruling so it could appeal. On April 22, 2002, the Justice Department issued an interim regulation prohibiting state and local officials from making public the names of INS detainees housed in their facilities.

Lawsuits have also challenged the holding of all "special interest" immigration proceedings in secret. *Detroit Free Press v. Ashcroft*,[125] filed in response to the barring of the press and Representative John Conyers (D-MI) from Rabih Haddad's deportation hearing, was successful at the district court level. Judge Nancy Edmunds ruled on April 3, 2002, that "it is important for the public, particularly individuals who feel that they are being targeted by the government as a result of the terrorist attacks of September 11, to know that even during these sensitive times the government is adhering to immigration procedures and respecting individual rights." Her opinion was unanimously upheld by a three-judge panel of the Sixth Circuit Court of Appeals, with Judge Damon Keith declaring that "democracies die behind closed doors."[126]

But the Third Circuit Court of Appeals had ruled differently in another case challenging the closure of immigration hearings, *North Jersey Media Group, Inc., and New Jersey Law Journal v. Ashcroft*.[127] After a district court judge rejected the government's blanket ban on secrecy, a three-judge panel of the Third Circuit Court voted 2–1 that the secret immigration hearings were constitutional. The US Supreme Court was expected to rule on the conflicting circuit court opinions, but it chose not to intervene. It is unclear whether the justices were motivated more by the Department of Justice claim that it was winding down its secret hearings or by their desire to leave intact what John Ashcroft called "an important, constitutional tool in this time of war."[128]

Material witness detentions

On April 30, 2002, Judge Shira Scheindlin of the US District Court for the Southern District of New York ruled in *United States v. Osama Awadallah*[129] that the government could not use a law that allows detention of material witnesses to hold people indefinitely for grand jury investigations. "Relying on the material witness statute to detain people who are presumed innocent under our Constitution in order to prevent potential crimes is an illegitimate use of the statute," she ruled. "If the government has probable cause to believe a person has committed a crime, it may arrest that person. But since 1789, no Congress has granted the government the authority to imprison an innocent person in order to guarantee that he will testify before a grand jury conducting a criminal investigation."

On November 7, 2003, this decision was overturned by the

US Court of Appeals for the Second Circuit, which ruled that Awadallah's detention as a material witness was valid and had not been "unreasonably prolonged."

Awadallah, who was attending college in San Diego, was arrested on September 21, 2001, and held in solitary confinement in various high-security prisons for the next twenty days. He testified before the grand jury on October 10, 2001, handcuffed to a chair. He was then kept in detention until December 13, 2001, on perjury charges, which were later dismissed by Judge Scheindlin.

Expanded FISA surveillance powers

A shadowy court structure, which few Americans even knew existed, is likely to play an increasingly prominent role if the regular federal court system insists on its powers to "check" the authority of the executive branch. The public recently got its first glimpse of the workings of the secret US Foreign Intelligence Surveillance Court (FISC), which was established under FISA in 1978 to review government applications for warrants to conduct "foreign intelligence" surveillance. In response to the Justice Department's assertion of broad new powers under the USA PATRIOT Act, the FISC stunned legal circles by writing a "Memorandum Opinion" on May 17, 2002, that criticized the FBI for refusing to play by the rules in its applications for FISA warrants and for its interpretation of section 218 of the USA PATRIOT Act. The memorandum was sent to the Senate Judiciary Committee, which released it to the public.

To contest this surprising ruling from a court that had never before made a public utterance, the Justice Department summoned into being an entity that had never before met—the three-judge Foreign Intelligence Surveillance Court of Review. A *New York Times* editorial sided with the FISC, arguing that its "revelations about the FBI's tactics are a powerful reminder of why the public needs to know more about how the government is prosecuting the war on terror."[130] On November 18, 2002, the Court of Review, in its debut performance, gave the government the ruling it wanted, stating that there was nothing in the USA PATRIOT Act's expanded surveillance powers that either contradicted FISA or the US Constitution.

"Enemy combatants"

Can US citizens be stripped of their rights if they are deemed "unlawful enemy combatants"? In Norfolk, Virginia, District Court Judge Robert Doumar twice ordered the government to allow a lawyer to visit Yaser Hamdi, an American citizen captured in Afghanistan. During the case *Yaser Hamdi v. Donald Rumsfeld,*[131] the government refused to provide the judge with documents supporting its assertion that Hamdi is an "enemy combatant," arguing that the judicial branch has no business interfering in the conduct of war. It finally handed over the "Mobbs declaration"—a statement from Michael Mobbs, identified as a special adviser to the under secretary of defense for policy, saying that Hamdi should be held incommunicado. The judge insisted on additional evidence, and the government appealed to the Fourth Circuit Court.

On January 8, 2003, a three-judge panel of the Fourth Circuit Court of Appeals held that no more evidence was needed to affix the label of "enemy combatant" on Hamdi and that his indefinite detention without access to a lawyer and the courts "conforms with a legitimate exercise" of executive war powers. There could be no judicial "searching review" of specific facts of the case, as that would be trespassing on executive war-waging powers. Since Hamdi had not been charged with a crime, he had no access to the due process procedures of the criminal justice system.

On December 3, 2003, the Bush administration filed a brief before the US Supreme Court, arguing that the justices should refuse to hear an appeal of the Fourth Circuit Court ruling in the *Hamdi* case, as this would interfere with the president's war powers. In a footnote to the brief it was stated that the Defense Department had decided to allow Hamdi access to a lawyer—not because this was his constitutional right, but "as a matter of discretion and military policy."[132]

The other American citizen who is being held incommunicado is Jose Padilla (Abdullah al-Muhajir). A former Chicago gang member who converted to Islam, Padilla's arrest on May 8, 2002, at Chicago O'Hare International airport was dramatically announced a month later by Attorney General Ashcroft at a press conference in Moscow (Russia). The United States, Ashcroft claimed, had disrupted an "unfolding terrorist plot to attack the US."[133] Soon afterward, deputy defense secretary Paul

Wolfowitz told CBS television, "I don't think there was actually a plot beyond some fairly loose talk and (Al Muhajir's) coming in here obviously to plan further deeds,"[134] but President Bush insisted, "This guy Padilla is a bad guy."[135] First held as a material witness, Padilla was declared an "enemy combatant" by President Bush and placed in military custody in a navy brig in Charleston, South Carolina.

"The government's position is unacceptable," the *New York Times* stated in a June 12, 2002, editorial. "Our Constitution guarantees that those suspected of crimes must be informed of the charges against them, be able to confront their accusers, consult with a lawyer and have a speedy and open trial. But that means very little if the government can revoke all those rights merely by labeling someone a combatant. And as Mr. Muhajir's case shows, the government is prepared to strip away the rights of American citizens as readily as those of foreigners."

Judge Michael Mukasy of the Southern District of New York twice ruled that Padilla should be permitted to consult a lawyer in order to challenge the "enemy combatant" designation.[136] The government hopes that the Fourth Circuit Court ruling in the *Hamdi* case can be applied to Padilla as well, although he was not captured in a "zone of active combat operations," and the Fourth Circuit panel declined to address "the designation as an enemy combatant of an American citizen captured on American soil." However, the judges repeatedly stressed the need to give maximum flexibility to the commander in chief as long as he decided we were still at war. "As the nature of threats to America evolves," the Fourth Circuit Court's chief judge J. Harvie Wilkinson III wrote, "the nature of enemy combatants may change also."

One wonders if the government will fix the label of "enemy combatant" to American citizens with the same care it took in declaring Afghan and Pakistani farmers, taxi drivers, and laborers to be "enemy combatants" before consigning them to the legal limbo of Camp Delta prison at Guantánamo Bay.[137] Citing military sources, Greg Miller wrote in the *Los Angeles Times* that at least fifty-nine of the prisoners have nothing to do with terrorism but were sent to Guantánamo over the objections of intelligence officers in Afghanistan who had recommended them for release. "There are a lot of guilty [people] in there," one officer stated, "but there's a lot of farmers in there too."[138]

"End-running the legal system"

On June 20, 2003, the public learned that an Ohio truck driver, Iyman Faris (formerly Mohammed Rauf), had pleaded guilty to supporting al-Qaeda and plotting to sabotage the Brooklyn Bridge.[139] Attorney General Ashcroft said that this guilty plea, which the naturalized American later tried to withdraw, had been sealed for seven weeks to avoid giving useful information to other al-Qaeda operatives and that up to fifteen other people were on the government's radar screen.[140] According to the June 23, 2003, issue of *Newsweek*, the Justice Department has been "working in the shadows" to track down al-Qaeda suspects, detain them in secret locations, and pressure them to accept plea bargains. "The Bush Justice Department is reluctant to throw terror suspects into the American criminal-justice system, where they can avail themselves of lawyers and use their rights to tie prosecutors into knots."[141]

In its June 18 issue, *Newsweek* had named Faris as one of the people identified as a "sleeper agent" by al-Qaeda's Khalid Shaikh Mohammed, who was captured in Pakistan in March 2003. After the magazine's journalists were unable to find any trace of Faris, they were told by law enforcement and intelligence sources that he "may be one of a small group of terror suspects who have been thrown into what one official calls 'a kind of limbo detention'—a new category that seems to be evolving outside the orbit of the criminal-justice system."[142] According to Kate Martin, director of the Center for National Security Studies, the Justice Department's departure from the rule of law "raises the specter of them being able to jail anyone they want in secret, and holding them incommunicado without access to a lawyer."[143]

Once Faris was publicly tied to al-Qaeda by Ashcroft, there were few expressions of concern about the government's methods. This fact alarmed veteran columnist Jimmy Breslin. In the New York newspaper *Newsday*, he spelled out what no one else was saying:

> Friday, the newspapers and television reported the following matter with no anger or effort to do anything other than serve as stenographers for the government: On March 1, give or take a day, in Columbus, Ohio, the FBI arrested an American citizen they say is Iyman Faris. There wasn't a word uttered. He vanished. No lawyer was notified. He made no phone calls and wrote no postcards or letters. He was a United States citizen

who disappeared without a trace into a secret metal world ... They held him secretly in an iron world for the next six weeks. This is plenty of time to hand out giant beatings ... In mid-April, again in deep secrecy, the government says Faris was allowed to plead guilty to plotting to pull down or blow up the Brooklyn Bridge ... This government's kidnapping of Faris/Rauf violated the laws handed down by Madison, Jefferson, Marshall. A small religious zealot, John Ashcroft, takes their great laws and bravery and using our new Patriot Act, turns it into Fascism ... There is not even the beginnings of anger about an American kidnapped by his government, over freedom being taken from us all, and bet me you won't see it back.[144]

In its June 23, 2003, issue, *Newsweek* publicized the case of another alleged "sleeper agent," Ali S. al-Marri, a Qatari national who was detained as a material witness in December 2001 and later indicted by a grand jury for credit-card fraud and making false statements to the FBI. He was facing trial in a federal court in Illinois when, on June 23, the attorney general announced that the criminal charges against al-Marri had been dropped. Although prosecutors said there was nothing to tie al-Marri directly to 9/11 and that he had not been "specifically tasked" to plot a chemical or biological attack in the US, he was termed an al-Qaeda operative and labeled an "enemy combatant."[145] His lawyer, Lawrence Lustberg, claimed that the government classified al-Marri as an "enemy combatant" because "we were raising powerful legal challenges" to the government's allegations. According to Lustberg, classifying al-Marri as an "enemy combatant" and depriving him of legal rights amounts to "end-running the legal system."[146]

The domestic war on terrorism: Are we on the right track?

Violating rights in times of perceived danger is an old American tradition that we have usually come to regret.[147] Today, as in the period immediately following the First World War, immigrants are feeling the brunt of government repression, but they are not alone. "Guilt by association" casts a wide net, which potentially can trap any Muslim citizen who makes a donation to the "wrong" charity, any Arab American who speaks out on US Middle East foreign policy, anyone whose appearance might attract the scrutiny of a citizen snoop, or anyone whose electronic profile might raise flags. The targeting by religion and national origin that is the federal government's weapon of choice in fighting terrorism has trickled down to the states, is amplified in the media,[148] and has its stressful counterpart in the "private sector." On the streets, on airplanes, in housing, in schools, and in employment, Muslims, Middle Easterners, and South Asians are increasingly the victims of hate crimes and discrimination, as the American-Arab Anti-Discrimination Committee's 2003 *Report on Hate Crimes and Discrimination Against Arab Americans: The Post–September 11 Backlash* amply attests.[149]

A detailed study of racial profiling based on law enforcement statistics reveals that profiling is a very ineffective method of fighting crime.[150] A scattershot approach to uncovering wrongdoing, it alienates the community from law enforcement rather than building the kind of trust that is the foundation of a healthy society and a critical part of intelligence gathering.

Because of its lack of transparency and accountability and its overreliance on unfounded suspicion and a dragnet-style hunt for the "enemy within," the administration now faces a growing credibility problem. On March 11, 2003, Senator Russell Feingold (D-WI), the only senator to oppose the USA PATRIOT Act, wrote to the attorney general and FBI head Robert Mueller "about some of the Department's conduct post–September 11—the selective enforcement of the immigration laws, the roundup and detention mostly of Arab and Muslim males, and the blanket targeting of mosques and Muslim Americans for surveillance. Mass detentions for public relations purposes and inflated estimates of the number of terrorists in our country can incite hatred of and violence against Arab and Muslim Americans and fuel suspicion in the Muslim world that our nation is fighting a war against Islam."[151] He made reference to a letter that FBI special agent and whistleblower Coleen Rowley had written to Mueller on February 26, 2003, in which she alleged that after September 11, the FBI "encouraged more and more detentions for what seemed to be essentially PR purposes" and that "particular vigilance may be required to head off undue pressure (including subtle encouragement) to detain or 'round up' suspects, particularly those of Arabic origin." Rowley had also questioned the FBI's estimate that there were some five thousand al-Qaeda terrorists in the United States, pointing out that Mueller had testified before the Senate Intelligence Committee on February 11, 2003, that there were "several hundred" people linked to al-Qaeda in the country.

The Justice Department's credibility has not been helped by reports that it is exaggerating its successes in the war on terrorism. In January 2003, the General Accounting Office stated that three-quarters of the "international terrorism" convictions for 2002 were wrongly classified and that the exaggeration prevented Congress and the public from understanding how much taxpayer money was being spent to prosecute terrorism.[152] Among the "terrorism" cases was one involving eight Puerto Ricans who were charged with trespassing on the island of Vieques, scene of frequent protests against the US Navy. The *Philadelphia Inquirer* looked into the fifty-six cases the Justice Department had labeled "terrorism" that were filed in the first two months of 2003 and found that "at least 41 of them had nothing to do with terrorism—a point that prosecutors of the cases themselves acknowledge." New Jersey prosecutors claim to have handled sixty-two "international terrorism" indictments in 2002, but on closer examination, all but two of these cases involved Middle Eastern men who were accused of paying other people to take their English exams and who were not linked to terrorism in any way.[153]

A growing skepticism about the Justice Department's classification of cases extends to its prosecution of terrorism-related cases. In April 2003, a district court judge in Denver, Colorado, reviewed FBI testimony and then ruled that two Pakistani nationals should not be denied bail, since the government failed to establish its claim that this was a terrorism case.[154] In Evansville, Indiana, the FBI publicly apologized to eight men who were paraded as terrorists and held as material witnesses in maximum-security jails after it was revealed that an estranged wife had made false accusations against them.[155] "Puzzling over motives of six men from Lackawanna: Terrorism or foolishness?" was the March 30, 2003, *New York Times* headline about the plea bargain accepted by Yemeni Americans who had admitted to attending an al-Qaeda training camp in Afghanistan. The government never made public any evidence that would back up its widely publicized claim that they were members of a "sleeper cell." As Matthew Purdy writes in the *New York Times*, "Ten years is a stiff sentence, but the three pleaded guilty after prosecutors made it clear that it could get worse ... they could face up to 30 years on gun charges. Defense lawyers feared treason charges, punishable by death ... Prosecutors held discussions ... about declaring the men enemy combatants and moving them out of the civilian judicial system." On October 12, 2003, the

Times devoted more than three entire pages to the "unclear danger" represented by the Lackawanna group, demonstrating "that behind Washington's sweeping proclamations is a more measured victory over a profoundly ambiguous threat."[156]

In the Detroit, Michigan, terrorism case, where the government's chief witness had proved unreliable, and in the case involving an alleged "sleeper cell" in Oregon, where James Ujamaa, an African American who had converted to Islam, also agreed to a plea bargain, strong doubts remain about the charges, which appear to some critics to be "overblown." The FBI counters that it cannot make all its evidence public.[157]

Could it even properly digest it? Is more information necessarily better information? Just as immigration offices are being overwhelmed by a blizzard of change-of-address forms, so FBI offices are reportedly struggling to keep up with the growing volume of tapes, transcripts, and photographs from ever-expanding surveillance operations. With very few Arabic language speakers on its staff before 9/11, it has added only a few hundred new translators for its counterterrorism efforts, 121 in Arabic and 25 in Farsi.[158] According to various studies, many old institutional problems remain. For instance, "secure areas" of airports are still not secure, ports and nuclear power plants remain vulnerable, and, as the GAO reported, nine federal agencies are still maintaining twelve separate "watch lists" with different kinds of information on known and suspected terrorists, have different policies on sharing the lists, and are still plagued by computer problems and poor communication.[159]

Two years after the attacks of September 11, the nation is no closer to understanding why they took place and what can be done to address the root causes of terrorism. Instead of focusing on solutions that actually work—on fixing specific flaws in the system, on building relationships of cooperation and trust, on tracking down concrete leads—the government has adopted a "guilty until proven innocent" approach to hunting down the "enemy within." In the process, it has devastated lives and dangerously eroded all of our rights, noncitizens and citizens alike. According to Amnesty International in its 2002 annual report, it has made the entire world a more dangerous and repressive place.

After the First World War, when the country was experiencing terrorist attacks in the form of anarchist bombs, Attorney General A. Mitchell Palmer ordered massive raids on homes, meeting places, and pool halls in scores of cities, arresting some ten thousand people, mostly without warrants or any kind of probable cause, and deporting up to a thousand immigrants. In a January 17, 1920, editorial entitled "Sowing the Wind to Reap the Whirlwind," the *Nation* magazine described a fearful United States in which hundreds of noncitizens were rounded up, held without any court appearances or bail, not given the opportunity to mount a defense, and not permitted to communicate with their families.

> If any of the persons, whether aliens or not, upon whom the Department of Justice has descended, have violated the law, they should be indicted, tried and punished for their offense ... Wholesale arrests and deportations such as we are now witnessing will not breed respect for government ... They will only ... increase many times the volume of discontent ... We shall not safeguard liberty by repressing it. The only way to end dangerous discontent ... is to remove its causes. Unless that is done, those who today are sowing the wind will before long reap the whirlwind.[160]

These words should resonate loudly in our own time.

Epilogue

By the beginning of February 2004—some eight months after this chapter was first drafted—growing sections of the public were challenging the government's version of the domestic "war on terrorism." Three state legislatures and some 240 cities and towns across the country representing thirty-five million people had passed resolutions against government measures that violated civil liberties and fundamental constitutional protections.

The resolutions passed by cities with large immigrant populations were explicit in their condemnation of ethnic and religious profiling. For instance, the Los Angeles City resolution, passed by a 9–2 vote on January 21, 2004, condemns portions of the USA PATRIOT Act that grant the attorney general the power "to subject citizens of other nations to indefinite detention or deportation even if they have not committed a crime" and Justice Department interpretations of the act and related executive orders that encourage "racial profiling by law enforcement and hate crimes by individuals in our community."

Lower court rulings in late 2003 and early 2004 held out hope that the rule of law might reassert itself. On January 27, 2004, US District Judge Audrey Collins, sitting in Los Angeles, ruled that the provision of the USA PATRIOT Act that bars providing "expert advice and assistance" to foreign "terrorist groups" is overbroad and a violation of the First and Fifth Amendments.

Two federal appeals court decisions, both decided on December 18, 2003, also put the Department of Justice on the defensive. A panel of the Court of Appeals for the Second Circuit ruled 2–1 that the government could not continue to hold US citizen Jose Padilla incommunicado as an "enemy combatant." His indefinite detention, the court stated, was a violation of the 1971 Non-Detention Act barring indefinite internment of citizens during times of war or national crisis without an act of Congress. The government immediately appealed to the US Supreme Court, which had already agreed to consider Yaser Hamdi's detention as an enemy combatant.

On the same day, a Ninth Circuit Court panel ruled 2–1 that the detention of prisoners at Guantánamo without access to US legal protections was unconstitutional and a violation of international law. While the administration was erecting a permanent prison and death chamber at Guantánamo and preparing to try some of the Guantánamo detainees before military commissions, its policies were being denounced not just by human rights groups and British high court judge Lord Steyn, who termed them "a monstrous failure of justice," but also by the uniformed military attorneys appointed by the Pentagon to represent some of the detainees. Five of them filed a Supreme Court brief in mid-January that calls the Bush administration a "monarchical regime" that has created "a legal black hole" in which one person, the president, has the power to prosecute, try, and execute sentences.

Will the US Supreme Court that appointed George Bush president choose to check the powers of the imperial presidency in its 2004 term? After agreeing to review the *Hamdi* case and to rule on the narrow issue of whether Guantánamo detainees could have hearings in US courts, the justices declined without comment to consider a case challenging the government's refusal to make public the names of hundreds of post–9/11 detainees. By permitting secrecy to prevail, is the high court signaling that there is little need for judicial—or public—oversight in how the executive branch conducts the domestic "war on terrorism"?

As we await Supreme Court rulings that will almost certainly have far-reaching implications for our constitutional system, the "enemy within" is proving elusive. After Guantánamo chaplain Captain James Yee and two Arabic language translators at Guantánamo were arrested on suspicion of espionage and "aiding the enemy," the charges against them were steadily scaled back. Captain Yee emerged from seventy-six days in solitary confinement to face accusations of adultery and keeping pornography on his government computer amid media reports that the documents found in his luggage as he was leaving Guantánamo might not even have been classified.

By the end of 2003, the government's high-profile prosecution of the so-called sleeper cell in Detroit was in turmoil after it admitted that it withheld evidence that its star witness, Yousef Hmimssa, had made up much of the story used to get convictions against two defendants. As the case unraveled, a federal judge sanctioned Attorney General John Ashcroft for twice violating a court-imposed gag order and making prejudicial statements about the case, and the FBI initiated an internal probe of its Detroit office.

In spite of these setbacks, there is no sign that the government is moving more cautiously in its targeting of Muslims and people of Arab descent. In a letter dated December 22, 2003, the Senate Finance Committee requested that the Internal Revenue Service turn over the donor lists and confidential tax and financial records of at least twenty-seven Muslim charities and foundations, on the grounds that they "finance terrorism and perpetuate violence."

A few weeks later, the FBI, with "evidence" supplied by the Washington-based Investigative Project, traced the "terrorism money trail" to Cleveland, Ohio, and arrested Fawaz Damra, the imam of the Islamic Center of Cleveland. He was charged with failing to reveal his ties to the Palestinian group Islamic Jihad when he applied for US citizenship in 1993, four years before Islamic Jihad was put on the government's list of terrorist organizations. The grand jury indictment against him also states that he failed to disclose an affiliation with groups that supported the Afghan resistance against Soviet occupation, a cause dear to the United States at the time. If convicted, the Palestinian American faces a maximum of five years in prison and can be stripped of his US citizenship and deported.

We learned from the leaked draft legislation entitled the Domestic Security Enhancement Act of 2003 that the Justice Department's wish list includes the power to strip of their citizenship Americans who provide support for even the lawful activities of a group designated as "terrorist." Will the government use the Damra case to test public and judicial acceptance of its citizenship-stripping powers even if PATRIOT II never becomes the law of the land?

"We the people" may just be beginning to discover how vulnerable we really are.

Nancy Murray
February 2, 2004

PART II

SUSTAINING AND REINFORCING
DEMONIZATION OF
ARABS AND MUSLIMS:
MANUFACTURING RACIST IMAGES OF
ARABS AND MUSLIMS

CHAPTER 3

"OUR ENEMIES AMONG US!" THE PORTRAYAL OF ARAB AND MUSLIM AMERICANS IN POST–9/11 AMERICAN MEDIA

Robert Morlino[1]

Introduction: Michigan storm warning

For those who channeled their anger, fear, and shock in the hours following the terrorist attacks of September 11 into concentrated hate, the requisite targets were easy to identify and locate. Some of them found Osama Siblani in Dearborn, Michigan, where the largest and most concentrated population of Arab Americans in the United States resides. Their voices threatened, indeed promised, further violence directed his way.

And though President Bush stood in the Islamic Center of Washington, DC, six days later and assured the world that the "war on terror" was not also the war on Islam, his words did little in the vast echo chamber of the mass media to counter the many other voices, some of them sadly trusted by the public, who instructed otherwise.

There was the infamous "Simply Kill These Bastards" column by Steve Dunleavy in the September 12, 2001, edition of the *New York Post,* the tabloid that shares its owner with the Fox News Channel. "As for the cities or countries that host these worms, bomb them into basketball courts," he wrote.[2]

In the *National Review,* there was Ann Coulter: "We should invade their countries, kill their leaders and convert them to Christianity ... We carpet-bombed German cities; we killed civilians. That's war. And this is war."[3]

National Review editor Rich Lowry to the *Washington Post*:

"If we flatten part of Damascus or Tehran or whatever it takes, that is part of the solution."[4]

On the subject of retaliation, a representative from the Institute for Public Accuracy asked Bill O'Reilly, "Who will you kill in the process?"

O'Reilly: "Doesn't make any difference."[5]

In mid-2003, the Washington, DC–based American-Arab Anti-Discrimination Committee (ADC) released a detailed report documenting violence directed against people perceived to be Arab or Muslim during the first year following 9/11. The ADC reported more than seven hundred violent incidents in the first nine weeks alone, and more than eight hundred cases of employment discrimination.[6]

Is that what Daniel Pipes meant when he wrote in the pages of the Manhattan Institute's *City Journal,* "Thankfully, some American Muslims ... understand that by accepting some personal inconvenience—and, let's be honest, some degree of humiliation—they are helping to protect the country and themselves" in an article that began by asking, "How should Americans now view and treat the Muslim populations living in their midst?"[7]

That question has been answered every day since it was posed, and rarely to the advantage of those about whom it was asked.

And the answering continues.

There was, for just one more recent example, the judge in Tarrytown, New York, who in 2003 asked a Lebanese American woman who appeared in court to resolve a parking violation if she was a terrorist. The woman, who was in court to contest a duplicate ticket for one violation (but not the original) was stunned but said nothing. Later, she reported, he did it again: "You have money to support the terrorists, but you don't want to pay the ticket." At that point, the woman collapsed. There was no court transcript, and the judge, 79-year-old William Crosbie, admitted to the first statement but not the second. Eventually, after the media reported the incident, he resigned.[8]

It is apparent that most Americans are no better informed about Arab and Islamic cultures than we were when the late Edward Said published his important book *Covering Islam*[9] in 1981. That the lessons of that work would go unheeded by the mainstream press is a reality compounded in the two years since the 9/11 attacks by coverage consumed with hysteria, sensationalism, and jingoism.

The relevance of media representations of Arab and Muslim Americans post–9/11 cannot be overstated in light of the ADC report. In fact, a comprehensive look at the issue would fill a volume on its own. This chapter presents one in-depth case study that reflects many of the mistakes repeated countless times in numerous other cases by the mainstream American media: the rush to judgment and assumption of guilt when reporting on Muslim and Arab Americans; the forced connection between the Islamic faith and terrorism; the failure to report all the facts when they were readily available; the reluctance or outright refusal to correct erroneous reporting; and the indulgence in speculation and defamation informed strictly by bias and ignorance. Following the case study are broader examinations of the issues it raises.

The Ptech incident

The Web site of Ptech Inc., a Massachusetts-based software company that specializes in enterprise architecture technology, contains several press releases marking various milestones. There's one dated January 28, 2002, announcing Ptech's recognition as one of *KMWorld Magazine*'s "100 Companies That Matter" for the second consecutive year. From December 2001, there's a profile written about the company and its CEO, run in the *Patriot Ledger* newspaper under the headline "Ahead of the Curve: Quincy-based Ptech Helps Big Business Stay Agile." The profile's author, Keith Regan, described Ptech as gaining "worldwide attention as a software company that has helped major government agencies, including some branches of the military, and Fortune 100 companies become more efficient."[10]

Understandably, however, there is not a press release noting the company's prominent mention on ABC's *Good Morning America* in late 2002.

"This just in."

On the morning of Friday, December 6, 2002, *Good Morning America* began with hosts Diane Sawyer and Charles Gibson informing viewers of a dramatic new development in the war on terrorism. Gibson led off with the alarming question, "Has al Qaeda infiltrated the FBI's computers?" He then gave viewers the headline: "Overnight the Feds Bust a Boston Area Software Company Suspected of Ties to the Terrorist Group." Calling it "an interesting story," Gibson teased the forthcoming news report by describing a "midnight raid" on a software company called Ptech, located in Quincy, Massachusetts.

The requisite loaded language was there for a sensational story. Raid. Al Qaeda. Infiltration. Terrorism. Boston. *Good Morning America* had a dynamic and compelling story for its viewers. As ABC News correspondent Brian Ross prepared to fill in the details, Sawyer urged him, "What on earth would prompt law enforcement officials to move on an American company, move in this quickly, this way?"

"Take a look at this remarkable footage," Ross replied as he described a late-night raid in the midst of a "driving snowstorm" by a team of US Customs agents—the "culmination of a top secret White House coordinated raid amid concerns the company was secretly controlled by al Qaeda activists or sympathizers."

With the important details established, Ross moved on to specifics, explaining that Yasin al-Qadi, a Saudi millionaire and one of Osama bin Laden's "money men," had financial ties to the company, and word of this connection spurred an investigation of the "highest priority" within the government.

And there was the final incendiary detail. Among the company's clients were a few government entities of relative note— the FBI, the US Air Force, NATO, the House of Representatives, and the Department of Energy, among others. "It really is startling to think that they could have access to central computer systems," Sawyer said.[11]

Those comments kicked off a rash of coverage in newspapers, on the radio, and on cable news, much of which emphasized many of the same bits of the story presented on *Good Morning America*. Even more startling than the horrific possibilities contemplated by the coverage is the prospect that the media's dominant characterization of what took place was flat-out wrong.

Less than two months after the events on December 6, 2002, a wholly different account of what took place at Ptech's headquarters that night appeared in the industry publication *Computerworld,* which had earlier published a report similar to that of *Good Morning America* and other major outlets. This new story presented several important details, not the least of which was that, according to representatives at Ptech, there was no dramatic "raid" of the company's offices at all.

In the *Computerworld* story, Ptech's CEO Oussama Ziade

presented his side of the story first reported the previous December. As Ziade, a native of Lebanon, told *Computerworld*, Yasin al-Qadi was one of the initial "angel" investors in the company in 1994 but was never an investor of record. Years later, following the September 11 terrorist attacks, a former Ptech employee saw a story on CNN about the Saudi businessman and his alleged financial connections to terrorist organizations. The former employee e-mailed the FBI, identifying al-Qadi as a Ptech investor. On Thursday, December 5, 2002, FBI agents went to Ptech's headquarters with a warrant and asked to investigate al-Qadi's connections to the company. Ziade granted permission immediately, and in return, US Customs promised him that word of the investigation would not get out. The agents on the scene even went to such lengths as parking their cars away from the company's building and entering its offices one by one through a rear entrance, escorted by Ziade. That same night, Ziade met with federal authorities in his lawyer's office. The feds assured Ziade that neither Ptech nor its employees were targets of the investigation.

The *Computerworld* story also recounted in detail the circumstances that connected, at least financially, al-Qadi and Ptech:

> Ziade said he then told investigators that al-Qadi had been a member of the board of directors of another company that had invested in Ptech when it was first starting in 1994. Ptech's first investment had come from venture capitalists in New Jersey, he said.
>
> Ziade, who came to the U.S. in 1985 from Lebanon and had contacts throughout the Middle East, made his first trip to Saudi Arabia in 1995 seeking additional funding for his young company. He had been told there was venture capital to be had there, so that's where he went.
>
> It was then that he met with al-Qadi and one of the largest investment bankers in Saudi Arabia. To his surprise, half a dozen other U.S. software and technology companies were there also looking for money.
>
> "When I was there, I attended a fundraiser for five different American companies," Ziade said. "There were investors there with common investments in dozens of U.S. companies." The companies, he said, are household names in the U.S. high-tech industry, though he declined to name them.
>
> Ziade was unsuccessful in persuading al-Qadi to invest more money in Ptech. When he approached the Saudi businessman a year later, he was told to look for investors in the U.S. Al-Qadi had given up on the company.
>
> In 1999, Ptech made another big push to raise more money—

and once again approached al-Qadi. Ziade and his executives, many of them Americans dressed in typical American garb, went back to Saudi Arabia to brief al-Qadi and others on the company's progress. When they finished, al-Qadi promised an additional $3 million. The money never materialized.

Ziade explains that by the time the interview with the investigators ended, so too had the search of Ptech's offices. It was early morning on December 6 at that point, and already the parking lot outside the company's offices was filling with reporters who had learned of the investigation.[12] It was at this point that *Good Morning America* was alarming viewers across the nation that the feared terrorist group may have gained access to the government's electronic infrastructure.

It didn't take long for the story to spread across the United States and around the world via newswires, and for the most part, the description of the government's visit to Ptech was that of an intense raid. Many outlets included some of the buzz words in their headlines. United Press International went with "Agents Look for Tech Firm Terror-Link."[13] The *Deseret News* in Salt Lake City, Utah, picked up the Associated Press (AP) wire story: "Customs Agents Raid U.S. Software Company."[14] Tech news outlets followed suit—*PC Magazine*'s Web site posted "Feds Raid Software Firm," and Ziff Davis Media: "Feds Raid Software Firm."[15] The Deutsche Presse-Agentur and Agence France Presse both had "raid" in their headlines.[16] So did the Associated Press in the United States. In its initial dispatch, the AP cited *Good Morning America*'s network, ABC News, as reporting that the company had been raided. (A later AP story by Curt Anderson, with a follow-up the next day, left out the word "raid" and noted that Ptech "consented" to a search.)

A few outlets, however, went without the "raid" descriptor. Cox News Service reported that a three-month investigation resulted in a search.[17] *Newsweek* posted a story online that noted, "Law-enforcement sources said the search was performed after a cooperating witness gave investigators access to the property on Thursday night." The story also included a detail absent from many other stories:

> Ptech may have recently taken steps to play down its possible connections with Qadi. Last month, the company's Web-site biography of the company's chief scientist, Hussein Ibrahim, described him as a former vice chairman of a company called

BMI Finance and Investment Group. A *Wall Street Journal* report recently alleged that Qadi was an investor in BMI, which Qadi's lawyer confirmed. As of today, the reference to Ibrahim's employment with BMI had been deleted from the biography.[18]

Though the wording implies a surreptitious effort on the part of Ptech, this detail was given low priority in the story and demonstrates an important fact about the immediate coverage—disproportionate reporting was being done in the rush to nail down the facts about Ptech. On the cable news networks, the disparity was exaggerated.

During the afternoon of December 6, MSNBC's talk show *Buchanan and Press,* a clone of CNN's *Crossfire,* got into the story with the network's resident "terrorism expert," Steve Emerson. Bill Press, the show's liberal host, asked Emerson first to tell the audience about al-Qadi and his membership in the "dirty dozen," a group of Saudi financiers suspected by the United States of funding Osama bin Laden's terrorist network. He asked pointedly, "If [al-Qadi] is definitely a member of it, what are we doing, doing business with his software firm?"

Never mind that there was, and remains, no evidence to support the characterization of Ptech as in any way belonging to al-Qadi. Immediately after discussing the dirty dozen, Emerson engaged in damning speculation before cutting out due to technical difficulties:

> EMERSON: The question is, how do these contracts get executed in the U.S. government to the highest levels, without anyone doing the due diligence?
> PRESS: Yes.
> EMERSON: That's the question, I think, we want to know. And I can't answer it other than to say that this is the—sort of the, I guess the concept behind 9/11. You hide under the radar screen. You insinuate yourselves under a legitimate cover. Ptech is no doubt a legitimate company, but *the best-case scenario is that moneys made by this company were being enumerated* [sic] *to al Qaeda.* The worst-case scenario not yet proven is that there was a bug or a Trojan horse in the software.
> PRESS: Well that's what I want to ask you about, Steve, because the other important question, I think is, is it possible for them to have gotten into these agencies by supplying some software in which were buried some so-called trap doors, as you say the Trojan horse, which would give them access to top-secret material inside all of these government agencies?
> EMERSON: I think that has been a very real—I mean, fright-

ening fear on the part of investigators, whether, in fact, something was embedded in the coded language of the software. So
far, as far as I understand, nothing has been found to substanti-
ate that, but the investigation is still continuing in terms of the
cyber analysis of the software DNA, but the other problem ...
    PRESS: I'm afraid we lost our connection there to Steve
Emerson.[19]

In light of all statements issued by the investigating agencies,
even at that early stage on December 6, the best-case scenario
for Ptech (or, rather, merely one of several better-case scenarios
than Emerson's) would have been that the company did receive
funding at one point that was in no way connected to terrorist
activity. (Ultimately, that would be proven most likely.) Further,
MSNBC competitor Fox News reported on the afternoon of December 6 that the government had cleared the company's software.[20] But no one on MSNBC's *Buchanan and Press* saw fit to
point out that fact.

    CNN's now-defunct studio-audience show *Talkback Live*
aired around the same time as MSNBC's *Buchanan and Press*.
Broadcast from Atlanta, *Talkback Live*'s format was similar to
that of daytime talk shows—a host would interview guests of
various backgrounds and viewpoints, and a live audience would
have opportunities to ask questions and comment. Major news
stories usually comprised the bulk of the show's discussion topics. On Friday afternoon, the show's host, Arthel Neville, teased
a live report from correspondent Bill Delaney by telling the audience that a Massachusetts software company had been raided
overnight. When Delaney filed his report, he took issue with the
use of the word "raid":

> DELANEY: Now, you used the word "raid," Arthel. We
> might want to be a little careful with that, because we have
> learned just in the past hour or so that it's *kind of hard to really
> call this a raid*. And the company doesn't believe it should be
> called a raid, since the CEO of the company walked Customs of-
> ficials into their offices last night, when Customs officials then
> began to download software.
>   Now, they did that to see if the software could in any way
> have been tampered with in a way that might enable hackers to
> break into any of the agencies that this software is sold to. Now,
> no less a personage than Tom Ridge, head of the U.S. Homeland
> Security Office, has said in the past hour or two that there is ab-
> solutely no evidence that any of the software here is or was or
> could be used for those purposes.[21]

Delaney's initial note about calling the search a "raid" under-
scores perfectly the lack of restraint employed by other outlet reporters and even others within CNN. It is also worth noting that
even at that point, just a few hours after the *Good Morning
America* broadcast, thorough reporting corroborated Ziade's description of events published months later in the *Computerworld*
article—one absent from most of the initial stories on the case.

Delaney also provided a less alarmist description of the chain
of events that led to the search at Ptech's headquarters. Other reports hinted at "desperate" pleas by employees of the company
to the FBI, begging the agency to investigate terror ties within
their offices. Delaney's report removed the hype and presented a
much calmer scenario:

> DELANEY: Now, Yasin al-Qadi was an investor in Ptech.
> And, beyond that, we have also learned—CNN's Kelli Arena
> speaking to sources close to this investigation has learned that
> the U.S. government has been looking at Ptech's relations to
> Yasin al-Qadi since right after 9/11.
>
> And that's because, right after 9/11, employees of this small
> company got in touch with U.S. law enforcement officials and
> said: "Hey, we just heard that Yasin al-Qadi"—whose name has
> been around a lot since 9/11—"is on a watch list. Well, this
> man," they said, "we actually met in Saudi Arabia on a com-
> pany tour with our small company a while back. And he was in-
> troduced to us," these employees of Ptech told government
> officials way back around 9/11. He was introduced to them in
> Saudi Arabia as an owner of their company.
>
> And that made them concerned enough to get in touch with
> investigators. Way back in 9/11, this investigation of Ptech's ties
> to Yasin al-Qadi began. It has gone on and climaxed last night
> with the CEO of this company, a gentleman named Oussama
> Ziade, leading Customs officials in here.[22]

Delaney's report also included comment from a Ptech vice
president, Joseph Johnson, who spoke to a key underlying issue
about the entire incident: the religious and ethnic affiliation of
some of the company's employees, CEO Ziade included. Most
of the stories published in the first few days pointed out that
many of Ptech's employees were indeed Muslim. One even noted
that the office included a separate prayer room for those employees of the Islamic faith. (In fact, according to a statement released to the media by the company, fewer than twenty-five of
the more than two hundred people Ptech hired in the course of
nine years were either of Arab descent or the Muslim faith.) The

significance of these details and their value in the currency of captivating news cannot be underestimated in considering much of the mainstream media's rush to characterize the Ptech search as a dramatic new twist in the war on terrorism:

> DELANEY: Now, as far as company reaction on camera, the only thing we've gotten so far is the reaction of a vice president, Joe Johnson.
> JOHNSON [recorded comments]: It doesn't come as a surprise to us. You know, I think that it's to be expected. We live in kind of different times right now, you know? So, we're an American company. We've been in business for almost nine years. We do have people here who are Muslims. They're American citizens.
> But we fully expected this. So, I don't think it's any different than when you go to the airport today and you have to go through additional security. You know, we kind of suspected that this might happen. And it's going to happen. We just have to kind of try to get through it and continue with our business.[23]

Later, in the *Computerworld* stories, as well as in several stories in the local *Patriot Ledger* newspaper, these themes would be revisited in the aftermath of the media meltdown, with the loyalty and patriotism of Ziade presented with as much weight as the actual substance of the case. Still, the CNN report by Delaney on *Talkback Live* explored many of the critical issues associated with the kind of irresponsible journalism practiced throughout the affair. After Delaney signed off, Neville turned to her panel of guests for comment, starting with Richard Bey, a television and talk-radio personality, who made a poignant observation.

> NEVILLE: And I go over to my panel now. And I want to start with Richard Bey on this one and ask you, when you hear about this investigation, what sort of thoughts come to mind?
> BEY: Well, it sounds like there's—listen, in this day and age, everything is worthy of an investigation if there's any kind of lead. It doesn't sound like there's a lot there.
> I wonder if they're going to be going over to Fox News Network, whose parent company, News Corps, is 20 percent owned by the Saudis as well? And maybe there's something nefarious going on over there with your competition. Can I say that?
> NEVILLE: You can you say anything you'd like, Richard.
> BEY: Thank you.[24]

Overall, despite Neville's initial description of the search, the CNN segment presented a reasoned and balanced examination even as MSNBC's report presented the opposite. A few hours later, the Fox News program *The Big Story with John Gibson* had its own report. Guest host David Asman also described the incident as a "raid." Of note in this story is the emphasis that correspondent Gregg Jarrett placed on the diagnosis of the company's software after the FBI's investigation, though he still reported that agents had "swarmed" the company's offices:

> JARRETT: David, the feds swarmed the building behind me. It's the headquarters of Ptech. That's an important software company. And what they did was they brought in their own computers. Now they didn't seize any equipment, they didn't seize hard drives, but they downloaded Ptech's software, and then they examined it today.
>
> And here is the most *important part of the story*. According to the federal government, all the software was screened. It came up clean. There were no security compromises. The government had feared that al Qaeda, through this company, had gained access to top-secret intelligence information of the military and the federal government.[25]

Jarrett's report included part of a statement by Blake Bisson, another Ptech vice president, whom Jarrett described as "very relieved," noting that the executive credited his Fox colleague Catherine Herridge with reporting the company's clean bill of electronic health.

> BISSON: According to a Fox News Channel report released in the early afternoon on Friday, December 6, the government said Ptech Inc.'s software was safe, after studying its code for evidence it might do anything other than advertised, such as allowing insiders to read sensitive data.[26]

The disparities in coverage on cable news were most acute during that first day of the story. Unfortunately for Ptech, print outlets had a lengthier attention span. The Saturday, December 7, edition of the *New York Post* carried a story on Ptech that was riddled with gross misrepresentations of what took place at the company's offices. "Anti-Terror Raid At Mass.-Based Software Firm" was the story's sensational headline, and from the start, the article emphasized the prospect that Ptech operated in some capacity as a funding cell of al-Qaeda:

> Federal agents yesterday raided a high-tech software firm and searched its offices and computer files for links to a Saudi businessman with suspected ties to Osama bin Laden's al Qaeda terror network.
>
> Federal officials said they are investigating allegations that the owners and some employees of Massachusetts-based Ptech Inc. may have funneled money to terrorists.

Attributed to vague "federal officials," the notion that Ptech's owners and employees were suspected of funneling money to al-Qaeda contradicts Ziade's account in the *Computerworld* article. He says the FBI assured him that no one employed at that time at Ptech was a suspect, and neither was the company itself. The *Post*'s article contained another distortion of the facts: "Ptech is reportedly controlled by Yasin al-Qadi, a wealthy Saudi businessman whose U.S. assets were frozen by the Bush administration after 9/11 because of his suspected role as a terrorist financier." This statement is attributed to no one is not supported in any way.[27]

On the same day, the *New York Times* ran a story that repeated some of the same suspect characterizations of the event, though it presented a layered, more nuanced version of the story. It still began with news of a raid by federal agents on a small software company in Massachusetts. As in the *Post* article, an unnamed government source was quoted, repeating the claim that al-Qadi had a current and controlling interest in the company, a claim that would never be substantiated:

> "The key thing here is that al-Qadi is on the terror financing list, and U.S. entities are prohibited by law from doing business with anyone on the list," said a senior law enforcement official who spoke only on the condition of anonymity.
>
> "We're pretty sure that he is the main financier of the company," said the official, although he would not detail evidence supporting that belief. "The question is, Was the company aware of his being on the list, and did they continue to deal with him despite the fact that he was on the list?"[28]

But the *Times* also included comments from Michael J. Sullivan, the US attorney in Boston, and they stood in sharp contrast to the alarmist tone conveyed by much of the coverage beginning with *Good Morning America*:

> This evening, however, Mr. Sullivan issued a statement seemingly playing down the question of whether Ptech software could have been used to access government data.
>
> "The search was conducted in connection with an ongoing financial crime investigation," the statement said. "Media characterizations of this as a terrorist investigation are premature."
>
> Mr. Sullivan also said a review of Ptech's computer systems had found "no reason to believe that the software has any secondary purpose or malicious code, or that there has been a breach of any kind."

"There have been no vulnerabilities identified in connection with any of the products provided by Ptech," he said. "There is no evidence to suggest that the system is susceptible to compromise or poses any security risk."[29]

Several stories published within two days of the incident focused on the search of Ptech's offices as part of a broader investigation into the financial connections of al-Qadi, stressing statements by officials such as Sullivan that there was no security compromise detected in the company's software and that the terrorism angle was "premature" with respect to the company. The December 7 Associated Press story by Curt Anderson, mentioned earlier, left out the word "raid" and characterized the event as a search that Ptech "consented to."

Smaller outlets continued to use the word, however. And, despite a wealth of reporting that should have reassured readers, a backlash was rapidly developing. An article in the Rhode Island *Providence Journal-Bulletin* quoted Hugh McKellar, editor of *KMWorld* (the publication mentioned earlier, which ranked Ptech among its "100 Companies That Matter"), as saying, "Ptech is not a shadow company. This is a legitimate organization."[30] Nevertheless, on December 8, the *Boston Globe* reported that the company had already received a barrage of hate mail,[31] and the *Patriot Ledger*, Quincy's daily newspaper, reported that the company had already lost a one million dollar contract and was in jeopardy of losing far more business in the hysteria created by the media frenzy.[32] The repercussions of the initial, sensationalistic coverage were revealing themselves already.

Focusing on local vs. national reporting

As the days went by and brought no evidence of wrongdoing on the part of any Ptech employee, national media outlets all but abandoned the story, as they often do when there's simply nothing new or compelling to keep viewers interested. At the local level, however, one publication kept with the Ptech story for several months—the *Patriot Ledger,* the daily newspaper of Quincy, Massachusetts.

For the *Patriot Ledger*'s reporters, the Ptech case presented a well to which many trips could be made, as their readers likely would sustain interest far beyond that of the national audience. Certainly, they benefited from having Ptech to write about at length. Nevertheless, the coverage in the *Patriot Ledger* is vital in two regards. First, the paper addressed at the local level the damage to the company's reputation; explored what happened in the aftermath of frenzied, if brief, national media attention; raised questions about the government agencies' handling of the case; and gave continued voice to Ptech's staff. Second, the paper did precisely what the national media did not do by spending time to cover the whole story, not just the parts that grab the attention of as many readers and viewers as possible. The difference between local and national coverage in this case is important because the comprehensiveness of the former exposes the flaws of the latter.

The *Patriot Ledger* first wrote about Ptech a full year before the search in December 2002. In the December 27, 2001, edition of the paper, an article in the business section profiled the company's growth from a struggling enterprise into a successful, competitive corporation with clients as high profile as the Federal Aviation Administration. In "Ahead of the Curve," Keith Regan interviewed Ptech CFO and COO George Peterson, who explained that one of the company's clients, a major utility company, had saved forty-seven million dollars in operating costs after implementing Ptech software in its IT department—a 3,500 percent return on investment. "Numbers like that sell themselves," Peterson told the *Patriot Ledger*. The article in 2001 also included several comments from the company's founder and CEO, Oussama Ziade. At that time, details such as Ziade's country of origin and his religious affiliation were unimportant and were not included. This story was, after all, strictly business.[33]

That of course changed the following year, when FBI agents descended on the town followed closely by a full contingent of national media reporters. The *Patriot Ledger* published its first story about the incident on Friday, December 6, reporting a midnight raid on the company and including most of the details found in AP and other national outlet stories, such as Ziade's Lebanese heritage. The local paper's reporters had the advantage of knowing the town on a more intimate level, and this story included comments from local sources at the story's conclusion:

> "They seemed to be honorable people. There was nothing suspect of them," said Thomas O'Connell, manager of Marina Bay Management Services, which rents office space to Ptech.
>
> O'Connell said he did not help Customs agents enter the office last night. Of Ziade, he said, "He seemed to be a savvy busi-

nessman and we never had an issue with him."

Amanda Ingles, a waitress at the Marina Bay Sandwich Shop in the Victory Road building, said Ziade's brother often came in to get his brother's lunch. She said Oussama Ziade was not friendly.

They came in regularly, she said, but stopped about two months ago.[34]

The quote from O'Connell is relevant, but the inclusion of Ingles's appraisal of the Ziade brothers' demeanor at this point is questionable, and her comments contributed, albeit unintentionally, to the cloud of suspicion rapidly forming over the Ptech executive. What percentage of customers would takeout restaurant employees, when pressed, describe as "friendly," and what exactly did Ingles mean when she said Ziade wasn't? And what was the significance of Ziade no longer patronizing the Marina Bay Sandwich Shop? Maybe the brothers decided to try another establishment, or simply didn't like the store's sandwiches anymore. There's no way of knowing. Though ultimately that question had nothing to do with the story, in the whirlwind of panic started by *Good Morning America*, minor and even irrelevant details could inspire a completely manufactured, ominous significance. A viewer who saw the reports on ABC or MSNBC then turned to the pages of the *Patriot Ledger* might find some significance in the sudden, seemingly drastic alteration in the eating habits of Ziade and his brother, but if there was a connection at all to warrant inclusion in the story, the burden was on the reporters to draw it.

The next day's edition of the *Patriot Ledger* contained no fewer than five full stories on the Ptech case, all on the first two pages—for the newspaper, the story was about as big as Quincy news gets. The lead story, "Raided Company Denies Terror Links," picked up where the previous day's story left off, further examining the investigation of al-Qadi investments and acknowledging the confusion surrounding the case:

Ptech officials said they cooperated fully with the investigation, flatly dismissing earlier reports of a clandestine, late-night raid by federal authorities. CEO Oussama Ziade allowed investigators into the building at around 8 p.m. Thursday to conduct the search, and the company plans to continue to assist the government's investigation, Johnson said.[35]

By now the media attention itself was part of the story. The article included a note about how it had already left Ptech scrambling to retain clients amid the controversy. The company told the reporters at that point that a one million dollar contract was in jeopardy. The *Good Morning America* piece came up as well:

> The company is considering demanding an apology from ABC News, which first broke the story about the government search during its "Good Morning America" program on Friday.
> "It just wasn't factual," said Blake Bissen, vice president of sales for the company. "It's obviously yellow journalism at its best. It's really sad."[36]

The story also included Michael Sullivan's comments about the media's characterization of the search as a terrorist investigation being premature. One of the other stories in the day's edition dealt exclusively with the fallout from the media coverage. Specifically, the story demonstrated the unfortunate effects of the national media's reporting:

> Other clients have also called saying they plan to pull their business, and Ptech has received a torrent of hate E-mails warning employees to "go back to the Middle East, you terrorists," Johnson said.[37]

The remaining articles on December 7 examine the various aspects of the story. One deals with the technical questions about Ptech's software and includes an expert stating that there probably wasn't any danger from its use.[38] Another story, in a way a follow-up to the earlier December 2001 profile, focuses on Ziade, but this time his Muslim affiliation became integral:

> Ziade, a Muslim, is an active member of the New England Islamic Center in Quincy Point, attending religious services most Fridays, the Muslim Sabbath. A member there Friday described him as devout.
> "He is a very gentle, wonderful man. He prays here all of the time," said Zaida Hassan Shaw, the center's office manager.[39]

By December 9, the *Patriot Ledger* stopped referring to the search as a raid and shifted its focus away from the investigation, which had diminished significantly. The newspaper focused instead on the effect of the negative attention on the company. On December 10, the paper published an editorial on the matter. It began, "The search of a Marina Bay software company last Thursday evening sounded like a really big story at first," and raised several unanswered questions about the investigation, advocating for government accountability in an event that had left its target "twisting in the wind." The editors wrote:

> Ptech has been damaged. It suffered the worst possible connection in the public eye—a suspected relationship with terrorists. By the time government spokesmen were backing off their suspicions late Friday, the story had been national news all day long.[40]

Interestingly, the December 10 editorial placed the burden of clearing Ptech's name squarely on the government, even though it alluded to overzealous reports in the media and their detrimental effect. Coverage in the paper would continue for several months, however, and this is the crucial point where local and national media parted ways: whereas the *Patriot Ledger* kept with the story as it became much less sensational, the national media simply moved on, uninterested in lingering on a story that turned out to be not nearly as dramatic as they had previously thought. In one sense, this is easily explainable. The impact of media attention on the Quincy-based company may have been interesting in Quincy, but across the country more important news was happening. Conversely, it was the elements of the initial, underreported version of the story worthy of national attention, and those elements are what caused the most damage. It is all but certain that the e-mails sent to Ptech and described above were the result of the national coverage on December 6. It would not be surprising if none of their authors had ever heard of the company previously.

Subsequent articles in the *Patriot Ledger* reported on financial problems inside Ptech, the continued backlash and responses from the local Muslim community, and updates on the status of the investigation. Oddly, by January 22, 2003, the paper was back to referring to the incident as a raid.[41] The next day, the paper reported that Senator Charles E. Grassley (R-IA) was calling for the FBI to further scrutinize Ptech's software for potential terrorist connections; this despite the fact that Homeland Security director Tom Ridge had cleared the company's software.[42]

Then in May 2003, the *Patriot Ledger* included the Ptech case as part of its analysis of the USA PATRIOT Act's effect on civil liberties. Ziade was quoted as saying that he didn't believe racial profiling had played a part in the event of the previous December:

> Oussama Ziade, owner of Quincy-based software developer Ptech Inc., said racial profiling played no part in a search of his business by federal authorities last winter.

Still, he objects to provisions of the Patriot Act that he believes encroach on Americans' civil liberties.

"I don't think this is the way to treat the issue at hand,"
Ziade said in an interview this week. "That's what the terrorists
want—for us to lose our values. We should never sacrifice our
liberties and civil rights."

Ziade's business was searched last December because of suspicion that it was connected to a terrorist financier from Saudi
Arabia. Ziade vehemently denied such a connection, and no
charges were filed against him or officials in his company.

The American Civil Liberties Union and other groups have
seized on the Ptech case and others around the country as examples of government abuse brought on by the Patriot Act.

"What we are seeing is an unprecedented amount of power
being assumed by the executive branch of the government,"
ACLU executive director Carol Rose said. "There has been a
fundamental shift in the system of checks and balances that has
protected our civil rights for the past 200 years."[43]

If anyone is in a position to decide whether racial profiling
played a part in the actual investigation by the government, it is
Ziade, and his belief seems justified in light of the coverage analyzed thus far. Instead, an overzealous media—not necessarily
motivated by discrimination, but rather by a combination of the
never-ending hunt for a ratings-boosting, sensational story and a
deferment to the biases of its audiences—made the company and
its employees victims of post–9/11 hysteria.

The problems don't end there, however. There is another ele-
ment to the immediate national media coverage of the Ptech investigation, one that is also perhaps the most disturbing. Howard
Kurtz, media columnist for the *Washington Post* and host of
CNN's media show *Reliable Sources,* wrote about an aspect of
the investigation not reported anywhere else, just one day after
Good Morning America broke the story. The revelations contained in Kurtz's piece portray competing media outlets, impatient
for a major story, entering into a quid pro quo arrangement with
the FBI long before the first agents ever arrived at Ptech's offices.

It's not uncommon for reporters covering criminal investigations to make arrangements with the agencies involved—deals
wherein the reporter agrees to hold the story until the agencies
are ready to move and, in exchange, is promised exclusive coverage or advance warning of an arrest. (This kind of arrangement
was a prominent part of the end of the 1999 film *The Insider*,
which dramatized the efforts of *60 Minutes* producer Lowell

Bergman to air a controversial interview. In the film, Al Pacino's Bergman discovers FBI agents who are close to making an arrest in the Unabomber case and calls the leader of the investigation, who warns him not to leak word of it. In exchange, he promises Bergman a "heads up," and CBS ends up with exclusive coverage of the eventual arrest, beating the other networks to the story.)

In the case of Ptech, according to Kurtz's article, as many as eight news outlets, including all three major broadcast networks, apparently knew about the investigation well ahead of the actual search on December 6. In "Out of the Scoop Loop: Feds Fail to Deliver on Promised Tip," Kurtz writes:

> Eight news organizations knew of the investigation in advance and agreed to sit on the story, according to government sources. But the news outlet that had been working on the case the longest, the CBS station in Boston, wasn't told that the raid was imminent.
> "We were promised that because we agreed to hold off, we would be told before the raid was held," said Joe Bergantino, a reporter for Boston's WBZ-TV. "In the end that didn't happen. We certainly were disappointed. We were lied to. It was an unsettling and disturbing development."

According to the article, the CBS affiliate WBZ began investigating Ptech when a local businesswoman contacted the station to inquire about the company's legitimacy after contacting the FBI to the same end and getting nowhere. When the authorities learned that Bergantino was snooping around, the Treasury Department told him to hold off for reasons of "national security." In exchange, he would get advance warning of the search.

Kurtz's article makes no mention of the fact that there wasn't really a raid at all, even though a report aired the day before on CNN, the network that airs *Reliable Sources*, raised issue with the term. In fact, Kurtz writes that the company had been raided and that Ptech was allegedly financed, in the then-present tense, by al-Qadi.

The most unnerving revelation from the article is the notion that the impatient news organizations actually influenced the chain of events that took place at the Ptech offices:

> Earlier this week, the media may have spurred the authorities into action. "We discussed with them that we were getting impatient with this," Bergantino said. "At one point we said we were considering going next week. There was never any threat."

ABC investigative reporter Brian Ross got word from his

sources Thursday "that other news organizations had violated the agreement and we should be aware something could happen in the next 24 hours." A major snowstorm had shut down the New York airports, so ABC dispatched staffers by train to a parking lot outside the Ptech offices in Quincy.

Bergantino went on to complain about being left out of the loop and missing out on footage of the midnight search, which for CBS must have constituted the broadcast news equivalent of pay dirt. Kurtz wrapped up his story by noting that "bragging rights are also important in television. The station's Web site boasted that the 'raid is the direct result of a WBZ4 I-Team investigation.'"[44]

In other words, Boston's CBS affiliate was taking credit for *creating* news that *wasn't*. And for all the news that wasn't—no one at the company was ever named a suspect, no arrests of any Ptech employees took place, the investigating agencies did not state a single instance in which the company's product was deemed unsafe in any way—the financial damage caused by the mere perception of wrongdoing was very real. Millions of dollars immediately lost, according to a statement released to the media by the company, and tens of millions in potential revenue gone. It's unlikely that CBS would be as willing to take credit for that.

As has been demonstrated in a multitude of high-profile cases, most recently including those of Richard Jewell and Wen Ho Lee, the power of an orchestrated smear campaign in the national media is overwhelming indeed, and the reason is as simple as it is infuriating.

There's a crucial difference between a criminal investigation and media reports of one. The instruments of the law that pursue suspects are blunt and, as has been demonstrated on countless occasions, make mistakes. Nevertheless, there is still a binding contract between those instruments and anyone subject to investigation, namely, that due process will be followed and, if the evidence vindicates the suspect, the suspect's name is cleared. With the media, there is no such contract. A newspaper or television news program can, at will, direct national attention on someone suspected of a crime, lending credence to the investigation by virtue of simply having done so. If *Good Morning America* or the *New York Times* or *Buchanan and Press* sees fit to devote its precious resources of time and energy to an investigation, surely it must be for a good reason. If the investigation turns up with nothing, however, those same news vehicles are under no obligation to spend as much time reporting the outcome as they did the mere possibility of the suspected crime. There is no contract, as Ptech, its president, and its employees learned. For all the coverage devoted to the story on those first two days, barely a fraction emerged concerning the aftermath. And nobody ran a correction for the use of the word "raid." All the flubbed details, soundings of alarm, and exaggerated warnings of disaster notwithstanding, the Ptech case demonstrates unequivocally the power of the wrong word.

And finally, in case anyone's *completely* missed the point:

raid *n.*
   1. A surprise attack by a small armed force.
   2. A sudden forcible entry into a place by police: a raid on a gambling den.
   3. An entrance into another's territory for the purpose of seizing goods or valuables.
   4. A predatory operation mounted against a competitor, especially an attempt to lure away the personnel or membership of a competing organization.
   5. An attempt to seize control of a company, as by acquiring a majority of its stock.
   6. An attempt by speculators to drive stock prices down by coordinated selling.
   —*The American Heritage Dictionary of the English Language,* Fourth Edition

"The Shoney's Three": Approaching lunacy and wingers with talk shows

The first anniversary of the September 11 attacks was a blockbuster media event. The cable networks had round-the-clock coverage, and the federal government's upping of the terror threat level to "orange" for the first time in the color-coded warning system's history added a sense of dread to the already complicated emotions of the entire week. It was amidst this highly charged atmosphere that *something* happened at a Shoney's restaurant in Calhoun, Georgia.

Three men, visibly of Arab descent, had a meal on the morning of September 13, 2002, at the Shoney's. Concurrently dining was Eunice Stone, a nurse from Cartersville, Georgia, and her son. At some point, Stone became convinced that the three men, whose conversation she could hear intermittently, were either plotting a terrorist attack on the United States or were making jokes about terrorist attacks and the 9/11 anniversary. Stone contacted the authorities, and within hours, the three men, who turned out to be medical students, were pulled over on a stretch of Florida highway known as Alligator Alley.

The event caused a media circus, coming directly on the heels of the anniversary, and television broadcasts were interrupted on the morning of September 14 with live images of the closed section of highway where the men's cars were stopped and the bomb squad was cautiously looking for explosives.

None were found. By the end of the day, the entire chain of events came simultaneously into focus and dispute. The three men—Kambiz Butt, Ayman Gheith, and Omer Choudhary—denied ever making comments, in jest or otherwise, about terrorist attacks or the 9/11 anniversary. They told the media that parts of their conversation had been misconstrued by Stone; specifically, her reports about comments along the lines of "bringing it down," which she associated with a building, were actually about an automobile. Eunice Stone in turn spoke to the media and defended her actions, maintaining that the men had indeed discussed a terrorist plot, possibly as a joke in response to what they took to be discriminatory glances by Stone and other customers. Ultimately, no charges were brought against the three men, though the investigation remained open as late as June 2003.

As with the Ptech case, many news outlets reported what would turn out to be erroneous information early on, even as the story developed. There was the matter of the first of the men's two cars reportedly blowing a tollbooth shortly before it was pulled over. At some point during the initial reports, this detail came out, in many instances reported as fact; the *Washington Post* reports on September 14, "The jangled saga began shortly after midnight this morning, when a car sped through a toll booth outside Naples, Fla., without paying the required 75 cents."[45] The three men denied that either of their cars had blown the tollbooth during their numerous television appearances over the following days, in some cases meeting skeptical or downright combative responses from interviewers on this point. After all, they would point out, the police *said* they blew the tollbooth, and surely the police weren't lying. In fact, when the video surveillance of the tollbooth taken that night came out, the charge was proven false. Amazingly, the same *Washington Post* article approached the terror question with skepticism and still got it wrong: "But so much didn't add up. If they were terrorists, why speak so loudly about their plans in a public place? Why pay for their meal with a credit card? Why blow through a toll booth?"[46]

Many reporters seemingly took on faith the premise that the three men had actually made a joke, ignoring what seems to be the likeliest explanation of what took place: Eunice Stone took notice of the three men. She saw that they are Arab in a restaurant that probably doesn't get many Arabs. She misunderstood the parts of their conversation she could make out and, as the government had instructed American citizens on numerous occasions, contacted the authorities to share her concerns. The authorities investigated and found that it was all a misunderstanding.

No problem, except when the media got involved. As a result of the hysterical coverage, which in all fairness focused as much on the possibility that Eunice Stone was a confused, prejudiced woman as the possibility that the men were threatening to blow up a building (and did so unfairly in both regards), the three men got booted from the medical school in which they were enrolled. Stone ended up being hospitalized with chest pains. The entire affair would be quickly forgotten, but it is worth remembering how far some in the media were allowed to go without reprisal.

By far the ugliest piece of work associated with the Shoney's story, and indeed one of the most blatantly anti-Arab pieces of writing post–9/11, came from none other than Ann Coulter, the conservative pundit/polemic whose edict "we should invade their countries, kill their leaders and convert them to Christianity" became infamous immediately following 9/11. (The *National Review* terminated its relationship with Coulter soon thereafter.)

Coulter wrote about the incident in her "Law and Liberty" column on WorldNetDaily, an online repository of conservative opinion. The column was posted to the site on September 18, 2002, nearly a full week after the event took place. The title was "So three Arabs walk into a bar ...," and it degenerated from there into a flat-out hate rant. First, Coulter set up the event by reprinting a few of Eunice Stone's accounts of the men's statements, out of context and with no attribution, as though she were quoting from a verbatim transcript of the event itself:

"If people thought Sept. 11 was something, wait till Sept. 13."
"Do you think that will bring it down?"
"Well, if that won't bring it down, I have contacts. I'll get enough to bring it down."

The phrases immediately following were base and ugly: "Patriot Eunice Stone took down their license plate numbers and called the police as the mirthful Muslims left. (I'd give you the names, but they're too complicated. There's a reason they use numbers at Guantanamo.)"[47] That kind of inflammatory, bigoted language is Coulter's preferred rhetorical vehicle. It earned her the following observation from *Guardian* reporter Jonathan Freedland: "In a couple of sentences, she can play with overt racism, soften it with a line so provocative she could only be kidding, then round off the performance with a sweeping smear of the liberal enemy. Coulter has turned riffs like that into an art form."[48]

In any case, Coulter saw fit to withhold the names of the men involved for the entirety of her column, instead referring to them as "the Muslims" no fewer than ten times. Once, she referred to them as "the Three Stooges." She also repeated the line about blowing the tollbooth: "That night, a little after midnight, one of the two cars being driven by the Muslims ran a toll booth—at least according to everyone but these beacons of truth." Of course, on that point, that's precisely what the three men turned out to be.

Coulter then accused the men of having "accused Americans, especially Southerners, of being ignorant racists," and to support her claim she excerpted a statement by "the sister of one" (of the nameless, villainous Muslims), but not surprisingly, the quote contained no such accusation.

And so the column went:

In point of fact, it is only by *not* reading that Americans have been deluded into spouting the Soccer-Momism about Islam being "a religion of peace"....

Non-terrorist Muslims are crying wolf when they play these games ... Instead of preying on America's hatred of prejudice, these aspiring Scottsboro Boys should capitalize on America's capacity for forgiveness, admit they did something really stupid, and stop lying.[49]

Coulter's views are justified every time she appears on Fox News or MSNBC, and her books sell enough copies that in June 2003, Random House announced that its Crown Publishing division would launch an all-conservative imprint, beginning with Coulter's latest offering to the world: *Treason: Liberal Treachery from the Cold War to the War on Terrorism.*[50]

Looking at the larger picture, it's easy to trace, back up a very slippery slope, the attitudes that shape a media environment tolerant of Coulter. In July 2002, Fox News talk-show host Bill O'Reilly became aware of a controversy stirring at the University of North Carolina, Chapel Hill (UNC). Among the reading requirements for a freshman orientation class was *Approaching the Qur'an: The Early Revelations* translated by Haverford College Islamic scholar Michael Sells. O'Reilly invited Dr. Robert Kirkpatrick, who selected the book, on his popular talk show *The O'Reilly Factor* for a discussion. "Boy, you're causing all kinds of trouble down there," O'Reilly began. "This is pretty controversial, is it? Why'd you choose it?" Kirkpatrick replied that, in the wake of the 9/11 terrorist attacks, the school was attempting to give its incoming freshman some idea of the basic tenets of Islam, which he speculated most Americans did not have. "We know what the basic tenets of Islam are," O'Reilly countered. "I mean, why, what's this going to do for any freshman coming to UNC?" (In fact, a 1995 report by the media watchdog Fairness and Accuracy in Reporting found that many Americans lack even the most basic understanding of Islam.[51])

During the discussion that followed, O'Reilly rejected the assignment on the premise that it constituted a forced religious indoctrination. Kirkpatrick disagreed and pointed out that students had the option to write a three hundred word essay about why they'd rather not read the book in lieu of actually reading it. "I wouldn't read the book," O'Reilly said. "And I'll tell you why, I wouldn't have read *Mein Kampf* either. If I were going to UNC in 1941, and you, professor, said, Read *Mein Kampf*, I would have said, Hey, professor, with all due respect, shove it. I ain't reading it."[52]

The segment on *The O'Reilly Factor* drew national attention, and, to their credit, newspapers and magazines across the country rallied in support of what was obviously a completely legitimate academic pursuit in their editorial pages. The *Buffalo News* called the attack on the assignment "anti-intellectual at best, and censorship at worst."[53] When the conservative American Family Association brought an unsuccessful lawsuit against UNC to halt the assignment, *American Prospect* columnist

Wendy Kaminer called it "the summer's stupidest whiniest law-suit."[54] And the *Lancaster Intelligencer Journal* wrote, "Educational institutions have an obligation to educate their students about the world in which we live. They must have the freedom to introduce students to books and texts which may clash with present mores."[55] Many editorials took issue with O'Reilly specifically. The *Philadelphia Inquirer* called the book "an anti-dote to babbling bobble heads like Mr. O'Reilly, who trade on stoking animus."[56] The *Bergen County (NJ) Record* wrote, "One conservative commentator compared it to having students read Hitler's *Mein Kampf* in 1941."[57]

O'Reilly addressed the criticisms leveled against him on his program, denying, absurdly, that he'd ever compared the Qur'an to *Mein Kampf*. The ABC News program *Nightline* did a segment on August 22, 2002, that O'Reilly took as an affront to his perspective. On his August 26 show, he quoted the segment: "'Popular television talk show host Bill O'Reilly of Fox News made the university's assignment a national cause. Why, he asked, should students study what he called "the enemy's religion"?' What he called the enemy's religion?" a befuddled O'Reilly responded. "Is *Nightline* serious? What religion's in play here, Buddhism? Where does the concept of jihad come from? Give me a break. And I never said the students shouldn't study Islam, I said they shouldn't be forced to study it in order to be admitted to the college."[58]

Of course, at the beginning of the controversy, during the original interview with Kirkpatrick, it was established that the students had the option not to read the book and instead write a brief essay on why they didn't want to read it. The idea that the students had to read the book to gain admittance is also mislead-ing. The assignment was for incoming first-year students—students who were *already admitted*—and the course was part of orientation. A student could have claimed to have read the book without having done so, thus avoiding the essay, and all but slept during the discussion of it, and there would have been no conse-quence. No damage to the student's GPA, no revoking of admis-sion to the school. Nobody at UNC was going to be forced to do anything except what they're supposed to do in college, which is to learn new things.

Perhaps not surprisingly, but satisfying nevertheless, O'Reilly couldn't even get students who had read the book and participated in the discussion to complain enough to justify his crusade against the assignment. In late September, long after the controversy had abated, O'Reilly invited two of the UNC first-year students onto *The O'Reilly Factor* for a debriefing, noting that hundreds of freshman had read the book even though the school had "backed off" the requirement because of pressure from his television show and others. He asked the two students for their thoughts on the book. The first, Paul Steinberger, responded, "I thought the book was good," and went on to say that he hadn't learned much about the day-to-day workings of Islam (thus debunking the indoctrination theory). The second student, Ryan Tuck, said, "Well, I thought it was a very important book to read, especially in wake of the attacks of September 11. I thought that these attacks, maybe, though, not directly influenced by our lack of knowledge to this culture, but, certainly, that bred our misunderstanding towards this group of individuals, this culture, this religion, and—"

At this point O'Reilly challenged Tuck on the issue of misrepresentation. When Tuck, a Christian, explained that he'd learned about many similarities between his religion and Islam, O'Reilly countered with a quote from the Qur'an that wasn't included in *Approaching the Qur'an*: "Oh, you who believe, do not take the Jews and Christians for friends. They are friends of each other, and whoever amongst you takes them for a friend, then surely he is one of them. Surely Allah does not guide the unjust people."

"Do you think it's fair, Mr. Tuck, that this kind of a quote was not given to you to digest as well as the nice things about the Koran?" O'Reilly asked. Tuck didn't appear convinced by the excerpt, so O'Reilly argued that the boys had been given a "propaganda tract" that excluded the negative elements of the religion. To that, Steinberger replied, "I think that we should have been allowed to read it and make our own judgments." Then, after some back and forth over the excerpt, Steinberger said, "That passage is not inciting terrorist acts. It is not saying, 'Go out and kill everyone.'" O'Reilly then invoked seniority, noting that he'd been through college *and* graduate school (twice!) and that in his estimation *Approaching the Qur'an* was an "agenda-driven vehicle."[59]

Ironically, the only lasting effect of the controversy was one that O'Reilly didn't welcome—the memory of his comparison between the Qur'an and *Mein Kampf*. In late May 2003, nearly a year later, O'Reilly appeared at Book Expo America in Los Angeles to promote his upcoming book. During a call-in question and answer session broadcast on C-SPAN2, he was again criticized by a caller for the comparison. O'Reilly angrily rejected the premise that he'd ever made it, as he had many times before. Ultimately, the attention he brought on himself would continue to haunt him, long after *Approaching the Qur'an* became as distant a memory in the minds of the UNC freshman as the rest of orientation.

There is also the case of Sami al-Arian, the University of Florida professor arrested in 2003 on charges of aiding a known terrorist organization, among others. From the get-go, the media all but self-applied the stamp of controversy. Just after the 9/11 attacks, O'Reilly had al-Arian on *The O'Reilly Factor* as a guest and proceeded to grill him about alleged connections to Palestinian Islamic Jihad. The interview caused an uproar; the university received threats and al-Arian was eventually suspended. He maintained his innocence throughout the following year and a half before his arrest and continued to do so as he awaited trial.

Whatever the outcome of the case, the lessons of the Ptech and Shoney's cases are still applicable. In fact, a detailed review of the media coverage of al-Arian's case, beginning long before the interview with O'Reilly, has already been written by *Salon* magazine reporter Eric Boehlert.[60] An analysis here would simply retread Boehlert's efforts, so instead I defer to them on this matter, except to note that, as of June 2003, coverage, fair and balanced or otherwise, has all but ceased since al-Arian's arrest. Partly this is due to the late trial date set for the professor—he won't appear in court to answer to the charges brought against him until 2005. His lawyers challenged the lengthy waiting period on the grounds that it denied al-Arian the constitutional right to a speedy trial; the government rejected the challenge, evoking the seemingly all-purpose "national security." O'Reilly invited the lawyers on his program and gave them airtime,[61] and the *St. Petersburg Times* continued to follow the story, featuring a short profile on al-Arian's daughter Leena that explores the anger and frustration she's lived with daily since the arrest.[62]

But effectively the story is over as far as the mainstream media is concerned. In a bizarre reversal, the arrest was the end, not the beginning, of a story that began on a national level with O'Reilly's first interview with al-Arian, during which the former advised the latter that, were he with the CIA, "I'd follow you wherever you went." Thus, the frenzied national coverage chronicled in Boehlert's *Salon* stories led to a self-fulfilling prophecy: for nearly two years, the coverage almost demanded its ultimate self-justification—the arrest. Who knows how much attention the eventual trial will receive? For now, al-Arian is in custody, and the media is all but finished with the matter.

The larger problem of ceaseless representations of Islam in the media strictly within the context of terrorism undermines even the efforts of those who work specifically against it. It's not all that difficult to find Arab or Muslim representatives on cable news. James Zogby, president of the Arab American Institute (and brother of political pollster John Zogby), and Hussein Ibish, spokesman for the American-Arab Anti-Discrimination Committee, are probably easily recognizable to the average cable news viewer, as they have made regular appearances on the networks in the past two years. It's not nearly as easy, though, to find an Arab or Muslim who's not on the air to answer to the host or another guest for an act of terrorism or indeed all acts of terrorism. The irony of course is that Zogby and Ibish represent groups whose primary concern as nonprofit, grassroots organizations is to advance more positive images of Arab Americans and protect their civil rights, yet in the venue that allows them to reach the most people—television—they are often painted into a corner where every point they wish to make must be prefaced with "Of course terrorism is wrong, but ..."

This is precisely what happened on the May 19, 2003, edition of *Scarborough Country*, a prime-time talk show on MSNBC. The show's host is Joe Scarborough, a former Republican congressman who, after leaving office in 2001, made the leap across the great yawning gulf that separates provincial ideologues from cable news pundits. *Scarborough Country*, launched in 2003, is an almost shameless imitation of *The O'Reilly Factor*. The format is the same, with Scarborough's "Real Deal" substituting for O'Reilly's "Talking Points Memo," the commentary that starts each show. In the wrestling matches with guests, Scarborough even adopts O'Reilly's rarely fulfilled promise to his guests, "I'll give you the last word." On May 19, Scarborough's first two guests were Zogby and Mark Regev, spokesman for the Israeli Embassy. The segment focused on the "violent detour of the road map to peace," as Scarborough put it—a series of suicide bombings and retaliations in Israel and the Palestinian territories. After noting that Hamas had claimed responsibility for the murders of thirteen people in four attacks over the preceding weekend, Scarborough introduced Zogby by playing a clip of a statement by a Hamas spokesman who essentially warned that more attacks would follow so long as conditions in the Occupied Territories continued to deteriorate. Scarborough then addressed Zogby, "Excuse me, but doesn't the road map to peace, Mr. Zogby, talk about a Palestinian state? And doesn't it demand a freely elected representative government?" Absurdly, Zogby was instantly positioned as a placeholder for the Hamas spokesman, and of course he was obliged to point out that Hamas doesn't speak for the Palestinians and that the group's actions directly oppose the peace process. Only after doing so could Zogby point out that the violence is cyclic on both sides and that the economic conditions in the West Bank and Gaza continue to deteriorate even as settlements expand. "You're right, Mr. Zogby. It's an awful, awful, awful situation," Scarborough replied.[63]

Osama Siblani is another frequent guest on politically oriented talk shows. Siblani, a native of Lebanon, is editor and publisher of the *Arab American News*, based in Dearborn, Michigan. The paper is noted as the nation's oldest and largest Arab American newspaper in "Arab Advocate," a story about Siblani by Lisa M. Collins that was published in the *Detroit Metro Times*. The story recounts Siblani's appearance in early March 2003 on *Street Beat*, a topical talk show on Detroit's UPN/CBS affiliate. The subject of that day's segment was the impending war with Iraq.

As reported by Collins, Tara Wall, the show's host and former liaison between the city of Detroit and Michigan's Republican governor John Engler, hosted a roundtable debate on the war with several guests, including Siblani. Before the taping began, Wall addressed Siblani: "Let me ask, are you Arab or Palestinian?" Siblani reportedly informed Wall that the question was akin to asking a Michigan resident if she were from the United States. In fact that was a polite way to put it. Wall's question was nonsensical and it exposed pure ignorance. How Wall could host a talk show on current events and know so little about them is totally amazing, but Collins reported that after the taping, Wall said to Siblani, "You can tell I watch a lot of Fox News. I love Bill O'Reilly." Siblani told her that had he known, he wouldn't have shown up. Indeed, during the segment, Wall took a cue from many cable news anchors, asking Siblani, "Shouldn't Saddam just leave?" This in the middle of a discussion in which she declared war "the only option."[64] Her other guests included another journalist, a Republican Party state vicechair, and the county director of Homeland Security, but it was Siblani who was called on to answer for Saddam Hussein, as though by virtue of *being Arab* he could provide the answer to the Iraq question better than anyone else.

The constant association between Arab or Muslim spokespersons and the looming threats of war and terrorism most certainly becomes ingrained in the minds of viewers. A *Newsweek* article by Keith Naughton recounts the repercussions of the 9/11 attacks on the Arab community in Dearborn, which is the second largest outside the Middle East. (Paris, France, has the largest.) Naughton wrote that immediately on that Tuesday morning, Siblani received a phone call. The voice on the other end said, "You had better pray to God that Arabs didn't have anything to do with this, or your ass will be next, Siblani." At least a dozen similar calls followed, "many urging the native of Lebanon to 'go back home.'" Naughton reported that the calls were for Siblani a premonition and a reminder of the violence that erupted in Dearborn after the Oklahoma City bombing—prior to 9/11 regarded the most atrocious act of terrorism committed in the United States, which proved to be the work of Timothy McVeigh.[65] In that case, Arab American businesses were burnt down and homes were vandalized. The role of the news media in fostering the attitudes that led to those crimes cannot be ignored. Immediately following the bombing of the federal building in Oklahoma City, Steve Emerson went on the air and called it almost certainly the work of Islamic extremists, based at that point on absolutely nothing save for his "expertise" in terrorism, which many have called into question.

It's also not surprising to find that many accused perpetrators of the worst acts of politically motivated violence in the United States are not perceived by the public as terrorists—so long they're not of Arab descent or the Islamic faith. In May 2003, federal authorities apprehended Eric Rudolph in connection with the 1996 Olympic Park bombing in Atlanta, Georgia, as well as attacks on abortion clinics and a gay nightclub. Two articles by Jeffrey Gettleman in the *New York Times* soon after the apprehension reported support for Rudolph in the areas of North Carolina where the FBI believed the suspect received food and shelter from local residents. Gettleman wrote that the FBI's suspicions about the residents' assistance to the fugitive led to animosity toward the agency; one resident was quoted as saying, "Nobody around here condones murder, but I think a lot of people weren't sure which side to be on." Indeed, the issue of Rudolph's perception in Murphy and Peachtree, North Carolina, touched explicitly on the question of whether the crimes he is accused of committing—killing one woman and injuring more than one hundred people at the Olympics, killing an off-duty policeman in one abortion clinic bombing, and the nightclub bombing—constitute terrorism. "He's a Christian and I'm a Christian and he dedicated his life to fighting abortion. Those are our values. And I don't see what he did as a terrorist act." So said Murphy resident Crystal Davis in one of Gettleman's stories.[66]

Maybe that's just the perspective of those who knew Rudolph. But the national media endorse and perpetuate the same double standard, according to separate reports by Fairness and Accuracy in Reporting (FAIR). One report, from 2000, asks, "Why is it that bomb suspects who are white and American generate roughly one-tenth to one-twentieth of the media interest of an Arab bomb suspect?"[67] Three years later, cartoonist Tom Tomorrow addressed this still-existent problem pointedly in his weekly political strip *This Modern World*. "You probably didn't hear about it," a caption over one panel reads, "but the FBI in Spokane just arrested a couple of terrorists for possession of secret military documents—including material relating to chemical, nuclear and biological warfare ..." Then, inside the panel, a concerned man responds, "That's terrible! Who were they? Iraqis? Al Qaeda? Hamas?" *This Modern World*'s contrarian penguin Sparky answers, "Um—white supremacists, actually." The man replies, "Oh—I thought you said they were terrorists."[68]

Another FAIR report, from 1995, concludes,

> The media is so full of reports on the "Islamic threat" from "radical Muslim terrorists" plotting "Islamic fundamentalist violence," one could excuse the average non-Muslim American for concluding that the "fundamentals" of Islam include a course in demolition training. No wonder that 45 percent of Americans, according to a recent poll, agreed that "Muslims tend to be fanatics."

The report also notes, "When reporting on 'Islamic violence' ... the media often identify Muslims by their religion," whereas one would be unlikely to read about "Christian violence" in a story about anti-abortion acts.[69]

Given the state of affairs described at the beginning of this chapter, it's evident that reports by FAIR continue to be ignored by the media. The same is true of Edward Said's book *Covering Islam*. That book prefaces all the problematic coverage analyzed here. The lessons of both simply didn't stand a chance against the onslaught of coverage that appealed to the least compelling ideas that resulted from the 9/11 attacks, if they were ever treated seriously in the first place. One need look no further than Oussama Ziade and the other employees of Ptech, the three medical students who were in the wrong place at the wrong time, Osama Siblani, or any one of the victims of racially motivated crimes reported in the 2003 ADC report to see why this is a problem.

CHAPTER 4

THE NEW COLD WARRIORS

Will Youmans

Introduction

The bundle of political and legal changes that give formal shape to the "war on terrorism" is not just the result of the initiative of ambitious bureaucrats. They were aided, conceptually informed, and validated by a robust network of elite groups and individuals. Interconnected by professional and personal relationships, this network is united ideologically by a broad set of views and goals given more currency after September 11, 2001. Namely, they argue that Islamism, or political Islam, is the greatest threat to Western civilization since international communism. Asymmetric warfare, or terrorism, is its primary tactic. They advocate aggressive governmental measures against Islamists of all shades, everywhere, with less than meager concern for the effects on Muslim populations in general. Though they are suave enough to routinely preface their statements with obligatory announcements that "fundamentalists," "extremists," or "Islamists" are a small minority of a large faith group, their prescriptions invariably punish a greater number of Arabs and Muslims in the United States and abroad. Underlying this campaign is the premise that the rights of Arabs and Muslims, regardless of citizenship, are expendable.

The notion that radical or militant Islamists pose a total threat to the United States, the Western world at large, and the principles of liberalism serves as the network's rhetorical base. A primary architect of this view is Bernard Lewis, an Orientalist whose scholarship was recognized by the current deputy secretary of defense Paul Wolfowitz as "truly objective, original—and always independent."[1] Wolfowitz paid tribute to Lewis for teaching "us" about the "complex" and "important" region in such a way that will help the United States create a "better world for generations."[2] One of Lewis's major theoretical contributions in the service of empire, as Lamis Andoni wrote, was to coin the phrase "clash of civilizations." It was later picked up by Samuel Huntington to articulate one of the most prominent American post–cold war visions. The United States and the West as a whole, he argued, were moving toward civilizational collision with the Islamic bloc after the demise of the Soviet threat. The current administration and establishment thinkers have adapted Lewis's tendency to reduce Arab politics to an inherently irrational, mindlessly antagonistic, and violent Islamic fanaticism.

Daniel Pipes and Steve Emerson have ridden the wave of confrontationalism reflected in the "clash of civilizations" thesis. The new cold warriors lobby for an attack on radical Islam—communism's substitute as the new threat to Western civilization—in all its forms, violent and nonviolent. For them, Islamism is the new totalitarianism and ultimately must be defeated. They argue that Islamic fundamentalists have infiltrated American society, exploiting its freedoms, and are poised to strike. The end of such alarmism is the adaptation of a confrontational foreign policy inward—the domestication of the war on terrorism. These new cold warriors provided the push for the monumental legal and policy changes after September 11, 2001, but pull came generously from the government, especially from the influential neoconservative quarters. One goal of this chapter is to show that this network of new cold warriors is more agenda-driven than scholarly or fair. This is evinced by the use of strategic hypocrisy and creative distortions that serve the ideological purpose of depicting Islam as the new enemy of the United States.

After briefly outlining the nature of this network, the chapter focuses on the work of two illustrious figures: Daniel Pipes, director of the Middle East Forum, and Steven Emerson, executive director of the Investigative Project. They are worth looking at because of their visibility in the media and proximity to government affairs—key elements of this network's *modus operandi*. Since September 11, 2001, the government's policies have approached conformity with their views—energizing their activities, which, in turn, actively encourages a confrontational foreign policy and an increasingly intrusive domestic campaign against American Muslims, Arabs, and their institutions. This chapter seeks to present the ways in which this network of private/quasi-public actors vilifies Arab and Muslim peoples and the repercussions of such a campaign.

The basics of the network

The primary organizational mode in the new cold war network is the policy-oriented research institute. As Daniel Pipes outlined in a talk at the Heritage Foundation in 1991, these elite creatures act a little like universities, foundations, publishers, wire services, world affairs councils, lobbies, and "government bureaus." Their wide range of activities includes sponsoring scholars and research, publishing books and journals, distributing newspaper columns, organizing talks and conferences, commenting to the media as experts, and attempting to influence government and public opinion "like a lobby." The end is to impact policy, "the business of applying knowledge—bringing specialized information and theoretical concepts to bear on issues of the moment." Such institutes have a "vantage point," or a specific agenda, and the audience is defined as the elite whose opinions shape foreign policy or other realms heavily dependent on specialists. Pipes describes this as a "top down" process that ultimately "applies equally to prominent issues" and "more obscure ones."[3]

The institutes in this network tend to center around the work of particular individuals. Though both have staffs, the Middle East Forum and the Investigative Project revolve around their directors, Pipes and Emerson, respectively. Pipes and Emerson fashion themselves as experts on the Middle East and terrorism, foreign and domestic. Emerson started the Investigative Project shortly after he produced a documentary called *Jihad in America* for PBS. The project is often touted as "the nation's largest archival intelligence center on Islamic terrorist activities."[4] Similarly, the Middle East Forum's repertoire of publications and events is dominated by Daniel Pipes.

The choir of institutes advocating more aggressive policies against Muslims and Arabs and in support of Israel has interlocking directorates and revolving doors. Analysts from different think tanks coauthor columns, organize conferences together, sit on the same boards of directors, list one another as experts, interview each other, and serve as research fellows or analysts at the same established think tanks, such as the Washington Institute for Near East Policy (WINEP), the Heritage Foundation, the Hudson Institute, and the Foreign Policy Research Institute. For instance, the deputy director of WINEP is Patrick Clawson. Daniel Pipes was a fellow there. Clawson sits on the board of governors of Pipes's Middle East Forum and was the senior editor of its journal, *Middle East Quarterly* (*MEQ*). Clawson has coauthored newspaper pieces with Pipes.[5] The current editor of *MEQ* is Martin Kramer, an Israeli academic who collaborated with Daniel Pipes to form an organization called Campus Watch, which monitors Middle East studies academics for subversive thinking, writing, and utterances critical of the United States and Israel. Kramer was a fellow at WINEP on numerous occasions.[6]

The relationship can also be financial. Emerson acknowledged that the Investigative Project received funding from the Middle East Forum, but declined to reveal his other sources.[7] Also, Pipes's Middle East Forum hired the public relations and lobbying firm BKSH & Associates after September 11, 2001, to represent Emerson and polish his image.[8] The same firm helped to arrange airtime for Emerson's 1994 documentary. Members of the network are used to grant credibility to each other. For example, Emerson calls on a Muslim named Khalid Duran as a source of information and to attest to Emerson's integrity.

The network extends from larger, institutional think tanks, such as American Enterprise Institute (AEI), the Hudson Institute, and Freedom House, to smaller specialized entities, such as the United States Committee for a Free Lebanon (USCFL), Middle East Media Research Institute (MEMRI), and the *Middle East Intelligence Bulletin* (*MEIB*). All the points provide more interconnections with government and the media. This demonstrates the span and influence of the network.

Pipes and Ziad Abdelnour established *MEIB* in 1999. It is a free monthly publication focusing primarily on Lebanon and Syria. Almost all of the articles are written by those closely affiliated with *MEIB*, though it does accept submissions. *MEIB* brings together individuals from several other organizations. Abdelnour is a Wall Street venture capitalist and president of the USCFL, an advocacy group united against Syria's role in Lebanon. The

USCFL has unabashedly pro-Israel views. In a clear emulation of the American Israel Public Affairs Committee (AIPAC), its Web site has written at the top, "The Most Important Organization affecting America's relationship with Lebanon," which comes from the *New York Sun*.[9] AIPAC's Web site features a parallel quote from the *New York Times*.[10]

The USCFL's "golden circle"—those who provide support to the organization and its goals—is an extensive list of neo-conservative thinkers, many of whom are in the Bush administration. The list includes Elliott Abrams, Douglas Feith, and, of course, Daniel Pipes. Also on the list is Richard Perle. The USCFL Web site displays Perle's article that declares, "Countries that harbor terrorists ... must themselves be destroyed,"[11] perhaps without realizing what such a doctrine has meant and could mean for their precious Lebanon. The USCFL Web site links up to an eclectic mix of organizations. Besides the usual suspects MEMRI, AEI, AIPAC, and WINEP, it connects viewers to the Christian Coalition, which it calls "America's leading grassroots organization."

MEIB editorial board members Matthew Levitt and Thomas Carroll worked in governmental agencies as counterterrorism functionaries. Levitt holds a dual post as a WINEP fellow. Carroll was with the Central Intelligence Agency (CIA) clandestine service. *MEIB*'s editor is a graduate student named Gary C. Gambill. He also serves as consultant for Freedom House, a neo-conservative club aimed at imposing liberalism everywhere in the world. Former CIA director R. James Woolsey heads it.

MEMRI selectively translates material from the Arab world to prove that Arabs are a hateful people. It offers consistent and unabashed pro-Israel political analysis. Dr. Meyrav Wurmser is currently a senior fellow at the Hudson Institute. She is a cofounder and was the executive director of MEMRI.[12] The Jewish journal *Forward* reported that she shared the ultranationalist values of the revisionist Zionist Ze'ev Jabotinsky. His main ideological contribution was that the Jews who settled Palestine could never coexist with the native Arabs and thus needed to construct an "iron wall" by force to maintain segregation and domination.[13] MEMRI was cofounded by Yigal Carmon of Israeli intelligence. Carmon is also connected to the Investigative Project and is named as an adviser for Emerson's *Jihad in America*.

The migration patterns and intercourse within the network, however, are less interesting and relevant than the interconnections between the network, the media, and the government. The name of the game, after all, is securing steady access to media channels and governmental agencies and officials. Pipes and Emerson have found success in these areas. The real achievement of this network was to build a professional field, an industry, out of alarmism about terrorism and Islam, while keeping close to power through links to intelligence agencies. Like other professions and industries, this network impacts governmental policies and people's lives, and does so through books, speaking tours, videos, and articles. Nearly every message they convey in writing or utter in the media involves the theme of militant Islam, its growth, its reach in the United States, and how Israel is an ally in the war against it. They have essentially made a profession of opposing militant Islam.

Access to media and government

Emerson has repeated the mantra that the American media is the "fourth branch of government."[14] Elsewhere, he quipped that it is "one of the principal—if not primary—vehicles through which people learn."[15] For Emerson, the media is "how history is made."[16] The centrality of the media to the network's goal of impacting policymaking cannot be understated. Like many other advocates for aggressive moves against Islamism, Emerson's relationships with both the establishment media and government are intimate. After employment with the US Senate Foreign Relations Committee between 1977 and 1982, he worked with media companies such as the *New Republic, US News and World Report,* and CNN as a special investigative correspondent.

After the PBS documentary, Emerson became known as a leading terrorism expert. He is still widely recognized as that despite several credibility-damaging gaffes. Most famously, he insinuated that Muslims were responsible for the 1995 Oklahoma City bombing.[17] After the crash of TWA Flight 800, he stated on Geraldo Rivera's CNBC show that he had "no doubt whatsoever ... that it was [destroyed by] a bomb." Always the opportunist, he used the tragedy to speculate that it was "not unconnected to the investigation of the Islamic Jihad operations in Tampa, Florida"[18]—an investigation that he had credibility resting on. In 2002, he suggested that FBI agents were "definitely investigating" whether "terrorists actually assassinated" Katherine Smith. Smith was the Tennessee motor vehicles inspector arrested for helping five Arab men get driver's licenses illegally. She was killed mysteriously the night before her arraignment. Emerson stated, "Definitely a firebomb, apparently, was put in the car." Besides assuming that the men accused of illegally obtaining the licenses were terrorists, Emerson contradicted existing news stories in which an FBI spokesperson told the *New York Times* that there was no evidence of an explosive device. Authorities were also investigating the possibility of suicide—something Emerson neglected to mention in favor of stereotype-based speculation.[19]

Still, since September 11, 2001, Emerson and the Investigative Project have grown into steady media sources. The *Chicago Tribune, New York Post, Los Angeles Times,* and others have quoted Emerson as an expert. The *Wall Street Journal* regularly publishes columns by him. NBC employed him as a terrorism analyst, and its networks featured him more than fifty times in the first two months after September 11.[20] Numerous news television programs featured his campaign to expose Islamists in the United States. One of the only major media channels that did not present his views continuously for some time was National Public Radio (NPR), which supporters of Emerson, such as Jeff Jacoby of the *Boston Globe,* attacked bitterly. Jacoby accused NPR of "bowing to a pressure campaign by Muslim extremists" in neglecting "this prophet."[21]

Even before September 11, 2001, Emerson testified before the congressional banking, judiciary, senate intelligence, and other committees more than a dozen times. He discussed topics such as "the terrorist infrastructure in the US, ... the protection of America's national infrastructure, and the threat of Islamic fundamentalism against the United States and the West." His range of expertise extended to a legalistic testimony on "Palestinian violations of the Oslo accords."[22] He appeared five more times after September 11, 2001, to call for an expansion of post–September 11 policy and legal measures. Emerson claims to have privately presented to the "Justice Department, FBI, Customs Service, National Security Council and the White House." Treasury Department officials acting against funds linked to terrorism consulted with him as well.[23] In 1995, US representatives Bill McCollum (R-FL) and Gary L. Ackerman (D-NY) sent every member of Congress a copy of Emerson's controversial documentary, *Jihad in America.* The conservative Carthage Foundation funded the distribution of the copies.[24] It

"played a real role" in the House's passage of the 1996 antiterrorism act, according to Representative Chris Smith (R-NJ).[25]
This act gave the government greater powers in the use of detentions and secret evidence in immigration legal proceedings.

Pipes has a more intimate relationship with the government.
He has held positions at the Departments of State and Defense,
including a place on the "Special Task Force on Terrorism and
Technology." Pipes was vice-chair of the Fulbright Board of Foreign Scholarships, a position appointed by the president. He has
worked on four presidential campaigns according to his biography on the Middle East Forum Web site.[26] Since September 11,
2001, he has testified in front of congressional committees twice.

In the one year after the destruction of the World Trade Center, according to Pipes, he produced "1 book, 8 long articles, 80
short articles," and made "110 television appearances, 120 in-
person lectures," with "360 mentions in the media ... and 450
radio interviews." Hits on his Web page increased from "300
per day before 9/11 to 2,000 after it." His e-mail list increased
from 2,000 to 14,000. So important is the media to his work
that his article dated one year after September 11, 2001, when
most public figures paid tribute, profiled his own increased visibility during the year and offered a few tidbits of advice for conservatives playing the media.[27]

Politically, Pipes is well-connected. He associates with the
neoconservatives in power. In April 2002, he cosigned a letter
drafted by the Project for the New American Century, a highly
influential center of neoconservative activity and offshoot of the
American Enterprise Institute.[28] The letter to George W. Bush argued that the United States should unquestionably support Israel
and its policies, since the two countries "share a common
enemy," namely, the "axis of evil" and terrorism. It made the
parallel complete by demanding that the United States cannot
advocate "Israel to continue negotiating with Arafat," since it
would be like the United States negotiating with "Osama Bin
Laden or Mullah Omar." Israel cannot be pressured to negotiate
while it is threatened with terrorism. Both the removal of Arafat
and the resumption of peace talks conditioned on an end to
Palestinian-sponsored violence became stated American policy.
The letter was cosigned by influential figures such as Elliot
Cohen, Richard Perle, R. James Woolsey, William Bennett, Kenneth Adelman, and other current or former government officials.

More recently, Pipes was announced as a presidential nominee for the board of directors of the United States Institute of Peace (USIP), a government-funded research institute designed to promote "the prevention, management and peaceful resolution of international conflicts." It was not without controversy, since Pipes's view on peace is infamously militaristic: "The strength of the U.S. military is the greatest peacekeeping force in the world. Peace is not achieved through weakness."[29] This view comports with his take on Israeli participation in a US-led peace process. When asked what Israel can do to bring peace, he replied, "There is no substitute for victory. The only way there can be closure is through victory, either Israeli or Arab"[30]—hardly the words of a peace-minded individual. In the past, Pipes has received funding from USIP for such projects as a study entitled "Muslims in the West: Can Conflict Be Averted?"[31] The implication of this federally funded report is that conflict between "Muslims in the West" and "the West" is inevitable. In other pieces, he suggests that Israel "raze" Palestinian "villages from which attacks are launched" and "capture or otherwise dispose of the PA leadership."[32] Pipes never forwarded any salutary proposals regarding the difficult peace negotiations. Ultimately, Bush pushed through his nomination when the board delayed making a decision.

Pipes has experience in academia as well. Harvard educated, he obtained a PhD in History in 1978. According to his press bio, he taught at the University of Chicago, Harvard University, and the US Naval War College.[33] However, not everyone accepts his scholarly credentials. Holly J. Burkhalter, a director for Physicians for Human Rights and member of USIP, stated that the institute's "only litmus test" for grants "is that the scholarship be excellent." She voiced concern that Pipes is "well-known for having made a career of imposing a different kind of litmus test, an ideological purity movement." Burkhalter suggested that it could have "a chilling effect" on scholarship.[34] Pipes himself believes that research institutes have a "vantage point." They must "explicitly take politics into consideration."[35]

Pipes has made it known that he seeks a wider audience than other scholars. He aims at influencing elite policymakers, primarily, and public opinion through the media. With a weekly column in the *New York Post* and an extensive sheet of publications in the mainstream media, Pipes is an active writer. He has written eleven books as the sole author and coauthored another eleven. He made more than fifty television appearances between September 11, 2001, and May 2003. Prior to September 11, he had made only around thirteen.

Beyond their careers in government, Emerson and Pipes could be described as functionally quasi-governmental. Besides being treated as official sources in the media, they serve some functions the government cannot. The FBI's former counterterrorism chief, Robert Blitzer, wrote in 1999 that Emerson "is better informed in many areas of terrorism than we were in the government."[36] Some officials believe this is because as a private entity the Investigative Project can spy on and infiltrate civic and political organizations without constitutional checks. Staff members pose as conference attendees, bear hidden microphones, and scan organization's publications. Similarly, Emerson serves as a conduit of information for foreign intelligence services such as Israel's.[37] As an increasingly influential figure in Washington, he may be able to get information to policymakers more effectively and with less political risk than the foreign agents could themselves. Also, censorship and pressure on dissenting academics is a lot harder for the government to pull off. Pipes and Stanley Kurtz have set up Web sites to direct pressure on academics who are publicly critical of Israel and the United States.[38]

Pushing for a militant domestic-foreign policy

Though Pipes and Emerson claim that Islamists are only a small percentage of Muslims, they contend that Islamists control Muslim institutions in the United States. Islamists blend into Muslim communities very easily. The key theme pushed by Pipes and Emerson is that there is a global Islamist movement united by the goal of destroying the United States (and Israel). A series of loosely connected terrorist cells have infiltrated countries all over the world for the goal of jihad. The doctrine of asymmetric warfare means that big-power politics do not provide a natural containment and stability of threats. International networks of political Islamists do not fight from a territorial base; rather, they are everywhere, including the United States, and based centrally in no one place but in networks of semi-autonomous cells. As a result, the two layers of federal policymaking—foreign and domestic—are merged together in the war on terrorism. Enemies of the state are not limited to foreign sovereign states anymore. Like the cold war, they can be anyone, anywhere. From this starting point, Emerson, Pipes, and their colleagues have shown little regard for the goodwill of the innocent Arabs and Muslims caught in the middle. They hardly utter a word about them. The Islamists are all that matter—rendering their disclaimer about distinguishing between militant and moderate Muslims functionally misleading.

Starting with the premise of an international Islamist threat, advocates of an aggressive domestic-foreign policy tend to agree broadly on several positions. With the necessary import of a security imperative into foreign policy, it demands support for other states waging war on the common enemy of political Islam, even if that means failing to differentiate violent strains from nonviolent activism. In the name of security, the Bush administration ushered in an avalanche of legal and policy alterations. It declared total war on terrorism, a nebulous and ill-defined tactic. The United States attacked Afghanistan and Iraq and, in the process, rewrote its basic strategic framework, while also dramatically revising its "diplomatic position" in relation to the rest of the world.[39] Domestically, civil rights have suffered, refugees and asylum seekers have fewer rights, and foreign students have lost access to American schools. Detentions of aliens and "enemy combatant" American citizens have also denied them due process rights.

The formula of security at all costs—even at the expense of minority groups and foreign populations—is borrowed from Israel, the network's primary model and ally.

The Israelization of the United States

The new cold war network has been effective at importing Israel's security statism to the United States. An elevated security imperative means moving closer to a police state and using whatever means necessary to stop terrorism, even if that involves employing excessive violence or submitting minority groups and foreign populations to collective punishment, surveillance, and intimidation. In effect, this means three things: first, enhancing the already intimate US-Israel relationship; second, employing the US government in Israel's campaigns against is own enemies, partly through eliminating the funding of groups hostile to Israel's military forces; finally, developing an antiterrorism framework that puts security above the rights of minorities and already collectively punished groups.

Emerson and Pipes argue that the war on terrorism was already being fought by Israel in the name of security. Therefore, not only is Israel an ally against the same enemy, international Islamic terrorism, but the United States could draw on Israel's experiences and tactics. Emerson and Pipes contend that when it comes to terrorism and the states that support it, American and Israeli interests comport. An integral part of Emerson's antiterror campaign is to increase US support of Israel. He consistently conflates the US and Israel as the same victim in the same war: "Rivers of blood have flooded Tel Aviv, Jerusalem, New York and Washington."[40] Often, he presents statistics that bind the two. For instance, he wrote in the *Wall Street Journal,* "More than 1200 Israelis and some 30 Americans have been killed in Israel" since 1988—without any mention of the Palestinian and Palestinian American casualties.[41] To draw the parallel complete, Emerson makes no distinction between the goals and tactics of Hamas, Hizbollah, and al-Qaeda. One of his testimonies to a congressional committee, "Terrorist Networks in the United States," included in its title, "The Structure of Osama Bin Laden, Al-Qaeda, Hamas and other Jihadist Organizations in the United States."[42] A reviewer of Emerson's book *American Jihad: The Terrorists Living Among Us* stated that Emerson treats these organizations interchangeably.[43]

The neoconservative agenda includes drawing the parallel as well. Neoconservatives tend to support the Likud, the right-wing Israeli party that Ariel Sharon belongs to. Richard Perle, of the Defense Policy Board, serves on the board of the company that owns the right-wing *Jerusalem Post,*[44] which features regular columns by Daniel Pipes. Pipes's association with the Israeli Right is symbolized by his relationship to an Israeli settler named Grayson Levy: he is Pipes's Web designer. He is in charge of presenting Pipes's face to the world. A man whose settler news service wrote, "There is no palestinian [*sic*] people, they have never existed, they are a figment of our imagination," works closely with Pipes.[45]

Drawing parallels between Israel and the United States is a conscious strategy designed by pro-Israeli advocates. The Luntz Research Companies, headed by Frank Luntz, a Republican pollster, and the Israel Project expressed this in a memo called "Israeli Communication Priorities 2003." It was written for the

Wexner Foundation, which funds "Jewish leadership initiatives." Even though Americans oppose budgetary increases, the memo states, "A national-security angle ... that clearly links the interests of both Israel and America" can convince the American public to support aid increases to Israel. Comparing Saddam Hussein to the Palestinians can do this. It recommends that just as "America had no choice" other than to remove Saddam Hussein, "Israel has no choice but to protect its borders and its people from terrorists who mean us harm."[46]

Emerson and company have used the war on terrorism to promote Israel's objectives. Emerson is closely linked to a small cadre of hard-liners, some of whom have worked for Israeli intelligence. He associates with former FBI associate deputy director Oliver "Buck" Revell, and a former FBI counterterrorism chief, Steve Pomerantz. He also colludes with Yigal Carmon, who was previously a high official with Aman, the Israeli military intelligence service, and a counterterrorism adviser to Israeli prime ministers Yitzhak Rabin and Yitzhak Shamir.[47] Carmon is a cofounder of MEMRI, the group that translates items from the Arabic press and offers unabashedly pro-Israel analysis. Vince Cannistraro, a former CIA official, witnessed Carmon fund raising in Washington, DC, to create a counterterrorism think tank. They invited him, but he refused because he "saw this was capped by Israeli intelligence" and "too political."[48] Carmon lobbies the US government to aggressively attack terrorism on the domestic front, even if that means altering the US Constitution.[49]

When Emerson centered on the financial support of the international terrorist ring he raved about, he was aiding Israel in combating groups such as Hamas and the Islamic Jihad. He testified before Congress that the Holy Land Foundation for Relief and Development, a nonprofit fund-raising organization, was linked to Hamas. Federal officials closed the foundation down after September 11, 2001. Emerson's focus on certain humanitarian groups followed an Israeli campaign for "an international crackdown on Islamic charities and private relief groups." Israel banned the Holy Land Foundation in May 1997, though the charity was based in Texas.[50] Under what has been called the "May 6 Decree," Israel could appropriate any of the charity's assets or money found in areas under its jurisdiction.[51] It shut down allegedly Hamas-affiliated groups in "Israeli-Arab communities and Palestinian areas under Israel's control."[52]

The US government's broad assault on Muslim charities is all within the antiterrorism framework that developed after the 1995 Oklahoma City bombing. A provision in the omnibus anti-terrorism bill, which was passed in a year as the 1996 Anti-terrorism and Effective Death Penalty Act, called for the prosecution of organizations and individuals providing funds to groups outlined by the State Department. The *New York Times* reported that Jewish groups welcomed the measure in order to eliminate contributions to political opponents of Israel.[53] The Anti-Defamation League cheered its passage.[54]

Government officials admitted that often the charities are unaware that terrorists use them as cover. Also, frequently, only a small portion of the funds or only a few employees will be involved in funding violence.[55] The government however punishes aliens who donate to certain organizations even if the money is for explicitly humanitarian purposes. For example, Ali Termos was detained and deported. The FBI pressed him and discovered his political connections; he gave three hundred dollars to support his nephews and nieces in a Hizbollah-run orphanage after Israel's attack on a UN camp in Qana left their parents dead.[56] He was held initially on a visa violation but detained and deported based on secret evidence. A related legal theory that punishes humanitarian donations to groups with militant wings is that donations to nonmilitary uses still free up money for terrorist activities. Emerson has been vigilant in showing no mercy for the humanitarian needs motive, which he claimed is often deceptive. He told Congress, "Terrorists don't openly raise funds for explosives or guns but rather for 'humanitarian' purposes, such as education or for orphans."[57]

With the same zeal for security, the United States has attacked *hawala* businesses. *Hawala* is an informal money wiring and banking arrangement that financially connects many impoverished third world residents to relatives working abroad. It is an important way for foreign workers to send remittances back to their families, especially where the banking infrastructure, and economy in general, is weak. Investigations show that it has also been used to exchange money within and between militant groups such as al-Qaeda. Though the lives and living conditions of tens if not hundreds of millions of people around the world depend on this service, the Unites States government is campaigning to close it down. Steven Emerson advocates an aggressive policy against *hawala* systems with any presence in the United States.[58] The impact this has on poor people in undeveloped parts of the world is not even considered—in the name of security. Thus, the rights and livelihood—or security—of the already impoverished are subordinated to the "security" of people of the United States and Israel. In other words, Arabs, Muslims, and others are just part of an expendable mass who fall outside the bounds of the new security imperative.

For Israel and the United States, security is their license to shape any policies no matter how many people are affected adversely. In Israel, policymakers debate the ethnic cleansing, or "transfer," of Palestinians as a security measure; US politicians accept the offensive invasion and occupation of a sovereign country as legitimized by security—hardly a new phenomenon in American history. However, the rhetoric is parallel, and the same personalities responsible for the occupation of Iraq advocate on behalf of Israel as well.

The new McCarthyites equate moderates with militants

For Pipes, the analogy is clear. Islamism is the new communism. One of the chapters of his book *Militant Islam Reaches America* is entitled "Echoes of the Cold War Debate." On a talk show, Pipes stated bluntly, "I think what Nazism or fascism was to World War II and Marxist/Leninism was to the Cold War, militant Islam is to this war."[59] To complete his own analogy, that would make him a mini-McCarthy. His policy suggestions are no less extreme than this absurd analogy. They follow from the dubious basis that al-Qaeda and other stateless movements are as threatening to world peace as Nazi Germany and the Soviet Union, industrialized states with powerful militaries, were. With militant Muslims lurking behind every door, Pipes argues for racial profiling, the use of secret evidence, enhanced surveillance, and so on. He contends, "Mosques are proved to be the planning grounds for militant Islam so this is where we should look." Muslims who work for the government "need to be watched for connections to terrorism."[60] Pipes and Emerson have written books taking up the *Jihad in America* theme. With articles entitled "Islamic Terror: From Midwest to Mideast" and "US Passport Holders: Potential Terrorists," the message is consistent: terrorists are everywhere, poised to attack. Civil rights must be compromised.

Though they claim to distinguish the moderates from the militants, they treat the Muslim community as a wholesale threat. Pipes and Khalid Duran, a frequent collaborator with Emerson, have written, "In its long history of immigration, the United States has never encountered so violence-prone and radicalized a community as the Muslims who have arrived since 1965."[61] Where is the subtlety of describing "a community" as "violence-prone"? There is no distinction between moderates and militants when discussing a general community. Daniel Pipes's Web site features a string of news articles and commentary on various topics, more vitriolic toward Islam in general rather than Islamism— the supposedly true target of Pipes's wrath. His Web log[62] featured a story on a swimming pool in France that became women-only for certain hours to accommodate religious Muslims. Pipes wondered alarmingly, "A sign of things to come elsewhere?" Another posted article reported that an Australian Muslim woman falsified an insurance claim because Islamic norms require that she follow her husband's wishes. Other articles deal with the demographics of Muslims in the United States and Canada. One headline reads that Muslims outnumber Jews in Canada. A *Los Angeles Times* article summarized Pipes's view that "increased Muslim populations in the United States, France, Holland and elsewhere around the world are a danger to Jews."[63]

In December 2002, Pipes wrote an article criticizing PBS for showing a documentary on the prophet Muhammad the night before it aired.[64] He charged that it was so favorable a presentation that it aimed to "proselytize." One example of his assault on nonpolitical Islam: he claimed that the video was misleading because it covered some of Muhammad's progressive views on women without mentioning the suffering of Muslim women today. To him, this was a whitewash. Later in the article, he claims that the documentary ignored scholarly reassessment of Muhammad's life, unlike the 1998 PBS *Frontline* documentary on Christ, "From Jesus to Christ: The First Christians."[65] Though he used "From Jesus to Christ" as a standard to reveal PBS's hypocrisy, it shows his own. Not once did that video include any discussion of the actions of present-day Christians who contravene Jesus Christ's teachings—he holds it up as a standard even though his criticisms of *Muhammad: Legacy of a Prophet* apply to it as well. This episode illustrates that even when a moderate's view of Islam is promoted, Pipes attacks it, further blurring the line he portends to draw between militant and moderate strains of Islam.

Before Steven Emerson became a terrorism expert, he was a full promoter of the anti-Saudi hysteria of the 1980s. His first major story covered the sale of US AWACS planes to Saudi Arabia. His critical view in the piece matched the pro-Israel lobby's position. The sale went through and is now considered the lobby's most significant congressional defeat yet. Emerson's first book expanded on the theme. *The American House of Saud* contends that American companies lobbied lawmakers for the Saudis "in exchange for lucrative deals."[66] Exorbitant lobbying is by no means a rarity in American politics. Only when it benefits Arabs is it problematic.

His scorn turned next to PBS. He wrote an investigative report for the *New Republic* charging that the 1989 PBS documentary *Days of Rage* was secretly funded by the Saudi government. Supposedly, this contravened a PBS policy against the receipt of funding from parties with a "vested interest."[67] Predictably, Emerson did not consider the funding from right-wing think tanks and the Middle East Forum he received for his PBS documentary a violation of that policy. Right-wing think tanks and pro-Israel groups have as much of a "vested interest" in his video as the Saudis would in a documentary sympathetic to the Palestinians—another example of Emerson's strategic hypocrisy.

Emerson and Pipes have actively worked to make moderate Muslims and their organizations appear militant. According to them, even mainstream and participatory Muslims use a veneer of moderation for nefarious Islamist ends. For instance, Emerson claimed in an interview with Daniel Pipes that Muslim "fundamentalists" want to "turn the United States into an Islamic country." His evidence was that "Ibrahim Hooper of the Council on American-Islamic Relations (or CAIR) openly declares that he would like to see the U.S. become a Muslim country."[68] The *Minneapolis Star Tribune* article cited in the interview does quote Hooper to that effect, but Emerson conveniently left out Hooper's statement that he was "not going to do anything violent to promote that." Hooper said he was "going to do it through education."[69] There, distinction between moderate and militant is functionally useless if the communications director of the largest Muslim civil rights organization is a "fundamentalist," the same term he uses to describe bin Laden. A more likely explanation of this is that Hooper is an outspoken critic of Emerson's.

CAIR is one of the several US Muslim organizations that Pipes and Emerson frequently disparage. Pipes suggested that CAIR is capable of violence. He wrote, "Violence comes potentially ... from groups which, like CAIR, apologize for and in other ways support Hamas."[70] Emerson claimed, "CAIR is Hamas with a K Street address in Washington."[71] Using Hamas as a referent defames CAIR while reaffirming the theme that Israel's war is America's.

Pipes charged the mainstream Muslim organizations—the American Muslim Council, CAIR, and the Muslim Public Affairs Committee—with "intimidating and silencing the opponents of militant Islam," and "raising funds for, apologizing for, and otherwise forwarding the cause of militant Islamic groups abroad, including those that engage in violence."[72] If not direct, their links to terror are indirect. Emerson accuses civil rights organizations of "creating a chilling climate where free speech on this issue has been suppressed,"[73] which assists terrorists in dodging the authorities. Emerson is yet to comment critically on the much more apparent chilling effect silencing the Arab and Muslim populations in the United States. On the contrary, he advocates for measures that end up intimidating the Arab and Muslim communities, then complains that civil rights groups have chilled his free speech. The absurdity is twofold. First, Emerson, with his congressional testimonies and multitude of media appearances, strikes no one as a silenced voice. Second, he suggests that the few organizations that can speak for a battered and scared community should be shut down.

His claim about a chilling effect by hegemonic civil rights groups is not the only example of Emerson's aptitude for hypocrisy. Though he often will leave sources unnamed, refuse to divulge where he gets funding from, and give little information about his past for "security" reasons, Emerson demands "truth in advertising" from US Muslim groups.[74]

According to Pipes and Emerson, the US government has not done enough in the war on terror. Pipes alleges that, as of late 2002, law enforcement in the United States "treads super gingerly" around people who "back" political Islam out of fear of being accused of "profiling."[75] This, he argues, follows the "strictures of American-based militant Islamic groups," which, he goes on to explain, means CAIR.[76] Part of the government's inadequacy, according to Pipes, is a problem of perception. The government and media just cannot face the truth about militant Islam's infiltration into US society. Not only was the soldier charged with tossing a grenade at other US soldiers in Kuwait part of a "sustained pattern of political violence,"[77] but the snipers who menaced the Washington, DC, area also were motivated by jihad,[78] just as Pipes claims, Saddam Hussein may have been behind the anthrax attacks.[79] Pipes asks, "When will officialdom acknowledge what is staring it in the face?"[80]

There is another reason why their disclaimer about differentiating moderates from militants is misleading. To Pipes, the threat is not just doers, but anyone who subscribes to or sympathizes with the ideology of Islamism, whether they use violence or not. Though Pipes rejects the label McCarthyite, he advocates the criminalization of holding a particular view. He asserts that the "Muslim population in this country is not like any other group" because "it includes within it a substantial body of people ... who *share* with the suicide hijackers a hatred of the United States."[81] A number of fundamentalists may be "peaceable in appearance, but they all must be considered potential killers."[82] He puts the number of "fundamentalists" at "10 to 15 percent" of the total Muslim population.[83] By simple syllogistic logic then, Pipes truly believes that 10 to 15 percent of Muslims are "potential killers."

To digress, Pipes's use of statistics has been one of his more creative traits. In an August 2002 *New York Post* column, he wrote about Muslim fundamentalists invading and ravaging Denmark. He concluded confidently, "Muslims are only 4 percent of Denmark's 5.4 million people but make up a majority of the country's convicted rapists."[84] When a letter to the editor several weeks later by two Danish officials challenged the credibility of this figure since Denmark does not keep religious statistics for crimes,[85] he replied with shady math. He wrote in response to the letter that official statistics show that 76.5 percent of rapists *"in Copenhagen"* (emphasis added) are immigrants—a category for which statistics are kept.[86] His first trick was to generalize a national figure for Denmark as a whole from numbers specific to Copenhagen. His second trick was to state that since Muslims are four-fifths of the immigrants to Denmark and 76.5 percent of convicted rapists are immigrants, it is reasonable to assert that Muslims "make up a majority of the country's convicted rapists." This assumes misleadingly that the religious breakdown of immigrants is the same as the religious breakdown of immigrants convicted of rape. In the end, it is only a possibility that most convicted rapists in Denmark are Muslim, not a fact as Pipes declared conclusively. The main reason for this point was to invoke the classic racist image of the predatory swarthy or colored man stalking white women. After his mathematical manipulations in the original article, he made a point to mention, "Practically all the female victims are non-Muslim." One wonders if he gathered that from the fact that practically all females in Copenhagen are non-Muslim.

Pipes is adamant about naming the enemy as Islamism in order to illustrate that "the problem goes beyond terrorists." Actions must be taken against those who in "non-violent ways" advance the militant Islam "agenda," including "funders, preachers, apologists, and lobbyists."[87] The Muslim population at large is a threat as well. He told the American Jewish Committee, "I worry very much from the Jewish point of view that the presence and increased stature and affluence and enfranchisement of American Muslims—because they are so much led by an Islamist leadership—that this will present true dangers to American Jews."[88] John Sugg, an investigative reporter, contacted Pipes to confirm this quote. Pipes did so and added that he would make the same comments to other groups such as Hindus, Evangelicals, Atheists, and scholars of Islam who also face "true dangers" as the Muslim presence in the US increases.[89]

While academics such as Fawaz Gerges differentiate violent and nonviolent adherents of Islamism, Pipes puts them together in one category. In his view, the political Islamist "who doesn't use violence today will use it tomorrow."[90] On *Lou Dobbs Moneyline,* Gerges challenged Pipes's view. He argued that "enlightened Islamists" are different from the "reactionary and fascist" ones, and that prior to September 11, "American policymakers made a clear distinction between mainstream and moderate Islamists and fringe Islamist movements who use violence and force." Pipes responded that "they are our enemy whether we—whether you recognize it or not."[91] For Pipes, his shining model is the ideological police state—where holding a view makes one an enemy of the state.

Like a good cold warrior, Pipes wants to enlist "the media, Hollywood, even academics" to join in the war against Islamism.[92] Pipes and Emerson have unleashed a full assault on one of the most accessible of these, academia. Their targets have been more than just Islamists, but anyone critical of American and Israeli policies. They have proceeded in two ways. First, they claim that Muslim radicals infiltrate American society as professors. Second, they criticize the entire field of Middle East studies as anti-American and anti-Israel.

One chapter of Emerson's most recent book, *American Jihad: The Terrorists Living Among Us,* seeks to illustrate that radical Muslims have sought refuge in ivory towers ("Jihad in the Academy"). Eric Boehlert pointed out in *Salon* that Emerson gives only one example to demonstrate this: "his already dubious charge against Al-Arian and USF." Still, he repeats the allegation that radical Islamists have infiltrated American academies, in front of congressional committees.[93] Following the lengthy campaign by Emerson against Dr. Sami al-Arian, the University of South Florida fired him. Dr. Al-Arian currently sits in solitary confinement, unable to fairly contest the evidence against him. The FBI investigated him for terrorist activities as they detained him.[94] If at least some of the evidence is from Emerson, it must be scrutinized openly, in the spirit of the American adversarial legal system. Emerson's earlier efforts include claiming to have proof that linked Muslims in Tampa Bay, Florida, to the bombing of the World Trade Center in 1993. John Sugg pointed out, "Emerson never delivered."[95] Some of the evidence Emerson presented against al-Arian came from Israeli intelligence.[96] It is unlikely that al-Arian will get a fair trial. One of the issues is to determine his relationship with the Islamic Jihad, a Palestinian militant group illegalized by Israel, and consequently, the United States.

The blueprint for the attack on Middle East studies comes from Martin Kramer, a fellow at the pro-Israel WINEP. His book *Ivory Towers on Sand: The Failure of Middle Eastern Studies in America* paints a picture of an overfunded field poisoned by political affiliations. Professors use their positions to advance political agendas, thereby failing to offer valuable insights into the actual events that define the Arab and Muslim worlds: the Egyptian-Syrian invasion of Israel in 1973; the Lebanese civil war; the Iranian Revolution; the Iraq-Iran War; the Iraqi occupation of Kuwait; the "explosion of Palestinian violence since 2000"; and Osama bin Laden and September 11, 2001.[97] The crux of Kramer's criticism of Middle East studies is that "time and again, academics have been taken by surprise by their subjects; time and again, their paradigms have been swept away by events"—which

amounts to a "failure." Presumably, shifting paradigms and sur-
prises are academically unique to Middle East studies. That is the
softest of the criticism. Pipes and others charge Middle East specialists with indoctrinating students and encouraging them to
commit acts of violence against Jews.[98]

Daniel Pipes's Middle East Forum established an organization, Campus Watch, to document professors and university
events critical of Israel. According to its Web site, Campus Watch
"reviews and critiques Middle East studies in North America"
with the benevolent intent of "improving them." Controversy hit
immediately, mainly because it published dossiers on individual
faculty members—a practice since discontinued. Campus Watch
still, however, encourages students and others to report statements and activities critical of Israel or the United States.

It claims to focus on five problems: "analytical failures, the
mixing of politics with scholarship, intolerance of alternative
views, apologetics, and the abuse of power over students."[99]
Campus Watch is apparently concerned with another "problem": that Middle East studies is "the preserve of Middle Eastern Arabs, who have brought their views with them."[100] To
empirically bolster its race-baiting, it cites that half the membership of the Middle East Studies Association is of Middle Eastern
origin. Even though these scholars are largely American citizens,
they "actively disassociate themselves from the United States." It
adds alarmingly, "sometimes even in public."

In the post–September 11 period, the defamation of Middle
East studies by Kramer, Pipes, and others has found a receptive
audience in Washington, DC. In June 2003, after much petition-
ing by these anti–Middle East studies crusaders, a US House of
Representatives subcommittee heard their allegations that federally funded international-studies programs at US colleges and universities are too critical of US foreign policy and should thus "be
more tightly regulated" and given less funding.[101] Stanley Kurtz, a
fellow at Stanford University's Hoover Institute and frequent contributor to the *National Review*, testified to this effect. The basis
for this campaign is that political views should be kept out of the
academy. In practice, they mean *certain* political views, of course,
since they never attack the outwardly political dispositions of the
pro-Israel and ultranationalistic academics they fraternize with.

Campus Watch: A case study in strategic hypocrisy

Pipes himself has a way of bouncing back and forth from what he considers scholarship of Islamic history to ideologically driven polemics about the threat of Islam. The dividing line is not so clear always. He does what his Campus Watch site targets dissident faculty for doing, mixing scholarship and politics. Of course, Pipes does not have an academic post anymore so he does not abuse "power" over students. With the rest of Campus Watch's criteria—"analytical failures, ... intolerance of alternative views, [and] apologetics"—he hardly stands on solid ground. The scholarship of the Middle East Forum, a research institute and parent to Campus Watch, is explicitly political. It serves to publish and provide "apologetics" for aggressive American and Israeli policies in the Middle East. The most hypocritical criterion is the one about the "intolerance of alternative views," since Campus Watch is refusing to tolerate views critical of Israel—certainly the "alternative" in the United States.

To cite Daniel Pipes's analytic failures is an easy task. One extremely troubling and under-discussed failure is worth reviewing. For having such an obsession over the mix of religion and violent ideology, Pipes has never critically written about or mentioned on television the Jewish Defense League (JDL), according to a search on his rich Web site.[102] Rabbi Meir Kahane, whose Chai movement is on the State Department's list of Designated Foreign Terrorist Organizations,[103] founded the JDL. While the Anti-Defamation League concedes, "Kahane consistently preached a radical form of Jewish nationalism which reflected racism, violence and political extremism,"[104] Pipes takes a cozy tone toward his views. For example, when asked if he had any connections to Kahane in a friendly interview, he merely said "none at all": his shortest response of all the questions.[105] In an article Pipes penned with Duran,[106] they only mention Kahane as a victim of "terrorism." The greater purpose is to imply a Muslim monopoly on terrorism. After repeating the charge that mainstream Muslim organizations are fronts for terror groups, Duran and Pipes write, this "brings us to the subject of terrorism." What they present next is revealing by what it omits as well as what it includes. They claim, "Since the November 1990 assassination of Rabbi Meir Kahane by an Egyptian, the immigrant Muslim community has been associated with a great num-

ber of violent incidents." The article obscures the fact that Kahane himself was a religious fundamentalist with a history of political violence. Instead, Pipes treats him as just a "rabbi," or
another Jewish victim of American Muslims, as he suggests in
another piece.[107] Kahane's murder, instead of offering insight
into the perplexing challenge of defining terrorism along ethno-
religious lines, is presented as the historical starting point of Islamic terrorism in the United States. In one swoop of the pen,
Pipes and Duran try to hide, then transfer, Kahane's long history
as a terrorist to the entire "immigrant Muslim community."
Elsewhere, Pipes has written that Kahane's assassination represents the inevitable conflict with Muslims in the West.[108]

Even where a discussion of the history of Jewish extremist attacks on Arabs and Muslims would fit into an article logically, as
with Pipes's *Commentary* article "American Muslims vs. American Jews," he leaves it out. To add some integrity to the "versus"
in the title, he could have covered the Anti-Defamation League's
record of espionage on Arab American organizations. Instead, the
article paints an exclusive picture of an American Muslim popu-
lace victimizing a hapless American Jewry. Jewish hostility toward
Arabs and Muslims in the United States has a well documented
though often neglected history. For example, in 1970 alone, JDL
members beat up Arab American "propagandists" and plotted to
hijack an Arab airliner.[109] In 1985, a bomb killed Alex Odeh, the
West Coast director of the American-Arab Anti-Discrimination
Committee, and injured seven others. The JDL is the primary suspect, though no one has been charged. In an affidavit submitted by
FBI Special Agent Mary P. Hogan, she states that an informant
with a tape recording of a meeting between leaders contacted
her.[110] It featured JDL figures Earl Krugel and Irv Rubin. The two
men discussed targeting mosques for acts of violence. The affidavit
states that Rubin expressed "his desire to blow up an entire building, but that the JDL did not have the technology to accomplish
such a bombing." Krugel pleaded guilty to conspiring with Rubin
to explode the King Fahd Mosque in Culver City, California, and
the office of Arab-American Congressman Darrell Issa (R-CA).[111]

Emerson also interprets the assassination of Kahane for similarly convenient analytical purposes. Instead of marking it as the
first act of homegrown Arab terrorists as Pipes does, Emerson considers it the first major government gaffe in the war on terrorism.
Officials investigating the home of the alleged killer, El Sayyid No-

sair, found forty-seven boxes of literature but made nothing of it under the assumption it contained merely religious material. Emerson asserts that it was the most significant collection of terrorist materials ever discovered in the United States.[112] This comports with his consistent message that the government is simply not doing enough to clamp down on the domestic terrorist threat.

If Emerson has ever made a critical comment of Kahane, it is not easy to find. The closest to critical comes from a 1995 article in which he referred to Kahane as the "militant Jewish leader."[113] Emerson claims to have condemned the JDL in his book *American Jihad: The Terrorists Living Among Us*. He complains, "No matter how many times I condemned the Jewish Defense League and Christian terrorists, they continued to bombard me with accusations that I was a racist and anti-Muslim."[114] Responding to accusations of bias during a televised debate in 1995, he claimed to go after all terrorists regardless of their background.[115] No investigative condemnations could be found in the research for this essay. The closest Emerson got was to list the JDL as one group "tied to international and foreign acts of terrorism."[116] Still, Emerson has not publicly presented any investigative research into the JDL, which was only mentioned twice in his book.

Conclusion

The primary problem with this network of confrontationalists that Pipes and Emerson are part of is that in the end they sound more like the enemy than they do people who should be granted influence with policymakers and access to media. The new cold warriors, like the militants they oppose, see a conflict between the West and Islam as imminent. They all believe that there is no alternative to violence, no matter how many innocent people suffer in the process. For both extremes, the world falls into two camps. Daniel Pipes wrote that there is a battle for the soul of Islam between moderates "eager to accept Western ways" and integration and Islamists "seeking strong rule,"[117] yet Pipes ultimately suggests targeting them both. That Pipes puts CAIR and the other US Muslim organizations, as well as millions of Muslim thinkers, professionals, and everyday people into the Islamist category demonstrates an extremity of thinking that nearly mirrors Osama bin Laden's. The innocents who fall in the middle between the bellicose ends fall victim—and neither extreme seems to really care.

Both radical Islamists and Pipes/Emerson are energized and motivated by this clash and do more to fuel it than to seek peace and reconciliation. They all seek more rather than less belligerency. While members of this network do not need to employ violence personally to get their points across, they actively encourage the employment of mechanized armies against civilian populations—with little regard for the human cost. The new Cold Warriors call for military action against Islamists and rogue regimes everywhere. Though Campus Watch accuses professors of being apologetic for Arab or Muslim terrorism, Pipes and Emerson always justify or ignore Israeli violence against Palestinians. Similarly, to them, the United States can do no wrong against innocent populations so long as it is in the name of fighting terrorism—an intuitively backward logic that will have grave future repercussions.

Though the praxis of security-based policy goals must be scrutinized, American policymakers should be advised to steer clear of overtly agenda-driven terrorism experts offering politicized bias as so-called prescriptions for security. American security will be threatened in the long run by elevating hatemongers to prominence and visibility. It further hurts America's already deficient credibility. Even if, in the end, Pipes, Emerson, and their cadre are only nominal players, those in power who give legitimacy to their voices will only set back the efforts of those trying to improve America's image, security, and policies. If security is truly the object of US administrations, they should leave it to objective and levelheaded specialists, not to pocketed political hacks.

However pragmatic this lesson, it is better to conclude with irony. The suspicion and mistrust with which Pipes sees Muslim populations in the United States and the West was clarified inadvertently in an interview he had about his book on the prevalence of conspiracy theories, especially in the Arab mind. He argued that conspiracy theorists are likely to organize conspiratorially themselves since they likely see it as a "good way of operating." In other words, "the conspiracy theorist becomes, himself, a conspirator." This suggests that "when you hear a conspiracy theory being alleged, watch out for the conspiracy. Look around carefully."[118] Pipes and Emerson have devoted the bulwark of their writing to demonstrating that an Islamist conspiracy effectively exists around the world and in the United States. Following Pipes's own advice to "look around," we can see him and Emerson involved in an open conspiracy with other warmongers hoping for a new cold war.

PART III

THE CONVERGENCE OF US DOMESTIC
SHIFT TO THE FAR RIGHT AND
THE PURSUIT OF GLOBAL EXPANSION:
THE CRIMINILIZATION OF
ARAB AND MUSLIM COMMUNITIES

CHAPTER 5

ROOTS OF THE AMERICAN ANTITERRORISM CRUSADE*

Samih Farsoun

The horrific attacks on the Twin Towers of the World Trade
Center in New York and the Pentagon in Washington, DC,
on September 11, 2001, have been defined by American analysts and politicians as a transformative or defining moment in
the modern history of the United States. It is a defining moment,
like earlier defining moments, that has rapidly changed American
governmental perception of international political reality and has
launched the US on a new political and military course intended
to address the new reality.[1] In the past century there were several
defining moments in American political history that had also set
American foreign policy on a new, overarching, comprehensive,
and determined direction. The Japanese attack on Pearl Harbor
was one, and the Korean War in the early 1950s was another.
What is unique about the September 11 attacks is that "this is the
first time since the war of 1812 that the national [American] territory has been under attack or even threatened."[2]

The Korean War globalized the anti-Communist and anti-

*This article originally appeared in *Holy Land Journal* 1, no. 2 (March 2003):
133–60. Permission to reprint this article from the journal's publisher, Contin-
uum Books, is gratefully acknowledged.

Some minor changes were made in the preparation of this manuscript regarding
capitalization and punctuation, as well as the form of documentation of sources.
Minor corrections also were made. The substance of the article remains unchanged.

I wish to thank Will Youmans for invaluable help in the research.

Soviet crusade that was already under way in Europe and set the US irrevocably on that path. The principal political-military strategy in the American anti-Communist crusade of the post–World War II era was *containment* of the Communist geopolitical sphere and *deterrence* against Soviet conventional and nuclear power. Longest in duration, this crusade, popularly labelled the cold war, with all its diplomatic and political conflicts, détentes, proxy hot wars, and the Vietnam War came to an abrupt end with the remarkable and unexpected collapse of the Soviet Union and of Communism in Eastern Europe and Central Asia.

In each of these major confrontations the American political elite and public intelligentsia formulated an overarching ideological framework that justified the new American policy direction and the derivative political-military strategy, and mobilized the American public and resources. However, the unanticipated collapse of Communism and the Soviet system early in the 1990s yielded no immediate visible enemy or challenge for the United States, as was the case earlier in the wake of the defeat of European and Japanese fascism. As a result, an ideological and policy vacuum emerged and led to a competition among policymakers, public intellectuals, and politicians to define the overarching character of the times and a vision for the future. Before she took office, National Security Adviser Condoleezza Rice wrote: "The United States has found it exceedingly difficult to define its 'national interest' in the absence of Soviet power."[3]

Ideology and strategy in the post-Soviet era

Several "visions" were promoted in the 1990s. Former president George Bush promoted the notion of the dawn of a "new world order"—of course American dominated and controlled— an ideological construct that was not fully defined by the elder Bush until after he lost the election to Bill Clinton.[4] Francis Fukuyama articulated a triumphalist thesis of the final victory of democracy and market capitalism and therefore the "end of history."[5] However, the ideological and policy establishment of the United States became more taken with a perceived new threat: "rogue states," especially those with the capability of developing "weapons of mass destruction," or those seeking such weapons, such as Iraq, Iran, Libya, North Korea, and others.

Although the United States mobilized a grand international

alliance of states, including many Arab states, to expel the Iraqi army from occupied Kuwait in 1991, the conflict was not elevated to the rank of a "defining moment" for the United States, nor to that of an overarching ideology and determined policy of ridding the world of "rogue states" once and for all. In retrospect, the Gulf War of 1991 was a regional conflict of importance to the strategic interest of the United States and its oil-producing client states, but not a "defining moment" in its own political history. It did, however, break the "Vietnam syndrome," the official and public fear of committing American troops overseas in order to avoid American casualties.

The Gulf War produced another significant lesson of contemporary international realpolitik: the huge American capability to project tremendous military might far beyond its borders. The overcoming of the "Vietnam syndrome" began with the Reagan administration's invasion of Grenada, a country without an army, and with its vigorous intervention in Central America through covert actions, particularly in Nicaragua. The illegal financing, supplying, and training of the Contras and other counterrevolutionary governments, organizations, and death squads in Central America paralleled as well the actions of mobilization and support of the successful "Islamic resistance" to the Soviet occupation of Afghanistan.[6] The Afghan intervention was the epitome of the return to aggressive, interventionist—and largely unilateralist in Central America—American foreign policy in the wake of the brief "retreat" brought about by the Vietnam debacle.

Beginning in 1992, the center-right, business-oriented administration of Bill Clinton followed, to a large extent, a path of multilateralism, interventionism, and the use of the United Nations as the forum for building international consensus for international intervention—not unlike the approach taken by the administration of George Bush the Elder in the war against Iraq. However, the military challenges of the 1990s were not deemed by the Clinton administration, or its functional intellectuals, to be too threatening to American geopolitical, economic, or strategic interests abroad, as was the Iraqi invasion and occupation of Kuwait. But the Clinton-era drive for military interventionism received a new and different justification: "humanitarian intervention."[7] The ideological concept of "humanitarian intervention" is not a new construct. It was used by European powers in their colonial conquests in the nineteenth century.[8] "Humanitarian intervention" was the justification for American intervention in Somalia and in Bosnia and Kosovo, under the umbrella of NATO. Indeed, the Clinton administration intervened militarily more times than all of the three previous administrations of Jimmy Carter, Ronald Reagan, and George Bush the Elder combined.[9] The strategy that evolved out of this "humanitarian interventionism" included "regime change." However, although Clinton's humanitarian intervention ended the egregious violence in the former Yugoslavia, it did not reverse the process of "ethnification, which is now consolidated and somewhat legitimated."[10]

The Clinton administration coupled the humanitarian military interventionist ideology with an economic-political foreign policy: the promotion and export of "free market capitalism," "economic globalization," and "electoral democracy." This ideological set and derivative policies, aptly labelled "neoliberalism," were intended not only to regulate economic investment and trade relations among the Western industrial powers and Japan (principally through the GATT, NAFTA, and WTO), but also to pry open and "reform" the economies of most countries of the "Global South," through the IMF and World Bank policy of "structural adjustment." But the ideology of neoliberalism remained current principally among the intellectual, professional, and political elites in the United States. It did not grip the imagination of the public, as most of the American people were much more consumed by accumulating wealth during the spectacular economic growth-bubble of the Clinton era, rather than by any international challenge.

The fly, as it were, in the "neoliberal" Clinton-era ointment was "terror attacks" on American armed forces and diplomatic installations in the Arab world and east Africa. Such attacks during the Clinton years included Somalia in 1993; the alleged planned attempt to assassinate George Bush the Elder in Kuwait in 1993; the Riyadh bombing in 1995; the Khobar bombing in 1996; the American Embassy bombing in Nairobi, Kenya, in 1998; the American Embassy bombing in Dar Essalam, Tanzania, also in 1998; the varied plots to launch millennium attacks in the United States and elsewhere in 2000; and the bombing of USS *Cole* in 2000. The attempted bombing of the World Trade Center in 1993 produced relatively little response. Also during this period, the confrontations with Iraq over UN-mandated inspections escalated and increased further the perception of the threat of a "rogue state" acquiring weapons of mass destruction.

These attacks did not generate a new overarching ideology or crusade, but they led to a new strategic military concept: "asymmetrical warfare."[11] This was especially suited to the new kind of enemy: stateless, transnational or subnational and mobile, motivated by religious, or other ideology or purpose (e.g., drug trafficking). The US government established offices and task forces to identify, monitor, and track what it considered to be anti-American "terrorist organizations." But, principally, the United States under Clinton "circled the wagons" and developed defensive security strategies for its diplomatic and military installations overseas, and, of course, satisfied itself with long-distance cruise-missile attacks against Osama bin Laden's al-Qaeda bases in Afghanistan and narcotics organizations in Colombia.

Prominent in the policymaking councils, and to a lesser extent in the news, were also the dilemmas of the "failed states," the new successor states of the Soviet system and the commensurate moral and humanitarian concerns associated with the tragedies of many Global South countries. With respect to the "failed states," "humanitarian military," political, and economic interventionism was the order of the times. The humanitarian rhetoric was deployed in order to justify military intervention in certain states experiencing lethal political chaos (Somalia), civil conflict, and ethnic cleansing (Bosnia and Kosovo). However, the genocidal Hutu-Tutsi ethnic conflict in central Africa did not lead to the deployment of Western military force to end the genocide. These and other conflicts prompted some American and British neoconservative intellectuals to call—on presumably moral grounds—for a "new imperialism," especially for the "failed states" of the Global South. As Martin Khor argues,

> The expanded theory of the "failed state" not only puts the blame onto the country concerned, but also opens the way to political and even military intervention in many countries— countries that are suspected to sponsor or tolerate "terrorism," and countries that are unable to develop sufficiently or in a way that would prevent conditions for "terrorism."[12]

Unabashed calls for the *need* to support a "new imperialism" to help the unfortunates of the non-Western world started shortly after the Somalia fiasco early in the Clinton era. Paul Johnson wrote an article entitled, "Colonialism's Back—and Not a Moment Too Soon."[13] Sebastian Mallaby also urged the

United States to "embrace empire."[14] Similarly, Max Boot argued "The Case for an American Empire."[15] These theorists distinguished the postmodern states of Western Europe and Japan from the "failed states" of the "premodern world" whose national patrimony is a base for, or can become a base for criminal activity (e.g., Colombia) and a safe haven for "terrorist organizations" (e.g., Afghanistan, Sudan, Syria, etc.). Therefore, according to this new ideology, there is a need for Western military intervention in the "failed states," "regime change" in those states, and protection of the Western-installed successor "elected" governments, as in Bosnia, Kosovo, and Afghanistan.

The emergence of the crusade against terrorism

The policies and ideology of "neoliberalism" were hailed by most in the West as the essential and incontrovertible means to economic growth, development, and prosperity not only in the West but also in the Global South. Government officials and functional ideologues who held to such an ideology either ignored or never admitted the negative consequences of such neoliberal policies on the great majorities of the peoples of the Global South. It is clear that such policies, imposed especially on the states in debt, threatened their independence, produced immense and increasing hardships on the great mass of its various peoples, generated processes of upward redistribution of wealth, and threatened as well the cultural authenticity and traditional values of the ordinary people.[16]

It was these issues, often articulated in cultural terms, that led one American academic, Samuel Huntington, to propose a controversial thesis about the contemporary world: that the coming global conflict in the wake of the end of the cold war would not be a conflict of power by states or coalitions of states over economic resources and markets, or over geo-strategic positioning, but rather a "clash of civilizations": "Cultural communities are replacing Cold War blocs, and the fault lines between civilizations are becoming the central lines of conflict in global politics."[17] For Huntington, Islam is the "Dark Force" in the world because of the "Muslim propensity toward violent conflict."[18] Thus, the inevitable clash between Islam and the West. Although Huntington's thesis was much debated in the United States, both for and against, it remained largely an academic and intellectual debate devoid of any official ideological acceptance, policy implications, or political-military strategy. It received a huge boost after the September 11 attacks.

Very quickly after the attacks, a virtual anti-Islamic and anti-Arab hysteria materialized in the American media, among some sectors of the American public, and among many politicians. This rhetorical and attitudinal hysteria was encouraged significantly by pro-Israel activists, politicians, public intellectuals, and columnists in all media. They quickly drew parallels between Islamic-inspired terror against Israel and Islamic-inspired terror against the United States. Some even declared the civilizational clash or war had started. Verbal and physical racist attacks, popularly and legally referred to as "hate crimes," were perpetrated against Arab Americans and Muslim Americans all over the country. The palpable torrent of verbal abuse, physical attacks, and harassment, which remarkably also reached into many university campuses, was so extensive that US government officials felt the need to voice their disapproval and warn the public against committing illegal "hate crimes." President Bush, Attorney General John Ashcroft, and others spoke out publicly against such attacks, and, in a symbolic gesture, Bush visited the Washington Islamic Center, the principal mosque in the city. He, like many officials, rhetorically took pains to distinguish between Islam and law-abiding Arabs, Arab Americans, and Muslim Americans, on the one hand, and terrorists who speak and act in the name of Islam on the other. At the time, such official governmental and media warnings and actions (joined sometimes by university officials) appeared to be hopeful signs that could possibly defuse the anti-Arab and anti-Muslim discourse.

Nevertheless, racist commentary, social profiling of Arab American and Muslim American air travellers, job and workplace discrimination, as well as other forms of illegal harassment and abuse increased and have persisted.[19] In November 2001, Ashcroft was reported to have said in a radio interview with a conservative radio host: "Islam is a religion in which God requires you to send your son to die for him. Christianity is a faith in which God sends his son to die for you." Moreover, conservative columnist Ann Coulter, seemingly in a fit of rage, proposed: "We should invade their [Muslim] countries, kill their leaders and convert them to Christianity." William Lind, coauthor of a pamphlet entitled *Why Islam Is a Threat to America and the West* and a leading conservative activist, said of Muslim Americans: "They should be encouraged to leave. They are a fifth column in this country."[20]

The storm of anger, outrage, and calls for action by politicians, public intellectuals, and the media emphasized the need to protect America and Americans from further attack and from the scourge of international Islamic terrorism. In this politically charged context, the US Congress passed a series of laws that launched, in the words of President Bush, a "war against terrorism." Congress passed the USA PATRIOT Act and voted a unique huge budget to fight the coming "war against terrorism." However, as Noam Chomsky has noted, "To call it a 'war against terrorism' ... is simply more propaganda, unless the 'war' really does target terrorism. But that is plainly not contemplated because Western powers could never abide by their own official definitions of the term, as in the US Code or Army manuals. To do so would at once reveal that the US is a leading terrorist state as are its clients."[21]

In short, a decade after the collapse of Communism and the end of the anti-Communist crusade, in the "defining moment" of the September 11 attacks, official America finally found a new crusade—the war on terrorism, an ideological construct that easily galvanized a population traumatized by the attacks, justified its domestic and international policies, and provided it with the moral high ground for all its forthcoming actions. The Patriot act curbed and eroded much of the long-cherished civil liberties in the United States. It was not surprising that the FBI made mass arrests of thousands of Arab and Muslim Americans without any legal basis. Most were arrested with no probable grounds other than the fact of their ethnicity or religion. This clearly violates the long-established legal principles of innocent until proven guilty and no detention for a long period without being charged.

Internationally, the United States launched the war on terrorism in an assault on Afghanistan with the purpose of eliminating Taliban rule in that country, effecting "regime change," killing the leadership and cadre of al-Qaeda that were based in that country, and destroying al-Qaeda's infrastructure. The United States also launched many other diplomatic, banking, financial, and intelligence actions in an international effort to cripple, if not eliminate the global network of al-Qaeda and allied organizations. It is in the context of claiming the high moral ground, and with self-righteous posturing, that the political leadership of the United States formulated the slogan "You are either with us or with the terrorists."

US officials, public intellectuals, and much of the American public were in no mood to inquire into the causes of terrorism or argue over what constitutes terrorism. Terrorism and terrorists were described as evil, which was enough to account for the attacks. Any questioning of the unilateral American definition of terrorism was brushed aside, and any local or regional opposition abroad to American policies was characterized either as terrorism or as coming from groups or states that support terrorism. This definition of terrorism, of course, does not include "state terrorism" that has long been practiced by the United States in Central and South America and by Israel in Palestine and by many other states allied to or clients of the United States. But it does extend to the so-called rogue states, which are neither American allies nor clients, but rather antagonists. Thus, the antiterrorism crusade incorporated policy and actions against the "rogue states" with the capability, or potential capability, of acquiring weapons of mass destruction, such as Iraq, Iran, Libya, and North Korea. Note here the contradiction that other states, such as Israel, India, and Pakistan, which have developed nuclear arsenals, are not classified by the United States as "rogue states."

The remarkable aspect of this political reality is the speed with which the ideology of antiterrorism and the crusade against "rogue states" became official dogma and popular discourse in the United States. This ideology now underlines all policies and actions of the government as well as the utterances of its political leadership, public intellectuals, and ordinary citizens. While much as this rhetorical hyperbole of the current Bush administration may be seen as politically motivated, it nevertheless is part and parcel of the effort to institutionalize in American society and internationally the ideology and policy of antiterrorism. In the United States, the institutionalization of the antiterrorism crusade included, in addition to the wide-ranging powers of the Patriot act, the creation of the Office of Homeland Security, now the Department of Homeland Security with a cabinet secretary, the shifting of the focus of the FBI mission, the National Terrorism Task Force, the restructuring and streamlining of the Immigration and Naturalization Service, etc. In a clear statement of this new Bush administration policy, Richard Haass, director of the State Department's Policy Planning Bureau, said:

> What you're seeing from this Administration is the emergence of
> a new principle ... I'm not sure it constitutes a doctrine ... [on]
> sovereignty. Sovereignty entails obligations. One is not to mas-
> sacre your own people. Another is not to support terrorism in
> any way. If a government fails to meet these obligations, then it
> forfeits some of the normal advantages of sovereignty, including
> the right to be left alone inside your own territory ... In the case
> of terrorism, this can even lead to a right to preventive, or
> peremptory, self-defense. You essentially can act in anticipation
> if you have grounds to think it's a question of when, and not if,
> you're going to be attacked.[22]

Of course this posture makes "sense" as long as the United
States is the one determining which state deserves to lose sovereignty. Thus, as with the crusade against Communism, America's
war against terrorism is redefining the terms and rules of engage-
ment of international relations in accordance with unilateral
American priorities, strategies, and diktats. Many states, including
several Arab states (Egypt, Saudi Arabia, and Jordan in particular) are being compelled through diplomatic, political, and economic pressure to accede to American policy and tactics in this
war on terrorism or face consequences, including sanctions or the
threat of the use of force. Through such a policy, using United
Nations resolutions, and through policies and actions of other international institutions (e.g., NATO, WTO, IMF and World
Bank, G-8) that are under American influence, the United States is
striving to institutionalize the war on terrorism internationally.

Most significantly for the Middle East, under the ideology of
antiterrorism, the Bush administration has progressively come to
accept the definition of the situation that Israel has promulgated
in its colonial war against the Palestinian Authority and population in the West Bank and Gaza Strip. It has aligned itself with the
policies and practices of the right-wing–led Likud government of
Prime Minister Ariel Sharon. The administration, in agreement
with Israel, has defined all resistance to Israeli occupation as "terrorism." Most egregiously, the United States, virtually alone in the
world, stood with Israel in its criminal onslaught on the Palestinian cities, towns, and refugee camps in March and April 2002 and
since. American politicians of all persuasions, along with the
media, columnists, and public intellectuals, ignored or dismissed
as false or exaggerated crimes against humanity and war crimes

committed by Israel's army throughout the reoccupied Palestinian population centers, especially Jenin and Nablus.

In the course of the rush to support Israel, American politicians and officials ignored the damning reports of Israeli practices by established and reputable human rights organizations such as Amnesty International, Human Rights Watch, and United Nations official findings. The United States was pivotal in scuttling the UN Security Council decision—a resolution it formulated and voted for—to dispatch a UN team to investigate the possibility of war crimes and crimes against humanity by Israel in its onslaught on the Jenin refugee camp. In short, the American government adopted Israel's definition of the situation in the Occupied Territories as one of "terrorism" and not of occupation. And Bush's America has come to accept Sharon's war on the Palestinian Authority and people (defined reductively as "Palestinian terrorism") as part of America's global war on terrorism. This evolved in the face of all the efforts by America's Arab allies (Saudi Arabia, Egypt, and Jordan), the historic Arab League peace offer at the Arab Summit in Beirut in March 2002, and European criticism. The recent characterization of the Israelization of American policy toward Palestine and the Middle East is, arguably, more like the Likudization of American policy. The convergence of American and Israeli policy is not limited to the Israeli-Palestinian conflict, but includes identical views and policies regarding Iraq and Iran as well. Ever since September 11, American and Israeli officials, media, and public intellectuals kept up a drumbeat of calls and arguments for widening the war against terrorism by an attack against the Iraq regime of Saddam Hussein.[23]

A debate erupted within the Bush administration on expanding to Iraq the war on terrorism, and on the question of unilateralism or multilateralism in American foreign policy. The hawks and unilateralists include the person and office of the vice president, the secretary of defense and practically all of his deputies, and the head of the National Security Council, whereas the more pragmatic, multilateralist, and diplomatic in approach are clustered around Secretary of State Colin Powell. It appears, however, that the hawks and unilateralists—who are also the domestic policy architects—seem to have the ear of the president, as evidenced by his speech on American policy on the Palestine-Israel conflict of June 24, 2002. The debate now seems largely to be closed, unless perhaps some policy failure ensues.

The hawkish approach is most worrying and dangerous in regard to nuclear strategy. In the classified Nuclear Posture Review (NPR), the Bush administration

> has directed the Pentagon to prepare contingency plans outlining the use of nuclear bombs against at least seven countries—Russia, China, Iraq, Iran, North Korea, Libya and Syria—five of which do *not* possess nuclear weaponry, and were newly added to nuclear targeting plans. The Posture Review also mandates that preparations be made for the use of nuclear weapons in the Arab-Israeli conflict, a confrontation between Taiwan and China, an attack by North Korea on South Korea, an Iraqi attack against Israel or another neighboring country, and other unspecified situations.[24]

Contrary to the previous American posture, the NPR expands the role of nuclear weapons, treating them as just another military option. Joseph Cirincione, the nuclear expert at the Carnegie Endowment for Peace foundation, explained: "We are saying that nuclear weapons are no longer the weapon of last resort but weapons of first choice."[25] Finally, no less serious is the intent of the Bush administration to develop the "missile defense shield," which, if deployed, will militarize space.

The Bush administration is clearly developing a strategic doctrine and military policy of striking first.[26]

> The Bush Administration is developing a new strategic doctrine ... Without abandoning containment and deterrence, the [strategy] will for the first time add "preemption" and "defensive intervention" as formal options for striking at hostile nations or groups.[27]

The discourse has become public. Jim Hoagland of the *Washington Post*, for example, advises the Bush administration to think big:

> The administration must now pursue other methods of preventing the region from becoming a chaotic platform for greater terrorism. That means more reliance on U.S. military might to support diplomacy. Events pull Bush toward a strategy of transforming the region by establishing a greatly expanded and intrusive U.S. military presence there. American forces would stay for years to help develop and shield new and democratic leaderships in Iraq and in a Palestinian state.[28]

Hoagland further contends that the conventional wisdom of waiting to strike Iraq and effect regime change until the Palestinian-Israeli conflict is resolved, or at least is stabilized, is now turned on its head in Bush administration thinking. "The greater the polarization between Israelis and Palestinians, the more likely a US invasion of Iraq becomes."[29] Bush has also authorized covert action to disrupt, capture, or destroy terrorists in as many as eighty countries. CIA covert action in these countries includes propaganda operations, support for foreign police and intelligence services, and direct lethal covert action against terrorist groups or individuals.

The unilateralist interventionist foreign and military-strategic policy is not only a global war against terrorism or the "rogue states," but also intends to reshape certain regions and the world itself according to its interests, and, equally significant, for permanent hegemony. "In 1992 ... the Pentagon envisioned a future in which the US could, and should, prevent any other nation or alliance from becoming a great power ... [The US should be] 'shaping' rather than reacting to the rest of the world, and [should be] preventing the rise of other superpowers."[30] This American vision is reminiscent of Israel's view, long supported by the United States, of the necessity of qualitative military superiority over all Arab armies.

The convergence of American and Israeli thinking goes beyond policy and strategy toward the Middle East. The emergent preemptive military doctrine that is being developed by the Bush administration is styled after Israeli policy and practice.

> Asked, for example, whether policy could be used to justify an attack on nuclear facilities in North Korea, [Secretary of State] Powell cited Israel's attack two decades ago on Iraq's Osiraq nuclear power plant after Israeli intelligence concluded the plant had the capability of producing weapons-grade plutonium.
>
> "The Israelis did it in 1981," he said. "It was clear preemptive military strike. Everyone now is quite pleased even though they got the devil criticized out of them at the time."[31]

In a trenchant critique, William Galston states that hardly anyone in the administration or in the respective political parties is debating the long-term implications of a unilateralist policy:

> A global strategy based on the new Bush doctrine means the end of the system of international institutions, laws and norms that the United States has worked for more than half a century to build ... Rather than continuing to serve as first among equals in the postwar international system, the United States would act as a law unto itself, creating new rules of international engagement without agreement by other nations.[32]

While being a "law unto itself" has long been an Israeli practice, one wonders how this transformation in American foreign
policy from containment, deterrence, and multilateralism to unilateralism, preemption, and aggression has come about. Moreover, how and why did American and Israeli policies in the
region converge so definitively?

Domestic roots of the American antiterrorism crusade: The rise of the secular and religious Right

This American alignment with Israel, politically and ideologically, is neither fortuitous nor unintentional in its present form. It
is, rather, the culmination of domestic American political and ideological currents that have long been in the making. My thesis is
that while the contemporary American crusade against terrorism
has deep domestic roots, it has been significantly influenced and
reinforced by Israeli action, rhetoric, and pressure *inside* the corridors of American power and in American public life. Indeed, it
is my contention, further, that support for Israel, the antiterrorism crusade, and their recent intersection have become *domestic*
American issues, and not merely US foreign policy issues. Thus,
the antiterrorism crusade and the unwavering and uncritical support for Israel's Likud policies and actions—not just toward the
Palestinians but also toward Iraq, Iran, and Syria—are part and
parcel of a policy direction that has both its domestic dimension
and its foreign policy side. Let us then turn to the domestic American context because, in discerning global tides, one must first
understand the domestic political currents.

The currents that have defined the contemporary American
global tides in the wake of the September 11 attacks have been in
the making for at least four decades, ever since the 1960s, during
which America witnessed the emergence and confluence of several
major sociopolitical movements that changed dramatically its political, social, and cultural landscape. These were the anti–
Vietnam War, the civil rights, the counter-culture, the women's,
and other liberalizing, radicalizing, and secularizing movements.
Just as significant was the "liberation theology" movement, imported from Latin America, that energized and liberalized the establishment churches and theological schools in the United States.

Together, these movements produced significant change in
the legal, social, economic, political, and cultural domains of

American society. But they also triggered a significant sense of threat (even outrage among certain social segments) to long-held American values, ethics, norms, and traditions among vast sectors of the population. These challenges generated considerable reaction among both elite and large segments of society, particularly in the South, the Midwest, and parts of the West, especially southern California. My contention, then, is that a confluence since the 1970s of neoconservative ideology and conservative religious theology in society in response to the liberalizing and secularizing challenges helped to push the American political center to the right and allowed the conservative currents to influence strongly, if not dictate, foreign and domestic policy.

In retrospect, the 1960s were more a socially polarized era than a radical one. Indeed, the decade witnessed the beginning of determined social, political, and cultural mobilization of American conservatives and the birth of the new Right. This was led by an unlikely alliance of the religious (Christian) Right and the secular, political neoconservative ideologues, helped by an increasingly conservative Jewish community. Moreover, along with economic transformations, a rightward drift in the politics of the United States and leading European countries occurred during the 1970s and afterward. Hence, the 1980s witnessed the coming to power of ideologically conservative leaders and parties in three major Western countries: Ronald Reagan in the United States, Margaret Thatcher in the United Kingdom, and Helmut Kohl in Germany. All three confronted and defeated labor union demands, dramatically reduced the cost and power of organized labor, and instituted other conservative policies.

In foreign affairs, Reagan, especially, instituted a belligerent confrontational posture toward the Soviet Union, describing it as the "evil empire." His administration was also behind aggressive interventionist, often illegal, practices in Central America against leftist regimes or movements, and in Afghanistan against Soviet occupation. The Nixon victory in 1972 (and even Carter's in 1976) and the Reagan and Bush Sr. victories in the 1980s were neither products of normal American politics nor accidental, but rather were products of the determined actions of the reenergized conservatives and the new religious and secular Right. In short, the role of the conservative and rightist sociopolitical movements in America have caused the shift, since the 1980s, of the American political center to the right, far from where it had been in the liberal Roosevelt era.

As part of this shift, the new Right has also come to set much of the political agenda and political discourse on both domestic and foreign policy issues in the country. As with the secular Right, the Christian Right's leaders were effective in shaping the public and legislative agendas and in checking some of the cultural trends of previous decades.[33]

> Religious conservatives have changed the American conversation. They have changed who participates in that conversation and what assumptions are brought to bear on it. They have changed the tone of the conversation, and they've changed the content of the conversation....
>
> ... The Christian right thrust the whole notion of values to the forefront of American life. Now these issues are not only *on* the table of politics, they *are* the table of politics ... Now the notion that religion is at the center of national life and not at its periphery is voiced not only by Republicans but also by Democrats.[34]

In short, the movement of the religious and secular Right to center stage of American politics and their presence in positions of power to a large extent explains the development of the aggressive interventionist antiterrorism crusade and the Likudization of American policy in the Middle East.

Permanent American economic and oil interests; strategic, military, and geopolitical interests; political stability—in particular that of key allies (Saudi Arabia and Gulf states, Egypt, Jordan, etc.); and the "security of Israel" are all critical factors in the making and conduct of American foreign policy toward the Middle East. This is true also of the domestic role of the pro-Israeli Jewish and secular lobbies, such as AIPAC and others. While acknowledging these long-established American political realities, and the obvious factors influencing American policy in the region since World War II, I am attempting to answer the question of why the current Bush administration policy has become so blatantly partisan toward Israel. My contention, therefore, is that in the context of the definite drift to the right since the 1980s, the roles of the religious and secular Right have been pivotal. All the more so in the wake of the September 11 attacks.

The Christian Right in contemporary American politics

The Christian Right began to assert its influence in the 1970s and burst dramatically on the scene in the 1980s. But its roots go much deeper. "To understand the New Christian Right, then you have to understand the American religious crisis of the late nineteenth century, the transformation of American politics in the 1930s and 1940s, and the cultural crisis of the 1960s and 1970s."[35] Two theological trends emerged in America: a liberal trend among the dominant Protestant establishment churches that emphasized ecumenism and liberal views, and the trend of the theological conservatives that stressed the Bible is inerrant, that Jesus is the son of God, and that God's Kingdom on earth will be established upon his return. The world, moreover, is getting worse, a belief that is interpreted "through a framework called *premillennial dispensationalism* ... All time is divided into ages or dispensations ...; we are in the next-to-last-age ...; Satan's agent, the Anti-Christ, will arise and eventually dominate the world; this will be followed by the second coming of Christ and the establishment of the Millennium."[36]

Tens of millions of people believe in this form of Bible prophecy. The First World War was pivotal; it had special meaning to the theological conservatives. "First, it proved pessimism was right; and second, according to Bible prophecy Jews would return to Palestine before the return of Jesus—*right before*—and the Balfour Declaration promised a Jewish homeland in Palestine."[37] Thus, the Dispensational Millennium is imminent. Many, like Hal Lindsey, one of the important Evangelical Christian writers—his *The Late Great Planet Earth* was a phenomenal hit—believe that the founding of the state of Israel in 1948 was a sign from God that the Last Days, Rapture, and Armageddon are upon the world.[38] This is the theological tradition that spawned the new Christian Right.

Perhaps contrary to some conventional social science interpretations, World War II and its aftermath produced in America a religious revivalism and a rightward drift of the political center as America mobilized for the anti-Communist crusade, during which time "'under God' was added to the Pledge of Allegiance [and] 'In God We Trust' made the national motto."[39] The revived conservative religious movement was symbolized by the emergence of the Reverend Billy Graham, who called himself "evangelical" rather than "fundamentalist." But this revival also included the Pentecostals or Charismatic Christians under the leadership of, among others, Oral Roberts. By the mid 1970s there was a very large constituency—"forty, sixty, eighty million, ready to be politicized" in a rightist direction because of the "secularizing court decisions, changing sexual mores, a society that seemed to be moving left politically and culturally."[40]

In 1972, Republican Richard Nixon reportedly received 80 percent of the evangelical, the other theologically conservative, and the Catholic vote. The passage of *Roe vs. Wade* (legalizing abortion) by the then liberal Supreme Court in 1973 particularly incensed the religiously conservative voters. Even Democrat Jimmy Carter, a "born-again Christian," was helped (56 percent of the Evangelicals and the Southern Baptists voted for him) by this same conservative constituency to win the presidency in 1976.[41] However, Carter proved to be basically a liberal and was disappointing to the revived conservative evangelical movement. He was thus largely abandoned in the second-term elections by this conservative constituency, many of whom in 1980 rallied around the conservative ideologue, Republican candidate Ronald Reagan. There is abundant evidence of the Christian Right's influence within the Republican Party and for its strong support for Reagan.[42]

Thus, with its role in the election of Reagan to the presidency and the Republican win and Democratic loss in the Senate, the Christian Right began its march to considerable influence within the Republican Party and to center stage in national American politics. The conservative religious movement had long been creating social, educational, media, and other institutions to serve and buttress its activity and influence. The Christian Right also developed and successfully used civil tactics, such as public protest, registering voters, voting, lobbying, and running for office on local, state, and national levels. The new breed of conservative or rightist evangelical leaders, for example, the Reverends Jerry Falwell, Pat Robertson, John Hagee, James Dobson, and Gary Bauer, created organizations to promote their political and social-theological agendas. Jerry Falwell launched the Moral Majority, and Pat Robertson launched the Christian Coalition in 1989, which under the leadership of Ralph Reed reached two million members in the late 1990s, albeit it has declined since its heyday. John Hagee broadcasts his religious and political messages over 230 television and radio stations. "Dobson's Focus on the Family is a colossus. It has a budget of about $130 million for 2000 ... It claims 2.1 million members ... with a staff of 1,300 ... [Dobson's] column appears in 550 newspapers."[43]

The Christian Right promotes social-political attitudes that are virulently anti-abortionist, anti-gay and anti-lesbian; for "family values" and prayer in schools; and against health care reform and other social issues. It also held strong anti-Communist attitudes during the cold war. Televangelist Pat Robertson extended strong "political (and in some cases, monetary) support for the Nicaraguan contras, the death squad governments of El Salvador and Guatemala, and the murderous proxy armies for South Africa's apartheid regime during the 1980s."[44] Indeed, Reagan's White House Outreach Working Group on Central America secretly met on a regular basis with more than fifty groups, including many Christian Right, secular neoconservative, and Jewish organizations, to coordinate media and lobbying activity in support of the Nicaraguan Contras, and again to bomb Iraq.[45] This is the very same political coalition that is behind the support of Sharon and his policies as well as the Bush administration's anti-terrorism crusade. Robertson, Falwell, Hagee, Bauer and many other Evangelical leaders are also viscerally pro-Israeli and anti-Palestinian. They see military aid to Israel as a Biblical mandate, and Israel itself as a fulfillment of Biblical prophecy. Take, for example, the following quotations from Robertson's Christian Broadcasting Network (CBN) Web site: "For the almost unbelievable truth is that all Israel will be saved. The fullness of Gentiles will climax with the fullness of Israel"; and, "Thus Jews, Israel, will eventually—and supernaturally—witness to the gospel, and with such explosive power that the world can scarcely be the same! Ah, there is God's future for ethnic Israel."[46]

Thus, despite the clear difference in the Christian evangelical vision for Israel, in which all the Jews would be converted to Christianity, and the Zionist Jewish vision of a permanent Jewish state, the alliance is solid. According to Ed McAteer, founder of the Religious Roundtable, who identifies himself as a Christian Zionist, "The best friends that Israel has are Bible-believing Christians."[47]

Pro-Israeli advocates have long—since the Truman post–World War II era—looked to liberals and the Democratic Party as the principal base of support for the Jewish state. Since the rise of the Christian Right they have received vociferous, determined, popular, and organizational political support from the conservative faction that they have charged with anti-Semitism, intolerance, and bigotry. Nevertheless, the cause of Israel has cemented a

Christian Right and Jewish American alliance that is forcing a change in the traditional constituency of both major political parties. Increasingly more Jews are supporting Republican candidates financially and through votes. It is significant that Jewish American support for House majority whip, Christian conservative Tom DeLay—who in May 2002 shepherded a strong pro-Israel, pro-Sharon resolution in the House of Representatives—has developed rapidly. The same applies to Trent Lott, the conservative minority leader in the Senate. Jewish support is cascading also on House majority leader Richard Armey, who suggested on a national television show that the Palestinians should be "transferred" out of the West Bank. This call by a major American politician, of course, is in favor of ethnic cleansing, in violation of all legal and moral conventions.

This unprecedented realignment of American political forces, especially in the Republican Party, has therefore had far-reaching political consequences both domestically and in foreign policy. "More than any single factor, it explains why there has been so little pressure from a Republican White House on Israel to curb its crackdown on Palestinians," according to an August 2002 article.[48] To Evangelicals,

> the attacks on Israel by Palestinian suicide bombers are an important test in the global fight against Islamist terrorism, a campaign fiercely backed by the Christian right....
>
> The White House is getting the message. At a meeting on April 10 ... [Republican] Senate minority leader Trent Lott informed Bush that Republicans were under increasing pressure from the religious right to back Sharon.[49]

The Christian Right was mobilized in support of George W. Bush in the primaries—its role was pivotal for his nomination in the South Carolina and "Super Tuesday" primaries,[50] as was also the case in the 2000 presidential elections. It has even become more frenetically energized in support of Israel by the intensified conflict in the Occupied Territories and Israel's assault on Palestinian-controlled municipal centers in the West Bank and Gaza Strip. It should be clear, however, that not all evangelical Christians are right wing. There are currents within the mainstream movement that have a more nuanced view of the Palestinian-Israeli conflict.

The Christian Right has since 1980 emerged as the most influential faction within the Republican Party.[51] As a consequence, it has burst on the national scene politically and forced its social and political agenda on the national discourse. Since the early 1990s, every Republican presidential nominee, including George W. Bush, appeared at the Christian Coalition conferences as indeed they did at the pro-Israel AIPAC gatherings. Lyman Kellstedt estimated in 1995 that conservative Christians comprise about a fourth of the population in the United States,[52] while 11 to 15 percent of the population has typically supported the Christian Right from the 1970s through the 1990s.[53] As many as four million people are members of Christian Right organizations, readily mobilized politically for specific and general Christian rightist causes and for electoral candidates. The campaign and election of George W. Bush has shown the importance of the Christian Right. Estimates indicate that without its support, including that in Al Gore's home state of Tennessee, Bush would not have carried the South and the border states to win in 2000.

The neoconservatives in modern American politics

The second principal pillar in the consolidation and influence of conservatism and rightist domestic and foreign politics in America is the secular Right. The contemporary origin of the new Right is in the 1980s under the umbrella of the "Reagan revolution." The principal elements of the new Right, or the "neoconservatives" as they are commonly known, are formerly liberal Jewish (and some Catholic) intellectuals who abandoned the Democratic Party coalition for Reagan and the Republican Party. Reagan's robust conservatism on both domestic and foreign policy issues attracted a collection of forceful and increasingly conservative public intellectuals.

Many neoconservatives joined Reagan's administration and translated his strong conservatism into policies and practices. These include several who are serving in the current Bush administration: Richard Perle, Douglas J. Feith, Donald Rumsfeld, Dick Cheney, Paul Wolfowitz, Lewis "Scooter" Libby, and Richard Haass, several of whom also served in the Elder Bush's administration; others act as conservative, if not right-wing public intellectuals. Many others became media pundits as syndicated columnists in major newspapers and have served often as "talking heads" on many TV programs. The ranks of this group were expanded by the addition of syndicated talk radio and TV hosts who together helped create, progressively since the early 1980s, a strong conservative, if not rightist, political culture in the United States. A new news network, Fox News, has distinguished itself as a neoconservative outlet.

The conservative political culture has narrowed the debate about issues and policies facing the United States. Such narrowness is pivotal in the easy passage of conservative policies and actions. A "stifling conformity, which muzzles public discourse on US foreign policy, the war on terrorism and Israel … but also on the threatened attack on Iraq" has set in:

> To enforce this abandonment of reasoned argument in the name of a witch-hunt against terrorists, a strange alliance of evangelical Christians in Congress has come together with leaders of American Jewish organisations who normally support the Democratic party.[54]

Grassroots groups also are active in this process of silencing alternative views and debate. A June 2002 opinion piece states,

> Recently, an estimated 1,000 subscribers to the *Los Angeles Times* suspended home delivery for a day to protest what they considered the paper's pro-Palestinian coverage. The *Chicago Tribune*, the *Minneapolis Star Tribune*, the *Philadelphia Inquirer* and the *Miami Herald* have all been hit by similar protests, and NPR [National Public Radio] has received thousands of e-mails complaining about its reports from the Middle East …
>
> [A correspondent at a large daily explains that newspapers] are "afraid" of organizations like AIPAC and the Presidents Conference. "The pressure is relentless. Editors would just as soon not touch them."[55]

As Reagan had encouraged the Christian Right to join the Republican Party and paved the way to its ascendance within the party, he also paved the way for secular right-wing ideologues and foreign-policy hawks to occupy important foreign-policy and national-security positions in the government. This action legitimized the nonreligious Right as much as his other action legitimized the religious Right. The trends Reagan set in motion in the 1980s escalated during the Bush father and son eras that bracketed, as the rightist ideologues put it, the Clinton period. The neoconservatives consolidated their political position by establishing many "think tanks" and research organizations, lobbying groups, newspapers, periodicals, and even TV and radio networks. Thus, neoconservatism is now a thriving industry.

And yet, unlike the Christian Right, the neoconservatives are small in number and do not have grassroots presence in the American body politic, except possibly for some of the grassroots constituency of the traditional Republican Party. Most of their influence resides in their articulate media presence, in the think tanks they established, and in the literature they have produced since the 1980s. But the bold theoretical and policy proposals they make persistently and relentlessly may also account for their influence. Their simplicity and boldness in the current context resonates with President Bush's theme of "You are with us or you are with the terrorists." It is also present because they have managed to intimidate dissent and narrow the public discourse to the constricted confines of their outlook. Many of these neoconservatives often advise the Israeli government to follow policies that are directly in contradiction to existing American policy. During the Clinton era, Richard Perle, chair of the Defense Policy Board, and Douglas J. Feith, Deputy Secretary of Defense in the Bush Jr. administration, coauthored a paper for the then prime minister Benjamin Netanyahu, entitled *A Clean Break: A New Strategy for Securing the Realm*.[56] It advised Netanyahu to make "a clean break" with the American-sponsored Middle East peace process.

The strange alliance that the Christian Right and the neoconservatives have forged inside the Republican Party, and through it on the national level, is unexpectedly influential in the corridors of American power in all branches of the government. Since the Reagan era, Republican support for rightist causes and for Israel has consistently increased. For Ralph Reed, the Christian Right activist and founder and former head of the Christian Coalition, "The Jewish community has played a strong role in keeping the Democratic party strongly pro-Israel and Evangelicals have played a similar role among Republicans."[57]

Israel's role inside the American body politic

What has furthered the sharp turn of the Republican Party to the right and to strong support of Israel are Israeli political actions *inside* the United States. Ever since its victory in the Israeli elections of 1977, the Likud Party and many of its leaders have been assiduously and systematically cultivating the conservative political forces—both religious and secular—in the United States.

> And the result of all this ... in the US is that a large and vocal
> Zionist Christian lobby has evolved, with influence in Congress
> and the ear of a sympathetic President.[58]

In 1987, Netanyahu edited a book on how the West could fight terrorism,[59] and founded the Jonathan Institute, an anti-terrorism "think tank" named after his brother, who was killed in the Israeli raid on Enteppe Airport, Uganda. In its first conference, then secretary of state George Shultz endorsed the view of terrorism that Netanyahu promoted. Shultz and other prominent Republicans still serve on the board of the institute. One should not underestimate the fact that the American conception of what constitutes terrorism is directly influenced by the Israeli definition. Israel has persistently promulgated such conceptions for decades now. Reaching out to conservative constituencies and courting their support against the US government's foreign policy is also a typical Israeli, in particular Likud, practice. When Netanyahu visited the United States as prime minister, he met with Reverend Jerry Falwell before he met President Clinton.[60]

As important in this increased Israelization and Likudization of the American body politic have been the actions of the well-organized and well-funded pro-Israel lobby AIPAC, and behind it the increasing number of pro-Likud American Jewish campaign contributors to the conservative and rightist candidates of the Republican Party. Jewish donations, which used to go principally to the Democratic Party, are now increasingly going to the Republican Party. The "power [of the pro-Israel lobby] is exerted within the political system from the local to national levels through soft money, and especially the provision of out-of-state funds to candidates sympathetic to Israel."[61] Thus the principal influence of the pro-Israel lobby is over elected officials in Congress and their staffers.

A sense of the power and influence of AIPAC is evidenced, for example, in its annual conference. The attendees in late April 2002 included *half* the US Senate, ninety members of the House, and "thirteen senior administration officials, including White House Chief of Staff Andrew Card, who drew a standing ovation when he declared in Hebrew, 'The people of Israel live.'"[62] On May 2, 2002, the House of Representatives passed a resolution by 352 to 21, with 29 abstentions, that expressed unqualified support for Sharon's Israel. On the same day, the Senate also voted a similar resolution, which passed 94–2. "That these votes occurred at the same time the Israeli army was slaughtering Palestinians in the West Bank sent the signal that no matter what Israel did it was OK with our senators and congressmen."[63] Congress often takes positions to the right of the White House, and far to the right of the State Department, in regard to Middle East policy.

Remarkably, the *Jerusalem Post* reported on May 6, 2002, that "Visiting Congressmen Advise Israel to Resist US Administration Pressure." An astonishing political act in which US congressmen are "seemingly permitted to travel to foreign countries at taxpayer expense for the purpose of publicly undercutting one's own government's foreign policy."[64] As important as AIPAC is as an Israeli lobby is the Conference of Major American Jewish Organizations, representing fifty-two Jewish organizations, whose "executive vice chairman, Malcolm Hoenlein ... has long had close ties to Israel's Likud Party."[65] Its influence is especially strong with the executive branch. The confluence of conservative perspectives (at least on Middle East policy) in the legislative and executive branches of the US government has certainly made that policy noncontroversial within the power structure of the American government, which has effectively silenced any reasoned debate on American Middle East policy and on the war on terrorism.

Since the end of the cold war, the key issue that has energized so vigorously the two ideological and theological pillars of American conservatism is Israel. Given the long-term American interest in Middle East oil, the right wing has focused US foreign policy on the region and on the war on terrorism. But for the two conservative allies, the war on terrorism is not a second or separate issue, but is the same as support of Israel.

> Since the beginning of the Israeli invasion [of the West Bank], the Christian right has joined forces with neo-conservatives and right-wing pro-Israeli groups in a vast campaign ... [that] defined the current conflict as part and parcel of America's own "war on terrorism," with Arafat as "Israel's Bin Laden." Negotiating with the Palestinians is thus a "moral compromise" and any pressure on Sharon dilutes America's "war on terrorism."[66]

Furthermore, "The hawks' reading of recent events emphasizes that opposition to US actions, while serious, has remained largely verbal. Neither Western Europe nor Russia nor China nor Saudi Arabia has seemed ready to break ties in serious ways with the United States."[67]

Even before the dust began to settle on the sites of the September 11 attacks, the twin allies of the American Right launched a campaign in the media emphasizing this and the other themes, such as not holding back Sharon from dismantling the Palestinian Authority; calling for war to overthrow President Saddam Hussein of Iraq and to reconstruct Iraq to suit American interests; pressuring the regional enemies of Israel—Syria, Lebanon, and Iran—to cease their support of terrorism; and finally, that the president should heed neither the advice of those in the State Department, the CIA, or other experts, nor that of America's Arab allies who, in any case, share the blame for terrorism against the United States.[68]

The debate within the administration, especially between the State Department on the one hand and all the rest of the national security and foreign policy establishment on the other, along with European and Arab criticism of President Bush's policy, has led him to weave an incoherent diplomatic pattern that has made his Middle East policy contradictory, or inconsistent at best. As a result, it has at times earned Bush the criticism, sometimes severe, of the ideological and theological Right. But as the conventional and popular wisdom has it, the president is "flying with the hawks" in his administration.

The June 24, 2002, speech that Bush gave as his vision for peace was, like his policy, incoherent. The speech was comprised of 1,867 words in which "more than one thousand words were devoted to criticizing and making demands of the Palestinians, while just 137 words dealt with what Israel should do."[69] Taking his cue from Sharon, Bush flipped the Palestinian dilemma on its head: it is terrorism that is forcing Israel to maintain the occupation, and not the occupation that is generating resistance and terrorism. He branded Arafat guilty of terror and called Sharon "a man of peace." He did not state that Israeli occupation is illegal and has to end in accordance with international law and United Nations resolutions to which the United States is a party. Instead, he called for a "provisional state"—an oxymoronic concept that has no standing in international law or conventions, and which later was reinterpreted by his aides as a "state" with "provisional borders"—for the Palestinians, contingent on *new* Palestinian leadership, a reformed authority, and a security apparatus that would enforce the security of Israel. In other words, he called for "regime change" for the "failed" Palestinian Authority. In essence, he called for a new Palestinian regime that is willing to accept Israel's conditions, now turned into American demands. Significantly, there was no statement in the speech regarding the Palestinian refugees, the largest segment of the Palestinian population, or their right of return.

This new American policy articulated in the Bush speech is unqualifiedly Sharon's blueprint. It ignores nearly completely the Arab League peace offer, except for the clause on normalization of relations with Israel even before the conclusion of the Palestinian-Israeli conflict. Aluf Benn of *Ha'aretz* confirms the point in an analysis accurately entitled "Ariel Sharon Agrees to His Own Ideas."[70] No wonder the Israelis were thrilled and the Palestinians were stunned, as the *New York Times* reported.[71] The American hawks have won, and Israel's Likud policy has become America's policy in the region. "Chris Patten, the European Commissioner for External Relations, says 'a senior Democratic Senator told a visiting European the other day: All of us here are members of Likud now.'"[72]

Conclusion

The September 11 attacks are a defining moment for American political history, as dramatic as any of the others that preceded it. The American response, a grand crusade against terrorism, has evolved as policy in the context of a conservative political culture, a conservative-dominated Congress, and a neoconservative administration. The neoconservatives (ideology) and the Christian Right (theology) have joined forces to push American politics to the right, and American foreign policy, especially in the Middle East, in an aggressive interventionist direction apparently intent on reshaping to their liking the political map of the region. The actions of the Israeli government helped this crusade and its ideological formulation directly inside the corridors of American power and in the public domain. Thus, Israeli policy and actions have become a domestic American issue, not just a foreign policy question. The American government, in agreement with the Israeli government, has given a unilateralist, self-serving definition of terrorism (excluding the practice of state terrorism long practiced by Israel and the United States and its allies and clients) and launched a war against terrorism that is changing the terms of international relations.

Whether it succeeds domestically or internationally, especially in the Middle East, will be determined by internal American political dynamics; by international, especially European, reaction; and by the situation on the ground in the Middle East. The United States is slowly and systematically institutionalizing the domestic structures for the war on terrorism. On the other hand, although the United States has succeeded in initiating some actions in the war on terrorism internationally, it has also run into difficulties in institutionalizing the measures, procedures, and structures it wants. With regard to the Middle East, the new American "neo-imperialist school" of thought wants to effect "regime change" in Iraq and Palestine and supposedly introduce "democracy" into the region by American military force. However, the key question is "how to bring these changes about? And how to do it without severe strategic damage to the United States?"[73]

Critiques of the hawkish Bush administration policies are beginning to emerge in the media and among elected congressmen and senators. The Bush administration is coming increasingly under attack for the business scandals that have rocked the stock market, the economy, and Wall Street. Domestic economic and political difficulties combined with some foreign policy failure(s) may push the administration to change its hawkish policy direction, especially if it believes that such a change would better serve its chances for reelection.

CHAPTER 6

AMERICAN GLOBAL REACH AND THE ANTITERRORIST CRUSADE OF GEORGE W. BUSH

Naseer Aruri

Today the world faces a single man armed with weapons of mass destruction, manifesting an aggressive, bullying attitude, who may well plunge the world into chaos and bloodshed if he miscalculates. This person, belligerent, arrogant and sure of himself, truly is the most dangerous person on Earth. The problem is that his name is George W. Bush, and he is our president.

> —Jack M. Balkin, Knight Professor of Constitutional Law and the First Amendment at Yale Law School, "The Most Dangerous Person on Earth," *Hartford Courant*, September 22, 2002

Introduction

This chapter provides a critical review of George W. Bush's war on terrorism and his foreign policy doctrine of preemptive/preventive war. The goal is to provide a context for understanding why and how the negative "legal" focus on Muslim/Arab Americans and residents was made easy at both the executive and legislative levels of the US government. Highlighted herein is how the ruling tripartite coalition of neoconservative, Evangelical Right, and pro-Israel politicians, think tanks, and organizations shape US foreign policy, and why their collective effort is, ipso facto, discriminatory against Muslims and people of Arab origin.

Bush and his predecessors: Strategic objectives

Since the collapse of the Soviet Union in the early 1990s, American foreign policy elites have been challenged to find and embrace a new-world-order vision and to define the US role in that order in the new millennium. A national security doctrine based on anticommunism would have to be replaced. With no more Soviet Union or communism to oppose, the containment policy based on superior military deterrence lost its raison d'être.[1] Hence, deterrence and multilateral cooperation gave way under George W. Bush to a policy of preemption, or even preventive wars, thus downgrading the role of diplomacy. The unprecedented assault experienced on September 11, 2001, transformed a parochial president into one whose foreign policy now dwarfs all other spheres of public policy. Nonetheless, George W. Bush's foreign policy may differ from his previous two predecessors in tactics and means but not in substance and strategic objectives, namely, how to develop and maintain US political and economic global dominance.

In keeping with the same foreign policy line since Gerald Ford and Henry Kissinger, George W. Bush's father inaugurated a post–cold war order in which "what we say goes." Bush Senior's new world order focused on matters affecting strategic resources, such as in the first Gulf war. Ambitious regional leaders such as Saddam Hussein would be taught a lesson: setting the pace in strategic areas belongs exclusively to the only surviving superpower. Although that lesson involved the use of overwhelming force, "Bush I" asserted US global predominance through forging coalitions and manipulating the United Nations to provide a diplomatic umbrella for neocolonial wars against Iraq, Panama, and other recalcitrant nations. Unlike his son, he did not abandon diplomacy in favor of unauthorized wars, and he stopped short of trying to topple Saddam and conquer Iraq. Both Bush I and Bill Clinton employed coercive diplomacy as well as the use of force. Clinton bombed the former Yugoslavia, invaded Somalia and Haiti, and bombed Iraq repeatedly.

Clinton's approach to maintaining US preeminence in the post–cold war period was to promote economic globalization as a powerful ideological tool that could contain nationalist and oppositional movements around the world. He replaced the anti-Soviet weapon with the seemingly benign tool of "free trade."[2] Penetration, thus, was targeting not only the natural resources of the global south, but also the markets, human resources, and ever-growing number of new customers. The globalization thesis of Bill Clinton postulated a new post–cold war dichotomy of integration versus fragmentation. The former applied to the United States, its allies, and the global economic and political machinery consisting of the G-8, the World Trade Organization, Asia-Pacific Economic Cooperation, the International Monetary Fund (IMF), and other such organizations.

Clinton's neoliberal approach, however, did not represent a departure from that of the Reagan-Thatcher era, in which deregulation at the national level was extended into the international arena. The IMF and other such institutions became Clinton's de facto means of global governance in a unipolar world. His dichotomy of integration versus fragmentation was more sophisticated and deceptive than Bush II's good versus evil. The forces of fragmentation were the global dissidents who were not enamored of free trade and not impressed by Clinton's promotion of "market democracies" and "economic enlargement."[3] Thus, the forces of good seeking "integration" and the evil forces promoting "fragmentation" were clearly separated.

Bush and his advisers have always shown contempt for Clinton just as the circle around Reagan considered Jimmy Carter a wimp. Nonetheless, Clinton's worldview did not depart substantively from that of Bush II, but it was much more subtle and nuanced. People throughout the world were not constantly challenged to be either "with us" or "against us," nor were they reminded about the consequences of not being "with us" and the "immorality" of straddling the fence.

Bush II is closer to Ronald Reagan than to any other former president in the objectives of his foreign policy, in the means to achieve these objectives, and even in the style of rhetoric employed to demonize his opponents and targets. Terrorism has suddenly become the focus of Bush's foreign policy, assuming a defining role, just as globalization was the overarching principle for Clinton's foreign policy and the Gulf War was the defining event for the president's father. However, the war on terrorism is not a concept original to September 11. In fact, it goes back more than two decades, when the neoconservatives who rule today with the Evangelical Right and the Likudniks made their mark on the Reagan administration. Reagan's crusade against "terrorism" treated the public to the unsubstantiated claims in the 1980s that a Libyan "hit squad" had entered the United States and tried to stalk the president during his first term of office.[4]

September 11 and the impact on Bush's foreign policy perspectives

The horror that befell America on September 11 sounded the alarm of future danger but afforded George W. Bush a unique opportunity to stake out a foreign policy turf and a context for a new American role in the twenty-first century. It provided a theme and a texture for his administration and summoned the American people to rally behind the flag. September 11 also equipped Bush with a sense of mission, unimpeded by constitutional restraints and unhindered by the Fourth Geneva Convention relating to civilian and prisoner rights in times of war.[5] Terror suspects, initially Afghanis and Pakistanis but now Iraqis and Muslims from other countries as well, are routinely apprehended and sent to Bagram Air Base in Afghanistan or to the Indian Ocean island of Diego Garcia. There, they are held not as "prisoners of war," thus entitled to protection under the Fourth Geneva Convention, but as "unlawful combatants," an ominous status, which strips them of any protection and has already facilitated their torture on non-American soil.

The tragedy of September 11 also had to be exempted from congressional investigation in order to clear the way for the open-ended response. According to Gore Vidal, "The first thing Bush did after we were hit was to get Senator Daschle and beg him not to hold an investigation of the sort any normal country would have done."[6] For Bush's advisers, September 11 was an opportunity to advance their agenda. At a time of such unprecedented calamity, a fearful and exasperated public would embrace Bush's call to rally around the commander in chief, raising neither questions nor reservations about the latest crusade. The display of imperial power would become, in fact, a substitute for diplomacy and statesmanship, as a stunned public eagerly awaited revenge, undeterred by the many possible consequences, such as the threat of blowback.[7] Arundati Roy related the story of one GI in pursuit of revenge:

> On March 21, the day after American and British troops began
> their illegal invasion and occupation of Iraq, an "embedded"
> CNN correspondent interviewed an American soldier. "I wanna
> get in there and get my nose dirty," Private AJ said. "I wanna
> take revenge for 9/11."[8]

Antiterrorism remains undefined and open-ended,[9] but it is
inherently racist, to the extent that the "evildoers" are Arab and
Muslim Americans, no matter how much Bush pretends to respect their religion and culture. Divorced from any cause rooted
in American foreign policy impact, by default it says the people
of Islamic faith and culture are degenerates. This is why it is especially easy to get an erosion of civil liberties focused on Muslims
and Arabs. The scare tactic of frequent announcements of terrorist threats (none of which has yet materialized) seems like a form
of deliberate psychological warfare against the American people
in order to keep everyone on edge and to pass laws trampling
civil liberties and constitutional rights. An op-ed by Jill Nelson,
which appeared in *USA Today*, captures the essence of this fear:

> Lost in the cacophony of military music, flying the red, white
> and blue and the patriotic rhetoric that marked the celebration
> of Independence Day and surrounds the war on terrorism is
> democracy's most wonderful and critical aspect: the right to dis-
> sent. Since Sept. 11, it's as if we've been terrified, not only by the
> terrorists, but also by an American government that demands
> silent acquiescence in whatever it proposes to do as part of its
> vague and thus far ineffective "war on terrorism."[10]

The Bush Doctrine

Clinton's interventions in Kosovo, Somalia, Haiti, and Iraq,
and those of Bush I in Iraq and Panama were rationalized in terms
of providing remedy for ethnic cleansing, starvation, autocratic
governments, the development of weapons of mass destruction,
and drug trafficking. Some of these so-called humanitarian interventions were justified as responses to presumed threats, thus they
were considered preemptive. The US invasion of Iraq waged by
George W. Bush, however, was not preemptive (i.e., military action
taken against an enemy that is about to attack) but preventive,
waged against the possibility that Iraq *might* someday strike with
weapons of mass destruction, either directly or through surrogates.

The new Bush Doctrine rationalizes military intervention as "preventive wars," not sanctioned by international law, as necessary to ward off potential threats. These are presumed threats to national security, mainly from "terror," as it comes closer to the gates of the now-broadened sphere of what is known as the "civilized world." That is a much more open-ended commitment than what had been assumed by Bill Clinton, and even Bush I, despite the rhetoric of human rights and democracy. It is also a commitment that keeps the United States in a permanent state of military readiness and a willingness to go after "evildoers" *long before they strike*.

The president and his warrior-intellectuals have dwelled on the theme of having to *anticipate* danger even at the expense of rendering the entire discourse hypothetical. The invasion of Iraq has neither a *casus belli* nor any multilateral authorization, either real or contrived. Seymour Hersh wrote the following with regard to Bush's haste to react preventively, risking a collapse of international order:

> Last September 24th [2002], as Congress prepared to vote on the resolution authorizing President George W. Bush to wage war in Iraq ... some Democrats were publicly questioning the President's claim that Iraq still possessed weapons of mass destruction which posed an immediate threat to the United States. Just the day before, former Vice-President Al Gore had sharply criticized the Administration's advocacy of preemptive war, calling it a doctrine that would replace "a world in which states consider themselves subject to law" with "the notion that there is no law but the discretion of the President of the United States."[11]

Neoconservative intellectuals and groups, such as the well-endowed Heritage Foundation, view the post–September 11 situation as constituting present and clear danger. John Hulsman, a Heritage Foundation researcher, for example, justified preventive strikes on the basis that the United States has no time to make sure that its interventions conform to the rules of war:

> With asymmetric warfare, there are no rules ... You have to move quicker, you have to be more aggressive to protect your people....
> ... There's no doubt that the US is the ordering power in the world. Whether we like it or not, that's a fact ... As the ordering power, the United States can say we will do things that will promote general global stability. It isn't fair, but it's not a debating society.[12]

This, in fact, is the essence of the emerging Bush Doctrine, which is nowhere better expressed than in the presidential graduation speech delivered at West Point Academy on June 1, 2002. Dismissing the adequacy of the cold war doctrine of containment and deterrence, Bush said:

> For much of the last century, America's defense relied on the Cold War doctrines of deterrence and containment. In some cases, those strategies still apply. But new threats also require new thinking. Deterrence—the promise of massive retaliation against nations—means nothing against shadowy terrorist networks with no nations or citizens to defend. Containment is not possible when unbalanced dictators with weapons of mass destruction can deliver those weapons on missiles or secretly provide them to terrorist allies ... If we wait for threats to fully materialize, we will have waited too long.[13]

Despite the fact that Bush himself and his father used depleted uranium in their wars against Iraq, the junior Bush assumes that today's dictators are much more "unbalanced" and thus more dangerous than the ones that the United States had to deal with during the cold war, be they antagonists or allies, a rather groundless suggestion. Moreover, as has been shown earlier, the policy of containment was in reality directed against nationalist leaders and oppositional forces, and not necessarily against the "dictators" of the Soviet Union and China, whose threats to the West were hardly existent, though widely assumed and publicized. Responding to this logic, Patrick Buchanan, a former member of the Reagan-Bush administration, foresaw danger in the approach and criticized it severely:

> Is this the new Bush doctrine: The USA asserts a right to launch preventive wars on any "rogue nation" caught building the kind of weapons we have had for half a century? If so, this is a formula for endless wars, almost certain to produce the very horror the president seeks to avert: the detonation of an atomic or a biological weapon on U.S. soil.[14]

The Bush doctrine emphasizes the need to identify and charge the enemy unilaterally and to punish US-designated aggressors by striking first and when not expected, anywhere in the world:

> The war on terror will not be won on the defensive. We must take the battle to the enemy, disrupt his plans, and confront the worst threats before they emerge ...
> ... Our security will require transforming the military you will lead—a military that must be ready to strike at a moment's notice in any dark corner of the world.[15]

The doctrine of "prevention" emphasizes the urgency of speedy action. It makes deliberations in Congress and consultations with allies or international lawyers impractical, if not indeed tedious and hindering. There is no time to study international treaties and conventions and assess their implications on the preemptive strikes.

Keeping America afraid and vigilant was a central theme in Bush's State of the Union Message in January 2002:

> I will not wait on events, while dangers gather. I will not stand by, as peril draws closer and closer ...
>
> Our war on terror is well begun, but it is only begun. This campaign may not be finished on our watch—yet it must be and it will be waged on our watch.
>
> We can't stop short ... History has called America and our allies to action, and it is both our responsibility and our privilege to fight freedom's fight.[16]

These words reflect aspects of what is known in American foreign policy as Wilsonian idealism, mixed with the idea of rollback, which was pitted against the containment policy during the early 1950s and later resurrected by re-assertionists/neoconservatives of the Reagan era. Waging the war "on our watch" and embarking on a historically ordained mission translate into a crusade rather than a policy, in which the pursuit of empire and the degradation of constitutional rights go hand in hand.

Bush sounded a similar theme in an address to the nation on September 7, 2003, which elevated Iraq to the "central front" of the "war on terror."[17] Totally disregarding the fact that the premises of his war on Iraq (that Saddam had weapons of mass destruction and threatened the security of the United States) were never proven, Bush conveyed that the war had the twin purpose of averting a threat and carrying out the white man's burden. Thus, he would lift up the oppressed and downtrodden with a civilizing mission that would appeal to American liberals, just as his incredible use of force would satisfy the neoconservatives:

> We have carried the fight to the enemy. We are rolling back the terrorist threat to civilization, not on the fringes of its influence, but at the heart of its power ...
>
> ... Together we are transforming a place of torture chambers and mass graves into a nation of laws and free institutions. This undertaking is difficult and costly—yet worthy of our country, and critical to our security.[18]

Pretending that Iraq was in some way responsible for the September 11 attacks in New York and Washington, Bush reiterated his doctrine of preventive war and the domino effect of inaction:

> And for America, there will be no going back to the era of before September the 11th, 2001—to false comfort in a dangerous world. We have learned that terrorist attacks are not caused by the use of strength; they are invited by the perception of weakness. And the surest way to avoid attacks on our own people is to engage the enemy where he lives and plans. We are fighting that enemy in Iraq and Afghanistan today so that we do not meet him again on our own streets, in our own cities.[19]

Despite such assertions, reiterated by Vice President Cheney on the September 14, 2003, Sunday morning television talk shows, and despite being on the record making the connection between September 11 and Saddam Hussein, President Bush had to publicly distance himself from Cheney, saying he never actually claimed that Iraq was responsible for what happened on September 11. In an article titled, "Bush: No Saddam Links To 9/11," the Associate Press reported, "President Bush said [September 17, 2003] there was no evidence that Saddam Hussein was involved in the terrorist attacks of Sept. 11, 2001—disputing an idea held by many Americans."[20] Yet, on March 18, 2003, Bush sent a letter to Congress in which he states that he was taking military action in Iraq "pursuant to the Constitution and Public Law 107-243, [which] is consistent with the United States and other countries continuing to take the necessary actions against international terrorists and terrorist organizations, including those nations, organizations, or persons who planned, authorized, committed, or aided the terrorist attacks that occurred on September 11, 2001."[21]

Feeling at ease with assuming contradictory positions, and feeling endowed with a moral mission, with fear occupying a central place on his agenda, the president had no problem rearranging priorities, unleashing his attorney general to trash civil liberties, dismissing international law, penetrating outer space with new armaments, overlooking corporate fraud, all in the name of homeland security. The commander in chief even felt free to cover up fraudulent deals with Enron and enabled other deals to escape the normal scrutiny, such as those of Dick Cheney with Halliburton and Richard Perle's with Global Crossing, among other unsavory deals.[22]

So much fear has been created because of September 11 that the term "terrorist" has replaced "communist" as the generic label by which active opponents of US hegemony are identified. It is becoming a domestic tool for gauging loyalty, cooperation, and goodness as well as evil, and even normalcy. It has certainly become a broad brush for demarcating the borders separating friend from foe, the righteous from the sinner, the virtuous from the mischievous. There is no middle ground; stopping the barbarians at the gate is a moral duty of all the civilized. Such absolutism negates an essential component of American political culture—compromise and bargaining, which is as American as apple pie. If George Bush is infallibly knowledgeable about what constitutes good and evil, truth and fiction, right and wrong, he may resort to whatever force at his disposal to impose his view on the entire world. Professor Peter Vernezze of Weber State University described the consequences of Bush's worldview this way:

> But perhaps the greatest danger of absolutism is that it is inimical to democracy. Democracy requires a full-blooded discussion of issues. By claiming he was leading a crusade against evil, the president short-circuited all debate on the recent war. How can you have a debate about whether to oppose evil? ... The problem with invoking God to your side in debates over abortion, capital punishment or gun control is that the other side becomes the devil and the compromise that our political system requires becomes impossible, for who can bargain with Satan?[23]

The pursuit of empire, relentlessly under way since the demise of the Soviet Union, has witnessed a corresponding erosion of international legality. International law was allowed to fall by the wayside, while the concepts of the balance of power and spheres of influence suffered serious erosion under the impact of US unilateralism and reliance on preventive wars. It is no accident that the United States has been giving short shrift to such treaties and international enactments as the Anti-Ballistic Missile Treaty, the Chemical Weapons Convention, the International Criminal Court, and the Kyoto Protocols, among other treaties intended to restrain the ambitions of states, since even before Bush II came to power. Such contempt for international law, coupled with the assault on civil liberties and constitutional protections, is being obfuscated by a created sense of moral mission and an aura of a sacred patriotism designed to leave no room for doubters and procrastinators. Even a touch of religion, a presidential sermon, would bolster the mission with a dose of legitimacy: "In tragedy ... God is near," declared the president, having ruled out any middle ground. Evil, after all, is clearly marked and readily identified:

> There can be no neutrality between justice and cruelty, between the innocent and the guilty. We are in a conflict between good and evil, and America will call evil by its name.[24]

According to Australian Broadcasting Corporation News, religion has become such a factor in the invasion of Iraq that the GIs were asked in a pamphlet to pray for Bush on daily basis, including the prayer "that the President and his advisers will be strong and courageous to do what is right regardless of critics."[25] Former presidential candidate George McGovern summed up Bush's divine mission thus:

> The President frequently confides to individuals and friendly audiences that he is guided by God's hand. But if God guided him into an invasion of Iraq, He sent a different message to the Pope, the Conference of Catholic Bishops, the mainline Protestant National Council of Churches and many distinguished rabbis—all of whom believe the invasion and bombardment of Iraq is against God's will. In all due respect, I suspect that Karl Rove, Richard Perle, Paul Wolfowitz, Donald Rumsfeld and Condoleezza Rice—and other sideline warriors—are the gods (or goddesses) reaching the ear of our President.[26]

You are either with us, thus against evil, or against us, thus a supporter of evildoers, the terrorists themselves. As a war on evil, this becomes an endless war, particularly since evildoers deserve extermination. Thus, the new nomenclature facilitates the erosion of law and order and promotes the unilateral exercise of force.

The dichotomy of George Bush is so absolute that there is little room for any distinctions between terrorism and resistance or cause and effect. In fact, the phrase "root cause" has been stereotyped and distorted as a scarcely veiled and disingenuous justification of the terror itself.

September 11 has so far produced an "axis of evil" and placed on the agenda the effects of weapons of mass destruction on American security, when in fact, Bush would be hard-pressed to demonstrate a logical connection between North Korea, Iraq, or Iran on the one hand, and the Twin Tower attacks on the other.[27] The problems that Bush has with his "axis of evil" are political in nature and hardly relate to any criminal matters that normally require police action, but manufacturing facts has become a familiar tactic for the Bush-Blair team, which did not hesitate to present plagiarized and falsified documents to the United Nations. An article appearing in the *Hindustan Times* stated:

> The US, and its sole effective ally, Britain, even tried to establish a false link between Saddam Hussein and 9/11 by cooking up and forging "evidence" of Iraq's uranium deal with Niger, and its global terrorist "network" (by doctoring a journal article).[28]

Moreover, Iran, whose reformist government has been struggling for years to foster normal relations with Europe and the rest of the world, does not meet Bush's criteria of terrorism. In fact, Iran made its own contribution to the war against the Taliban. Despite that, however, the neoconservatives lean toward regime change in Iran in accordance with the Bush Doctrine. That may not necessarily happen in the near future and may not be an Iraq-style invasion, but according to a BBC report, "destabilization through covert action" during a Bush second term remains an option.[29]

A Hobbesian world

In this "war on terror," the president seems to be driven by a feeling that the world in which we live today is a Hobbesian world, a bad neighborhood, unstable, and in need of a firm hand. The responsibilities of the lone superpower in such a "grim landscape," a phrase used by Robert Kaplan (*Eastward to Tartary*), are unambiguously clear: We cannot remain in the shadows. Face it with staunch determination and undoubted resolve.[30] So impressed was Bush by Kaplan's book that he asked his staff to invite the author to the White House for an on-the-job training session, in which Kaplan and possibly national security adviser Condoleezza Rice would add intellectual content to Bush's instincts, gut feelings, and unstructured inclinations. After all, the president was accustomed to seeing things in black-and-white terms and did not have the intellect to operate in a complex and internationalist world. Presumably, he could not have escaped the resonating effect of Kaplan's warning about chaos and instability, as well as his counsel that great powers respond with "leaders who know when to intervene and without illusions."[31] This dark view of the world, reinforced by the events of September 11, has given Bush an incontestable sense of mission.

Kaplan concluded after his seminar with Bush:

> I think Bush's view of the world is that American predominance
> is tenuous ... The world is a bad place with a lot of bad people
> who can do us harm and the most important moral commitment
> for America is to preserve its power.[32]

Foreign policy, thus, cannot be guided by "sentimental illusions" such as democracy and human rights or misguided concerns about state tyranny, when order has to be reestablished. In
fact establishing order was what had driven Reagan to send
troops to Lebanon in 1983, and later to Grenada. It was the reason behind George H. W. Bush's invasion of Panama and later
Somalia. The rhetoric associated with George W. Bush's adventures in Afghanistan and Iraq mixes order and stability with
democracy and liberty, but his agenda is not much different from
that of his predecessors—unrivaled global predominance.

George W. Bush's advisers, many of whom are retreads from
the Reagan era, overwhelmingly believe in using force preventively, irrespective of evidence or a *casus belli*. Paul Wolfowitz,
deputy secretary of defense, for example, postulated that that
there is no need "for proof beyond reasonable doubt." The emphasis must be on "intentions" and "capability," says Wolfowitz, who has been urging an invasion of Iraq since the late
seventies and who was a signatory to the 1998 letter addressed
to President Clinton urging a war against Iraq.[33] For him, there
is no need for the "proof," if we know the "intentions" and "capabilities." On the question of Iraq in 2002, Wolfowitz said,
"Proof beyond a reasonable doubt is the way you think about
law enforcement. And I think we we're much closer to being in a
state of war than being in a judicial proceeding."[34] Such configu-
ration of the calculus of warfare and the cost-benefit analysis has
become acceptable to a hawkish pro-Israel circle, sometimes referred to as "chicken hawks" because none of them has fought
in a war but they seem to have no problem committing millions
of the underclass to war.

The forces behind Bush's thinking
post–9/11 and their rationale

The following statement by Michael Lind is quite revealing
about the men behind Bush's foreign policy and war against Iraq:

As a result of several bizarre and unforeseeable contingencies—such as the selection rather than election of George W Bush, and 11 September—the foreign policy of the world's only global power is being made by a small clique that is unrepresentative of either the US population or the mainstream foreign policy establishment....

Most neoconservative defense intellectuals have their roots on the left, not the right. They are products of the largely Jewish-American Trotskyist movement of the 1930s and 1940s, which morphed into anticommunist liberalism between the 1950s and 1970s and finally into a kind of militaristic and imperial right with no precedents in American culture or political history.[35]

George W. Bush has already surpassed both of his predecessors in employing unbridled force, disregarding diplomacy and coalitions, and degrading economic globalization. Having already devastated two spent nations—Afghanistan and Iraq—while threatening to extend his campaign to an expanding list of what he calls the "axis of evil," he has, indeed, globalized state terrorism. The merciless onslaught he unleashed on Iraq on March 19, 2003, has effectively signaled a unilateral dismantling of the post–World War II international structure. The invasion of Iraq, dubbed by Bush's secretary of defense Donald Rumsfeld as "Shock and Awe," was described by consumer advocate and former presidential candidate Ralph Nader thus:

[Rumsfeld] wants the whole world in "awe" of the mighty military superpower in preparation for the next move against another country in or outside the "axis of evil".

This is truly an extraordinary time in American history. A dozen men and one woman are making very risky consequential decisions sealed off from much muted dissent inside the Pentagon, the State Department, the CIA and other agencies that have warned the President and his small band of ideological cohorts to think more deeply before they leap. They are launching our nation into winning a war that generates later battles that may not be winnable—at least not without great economic and human costs to our country.[36]

Not only has Bush trampled the US Constitution, but he also rendered the United Nations inoperable, having effectively reduced the permanent members of the Security Council to one. One of his principal neoconservative advisers, Richard Perle, who together with Ariel Sharon kept on urging a war against Iraq, wrote an article in the London *Guardian* celebrating the "death" of the United Nations:

This new century now challenges the hopes for a new world order in new ways. We will not defeat or even contain fanatical terror unless we can carry the war to the territories from which it is launched. This will sometimes require that we use force against states that harbor terrorists, as we did in destroying the Taliban regime in Afghanistan....

... The chronic failure of the Security Council to enforce its own resolutions is unmistakable: it is simply not up to the task. We are left with coalitions of the willing. Far from disparaging them as a threat to a new world order, we should recognize that they are, by default, the best hope for that order, and the true alternative to the anarchy of the abject failure of the UN.[37]

The glee of Bush's circle of neoconservatives was expressed in the open during what was billed as a "black coffee briefing on the war on Iraq" held March 21, 2003, at the American Enterprise Institute (AEI). Both Richard Perle and colleague William Kristol, editor of the *Weekly Standard,* mouthpiece of the neoconservatives, ridiculed the United Nations. Kristol said it "did not matter much," while Perle suggested that as a security institution "its time has passed," though it might still be of some use in health matters and peacekeeping.[38] In an article that appeared in the daily newspaper *Ha'aretz,* Israeli journalist Ari Shavit ventured to guess that if twenty-five neoconservatives had been sent away from Washington to a desert one year ago, there would be no war in Iraq today. He wrote:

In the course of the past year, a new belief has emerged in the town: the belief in war against Iraq. That ardent faith was disseminated by a small group of 25 or 30 neoconservatives, almost all of them Jewish, almost all of them intellectuals ... Their philosophical underpinnings ... are the writings of Machiavelli, Hobbes and Edmund Burke. They also admire Winston Churchill and the policy pursued by Ronald Reagan. They tend to read reality in terms of the failure of the 1930s (Munich) versus the success of the 1980s (the fall of the Berlin Wall).[39]

Globally, American war and diplomacy aim to use Iraq as the context for limiting the spread of nuclear weapons on US rather than UN terms, and to warn the European Union that its lifeline is now controlled by the United States. No more autonomy will be allowed in the new world order of George W. Bush for other permanent members of the security council. The dollar will be "defended" against the Euro, and Iraq's dealing with the latter will be nipped in the bud before it penetrates OPEC. Thus, this is a "war" beyond regime change, beyond weapons of mass destruction, and beyond the Middle East region as well. The objectives are not only regional, but global. The ultimate aim of the neoconservatives is unquestioned US supremacy, a new unipolar world. For them, the Iraq invasion would rearrange not only the World War I map of the region, but also that of World War II. The post–World War II structure of international relations is to be dismantled as long as the neoconservatives remain in power.

At the regional level, the kind of democracy represented by the ailing Karzai regime in Afghanistan is likely to be the neoconservative recipe for Iraq and Palestine, should they and Sharon have their way. The successors of Yasser Arafat and Saddam Hussein would have to accommodate the concerns of Washington and Tel Aviv in the name of fighting terror, even as Sharon conducts one of the most devastating campaigns of destruction and ethnic cleansing since the conquest of 1948. Meanwhile, America's energy needs and Israel's colonial conquests would be secured in the name of advancing democracy and promoting reforms as the guarantors of security and regional stability, even as instability threatens the entire region. But will George W. Bush be more successful than Sharon was when the latter embarked on his own grandiose scheme in Lebanon in 1982?[40]

The Israeli connection

Israel has been pushing for an invasion of Iraq in order to accomplish what it had failed to accomplish in 1948, 1956, 1967, 1978, 1982, and throughout the seven years of Oslo.[41] For Israel, the war on Iraq constitutes a post-Oslo strategy. As Bush II tried to complete what his father left unfinished, Israel was revisiting 1982 all over again. That is why the 2003 Anglo-American invasion of Iraq was not only a continuation of the same war that began in 1990–91, but also a war whose broader agenda includes reshaping the strategic landscape in the Middle East and central Asia. It is a war of the civilian hawks in the Pentagon and their allies in a number of right-wing and pro-Israel think tanks, such as the Hudson Institute, the AEI, and the Jewish Institute for National Security Affairs (JINSA), among others.[42] In fact, the US occupation regime in postwar Iraq was initially assigned to Jay Garner, a pro-Israel general with close association to JINSA.[43] His replacement, Paul Bremer, is not only well connected to corporate America, but also associated with William Bennett's right-wing organization Americans for Victory Over Terrorism.

American and Israeli interests coalesce in the hope of redrawing the Middle East maps of both the World War I and World War II periods. A central objective of the war has been all along to settle the Arab-Israeli conflict on terms wholly agreeable to General Sharon's cabinet, the most intransigent and extremist cabinet in Israel's history. More about this later.

The adventure would also aim to deprive Saudi Arabia of leverage over oil prices, intimidate Syria, and manipulate the domestic balance in Iran, which Israel regards as a strategic threat. In a hardly veiled threat to Iran, Richard Perle said that the fall of Saddam Hussein would be an "inspiration for Iranians seeking to be free of their dictatorial mullahs."[44] Michael Ledeen, a fellow of the AEI and a former consultant working with National Security Council (NSC) head Robert McFarlane, who was involved in the transfer of arms to Iran during the Iran-Contra affair, said this conflict was part of a "longer war" and "such terrorist-sponsors as Iran and Syria knew that."[45]

Six months after the invasion of Iraq, Israel continues to blow the trumpets against Iran. According to an article by Terrel E. Arnold, Israeli foreign minister Silvan Shalom expressed the view that "Iran is fast approaching the point of no return in its efforts to acquire nuclear weapons capability."[46] Such alarmist soundings represent a supreme irony, especially when they come from the state that has a stockpile estimated at 250 weapons, refuses to allow any inspection by the International Atomic Energy Agency, and refrains from joining the Treaty on the Non-proliferation of Nuclear Weapons. As of fall 2003, the debate about the lying and deceit by top policymakers in the Bush administration had not yet included Israel as a vital source of the shabby intelligence that led to war and put thousands of Americans and Iraqis in harm's way. How long Israel will remain insulated from that debate, which has not even spared the president and close associates, will depend on whether Israel will remain the sole issue beyond discussion in American domestic politics, no matter what harm befalls the national interest.

Barely one week into the invasion of Iraq, both Rumsfeld and Colin Powell made public threats against Syria, with the latter using the annual American Israel Public Affairs Committee meeting in Washington as his platform. According to a United Press International story, contingency plans to extend the attack on Iraq to Syria, ultimately thrown out by Condoleezza Rice with the president's approval, were drawn by Douglas Feith, assistant secretary of defense for policy, with the approval of Rumsfeld and the urging of Wolfowitz, all of whom are close to the Israeli Likud. The news story continues:

> The latest Pentagon press for action against Damascus was bolstered by the visit of Israeli National Security Adviser Efrian Halevy, who visited Washington on April 12–14....
>
> According to a *Ha'aretz* report of April 13, Halevy and another senior aide to Israeli Prime Minister Ariel Sharon, Dov Weisglass, were visiting Washington to "suggest that the United States take care of Iran and Syria because of their support for terror and pursuit of weapons of mass destruction"....
>
> The meeting with Halevy took place in the president's conference room with only top NSC officials and White House advisers in attendance, administration sources said.
>
> In response to Halevy's entreaties for action, Rice repeated her assertion of no more military adventures for the rest of Bush's first term.[47]

Meanwhile, the invasion of Iraq was linked squarely to the Likud by Eric Margolis, foreign affairs columnist for the *Toronto Sun,* citing the proximity of their views to those of the American neoconservatives:

> My view is that Israel, through the neo-conservatives in the States, has played a primary role in engineering the war ... They do not speak for all Israelis. They speak for the Likud Party and further-right elements in Israel, and they believe what's good for Israel is good for the United States ... Remember that the neocons have all been consistent in saying that Baghdad is the first step and that Iran is next. And Gen. Sharon said the day after the American army enters Baghdad, it should march on Teheran. The Israelis know perfectly well that Iraq is not a major threat to them at this point, but may be at some point way down the road if allowed to develop. I think Iran is their principal target.[48]

None of these objectives has anything to do with Bush's declared concerns about a threat to the security of the United States. Israel's supporters in the administration, think tanks, media, and Congress, who kept on beating the drums of war, viewed it as providing cover for Israel to expedite what Israeli professor Tanya Reinhart has called "a slow steady genocide," as well as the creeping ethnic cleansing (known as "transfer" in Zionist parlance) ongoing in the Occupied Territories since summer 2002.[49] The Israeli connection to Bush's war on terror was exposed in the

Israeli press during 2002 by a number of respected Israeli analysts, including Meron Benvenisti, the former deputy mayor of Jerusalem, who made the link in the daily newspaper *Ha'aretz* between Israel's advocacy of an American war against Iraq and Israel's overall objective of ethnic cleansing in the West Bank.[50]

Moreover, attitudes of the Israeli leadership were underscored by Israeli public opinion: a survey in the largest-circulation Israeli daily *Ma'ariv* conducted in August 2002 revealed that 57 percent of Israelis were in favor of an American attack on Iraq to unseat Saddam Hussein.[51] Israeli commentator Gideon Levy wrote in *Ha'aretz* about the many senior army generals who were upset by the delay of the US invasion of Iraq and their gleeful attitude as the bombs began to fall on Baghdad:

> It was apparent already during the waiting period that the lengthy anticipation was hard on them: They considered every postponement a terrible mistake and every debate about the justification for the war was heresy. Now that the forces are finally on their way, their enthusiasm bursts forth, not merely about the very outbreak of the war, but about the sophisticated equipment being used. The smart bombs and the guided missiles, the satellite navigation and the turbofan engines, the Stealth bombers and the mega-bombs are firing their imagination.[52]

Israel's role in the invasion of Iraq was kept out of the public debate, as many media pundits refrained from raising it. Michael Kinsley of *Slate* described the silence aptly thus:

> The lack of public discussion about the role of Israel ... [was] the proverbial elephant in the room: Everybody sees it, no one mentions it.[53]

With the invasion over and "victory" declared, however, this fact was lamented by Israeli officials and by certain American Zionists, who considered the silence truly dishonorable, if not a colossal failure to acknowledge the good deed of a worthy ally. The lack of credit given to Israel for America's "victory" in Iraq led one disgruntled person, for example, to write about the exclusion of Israel from the "coalition of the willing":

> Our capable ally [Israel] not only supplied us with weaponry for use in Iraq, including Israeli-armored bulldozers and Israeli-made pilotless planes, but ... '[helped] to train soldiers and Marines for urban warfare, conducting clandestine surveillance missions in the western Iraqi desert and allowing the United States to place combat supplies' within her borders. We also

went to the Israelis for advice on such things as how 'to spot a suicide attacker on his way to attack, how to deal with road-blocks, overpowering a suicide bomber.'"[54]

Paradoxically, it did not seem necessary for those who acted as architects in Washington prior to the invasion to insist on credit; in fact, linking the numerous Jewish Americans from the neoconservative movement to the invasion was considered in the politically correct circles as an expression of anti-Semitism. It was no secret that the leading war advocates in the US included Israel's best friends and close associates of its right-wing military and political leaders. The list includes, among others, Richard Perle, former head of the Defense Advisory Board and resident fellow of the AEI, and his close friend and political ally at AEI, David Wurmser of the Hudson Institute.[55] Mr. Wurmser's wife, Meyrav, is cofounder, along with Colonel Yigal Carmon, for-merly of Israeli military intelligence, of the Middle East Media Research Institute (MEMRI), which translates and distributes articles that specialize in Arab bashing.[56] Other senior Bush ad-visers responsible for this war include Paul Wolfowitz, deputy defense secretary; his next in line, Douglas Feith; Lewis "Scooter" Libby, chief of staff of Cheney's office; Michael Rubin, a specialist on Iran, Iraq, and Afghanistan, who recently arrived from yet another pro-Israel lobby, the Washington Insti-tute for Near East Policy; and many others.

Much has been written about the extraordinary role these hawks have played in the formation of Bush's foreign policy and their ties to the American Jewish community, leading some to charge anti-Semitism. One of the targets of these charges, Patrick Buchanan, responded in a comprehensive article charging the neoconservative cabal of having dragged this nation unnecessar-ily to war, and raising the question, "Whose War?"[57] According to Buchanan, even the right-wing, pro-Israel magazine *New Re-public* (which cannot possibly be labeled anti-Semitic) did not hesitate to carry an analysis by Harvard professor Stanley Hoff-man characterizing the neoconservative cabal as constituting the "fourth power center" in Washington:

> And, finally, there is a loose collection of friends of Israel, who
> believe in the identity of interests between the Jewish state and
> the United States. These analysts look on foreign policy through
> the lens of one dominant concern: Is it good or bad for Israel?
> Since that nation's founding in 1948, these thinkers have never

been in very good odor at the State Department, but now they are well ensconced in the Pentagon, around such strategists as Paul Wolfowitz, Richard Perle and Douglas Feith.[58]

Meanwhile, administration hawks pushing this war, such as Cheney, Rumsfeld, and Rice, are all on record supporting Sharon's draconian measures in the Occupied Territories. Rumsfeld is the first senior US public official to use the phrase "the so-called occupied territories" in describing the West Bank and the Gaza Strip. Rice defended the Israeli strategy of preemption instead of deterrence or containment, and she considers that policy worthy of duplication in Iraq and on a global scale. Her objection to extending the invasion to Syria was linked purely to the factor of the presidential campaign. The message of the neoconservative cabal has been crystal clear: New rules of international conduct are being drafted. The war on Iraq, the aerial bombardment of Yugoslavia in 1999, and the full-scale invasion of Afghanistan in 2001 illustrate that the theater of operations for the US military is now worldwide, placing the post–World War II international system in great jeopardy.

Testing the Bush Doctrine in Asia

Within hours of the September 11 attacks in New York and Washington, President Bush declared a "war on terrorism," which signaled the beginning of a broad strategic play to reshape the map of the Middle East and central Asia and to expand US hegemony. The initial agenda included the overthrow of the Taliban regime in Afghanistan and its replacement by a more compliant regime from the Northern Alliance, which had demonstrated equal brutality during the 1980s quagmire. The US-installed, hapless regime of Hamid Karzai is touted already as the product of a "nation-building" project after a quick military "victory" was declared with virtually no US casualties.

The re-conquest of Afghanistan was largely viewed in the United States as a vindication of the hawks in the Bush administration, who utilized the threat of terrorism to advance their strategic agenda—oil, bases, and hegemony. In fact, the US military bases under construction since the war on terrorism began have an inconspicuous proximity to the projected pipelines that constitute a precious dividend of this war. Washington is already consolidating its strategic position in that region by building military bases in Kazakhstan and bridges, rail lines, storage depots, and communication centers in Uzbekistan. Moving US bases from Turkey eastward, from Western Europe to Eastern Europe and from Saudi Arabia to Qatar is part of the strategic reshaping of the new landscape resulting from the invasions of Afghanistan and Iraq. Ian Traynor described the evolving connection between the Middle East and central Asia this way:

> The past two years have seen a rapid expansion of American deployments across thousands of miles stretching from the Balkans to the Chinese border and taking in the Caucasus, central Asia, the Middle East and the Indian subcontinent.
>
> From Camp Bondsteel in Kosovo, a result of the 1999 NATO campaign, to the Bishkek airbase in Kyrgyzstan, appropriated for the Afghanistan war, the Americans are establishing an armed presence in places they have never been before.
>
> Thirteen new bases in nine countries ringing Afghanistan were rapidly established as Russia's underbelly in central Asia became an American theatre for the first time [*sic*]....
>
> Further plans are in the pipeline to move US assets out of Germany, where they have been since 1945, into the new NATO countries of eastern Europe, notably Poland as well as Romania and Bulgaria on the Black Sea, prized for their proximity to Turkey and the Middle East.[59]

Combating "terror" thus becomes the prelude to and justification for an expansionist foreign policy that might be aiming to redraw the strategic global map. Afghanistan and Iraq are sufficiently weak as to make them appropriate candidates for testing the Bush Doctrine.

Although a central objective of Bush's foreign policy is geared toward maintaining and creating stability in a presumed turbulent world, America's actions in central Asia and the Middle East may very well induce anarchy and spread violence in some areas along the Himalayan Mountains. How long will the improved relations between the United States, on the one hand, and Russia and China, on the other, last in view of the fact that American military bases and oil pipelines penetrate their traditional spheres of influence?

That ominous phrase used by Paul Wolfowitz after September 11 about "ending states" is a sign of what is to come should the test in Iraq yield a green light for a further advance throughout the region. The entire Middle East would be destabilized as the new guiding rules add client regimes, such as Saudi Arabia and Egypt, to the list of predictable targets in order to effect a radical change not only in geography and geopolitics, but in political culture as well.[60] Such a comprehensive, megalomaniacal scheme was set forth by Norman Podhoretz, a neoconservative/Likudist guru, in the September 2002 issue of his magazine, *Commentary*. Changes in regime, he proclaimed, were "the sine qua non throughout the region." They might "clear a path to the long-overdue internal reform and modernization of Islam."[61]

There is also a potential conflict in the Indian subcontinent that may involve the use of weapons of mass destruction that Bush has committed himself to destroy. India could undergo a major strategic transformation after decades of being Russia's ally against China and the United States, raising the question of whether the United States is now ready to assume the position of the former Soviet Union vis à vis India. There is a similar question about the possibility that India might also serve as a strategic buffer for the United States, keeping Russia off the Arabian Sea and Indian Ocean. Does the United States also hope to use India's demographic depth as a human barrier against China's regional ambitions? If so, Pakistan is certainly destined to lose its strategic position, after renouncing its alliance with the Pashtuns and putting all its eggs in the American basket at a time that it is being relegated to one of the dispensable parties with demonstrated public sympathies to the "terrorists." Pakistan's mosaic structure, which resembles that of Afghanistan, may become vulnerable to US-Indian pressure, making the Kashmir issue look like child's play by comparison, with horrendous consequences for the region's stability.

As Lloyd Richardson of the Hudson Institute told the *Financial Times*, India has the "economic and military strength to counter the adverse effects of China's rise as a regional and world power. India is the most overlooked of our potential allies in a strategy to contain China."[62] A recent classified US Department of Defense document revealed by *Jane's Foreign Report* argues, "China represents the most significant threat to both countries' (India and the U.S.) security in the future as an economic and military competitor." It goes on to observe "that U.S. relations with its 'traditional' allies in Asia—South Korea and Japan—have become 'fragile,' and concludes that 'India should emerge as a vital component of US strategy.'"[63]

The Bush Doctrine and the Palestine-Israel conflict

The Palestinian-Israeli conflict effectively begins for George W. Bush with the suicide bombings of 2001, rather than in 1948 or even 1967. Hence, Bush's Middle East policy is shaped and re-shaped by a worldview influenced by domestic considerations, derived from the horrors of September 11, and revamped by the experiences of the likes of Ariel Sharon, whom he has called "my teacher" and a "man of peace." The Israeli rampage through Palestinian towns and refugee camps, ongoing since March 2002, was described broadly as a form of self-defense and part of a campaign to root out the "network of terror," despite the "preventive" nature of the so-called incursions and despite the wanton destruction and the almost daily killing of civilians. It is a view not dissimilar to that of Reagan and former secretary of state George Shultz, whose expressed admiration for the Israeli model of fighting "terrorism" was highly publicized. For example, Reagan, who accepted the Israeli approach as a model for fighting "terrorism," associated himself with the Israeli raid on Tunisia in October 1985, which took the lives of seventy Tunisians and Palestinians, in retaliation for the killing of three Israelis in Cyprus. Reagan called it a "form of legitimate self-defense" and saw no violation of the Arms Export Control Act, which prohibits the use of US-supplied armaments for offensive purposes.[64]

Bush did the same thing in Jenin after the April 2002 atrocities, in which American-supplied Apache helicopters, bulldozers manufactured by Caterpillar, and other military equipment were utilized by Israeli forces to commit crimes against humanity in the Nuremberg sense of the phrase. Today, we see US military commanders stopping by Israel to pick up some wisdom from Israeli war criminals about fighting urban warfare in Iraq. It has been reported that the US military has also been purchasing militarized bulldozers from Israel to use in Iraqi cities and slums.[65]

September 11 was initially thought to be a wake-up call for America to reassess its foreign policy toward the Arab-Israeli conflict and indeed toward the Muslim world. A *Boston Globe* article claimed, barely one month after the Twin Towers attacks, that President Bush was about to unveil a plan for settling the Palestine-Israel conflict on the basis of a "vision" of two states existing side by side after Israeli withdrawal and an end to the 1967 occupation.[66] The president went out of his way to host

Muslim American leaders for the 2001 Ramadan holiday at the White House and to seek photo opportunities during a visit to the Washington Islamic Center, while repeating his message to Americans that Islam is a religion of tolerance and peace. The top Democrats in the Senate and House arranged for a rare meeting in Congress with leaders of the Arab American community in October 2001, ostensibly to learn from them about root causes. All of this sudden concern seemed to vanish as quickly as it had appeared. It had been widely assumed by the US foreign policy establishment that the road to Baghdad goes through Jerusalem, but the neoconservatives persuaded Bush that peace in Palestine lay through war on Iraq.

Meanwhile, after the invasion of Iraq, Bush came under some pressure to push for a solution in the Middle East beyond the failed mission of Admiral Anthony Zinni and the Powell Kentucky speech during autumn 2001, both of which were sabotaged by Sharon's policy of assassinations geared to invite suicide bombings in Israel.[67] Arguing that the road to Jerusalem is through Baghdad, and conquering Baghdad—yet failing to produce the highly publicized weapons of mass destruction—Bush decided to revive his speech of June 24, 2002, and make public the subsequent "road map," after it had been postponed three times in deference to Sharon.

As a "performance-based" document, the road map placed the onus on the Palestinians, making their position effectively probationary. It had neither a binding time schedule nor a tangible endgame. Now, after the Powel Louisville speech of November 2001 became irrelevant and the Saudi initiative of winter 2002 was consigned to the dustbin of history, the self-designated "catalyst for peace" in Washington was pushed toward diplomacy, albeit mildly, by the so-called Quartet (Russia, the EU, the UN, and the US). Meanwhile, Sharon's "security" measures failed to ensure Israeli security or to force the Palestinians into submission. In these circumstances, the Bush administration, emboldened by a military "victory" in Iraq, yet embarrassed by a mounting Iraqi resistance and an increased death toll of US GIs, decided to delve into personal diplomacy. The president traveled to the Aqaba summit in Jordan on June 4, 2003, to demonstrate that not only does he excel in war but also in peace. His diplomacy, however, floundered when he failed to demand that Sharon must fulfill his obligations under the road map, citing fourteen Israeli reservations, which rendered the document superfluous.[68]

His meetings with Sharon and the American-picked Palestin-ian prime minister Mahmoud Abbas at the White House at the end of August 2003 ended exactly as Sharon wanted. Again, the threshold of requirements for Abbas was raised even higher, causing him to fail in the absence of anything tangible to deliver to his captive constituency. Conditionality has totally over-whelmed reciprocity; performance has been made the responsi-bility of one side; and resistance (re-labeled "terror") instead of occupation has become the problem. Abbas went home empty-handed, despite the cosmetics, while Sharon would brag to his ultrarightists that concessions were not in the lexicon. In fact, Sharon was so emboldened by Bush's green light that he rein-stated checkpoints, which he had suspended apparently only for the duration of his Washington visit. He also gave a speech to the National Security College of Haifa University shortly after his return in which he said, in effect, that the road map has no standing without Israel's famous fourteen reservations. These in-clude a Palestinian renunciation of the right of return, dismantle-ment of the Intifada infrastructure, suspension of the March 2002 Saudi initiative, and keeping the United States, instead of the four sponsors, in real charge of the road map process. He further emasculated the road map by repeating his preference for a series of long-term interim agreements that would be deter-mined not by a planned schedule, but by developments on the ground. That is, he would use his own judgment as to whether Palestinian performance warrants Israeli compliance. Yet, not a word from Bush, who apparently decided that his electoral con-cerns outweigh the broader interest in Middle East stability.

Israel's intransigence and the uncompromising stand of Ariel Sharon have won decisively an unqualified approval of George Bush. He even instructed his UN ambassador to veto a security council resolution calling on Israel to rescind its decision to "re-move" Palestinian president Arafat on September 17, 2003. A similar general assembly resolution was subsequently opposed by the United States, accompanied by Israel, the Marshall Is-lands, and Micronesia. That seems to spell a clearer end for the so-called peace process, a matter that challenges the Arab world and the PLO to withdraw their acceptance of the two-state solu-tion, ongoing since at least 1988, but not likely to happen in the short term. For now, the neoconservatives' preference for Baghdad rather than Jerusalem as the avenue for a settlement is the one that stands in Bush's White House. A credible and lasting settlement, however, may have to await a regime change not only in Iraq, but also in Israel and maybe in Washington.

The domestic test of the Bush Doctrine

The ongoing debate regarding Bush's handling of the war, particularly the record of lies and distortion of intelligence reports, the mounting deaths of US soldiers, and the rising cost of the war to the tune of eighty-seven billion dollars requested by Bush in September 2003, must also be considered as a debate of the Bush Doctrine. The most interesting reality of this debate is that the striking opposition is coming from unlikely sources—the US foreign policy establishment, congressional circles, and the mainstream media. The quarterly journal *Foreign Affairs,* organ of the American Council on Foreign Relations, has one article after another by establishment figures, including James Rubin, former assistant secretary of state, expressing concern about Bush's deviation from the traditional parameters of US foreign policy.[69]

Likewise, Senator Edward Kennedy of Massachusetts said in an interview with the Associated Press on September 18, 2003, that the case for going to war against Iraq was a fraud "made up in Texas" to give Republicans a political boost. He added that the Bush administration has failed to account for nearly half of the four billion dollars the war is costing each month.[70] The prominent senator said he believes that much of the unaccounted-for money is being used to bribe foreign leaders to send in troops, and described the administration's current Iraq policy as "adrift." He expressed doubts about how serious a threat Saddam Hussein posed to the United States in the battle against terrorism and charged administration officials with relying on "distortion, misrepresentation, [and] a selection of intelligence" to justify their case for war.

Criticism of Bush's foreign policy is also coming from a number of foreign policy establishment writers, such as John Newhouse. His new book, *Imperial America: The Bush Assault on the World Order,* represents an indictment of unilateralism, diktat through the use of force, and disregard for diplomacy. H.D.S. Greenway of the *Boston Globe* admired the substance and the tone of the book, which speaks of the "administration's missed opportunities since September 11, 2001, when … even countries that might not have traditionally loved us offered their hand." According to Greenway:

> Newhouse argues that a lasting coalition against terror could have been built to this country's advantage. Instead, President Bush, in stark contrast to his father, adopted the attitudes, prejudices, and strategies of America's far right, which for the first time has gained ascendancy in foreign policy to the detriment of this country's long-term security.[71]

On the Middle East, Greenway added, "One dream of the new right radicals is a wave of democracy sweeping over the Middle East that would destabilize the old monarchies and regimes. The influence of Israel's right-wing Likud Party over many in the Bush administration is a Newhouse theme." Remarkably, Newhouse ventured into a hostile terrain, which has been giving Democratic presidential candidate Howard Dean nightmares, and which may also be costly to Newhouse himself:

> [A] cohort in the Pentagon has operated, in effect, like an extension of the Likud leadership and has scared other governments with talk of redrawing the political map of the Middle East and implicitly turning the region into a US-Israeli co-management sphere.[72]

As for the establishment press, the coverage during the period leading to war, during, and after was rather supportive, and some of the cable television media acted as cheerleaders for the administration. The phenomenon of the "embedded media" left much to be desired in a society that prides itself on free press and free expression. Later, however, we began to see a critical tone and an interrogative attitude. Professor Immanuel Wallerstein wrote the following about the new critical spirit in the establishment media:

> The fact is that the Establishment press in the United States is and always has been solidly centrist. For a year after 9/11, indeed up until three months ago, this centrist press sounded like they simply took the press releases from the White House and endorsed them. Now suddenly, this is no longer true. Indeed far from true. One only needs to take a look at the four main TV channels (CBS, NBC, CBS, and CNN) [sic] or read the main news magazines (Time, Newsweek, U.S. News & World Report) or the principal newspapers (N.Y. Times, Washington Post, L.A. Times, Boston Globe). What one sees is article after article— news stories, opinion pieces, editorials—quite critical of the Bush administration—of its policies in Iraq, or rather of its "fail-

ures" in Iraq, and of its inability to counter the persistent and growing recession and unemployment in the United States.[73]

One example of the scathing criticism of Bush by the establishment media comes from Paul Krugman, op-ed columnist for the *New York Times*. He accused Bush of having lied more than any other president in the past and having abused people's patriotism after September 11. He said the following in an interview on September 15, 2003, before a party to launch his latest book, *The Great Unraveling*:

> Bush is a leader of a movement that wants to smash the system as we know it, the social contract, the safety net that was built up since Franklin Roosevelt ... Certainly there is nothing in modern American history that resembles this.[74]

The *Financial Times* has also been equally critical of US foreign policy under George Bush, placing the blame for the discord in US-European relations not only on some of the European nations but on Washington as well:

> The Bush administration must bear much of the blame, with its prickly unilateralism and fundamentalist division of the world into good and evil. Its insistence on trying to run the world with "coalitions of the willing" has caused extraordinary bitterness among old allies. But the EU is also at fault, because its leading governments have been so divided, although their voters were far more united.
>
> A recent opinion poll by the German Marshall Fund ... shows that the war has had a disastrous effect on European attitudes towards US leadership. Every single European country polled, except Poland, showed a large majority disapproving of US foreign policy. In Germany and France more than 80 per cent disapproved. In Britain it was 57 per cent.[75]

Another *Financial Times* article refers to bureaucratic inertia and fragmentation of the decision-making process at the level of the National Security Council in Washington in matters of national security in ways that compromise the integrity of foreign policy and impede rationality and sound coordination:

> As the human and financial toll rises in Iraq, as the Bush administration returns cap in hand to the UN, as a videotape surfaces of spritely Osama bin Laden, as hope is swamped in blood in the Middle East and as North Korea issues ever more shrill nuclear threats, the White House's handling of foreign policy has gone from political asset to something akin to a liability. Ms. Rice's reputation is having to weather a harsh reassessment.[76]

Most surprising was the criticism launched by the normally tame UN Secretary-General Kofi Annan, who warned President Bush on September 23, 2003, that his doctrine of preventive military intervention poses a fundamental challenge to the United Nations and could lead to the law of the jungle. In a speech shortly before Bush addressed the UN General Assembly, Annan said:

> My concern is that, if it were to be adopted, it could set precedents that resulted in a proliferation of the unilateral and lawless use of force, with or without credible justification.[77]

He also berated UN members for not increasing the number of members of the Security Council for fifty-eight years. According to Annan, sidestepping the United Nations in waging war against Iraq or elsewhere called into question the entire structure of collective action forged when the United Nations was created out of the ashes of World War II.

All of this criticism coming from the traditional foreign policy establishment and mainstream press does not augur well for Bush's unilateralism and preventive action. If the economy remains in the doldrums and the body bags continue to arrive home during the forthcoming presidential campaign, the entire global strategy of the neoconservative cabal might be subjected to public scrutiny. Yet, it is far from certain whether a Democratic administration would scale down America's adventures overseas to a significant degree.

The real question, in the end, is whether America's imperial wars will prove to be a stopgap measure to slow down the dwindling American competitive advantage and prolong the life of unilateralism, or will they prove too costly and counterproductive that a major reassessment would be acclaimed as enlightened self-interest?[78] Will the silent rational voices in America finally react and move to protect the republic from the empire, to reenergize international law, and to arrest the moral corrosion of an otherwise vibrant society? Will these voices be raised to reclaim the Constitution and to ensure that the civil rights of dissidents and ethnic minorities, particularly those of Arab and Muslim Americans, are duly protected? Today, the abuse is reserved for Arab and Muslim Americans, but tomorrow different minorities could be the victims, as in the past when Japanese Americans, African Americans, and Native Americans, among other minorities, were the culprits, the scapegoats, and the targets of permissible prejudice.

America's "war on terror" is likely to remain a slogan as long as the society refuses to address the question of the root cause, and consider the true definition of terrorism in a manner that no longer exempts the state terrorists in Washington, Tel Aviv, Moscow, and countless other world capitals. In the end, the connection between injustice and terror will continue to challenge organized force as a remedy for the scourge of terrorism. Karen Armstrong, a respected authority on Islam, expressed it this way:

> Terrorism is wicked and abhorrent, but it has not come out of the blue. If we simply write off these movements as irrational and inexplicable, we will feel no need to examine our own policies and behaviour. The shocking nihilism of the suicide killers shows they feel they have nothing to lose. Millennial or fundamentalist extremism has risen in nearly every cultural tradition where there are pronounced inequalities of wealth, power and status. The only way to create a safer world is to ensure that it is more just.[79]

Similarly, Canadian mainstream journalist Anthony Westell posited that George Bush is not winning the war he launched on terrorism, just as many others before him who failed to understand the grievances of the terrorists:

> From the beginning, Mr. Bush has ignored the lesson of history: Terrorism can be contained but not defeated by armed force, no matter how smart the bombs. The Nazis had total control when they occupied France ... but they could not defeat the organized resistance. The might of the British army, emergency laws and special courts could not defeat the IRA; an uneasy peace descended only when both sides realized that neither could defeat the other. Israel, with all its tanks and helicopter gunships, cannot stop the Palestinian suicide bombers.
>
> Terrorism can be defeated only by political measures that, over time, remove the grievances that breed terrorists.[80]

THE INTERLOCKING OF RIGHT–WING POLITICS AND US MIDDLE EAST POLICY: SOLIDIFYING ARAB/MUSLIM DEMONIZATION

Elaine C. Hagopian

Introduction

Much has been made of the power of the pro-Israel, Zionist lobby in the United States. It is true that the lobby has exercised great influence on congressional members and US administrations in past decades. The lobby's influence resulted from the confluence and compatibility of US and Israeli strategic interests. Former American Israel Public Affairs Committee (AIPAC) executive director Thomas Dine, in his speech of April 6, 1986, to the twenty-seventh annual AIPAC Policy Conference, stated the following:

> ... we are here on behalf of our common cause—to expand, to deepen, to enhance the partnership between Washington and Jerusalem.
>
> This administration, this Congress, and this community—together with Israel—are engaged in changing the entire basis of U.S.-Israel relations. And I submit to you, these changes in the strategic, economic, and diplomatic spheres will be felt for decades to come.
>
> Let me ... share with you what Secretary of State George Shultz recently explained. He said the point of strategic cooperation is, and I quote, "to build institutional arrangements so that eight years from now, if there is a secretary of state who is not positive about Israel, he will not be able to overcome the bureaucratic relationship between Israel and the U.S. that we have established." Think about that. For a secretary of state to feel that way—think about how far we have come.[1]

With the emergence of pro-Likudnik neoconservatives ("neocons") in the present Bush administration, the major lobbying organizations found their mirror image in key government positions. Undergirded by the Christian fundamentalists, they have been able to participate with the neocons in shaping US foreign policy in the Middle East. This development also brought Israel, under Prime Minister Ariel Sharon, into direct policy partnership with the United States. Given the priorities of both states in reinventing regional states to comply with American and Israeli interests, ipso facto this meant defining Arab/Muslim states and/or movements within them as terrorist or supporters of terrorism. Other attributes such as allegedly having weapons of mass destruction and undemocratic governments were also attached to them. Given that the states and movements designated were primarily identified as Muslim—Arab, Iranian, Pakistani, and others—there could be no other outcome but a concretizing of demonization of Arabs and Muslims. This chapter will focus on particular cases that elucidate the specific interlocking of right-wing politics and US policies in the Middle East. These cases stigmatize Arabs and Muslims and reinforce targeting members of these communities in the United States, citizens and noncitizens, for discriminatory abridgement of their civil rights.

Brief context: Post–Iraq war reshaping of the Middle East

For more than eight decades, Western powers have sought to remap and reshape the strategic landscape of the Middle East. The war on Iraq represents another chapter in Western imperialism, only on a much grander scale. This time the United States is partnered with Israel. Both seek to weaken the regional states by isolating them one from the other, as well as fostering possible further regime change.

Of the six countries covered in this chapter—Iraq, Lebanon, Iran, Syria, Palestine, and Saudi Arabia—three (Iraq, Lebanon, and Iran) have recognized and established alternative exile leadership founded and groomed in the United States. The three are all distinguished by the fact that they attached themselves to the pro-Israel, Zionist lobby; related think tanks; and neocons/Likudniks in the Bush administration. For the other three—Palestine, Syria, and Saudi Arabia—alternative leadership connections with US government officials and/or the Zionist lobby and related think tanks are neither well developed nor recognized.

The three countries

Iraq

The Iraqi National Congress, headed by Ahmed Chalabi, favored by the Pentagon but not liked by the CIA and State Department, has its leaders and followers in Iraq now competing for power. For more than a decade, Chalabi and his colleagues in the Iraqi National Congress were the political protégés of the Zionist lobby and think tanks, who in turn connected them to the neoconservatives in the Pentagon. Moreover, Chalabi and his supporter Kanan Makiya frequented and still frequent Israel, promising "liberated" Iraq's recognition of and robust economic relations with it (i.e., normalization).

Lebanon

A significant set of Lebanese American right-wing leaders and their organizations have been working in tight cooperation with, among others, Daniel Pipes's Middle East Forum, the Zionist-oriented Hudson Institute, and leaders of the right-wing Americans for Victory Over Terrorism (AVOT), headed by William Bennett. They are promoting former Lebanese general Michel Aoun, a Christian, to head the Lebanese government.

Iran

Presently, exiled Iranian monarchists are following the Iraqi National Congress route by developing an alliance in Washington with influential neocon/Likudnik think tanks, the Zionist lobby, and Pentagon officials. The former Shah's son, Reza Pahlavi, is in the forefront of this effort, but he may eventually become only a figurehead.

The other three

Palestine

Alternative leadership to Yasser Arafat is not presently being groomed in the United States. Nonetheless, in spring 2002, an obscure Palestinian banker from Nablus who was living in Ramallah, Omar Karsou, was hosted by Meyrav Wurmser, director of the pro-Likud Hudson Institute's Center for Middle East Studies, among others. He did the rounds in Washington, but never quite took off as a potential alternative leader. The United States and Israel handpicked the first Palestinian prime minister, Mahmoud Abbas, also known as Abu Mazen, in summer 2003, primarily because they expected him to accept terms unacceptable to Palestinians. He was groomed by default, but failed to deliver what the United States and Israel required. Arafat appointed Ahmed Qurei, also known as Abu Ala'a, as the second prime minister in October 2003. Within days, he threatened resignation, but as of January 2004 he had not resigned.

Saudi Arabia

It does not appear that an alternative leadership is being openly groomed in the United States, but there are organizations in the United States that represent the contradiction that is Saudi Arabia and US foreign policy regarding the kingdom. The Saudi-American Forum is sponsored by the National Council on US-Arab Relations (NCUSAR) in Washington, DC, founded by John Duke Anthony, a Gulf specialist. This forum tends to portray the importance of Saudi Arabia to US interests, while also pointing out some of the issues between the kingdom and the United States. A "Saudi-US Relations Information Service," aimed at improving understanding of Saudi Arabia, has recently been added to the forum. NCUSAR and its affiliates are funded by American corporations, especially those in the oil industry. On the other hand, there is the Saudi Institute, allegedly an independent human-rights watchdog group based in McLean, Virginia, headed by Ali al-Ahmed, a Shia Muslim who grew up in Saudi Arabia. This organization is very critical of the Saudi regime, Wahhabism, and Saudi education. It is well funded, but the source is not known. Alain Gresh notes, "Many Saudis are convinced that the United States aims ... to divide the kingdom, creating a Washington-friendly Shia republic that would control oil."[2] Is there any truth to this? A link to the Saudi Institute's Web site is found on a pro-Israel Web page, Kesher Talk.[3] The institute does not identify its board of directors or its staff. Also, there are Saudi reformer intellectuals and intelligentsia who address the Saudi government directly in order to preserve Saudi independence.

Syria

There is no plausible pro–US/Israel Syrian exile alternative leadership that is organized similar to that of the Iraqis, Lebanese, and Iranians. Syrian critics of Syria tend to address their society and government directly, seeking reform from within and not an alliance with Israeli supporters and US officials. However, the self-styled Syrian American dissident Farid Ghadry "informally unveiled his Reform Party of Syria" at the American Enterprise Institute (AEI) in May 2003 and affirmed his determination "to go public with his opposition efforts."[4] Ghadry, allegedly a member of AIPAC,[5] is welcomed by the Zionist lobby and think-tank network, but it is unlikely that his party will be seen as a viable alternative to the present Syrian regime in the foreseeable future. Authentic Syrian reformists and opposition groups do not take Ghadry seriously.

Possible sources of resistance to US designs

The United States is now deep into the reshaping and remapping of the Middle East and Central Asia. The neoconservative strategists in the United States act on the belief that, as the lone superpower, the fate of the United States in the Middle East and in other target areas will be different from that of former colonialists and imperialists. Nonetheless, we can expect and are witnessing increased resistance to American designs in the region. The resistance in the Middle East and Central Asia is coming from Islamist organizations, some reformists/nationalists, some fanatics, and some from fringe "Islamic" networks who appropriate the various grievances to legitimize terror strikes against American, British, Israeli, and affiliated foreign diplomatic missions and business targets.

Although secular Arab nationalists are surfacing in both Iraq and Egypt,[6] the Islamist route is more feasible, given American/Israeli and conservative indigenous Arab government efforts to destroy secular opposition groups in earlier years. Hence, for example, while secular forces in Egypt—long held in check after Gamal Abdel Nasser's death—are reasserting themselves, it is the Islamists—many of whom were released from prison by Anwar Sadat after Nasser's death in 1970 to counter remaining Nasserist political tendencies—who form the main opposition to American policy and power in the area. In Lebanon, it is Hizbollah and some newer Sunni-based groups. In Syria, a country that claims to oppose US actions in the Middle East, the military is the only organized force, but its capability is inadequate to deter definitively the United States or Israel. The Syrian Ba'ath Party is secular, but it serves as a tool of control for the political and military elites. According to Syrian analyst Dr. Murhaf Jouejati in a spring 2003 talk at Harvard University,[7] Islamists are resurging in Syria and may play a future role. In Saudi Arabia, after the joint Saudi/American repression of a secular opposition movement in the 1960s, it can only be "Islamic" terror networks, internal fanatics, or reformist Islamists who respond to the US role in the area.

In 1979, the United States sought Saudi and Pakistani help in creating and training the mujahideen to fight the Soviet Union for a decade in Afghanistan. Islam is diametrically opposed to atheism, which the Soviet ideology represented. From the mujahideen were spawned the Taliban and Osama bin Laden's al-Qaeda network, both of which still seem to be active. In Iraq, the United States is faced with secular and Sunni/Shia Islamic resistance, competition between Shia groups, Kurdish ethnic discontent with possible competitive civil strife between the two major Kurdish factions headed by Mullah Mustafa al-Barzani and Jalal Talabani, and the problematic Turkish interest factor. Individuals and groups with either or both Islamist and secular tendencies are struggling to regain influence in their countries by promoting resistance to US dominance through domestic reform and indigenous formulated democratization. They are, as yet, weak.

Regional analysis: Six countries

Iraq

The attempts to pacify Iraq and install an "interim" or "transitional" government are well known. In May 2003, the United States announced that it was not possible to form the promised interim government in the immediate future, an announcement that angered Iraqis. Instead, L. Paul Bremer, US Civil Administrator and head of the Coalition Provisional Authority in Iraq, appointed a twenty-five person Iraqi Governing Council with limited powers and charged them with writing a new Iraqi constitution. The council is seen by significant sectors of Iraqi society and the Muslim world as a tool of the US occupation. One council member was killed in September 2003; others continue to come under attack.

Clearly, Iraq is a major component of the reshaping and remapping of the Middle East to suit the strategic interests of the United States as well as Israel. Israel has long sought regime change in and/or weakening of key Arab states and Iran to prevent them from deterring Israel's dominance of the Middle East under the US umbrella. For the United States, Iraq forms a key area in the effort to establish an arc of control over the oil-rich and strategic Middle East and Central Asia in partnership with Israel. The movement of American military bases and/or "assets" eastward, from Western Europe to Eastern Europe; from Turkey to Iraq and Central Asia in Kyrgyzstan,[8] Uzbekistan, and Afghanistan; and from Saudi Arabia to Qatar is meant to secure this area and its oil resources as a barrier to the emergence of China and/or Russia and China together as a superpower that could challenge US global hegemony.[9] In this latter effort, as well as for mutual security interests, there is a growing Israeli-Indian alliance with US strategic goals in the area, as evidenced by Israel's military aid to India.[10] Additionally, the Zionist lobby in the United States actively pursues Indian immigrants as allies and supporters.[11] Conn Hallinan suggests,"The freshly-minted U.S.-India Institute for Strategic Policy is an organization to watch and one that may help reveal the next target of American power: containing China."[12]

Discreet talks took place recently in Washington between senior advisers to the Pentagon and to the Indian government "on the prospects for a new security system for Asian-Pacific democracies, a kind of Asian NATO, anchored by the United States and India."[13] Israel is a part of this growing alliance. It sold to India, with Bush administration approval, three Phalcon Airborne Warning and Control Systems aircraft with their advanced technology. In October 2003, Sharon visited India to pave the way for the signing of the sale of the Phalcon early warning radar system. It was signed on October 10, 2003, by an Israel defense ministry official.[14] Israel is also scheduled to sell to India the Arrow 2 antimissile system. These two systems could shift the balance of power to make India invulnerable to missile attacks from Pakistan or China.[15] Additionally, reports have it that the United States has been collaborating with Israel to deploy "US-supplied Harpoon cruise missiles armed with nuclear warheads in Israel's fleet of Dolphin-class submarines, giving the

Middle East's only nuclear power the ability to strike at any of its Arab neighbors ... The sea-launch capability gives Israel the ability to target Iran more easily."[16] However, the report has been questioned by Ted Hooton, editor of *Jane's Naval Weapon Systems* in London. He told the Associated Press that "the weight of a nuclear payload would put the Harpoon out of balance, limiting its range and accuracy."[17]

Coincidentally, the right-wing Hindu nationalist government of the Bharatiya Janata Party (with an ideology similar to Zionism) has actively sought the support of the US Zionist lobby to "pressure" the Bush administration to "contain" Pakistan, India's alleged main foe and contender for water-rich Kashmir. The Zionist lobby is also seen by India as the main route to the Pentagon neocons, especially after the US conquest of Iraq set in motion the American attempt to reshape the region.[18] There appear to be no imminent US plans to pen in Pakistan.

Given the above, the importance of Iraq is clear. The United States expected the conquest of Iraq to give it a commanding platform to enforce its plans for the whole region. The plans include isolating Arab states one from the other, projecting power from the conquest of Iraq to effect changes in Arab political behavior, and imposing an unjust settlement on Palestinians. Moreover, the new Iraq is expected to normalize with Israel, the US partner in this enterprise, without conditioning normalization on real progress in justly resolving the Palestine/Israel conflict. A further expectation is that Iraq must offer Israel oil security through a proposed pipeline from Iraq to the port of Haifa.

As is evident, the Bush administration was clearly ill informed about the sociopolitical dynamics of Iraq's diverse population and its rejection of American "liberation." There are competing Shia organizations vying for power. Shias constitute 60 percent of the Iraqi population. The recently killed Ayatollah Mohammed Baqir al-Hakim, the former leader of the Iranian-backed Supreme Council for the Islamic Revolution (SCIRI), returned to Iraq after twenty-three years of exile in Iran. He received a tumultuous welcome from his followers. Well financed by Iran, al-Hakim's political apparatus brought in busloads of supporters from within a one-hundred-mile radius to the holy city of Najaf to attend his homecoming. He also commanded a five-thousand-strong militia force allegedly funded by Iran. In the past, he had called for an Islamic Republic of Iraq, but he did not actively oppose the American occupation.[19] His brother Abd al-Aziz al-Hakim serves on the Iraqi Governing Council.

Competing with the SCIRI is the older al-Da'wa al-Islamiyya Party ("the Call"), founded in 1958. The party had coordinated with Sunni Islamic organizations in the past. During the Iraq-Iran War of 1980–88, some Da'wa members either fought with Iranian military units or dropped out of political activity. Da'wa members also attempted to assassinate Saddam Hussein in 1982 and again in 1987. The Da'wa party was anti-American in the 1980s and 1990s. Its members launched bombings of the US and French embassies in Kuwait in December 1983. However, Da'wa split in the 1990s when some of its component groups decided to work with the United States. Four other groups that trace themselves back to Da'wa are now part of the umbrella SCIRI.[20] The head of the Islamic Da'wa of Basra, Izz al-Din Salim is a member of the Iraqi Governing Council.

There are numerous other Shia groups and clerics also competing for a slice of the political pie. Ayatollah Muqtada al-Sadr has been actively seeking followers opposed to the American occupation. He is the son of a revered religious scholar, Mohammad Sadiq al-Sadr of the old Islamic Da'wa party, who opposed the secular Ba'ath Party of Saddam Hussein. The latter had Muhammad assassinated in 1999. Muqtada al-Sadr has formed his own movement, Jamaat al-Sadr al-Thani ("the Sadr II Movement"). He is young, thirty years old. He is known as a firebrand who opposed the late Mohammed Baqir al-Hakim and Sayyed Abdul Majid al-Khoei, also murdered shortly after his return to Iraq in spring 2003. Al-Sadr was alleged to have had a hand in the death of al-Khoei. Al-Sadr has a following among the two million Shia who live in Sadr City (formerly Saddam City), a poor Shia area of Baghdad. He is also opposed to the Grand Ayatollah al-Sistani, who heads the Hawza al-Ilmiya, the highest seat of learning in Najaf. Al-Sistani is from Mashhad, Iran. Al-Sadr labels al-Sistani a quietist on the American occupation. On October 13, 2003, in Karbala, " ... Sadr's Mahdi [rightly guided] Army militia engaged in a running gun battle with supporters of Sheikh Ali Hussein Sistani in a struggle for control of the shrines to Abbas and Hussein. The tombs of the seventh century imams are regular pilgrimage sites and their guardians are accorded respect and power among the Shiites."[21]

Unlike the other Shia clerics, al-Sadr believes in the wilayat al-faqih, which upholds the late Iranian revolutionary leader Ayatollah Khomeini's view advocating the role of clerics in both religious and temporal affairs. However, he insists that the supreme jurisprudent should be Iraqi, not Iranian. Most Shia in Iraq believe that the role of clerics is uniquely spiritual. Al-Sadr has been able to get out crowds on various occasions. His youth and lack of high religious status are seen by some as drawbacks, while others believe he may become a strong opposition leader. He champions the poor, opposes the American occupation, and condemns the members of the Iraqi Governing Council as infidels. It is alleged that he has received substantial financial support from Iran, whose aim, it is further alleged, is to disrupt Pax Americana in Iraq. In fall 2003, he declared his own government, which few take seriously.[22] Nonetheless, he is viewed increasingly as a disruptive force to be reckoned with by the Iraqi Governing Council and the American occupation.

"The political competition between the clerics, and by extension their emotional constituencies, threaten to revive the old divisions between Iraq's Shi'ites that were exploited and encouraged for over 35 years by the Baghdad Government."[23] "The destruction of the Ba'athist regime did not end the longstanding fights among its opponents. SCIRI, the Sadr II Bloc, al-Da'wa, and followers of Grand Ayatollah Ali Sistani conducted an underground war against one another, struggling for control of key symbolic spaces."[24]

During the Iraq-Iran War, most of the Shia remained loyal to Iraq and fought alongside their Sunni brothers, excepting some Da'wa members. Will that "solidarity" continue, given the history of Sunni-Shia relations in general, and given the fact that the 20 percent Iraqi Sunni population served as the base of the Iraqi government's authority from the inception of the state of Iraq? Others during the Iraq-Iran War took up residence in neighboring Shia Iran. The question today is just how much "theological" influence Iran, especially the powerful Supreme Leader Ayatollah Ali Khamenei, has had on Iraq's Shia. Two facts to note: First, "Thousands of Shiite and Sunni Muslims marched peacefully through Baghdad on Monday [May 19, 2003] in a religious rally that turned into a largely political protest against the American military presence and its plans for a future Iraqi government."[25] Second,

Whereas Iran ... gradually gave the clergy an increasing role in the running of the community affairs culminating in the Islamic revolution of 1979, Iraqi Shias have known no such political activism on the part of their religious establishment....

The Iraqi ulema [learned men] ... have stuck [to the position enunciated by] the late Grand Ayatollah Abul Qassem al-Khoei, actually going on record saying that he did not find Ayatollah Khomeini's [the original 1979 revolution leader] theory of the Velayat-i-Faqih [wilayat al-faqih] (leadership of the learned scholar) acceptable because it included the exercise of temporal authority. [Only Muqtada al-Sadr differs on this matter.]

The Shia religious endowments in Iraq have focused their energies on providing a spiritual leadership that has only extended to carrying out charitable works ... Political leadership and active politics, thus, remain the domain of the *non-cleric Iraqi Shias*."[26]

The Iraqi Kurds have experienced a period of relative sovereignty in the north since the end of the first Gulf War, bringing together the competing Kurdish Democratic Party (KDP, affiliated with Barzani) and Patriotic Union of Kurdistan (affiliated with Talabani). The Kurds have said they would accept a federal status within Iraq. The Turks, with a larger Kurdish population, are wary of Kurdish nationalism. Not to be forgotten is the fact that a Kurdish Republic, Mahabad, supported by the USSR, was proclaimed in 1946 in the heart of the USSR- and Iranian-contested Azerbaijan. In 1947, Soviet leaders withdrew support, opting to pursue Iranian oil concessions. Mahabad collapsed. Barzani had been a general in the Mahabad military. He returned to Iraq after Mahabad ceased to exist. In the late 1960s and early 1970s, he cooperated with the American CIA, whose stated goal was to overthrow the Iraqi Ba'ath regime. In return, the United States would back the Kurdish nationalist struggle for autonomy in northern Iraq. In the end, the United States reneged on its promises to Barzani, using his followers primarily to sap Iraq's strength while preventing the Kurds from prevailing.[27] Barzani's son now heads the KDP-Iraq. Kurds yearn for statehood, denied to them after World War I by the British (and the Turks). Will they be satisfied with American-conceived federalism, if actually implemented? Some Kurds doubt that the Americans will keep their promise of federal status.[28] Will the Kurds again fight among themselves? How will they react to American control of oil fields in their area, from which they assumed they would benefit? What will Turkey do? As of October 2003, the Turks were considering sending

10,000 troops to help the coalition forces stabilize Iraq. Iraqis in general and the Kurds in particular object to Turkish troops, and, as a result the offer was subsequently dropped.[29] Kurds fear Turkish intent is to preclude any Kurdish national formation in Iraq.

The shakedown in Iraq has not happened to date, and it is too early to project the future. Nonetheless, it is safe to say that it is not what the United States imagined it would be. Fearing the rise of the Shia, Secretary of Defense Donald Rumsfeld stated that the United States would not tolerate the election of an Iranian-styled theocracy. Karen Armstrong argues that should a free election take place and a Shia government come to power, it should be given a chance to demonstrate what many of their thinkers have expressed, that is, a commitment to a democratic ethos. She notes,

> Like any religious tradition, Shi'ism has had its share of belligerent, narrow-minded hardliners, but from the very beginning, leading Shia thinkers promoted ideals that are familiar to us in the west, not least that criticism of their own society is the basis of the democratic ethos. After decades of Saddam, western-style secularism may not appeal to many Iraqis, and Shia leaders, who have so bravely opposed the Ba'ath regime, are likely to be more respected than an Iraqi exile parachuted in by the Americans.[30]

Most of the Shia clerics and followers are espousing this point of view. Hence, if elected, Iraqi Shia clerics—excluding Muqtada al-Sadr—would not be the ultimate political authority, as in Iran, but elected Shia could promote a political culture that included Shia values.

The late al-Hakim's SCIRI was funded by Iran. However, al-Hakim, before his death, committed himself to democracy and to not actively opposing the US occupation. The Basra branch of Da'wa has demonstrated its cooperation with the Coalition Provisional Authority by agreeing to have its leader become a member of the Iraqi Governing Council. Given that most Shia clergy do not accept the wilayat al-faqih, might the Iraqi Sunnis find it easier to embrace a Shia-dominated government of both lay and clerical Shia? How would the Kurds feel about it, even if granted federal status? In fact, how would Sunni-dominated Gulf states with significant Shia populations feel about it? After all, a contiguous Shia-populated area is now "out of the bag" since the American conquest: Iraq, Iran, Bahrain, Eastern Saudi Arabia, and other Gulf states, as well as Shia in Afghanistan, Pakistan, and India.[31] Will the United States, goaded by Israel, take action against Iran under the pretext and/or belief that Iran is developing nuclear capability and is broadening its leverage in the area through Iraqi Shia? Indeed, will Israel get the green light from Washington to take action against Iran? Certainly the neocons and Israel favor weakening and isolating both Syria and Iran, thereby producing a contiguous string of toothless opponents, i.e., Lebanon, Syria, Iraq, and Iran. The October 2003 bombing of a Syrian site under the pretext that it was a training camp for Palestinian Islamic Jihad had all the fingerprints of the neocons on the operation and elicited a scripted Bush approval for the action.[32]

Back in July 2003, in Najaf, the center of Shia Muslim authority in Iraq, "A conference of 900 Iraqi notables have [sic] demanded the quick establishment of an Iraqi government to combat the lawlessness and insecurity"[33] in the country since the overthrow of the Ba'athist regime. The organizers did not seek Paul Bremer's approval for the meeting. Bremer had already announced plans to appoint twenty-five to thirty people to a council, which would then name candidates for senior ministry positions under his authority. The Najaf meeting "was attended by lawyers from all over the country, with the exception of the northern Kurdish region, and representatives of the main political parties including monarchists, liberals and the US-backed Iraqi National Congress."[34] (No mention is made of whether or not Muqtada al-Sadr attended.)

> The country's most senior Shia cleric, Grand Ayatollah Ali al-Sistani issued a fatwa, or religious ruling, in Najaf ... criticizing US plans to appoint a governing council and demanding elections instead, so that Iraqis can elect their own constitutional convention. According to the fatwa, "There is no guarantee that the [US-backed] council would create a constitution conforming with the greater interests of the Iraqi people and expressing the national identity, whose basis is Islam and its noble social values."
>
> ... the central role being played by Ayatollah Sistani in Najaf was confirmed when Ahmad Chalabi, leader of the Iraqi National Congress, travelled to the town for discussions on how to form a national government.[35]

The Najaf meeting notables, led by Ayatollah Sistani, stated clearly that they seek to combat the US/British occupation by diplomatic means. The conference was a show of "muscle" to Bremer's authority, and indeed, the Coalition Provisional Authority can be said to be in a tug of war with Iraqi sectors regarding Iraq's future.

Israel and Palestine: The road map

The Madrid/Oslo process failed because its legal framework, supposedly United Nations Security Council (UNSC) Resolutions 242 and 338, which recalls the terms of 242, was really the Camp David I (1978) autonomy plan for Palestinians in the Occupied Territories presented by Menachem Begin and embedded in the nonstarter Framework for Middle East Peace. That same framework was automatically resuscitated in the road map for Middle East peace, also claiming UNSC Resolutions 242, 338, and 1397 (which reiterates the Tenet and Mitchell plans) as its legal framework.

Directly after 9/11, Bush Junior called for a Palestinian state, which gave the impression that he understood the Israeli-Palestinian conflict to be a core issue requiring immediate American attention. However, after visits from Sharon and coaching from the neocons/Likudniks in his administration, he embraced completely their view of the Israeli-Palestinian conflict as part of the war on terrorism, rather than one of occupation. Their approach called for war on Iraq and removal of Saddam Hussein as the route to dissolving the Israeli-Palestinian conflict. Palestinians—and the other Arab States—would be substantially weaker, isolated, and would have no recourse but to accept whatever terms may be offered. In the meantime, Bush gave full rein to Sharon to destroy Palestinian society.

Bush's speech of June 24, 2002, which some say could have been written by Sharon,[36] called for the replacement of Arafat and a cessation of Palestinian violence as preconditions for any negotiations on the future of Palestinians. The issue fell off Bush's screen as Iraq heated up. It was brought back by British prime minister Tony Blair, needing to balance his unpopular commitment to the Iraq war and to Bush with a show of concern for Arab sensibilities over Sharon's destruction of Palestinian society.

A Performance-Based Road Map to a Permanent Two-State Solution to the Israeli-Palestinian Conflict,[37] dated December 20, 2002, was put forward by the United States, the European Union, Russia, and the United Nations—popularly referred to as "the Quartet"—and released on April 30, 2003. The road map had all of the flaws of Madrid/Oslo. Nonetheless, the Palestinians accepted it, feeling they had no other alternative. Sharon's cabinet "accepted" it on May 25, 2003—conditioned on fourteen amendments, which the Bush administration said it would take into consideration. The amendments would effectively stalemate "negotiations" and preclude the establishment of a viable Palestinian state. Sharon announced two pre-conditions, which were part of the fourteen amendments: Palestinians would have to full stop and dismantle the resistance (terrorism), as originally stated in Bush's June 24, 2002, speech,[38] and they would have to renounce the legal Refugee Right of Return. Given the fact that the powerful Israeli military was unable to stop Palestinian resistance, Sharon set an impossible condition for the then newly appointed prime minister Abbas, especially since there was no guarantee of viable statehood in return. No Palestinian leader can renounce the legally based Palestinian right of return, although there have been and are continuing attempts by some to do so.[39] The refugees make up approximately 70 percent of the Palestinian population. They insist that their right to return be recognized by Israel; then, and only then, can mutually acceptable, rights-based compromises be made. Moreover, during Secretary of State Colin Powell's visit in early May 2003, Sharon also made it clear that "any talk of changing Israel's settlement policy" was not "on the horizon."[40] Clearly, Sharon's actions were aimed at setting up the Palestinians to take the blame for "failed" negotiations. Sharon also excluded reference to a *viable* Palestinian state at the June 2003 meeting in Aqaba, Jordan, with Bush and Abbas. The road map was disabled by Sharon's refusal to comply, continuing as he did to target Palestinian resistance leaders for assassination, and by insisting on his fourteen amendments.

The road map had three phases. Phase One was "Ending Terror and Violence, Normalizing Palestinian Life, and Building Palestinian Institutions." International lawyer John Whitbeck noted the following about the first phase:

> If one reads this "road map", it is apparent that it builds on a false premise to reach a fantastic (in the literal sense of "fantasy") conclusion. The premise is that the problem in Israel/Palestine is Palestinian resistance to the 36-year-long occupation, not the occupation itself.[41]

In the first phase, Palestinians were to stop all resistance (violence). Simultaneously, Israel was called upon to end incitement against Palestinians and take no actions that would undermine trust. These included deportations; attacks on civilians; confiscation and/or demolition of Palestinian homes and property; and destruction of Palestinian institutions and infrastructure, which was already too late. Israel was also to dismantle "unauthorized" Israeli settlement outposts built since March 2001, and freeze all other "authorized" but still illegal settlement construction. Under the Geneva Conventions, these actions, and even more, are duties of the occupying authority. They are not concessions.

The other two phases, if the first phase succeeded, would have been to focus on "the option" of creating an independent Palestinian state with provisional borders and attributes of sovereignty, a legal oxymoron, and then to deal with final status issues: borders, refugees, settlement, and Jerusalem—the same issues left to the end of Oslo, which were not resolved—leading to a "viable" Palestinian state. The road map also called for international efforts to promote a comprehensive peace on all tracks, including Syria-Israel and Lebanon-Israel without specifying any goals or procedures, and for Arab normalization with Israel.

In spite of the fact that Bush announced he would not impose a settlement on the parties, giving Sharon the "right" therefore to insist on his own terms, Sharon's government, and its supporters in the United States, objected to three of its main features, which were part of the conditional "acceptance" of the map. These were the requirement for concurrent and parallel steps by the Palestinian Authority and Israel, which Israel views as a deviation from Bush's June 24, 2002, speech; the identification of Israel's presence in the territories as an occupation; and reliance on the Quartet parties to evaluate the performance of both parties.

The Zionist lobby, supported de facto by the neoconservatives, led by AIPAC and the Conference of Major American Jewish Organizations and supported by the Christian fundamentalists, was against the road map. They focused on the "concurrent and parallel steps" provision to express their disapproval, rejecting what they refer to as the "symmetry of blame" implied by the provision. They activated more than 80 senators and 280 representatives to send a letter to Bush to reject this provision.

These same parties objected to the designation of Israel's presence in the territories as an "occupation." Sharon startled his coalition government by stating on May 26, 2003, that keeping "3.5 million Palestinians under occupation is bad for us and them."[42] Although Sharon was referring to occupation of the people and not the land, he retracted the word "occupation" the next day, saying he should not have used it. Israelis and their supporters have always insisted that Israel is not an occupying power. They argue this on two points: (1) Since the West Bank and Gaza were not sovereign areas—Jordan's annexation of the West Bank after the 1948 war was never recognized, and Egypt simply administered the Gaza Strip—how could Israel occupy them; and (2) since the areas are part of ancient Eretz Israel, how could Israel be occupying its own land?

Needless to say, the "legal" argument does not hold up, especially when one notes that Israel annexed the Golan Heights, part of the sovereign state of Syria. The other is a matter of biblical mythology, which has no place in international law. Writing in the *New York Sun* in spring 2003, the Anti-Defamation League's Abraham Foxman worried that, according to the road map, "the core of the problem is Israel's 'occupation' of the territories," which he said does not exist. Focusing on the third main Israeli objection to the road map, Foxman blamed this heretical notion of occupation on the partners in the Quartet and "called on the pro-Israel lobby to do all it can to keep 'peacemaking' in the hands of the US, where it could be kept under strict supervision and continue to focus attention on Palestinian shortcomings."[43]

Nonetheless, how is one to interpret Sharon's statement on occupation? It appeared to be a strategy of symbolism employed to give the impression of change and movement. The strategy was aimed at offering the Palestinians the 42 percent or less of the West Bank that Sharon had previously stated would be his maximum offer and made it sound "generous." Given the fact that the "separation (read 'apartheid') wall" continues to be built around the Palestinian areas, and given the terms laid out in one of the fourteen Israeli amendments to the road map, it is clear that the goal was never a viable Palestinian state. The amendment states,

> The character of the provisional Palestinian state will be determined through negotiations between the Palestinian Authority and Israel. The provisional state will have provisional borders and certain aspects of sovereignty, be fully demilitarized with no military forces, but only with police and internal security forces of limited scope and armaments, be without the authority to undertake defense alliances or military cooperation, and Israeli control over the entry and exit of all persons and cargo, as well as of its air space and electromagnetic spectrum.[44]

Essentially, the road map is actually dead, and it is highly unlikely that even a "provisional state" will be reached.

Israel's tourism minister, Benny Elon, came to the United States in early May 2003 to address the Christian fundamentalists and to persuade members of Congress that a Palestinian state in the spirit of Bush's stated vision, i.e., a viable state in the Occupied Territories, will only feed terrorism, and that Jordan is Palestine.[45] While Sharon has always embraced the "Jordan is Palestine" thesis, he has not publicly endorsed Elon's plan. Nonetheless, Sharon did not object to Elon's visit or presentation of his ideas.

Meanwhile, the *Jordan Times* reported that just as Powell was visiting Israel in early May to promote the road map, "Israeli police launched a huge raid in northern Israel ... against a local Arab [Israeli citizens] political party, the Islamic Movement, nabbing fourteen of its members who are suspected of 'laundering money' to the Palestinian resistance group Hamas."[46] At the same time, Sharon transferred a Palestinian from Jenin to Gaza, in violation of the Fourth Geneva Convention, for a period of two years.[47] In October 2003, Sharon deported sixteen people from the West Bank to Gaza.[48] He allowed the murder of members of the International Solidarity Movement (ISM) and a British filmmaker, and he instituted a policy whereby Gaza visitors must sign waivers absolving the army from responsibility if it shoots them. Visitors must also declare that they are not ISM peace activists.[49] More recently (January 2004) Israel issued a new law requiring foreign passport holders to apply for a permit to enter the Occupied Territories, further isolating Palestinians. Sharon's policy of targeting Palestinian resistance leaders for assassination never stopped, in spite of the July 2003 "cease-fire" agreement with Abbas. These facts, combined with the continuous assault on Palestinians in the territories and the construction of the wall, appear to be Sharon's flaunting of his exemption from any criticism or pressure from the Bush administration, hence from the international community as well. As of October 2003, Bush has tolerated all of Sharon's actions. The mild rebuke Bush conveyed to Sharon over the June 10, 2003, targeted attempt on the life of Hamas leader Abdel al-Aziz Rantissi was immediately criticized by the Zionist lobby and its supporters in Congress. Within days, Bush reversed himself and expressed strong support for Israel's attacks, and shifted his focus to Arab leaders and the Palestinian Authority, demanding that they deal with Palestinian "militants."[50]

Conclusion and prospects

It is clear that Bush will not pressure Israel to embrace and thus resuscitate the already defunct road map. Bush's political advisers see an opportunity to make unprecedented inroads on Jewish support for the Democratic Party in 2004 and have thus warned him against pressing Sharon into "major" concessions. They insisted that the president would not only risk reducing his high approval ratings from traditionally liberal US Jews, but he could also disappoint his core Christian fundamentalist supporters. "In fact, Sharon and the Bush neocons are rushing to fulfill Sharon's objectives in the Palestinian territories, i.e., limiting Palestinians to a walled-in ten percent of pre-1948 Palestine, i.e., the 42% or less of the West Bank suggested by Sharon as the maximum offer to Palestinians, before the American presidential election. Sharon fears that Bush may not be re-elected, and is trying to create a fait accompli before Bush's term ends."[51] As H.D.S. Greenway noted in early May 2003 after the release of the road map:

> But now that the "road map" for ending the Israel-Palestine conflict has been published, the real test of strength between the warring ideologies is about to begin. Will President Bush remain engaged to press both the Israelis and the Palestinians down the path to peace [such as they conceive it] as Colin Powell would wish it? Or will the neo-conservatives, in and out of the Pentagon, who have close ties to Israel's right wing Likud party prevail, permitting Israel's Ariel Sharon to impose a peace that leaves Israel de facto in charge and the settlements largely intact? Put your hopes on the former, but your money on the latter.[52]

Given the weakened situation of the Palestinians, the ill-fated Palestinian prime minister Abu Mazen's role under the short-lived road map was basically to facilitate the surrender of Palestinian national and individual rights in return for a weak mini-"state." Abbas's ability to deliver the surrender was never possible. Nor can the new prime minister, Ahmed Qurei, deliver surrender to Sharon. Instability and violence in the area will likely continue until such time as a just peace is constructed from within the terms of applicable international law and existing UN resolutions. Ultimately, the only real answer is to have an American-backed UN force in the area to facilitate the removal of the occupation in all of its forms, and to assist the Palestinians in achieving viable statehood under a democratically elected government. The United States needs to reach a point where it too understands that. In the meantime, the

Palestinian nonviolent resistance efforts, joined by the protective efforts of ISM—now under literal fire from the Israel Defense Forces—struggle to provide an alternative to violent resistance.

The recently announced (October 2003) Geneva accords, the unofficial secret agreements made between Israeli and Palestinian delegations led respectively by Yossi Beilin and Yasir Abed Rabbo, recently signed and peddled to both the Israeli and Palestinian peoples (December 2003), also appear to be doomed. Three major issues bode ill for its future: (1) no recognition of the Palestinian refugees' legal right of return, to which the refugees will not agree; (2) recognition of Israel as a Jewish state, putting in question the future of the one million or more Palestinian citizens of Israel; and (3) the replacement of all previous UN resolutions related to Palestinian legal claims. In return, Israel would allow a Palestinian state in Gaza and the West Bank; remove most, but not all, settlements; annex particular areas with Israeli settlements, especially those in expanded East Jerusalem, while offering other, but unequal in quality, land to Palestinians; and "share" Jerusalem as the capital of both states. Sharon's government will not accept these terms, nor do they satisfy minimal Palestinian legal claims.[53] Nonetheless, the Palestinian Authority has unofficially approved them. A careful reading of the accords clearly spells out that what is offered is a larger Palestinian bantustan than previously proposed, and one tightly controlled by Israel politically and economically.

Given the determination of the neocon-dominated Bush administration to ensure no real concessions to Palestinian national claims, the October 2003 Israeli bombing on a site north of Damascus must be seen as a renewed neocon effort to weaken all Arab actors. Palestinian endorsement of the unofficial Geneva accords will gain the Palestinians nothing. It may weaken their legal claims at a future time when the chaos of the area will demand new efforts.

Syria

From its outset as a state, Israel identified three Arab states that were possible threats/deterrents to its ambitions in the Middle East: Egypt, Iraq, and Syria. Egypt was retired through the 1978 Camp David peace treaty. Iraq has now been conquered, and efforts are underway to reshape its political institutions and leadership to US specifications, which include recognition and cooperation with Israel. Syria remains, albeit weakened and relatively isolated. These three Arab states carried the mantle of secular Arab nationalism, understood as a threat to US interests and feared by Israel as the basis for a unified Arab state that could potentially challenge Israel. Israel has added post-Shah Iran to its list of "feared" states. Syria has no parity with Israeli technology and military might. However, Syria and Iran have supported the Lebanese Hizbollah—nemesis of Israel's occupation of Southern Lebanon—which has provided Syria with some political leverage. Syria has also kept troops in Lebanon and has basically called the political shots there.

Clearly, Israel and its US supporters would prefer to see Syria (and Iran) militarily humbled and politically revamped to suit their interests. These two states were on the Bush administration's agenda for regime change, along with several other "rogue" states. However, given that the United States is bogged down in Iraq in a manner the postwar planners—Rumsfeld and his Pentagon neocons—did not expect or anticipate, Bush has, at the time of this writing in October 2003, approved of essentially "subcontracting" Syria and Iran out to Israel, buttressed by US military force in Iraq and staging bases throughout the region. Weakening both countries and encouraging pro-Israel/United States behavioral change is an Israeli prime objective. The neocons/Likudniks and the Israeli government seek dominance in the region and imperialistic economic "normalization" without conceding much of anything on the Palestinian issue in return. The October Israeli bombing of a nonactive Palestinian training camp was the first shot in this US-approved heightened Israeli military mobility. The strategy and goals of this fall 2003 effort are not new. They were planned much earlier, before the neocons came to power.

In 1996, the neocons/Likudniks (Richard Perle, Douglas Feith, and Wurmser, among others) presently in the American government and pro-Israel think thanks sent a strategy plan, *A Clean Break: A New Strategy for Securing the Realm,* to the incoming Israeli prime minister Benjamin Netanyahu. It calls for the removal of Saddam Hussein and focuses specifically on Syria (and Iran). It says:

> Syria challenges Israel on Lebanese soil. An effective approach, and one with which Americans can sympathize, would be if Israel seized the strategic initiative along its northern borders by engaging Hizballah, Syria, and Iran, as the principal agents of

aggression in Lebanon....
Given the nature of the regime in Damascus, it is both natural
and moral that Israel abandon the slogan "comprehensive
peace" and move to contain Syria, drawing attention to its
weapons of mass destruction program, and rejecting "land for
peace" deals on the Golan Heights.[54]

In short, the strategy called for the abandonment of the Oslo
process, although weak and deficient from the beginning, and a
return to Israel's policy of "preemptive" strikes, offering only
"peace for peace" not "land for peace." The neocons/Likudniks
share with the Israeli right the dream of Eretz Israel (all of pre-
1948 Palestine).

Syria's early independence years were marked by one coup
d'etat after another.[55] The country was highly unstable until
Hafez al-Assad took over in 1970 and governed Syria through
the Ba'ath Party and the military with an iron fist. He offered
stability and dignity, albeit grudgingly acknowledged by the Syrian people, but restricted freedom of expression and opposition
groups.[56] His ophthalmologist son, Bashar, "inherited" the presidency in 2000, upon the death of his father. Although he was
"voted" in as president by the established order, he has been unable to consolidate his power. He did initiate what is now called
the "December Spring," some six months of attempted liberalization of the Syrian political and economic scene. The old elites,
whose lucrative interests were threatened, closed down liberalization and arrested those who expressed their views freely regarding democratizing Syria. Nonetheless, Syria is not Iraq, and
it does have a nucleus of civil society organizations.

Syria is somewhat stagnant economically and politically,
which contributes to its weakness. It is politically pragmatic, yet
carries the burdens of the last Arab state to carry the mantle of
Arab nationalism, even if symbolically. It opposed the US war on
Iraq, but did not embrace Saddam Hussein. Syria understands
that it is weakened by the US conquest of Iraq, but struggles to
do a balancing act between its state and Arab nationalist interests. The unleashing of the Israeli bombing after thirty years of
observed cease-fire agreements presents Syria with narrowed options. Surrounded now by Turkey, Israel, and the United States
from its position in Iraq, Syria is under great pressure to accede
to US-Israeli demands for behavioral change. The further blow
of the American congressional passage in October 2003 of the

Syria Accountability and Lebanese Sovereignty Restoration Act—passed by the Senate in November 2003, and signed by the president on December 12, 2003—is aimed at removing Syrian leverage in Lebanon and establishing a pro-Israel Lebanese government, and a neutralized Syrian government at a minimum, but preferably a pro-Israel regime at a maximum.

Although contingency plans for US strikes against Syria after the invasion of Iraq in spring 2003 were drawn up by neocon/Likudnik Douglas Feith, Undersecretary of Defense for Policy, and approved by Rumsfeld, that effort was stopped by National Security Council head Condoleezza Rice. Bush's chief domestic adviser, Karl Rove, and Powell concurred in her decision. The focus had allegedly shifted to getting the president reelected and not creating any further entanglements beyond Iraq. Any movement on Syria was considered to be pushing Bush's luck.[57] That did not mean, however, that the neocons who were setting strategy in the Bush administration gave up their goal of weakening and isolating Syria (and Iran). Rather, they allegedly advised Bush to "subcontract" that effort to Israel, which became obvious in October 2003.

Before that latter decision was made, Powell flew to Damascus, on May 2, 2003, at the height of the American occupation of Iraq, to meet with President Bashar Assad. Powell sought to impress upon him that the regional picture had changed, and that Syria needed to recognize that fact and change its behavior. He charged Syria with sponsoring terrorism, promoting extremist groups opposed to peace with Israel, and acquiring chemical weapons. He also charged that Syria's troops in Lebanon were an army of occupation—previously endorsed by the United States—and that it allowed fugitives from Saddam Hussein's regime to enter Syria and sent men and weapons to resist US forces in Iraq.[58]

What the United States wanted was for Syria to close down the offices of representatives of Palestinian resistance groups, stop support for Hizbollah, get its troops out of Lebanon, destroy its alleged weapons of mass destruction, cease exploiting its alliance with Iran, and seal its borders with Iraq. Syria reportedly "froze" the activities of Palestinian representatives in Damascus. In any case, Syria had not allowed them to launch any attack against Israel from Syrian soil over the past decades, and US intelligence knew that. They are basically "for show" offices that allow Syria to keep its symbolic Arab nationalist credentials, as well as to cultivate leverage over the Palestinian resistance movement. Syria has allegedly sealed its 340-mile border with Iraq, at least insofar as possible given the length of the border. Nonetheless, in late June 2003, US troops crossed into Syria in "hot pursuit" of alleged escaping Iraqi officials, wounding five Syrian soldiers and killing numerous Syrian villagers.

On the issues of Hizbollah and Syrian troops in Lebanon, the United States will continue to pressure Syria, as US-Israeli goals are to eliminate all resistance groups in the area and Syrian leverage in Lebanon. According to Syrian analyst Dr. Murhaf Jouejati, Syria will not willingly comply on Hizbollah, as the latter is too popular throughout the Arab world.[59] Syria has restrained and will continue to restrain it however. Syrian troops will remain in Lebanon for as long as possible and based on mutual strategic purposes related to Israeli designs on Lebanon.

Congressman Tom Lantos, a right-wing supporter of Israel and ranking Democrat on the House International Relations Committee, cosponsored the Syria Accountability and Lebanese Sovereignty Restoration Act, "which ... [gives] the president the authority to impose severe sanctions on Syria if it does not meet certain conditions."[60] By July 1, 2003, the combined efforts of right-wing Lebanese Americans and the pro-Israel lobby and institutional networks in the United States gathered the support of more than 250 representatives and 58 senators for the act. A House of Representatives hearing was set for July 15, 2003, featuring the testimony of the undersecretary of state for arms control, John Bolton.[61] The hearing was finally held in September 2003. The act was passed by the House in October 2003, and the Israeli bombing of Syria came shortly thereafter, announcing de facto the Bush administration's "subcontracting" of subduing Syria and Iran to Israel, as noted above.

It mattered not that in May 2003 Iranian president Mohammad Khatami visited Lebanon and Syria primarily to caution each country to recognize the new realities in the region, hence to avoid any semblance of action against Israel. He said that "his country did not wish to participate in any activity that could lead to escalating tension in the Middle East, adding that Israel shouldn't be given any excuses to utilize American forces for its own interests."[62] Apparently, Israel had no need of "excuses." It manufactured its own to bomb Syria this past fall. Khatami went on to stress the importance of democracy in all types of regimes and argued that Islamic countries were not in need of democratic paradigms imposed by outsiders.[63] He was responding to US demands that Arab regimes democratize.

Syrian intellectuals and outside analysts have argued that democratization (not as the United States understands it, i.e., a compliant government with trappings of democracy and a market economy open especially to US capitalism) is the only way that Arab countries can defend themselves against foreign occupation and internal dissension. The discussion began long before the present crisis in the area. On September 27, 2000, ninety-nine Syrian intellectuals within Syria and elsewhere in Europe published a statement in the popular Arab newspaper *Al-Hayat*, calling for specific reforms. The signers were professional people, artists, lawyers, and educators, not political ideological has-beens.

Facing the present reality, a new surge of calls for reform emerged.[64]

> About 140 leftists, rightists, Muslim Brothers and ordinary citizens signed a manifesto published by the Damascus Center for Theoretical and Civil Rights Studies declaring that a strong internal front based on freedom for all was the only effective defense against American and Israeli aggression. As the war against Iraq has proved, the signatories wrote, one party rule and repressive security services cannot protect a country's independence and dignity. A population that feels persecuted and repressed cannot defend its own state.
>
> On April 21, Akhbar al-Sharq said Tayyib Tizini, a well-known Professor of Philosophy at Damascus University, had called for a national democratic dialogue. "Please start to open the circle from inside," he urged the authorities, "before some foreign power opens it from outside!"[65]

Perhaps Lebanese Hizbollah leader Sayyed Hassan Nasrallah said it best in a speech dated April 23, 2003:

> The greatest lesson to be learned from the U.S.-led invasion of Iraq ... is that a country that is fragmented or ruled by repression has no future when faced by a superior enemy. We [Arabs] and our regimes must learn the lesson ... an army and intelligence organizations can protect a regime against an unarmed people, but when they face a greater power, they can't protect the regime. It is the people who protect it.[66]

The Syrian intellectuals who published their call for reform in the *Al-Hayat* newspaper and the 140 who signed a manifesto of reform published in Damascus are understood as Syrian nationalists calling directly on their government to democratize. They are not a foreign-sponsored (read "US-Zionist lobby") opposition. They are authentically nationalist and credible. The May 2003 announcement at the AEI of the Reform Party of Syria headed by Farid Ghadry, attempting to secure the mantle of reformer and regime opponent, is neither popularly recognized nor solidly established in Washington power circles in the same way as the alternative exile leadership of Iraq, Lebanon, and Iran have been and are. Nonetheless, Ghadry, an opportunist par excellence, indicated at the AEI meeting that he expected to form a government in exile soon.[67]

Ghadry was born in Aleppo, Syria, in 1954. His family moved shortly thereafter to Lebanon. There, Ghadry attended the Maristes Brothers (Roman Catholic) School and came into contact with right-wing Lebanese who favored a Christian-dominated state in Lebanon. In 1975, the Ghadry family moved to the suburbs of Washington, DC. Trained in finance and marketing at the American University in Washington, Ghadry worked for several companies. Ultimately he owned a chain of American coffee shops, Hannibal's Coffee Company, that went bankrupt in 1996.[68]

In October 2001, Ghadry, joined by several other Syrian Americans who now make up the Executive Committee of the Reform Party of Syria—Abdulwahab Chaalan, Baschar Najjar, Najat Ashkar, Abboud al-Sultani, and Chukri al-Samih—founded the party. They modeled themselves on Ahmed Chalabi's Iraqi National Congress. Ghadry himself allegedly became a member of AIPAC[69] and began to insinuate himself in the circles of power pursued by the established exile alternative leaders.

Ghadry and his colleagues hold similar political positions to those of the established alternative leaders, their organizations, and the Zionist lobby and its related institutional network. The party leadership supports regime change in Syria; the Syria Accountability and Lebanese Sovereignty Restoration Act, which places sanctions on Syria until it complies with American demands as noted above; and recognition of Israel, which Ghadry has visited, with full economic relations. Given Ghadry's earlier history, it is not surprising that he is supported by those Lebanese American organizations that support Michel Aoun as an alternative head of state for Lebanon (see the Lebanon section below) and that are themselves linked to the Zionist lobby and institutional network. Ghadry and his colleagues would prefer US military action against Syria to force regime change but were pleased by the Israeli bombing. They continue to push in Washington circles for punitive actions against Syria.[70]

In spelling out his party's vision of reform, he says the Ministry of Foreign Affairs should

> ... envision a new plan of diplomacy to consult closely with the US on momentous issues but more importantly to open the dialogue with Lebanon to leave peacefully and to vacate fully its armed forces. On parallel tracks, Hizbollah and other remnant Palestinian organizations will be asked either to leave Syria or to change their ways by renouncing violence and by re-inventing themselves for true peace ...
>
> ... the minister shall then seek the help of the US in opening a dialogue with Israel to attain a peaceful solution to the Golan Heights until a trust is built with Syria ... The very thing that Arabs truly misunderstand about Israel, as a country, is that its people want to live in peace and prosperity.[71]

Ghadry goes on to call for the usual market reforms cherished by the United States, and thus curries favor with the powers that be in the government. Ghadry claims that "the party is enjoying the tacit support from many organizations and people in the U.S. administration and think tanks in Washington [and] we are active in lobbying the U.S. Congress and cultivating the media."[72] However, he and his party have not been embraced seriously by the power centers in the United States. Unlike other established alternative leadership groups, there are no Syrian facade organizations equivalent to the Coalition for Democracy in Iran, for example, or a congressional bill such as Republican Senator Sam Brownback's Iranian Democracy Act (see below). The Zionist lobby and institutional network nonetheless enjoy the propaganda value of having a dissident Syrian voice available to them.

It is not likely that Ghadry's efforts will see fruition. Syria is an immensely nationalist country. Moreover, the resurgence of Islamism in Syria ensures for the foreseeable future that Ghadry and his opportunistic colleagues would win no grassroots support there. Nor, it seems, would the United States try to forcibly install a leader and party who would generate rapid resistance. The United States may be learning some lessons from Iraq and Afghanistan.

Young President Assad—in his late thirties—has his task cut out for him: how to heed the call for democratic reform with which his own thinking resonates when faced with an entrenched bureaucratic elite that benefits from the system as it exists? However, both Syria's geopolitical reality plus other demands that will be made on the Syrians under the Syria Accountability and Lebanese Sovereignty Restoration Act will cut deeply into Syria's ability to maneuver politically. Syrians want the 1967 Israeli-conquered Golan Heights back; Sharon is not willing to return them. Syria has no real leverage to force their return. The United States will basically back Israel. Clearly, the Syrian military cannot resist *effectively* either Israeli or US select strikes. However, a democratized Syrian society could possibly put forward a credible public resistance to yielding to US-Israeli demands. The question is, how fast can Syria democratize? There is not much expectation that it will be anytime soon, although self-determined reform is the only long-term viable option for Syria.

If the entrenched elites choose to rely on the military and intelligence as their main foundation for resistance and/or negotiations with the United States and Israel, they will lose and suffer the sanctions embedded in the Syria Accountability and Lebanese Sovereignty Restoration Act, or worse. Given its depressed economy, Syria can ill afford further restrictions. Other regional factors could alter the situation, such as the growth of Islamist groups in Turkey and Syria. The reaffirmation of solidarity between Iran, Syria, and Lebanon made during Iranian president Khatami's May 2003 visit to Lebanon and Syria was basically a show of unity to make the need for studied caution regarding Israel and the United States palatable. It has not sufficed to checkmate Israel.

Of interest is an alleged conversation between Assad and Powell during his May 2003 visit. David Ignatius recounts in the *Washington Post*, "Assad asked him a blunt question: 'Where is our road map?'"[73] This could be understood in two ways: (1) Assad wanted a clear understanding of what the now defunct road map meant when it talked about dealing with the Syria-Israel and Lebanon-Israel tracks; and (2) it was a way of signaling the United States that Syria wants to cooperate further with it. Syrian cooperation in providing intelligence to the United States on terrorists is now seen as insufficient to persuade the United States to restrain Israel, if it ever wanted to do so in the first place.

Although it is clear that Syria is not a direct threat to the United States, Israel (along with Ghadry's reform party) wants to see Syria diminished and separated from Lebanon for its own regional interests. The United States does not object to this and would welcome the reining in of Hizbollah. Interestingly, Syria signed major oil and gas exploration contracts in early June 2003 with two US firms, to which the Bush administration did not object in spite of the fact that Syria remains on a State Department list of state sponsors of terrorism. It appeared that the Bush administration was applying a carrot-and-stick policy toward Syria, as one Western diplomat noted.[74] However, as noted above, Bush signed the Syria Accountability and Lebanese Sovereignty Restoration Act, which changes economic relations with Syria.

Lebanon

Lebanon's Maronite Christian population was always seen by Israel as offering fertile ground for initiating fragmentation within Arab states and legitimating Israel's sectarian-based state.[75] It should be noted for the record, however, that not all Maronites embraced Israel. Nonetheless, in the 1970s, Israel found Maronite Phalangist leader Bachir Gemayel and his Lebanese militia forces. The Israelis trained and supplied them. Israel invaded Lebanon in 1982, with an earlier incursion in 1978, with the dual purpose of destroying the Palestine Liberation Organization leadership and guerrillas located there and creating a client Christian-dominated state. In the end, Israel did not succeed. Nonetheless, it continued to occupy Southern Lebanon in conjunction with a pro-Israel, renegade, Christian-dominated Southern Lebanese Army until the Lebanese Shia Hizbollah movement forced them out in April 2000.

The scene shifted to the United States, where a number of prominent Lebanese right-wingers reside. With the encouragement of right-wing, pro-Israel leaders such as Daniel Pipes, the United States Committee for a Free Lebanon (USCFL) was formed. Pipes and other pro-Likudists serve on its board. Among its leaders are Ziad Abdelnour, a successful businessman; Walid Phares, an academic teaching in Florida and a member of the ultra–right-wing Guardians of the Cedars; and Habib Malik, the son of the late American University of Beirut professor Charles Malik, whose disdain for Muslims was palpable.[76] Incidentally, Ziad Abdelnour and Habib Malik are listed on Pipes's Middle East Forum Web site along with Pipes, Laurent Murawiec, William Kristol, Martin Kramer, Robert Satloff, and Joseph

Farah, among others, as expert speakers on Islam and the Middle East.[77] With the help of Pipes and his colleagues, the USCFL leaders presented testimony before congressional committees and the United Nations particularly aimed at removing the Syrian forces from Lebanon. Behind the scenes, they worked on ideas about how to create the nucleus of a Christian state in Lebanon.

The success of Hizbollah in ousting Israel and the renegade army from Southern Lebanon did not deter the efforts of the partnered pro-Likudists and Lebanese in the United States. In anticipation of the fall of Iraq and the changed dynamic in the region, the Hudson Institute, a well-known right-wing, Zionist think thank, whose leadership is tied into the neocons/Likudniks in the American government, held a conference on March 7, 2003. It was entitled "Discourses on Democracy—After Iraq: Can Lebanese Democracy Be Revived?" The main speakers were Dr. Jeanne J. Kirkpatrick, former US Ambassador to the UN under Reagan, and associated with AVOT; Dr. Walid Phares, also with AVOT and at that time senior fellow at the Foundation for the Defense of Democracies, another right-wing organization; Ziad K. Abdelnour, president of the USCFL; Dr. Jean Aziz, director of the Freedom and Human Rights Foundation in Beirut; Congressman Eliot L. Engel (D-NY); General Michel Aoun, who led a challenge to the Syrian presence in Lebanon after the 1982 war; and Frank J. Gaffney Jr., director of the Center for Security Policy, a neocon think tank, a supporter of the Coalition for Democracy in Iran (CDI), and also with AVOT.

The USCFL is joined by the Lebanese Canadian Coordinating Council (LCCC), which is also promoting General Michel Aoun. On both organizations' Web sites, they called on people to "Help Lebanon, support the Syria Accountability and Lebanese Sovereignty Restoration Act" by signing a provided petition.[78] Another Lebanese Christian right-wing organization, the Lebanese Information Center—not to be confused with any Lebanese government body—sent a position statement to the Hudson Institute conference entitled "Revival of the Lebanese Democracy." Its position is identical to those of the USCFL and LCCC. It states specifically that there should be a cessation of hostilities between Lebanon and Israel. An interesting part of their position calls for the "cancellation of all mass naturalizations issued during the last twelve years," an issue that has been under serious consideration in Lebanon. The aim is to reduce the number of Palestinians, in particular, holding citizenship in Lebanon, allegedly obtained through special connections.[79]

These partners—joined also by other Lebanese American organizations, including the Lebanese American Council for Democracy in Washington, DC—have now fixed on Aoun, a Christian, as a possible figurehead leader for right-wing forces in Lebanon.[80] It is not without coincidence that when Powell visited Lebanon in early May 2003, demonstrations were held by the Aounist group Free Patriotic Movement. They carried posters that called the Lebanese president Lahoud, the speaker Nabih Berri, and the prime minister Hariri "puppets," and they screamed "Syria Out Now." Their message was clear: "No to Syrian occupation." The occupation serves as the vehicle for promoting their right-wing agenda. Focus on the occupation is aimed at delegitimizing and further weakening Syria. The Lebanese government is well aware of the fact that the partnered Zionist and Lebanese right are promoting these efforts and that the post-Iraq period was seen by them as an opportunity to carry out the long-desired Christian-dominated Lebanon as an Israeli client state. As a result, the reshuffled Lebanese Cabinet, post-Iraq war, fielded pro-Syrian ministers. For President Lahoud, immediate removal of Syrian troops would weaken Lebanon and leave it prey to Israeli designs, in a real sense, occupation by proxy. Hence, Lebanese officials—against the wishes of a vociferous opposition—expressed continued support for Syria's presence in Lebanon because of the concern about Israeli designs. This does not mean that they support open-ended Syrian occupation. Almost all Lebanese want the Syrian occupation to end in the near future.

In May 2003, the Lebanese Army found and arrested alleged "terrorists" who were attempting to launch a rocket attack on the US Embassy in Beirut. The army announced that the arrests were made possible with the assistance of the Syrian Army. Both countries wanted to demonstrate to the United States their cooperation in the war on terrorism, with which Syria has been a prime collaborator. However, the Lebanese American Council for Democracy claimed, without evidence, that the foiled plot was really a plot by the Syrians.[81] This latter organization worked to orchestrate the passage of the Syria Accountability and Lebanese Sovereignty Restoration Act.[82]

During his visit to Lebanon in May 2003, Powell called upon Lebanon to disarm Hizbollah and place Lebanese troops on the border with Israel, in essence to be responsible for Israel's security. Lebanese officials indicated that they will not ask Hizbollah to stop its resistance posture against Israel's remaining occupation of Sheba'a farms. Moreover, Prime Minister Hariri expressed concern to Powell about the then newly released road map, especially since it did not call for the right of return of Palestinians; hence, their destabilizing presence in Lebanon would continue. Lebanon and Syria announced their continuing solidarity, a solidarity born of pragmatism. Their solidarity and "refusals" are challenged by the United States and Israel, and that message was made clear by the October 2003 Israeli bombing of a Syrian site. Iran can only do so much to buttress Syria and Lebanon. Jordan may become a factor if it appears that Sharon will move to create pressure conditions to push more Palestinians into Jordan, thus threatening its status as the Hashemite kingdom. Clearly, both Lebanon and Syria seek leverage in negotiations from each other and Iran as they face American-Israeli demands.

Saudi Arabia

The United States gained the Saudi oil concession in 1933 and established an American intelligence infrastructure there with a modest, oil-related military presence. As the Arab world decolonized after World War II, the spread of Arab nationalism gave rise to various opposition movements in the kingdom. Inspired by Nasser's secular nationalism in the 1960s, resistance took on the form of an armed struggle, led by the Arabian Peninsula People's Union operating out of North Yemen. It claimed to represent all classes of Saudi society. It succeeded in blowing up parts of the Tapline pipeline, the US military headquarters at a hotel in Riyadh, part of the biggest Saudi air base, and other sites. Nonetheless, Saudi and US security forces were able to put them down.[83] The Saudi monarchy served US interests, while Nasser's secular nationalism was perceived as threatening them.

The United States had never questioned the fanatic form of Islam on which the Saudi monarchy was based. It was in the interest of the United States to maintain the decadent regime's dependency for its security and hold on power. The Saudi regime itself could not stray far from its legitimizing base in Wahhabism, even though the bureaucratic needs of running a state required deviation. The Saudi government allowed the religious police and establishment sweeping powers to compensate for any deviations of the regime from Wahhabism. The United States utilized Saudi money and volunteers to train the Islamic mujahideen—composed of Muslims from Arab and non-Arab countries—to fight the USSR in Afghanistan in 1979. The United States saw Saudi Islamic fanaticism as a bulwark against the Soviet Union's effort to insinuate itself into the strategic Middle East. As such, the United States turned a blind eye to the realities of Saudi society. The Saudi regime maintained itself in two ways: (1) It funded opposing movements in the region, such as the Lebanese Phalangists and the Palestine Liberation Organization, and gave money to the Syrian regime as a way to avert possible Syrian disruptive activities in the kingdom; (2) It gave money to support numerous *madresahs* (Islamic schools). Many promoted Wahhabism and mujahideen opposed to evolving US domination in the region. With the fall of the USSR officially in 1991, the region came to focus on US policies. While the Saudi government continued to cooperate with the United States, there was growing discontent in the kingdom and elsewhere in the Arab/Muslim world. Saudi support for the first US Gulf war exacerbated regional perceptions of US-Saudi cooperation as unimpeded US imperialist/colonialist designs on the area, undergirded by a decadent regime. Both the United States and the Saudi government did not acknowledge the growing opposition to American dominance and Saudi compliance.

The horrendous attacks by al-Qaeda on US targets, causing deaths in the thousands, were wake-up calls regarding US policies in the area that went unheeded by the Bush administration. Fifteen of the nineteen who carried out the attacks were Saudi. Rather than recognize the attacks as evidence of vast discontent with US policies in the Arab/Muslim region, the Bush administration declared a "war on terrorism," not a reevaluation of American policy. Those events were grasped to rationalize the neocon policy of preventive war and expansion of American dominance. Saudi reluctance to support the US war on Iraq in March 2003, given its unpopularity in the country and in the region, soured US-Saudi relations, even though there was eventual cooperation. With increased terrorist incidents against Western targets in Saudi Arabia, the United States had to take notice that there are select layers of Saudi society and royalty that support those acts. The kingdom presents a dilemma for the US government in that the existing Saudi government is cooperating with the United States, yet it is not a popular government domestically. Alternative leadership that could straddle domestic concerns and US pressure is not in sight. Nonetheless, the neocons are determined to subdue Saudi Arabia and open it to Israeli interests.

Using the fact that fifteen of the 9/11 terrorists came from Saudi Arabia, the neocons/Likudniks undertook a campaign to threaten Saudi Arabia. Richard Perle invited Rand analyst Laurent Murawiec, a former associate of Lyndon LaRouche, to present a briefing on Saudi Arabia before the Defense Policy Board, then chaired by Perle, in July 2002. Murawiec said, "The United States should demand that Riyadh stop funding fundamentalist Islamic outlets around the world, stop all anti-U.S. and anti-Israeli statements in the country, and prosecute or isolate those involved in the terror chain, including in the Saudi intelligence services." He said further, "If the Saudis refused to comply, Saudi oil fields and overseas financial assets should be 'targeted.'"[84]

In spite of the fact that the United States will continue to be "dependent" on Saudi oil for the foreseeable future, Saudi Arabia understands that the United States is trying to reduce Saudi political weight in the Arab region. Withdrawing most of the US military from the kingdom sends both the messages "We don't need you anymore" and "Qatar serves our military needs better as we move our bases eastward," rather than the move being a concession to the fundamentalists. The June 2003 car bombings in a gated community of Riyadh, killing and injuring scores of foreigners including Americans, demonstrated the seething anti-Western, anti-US feelings within the kingdom. The Saudi government and Powell linked the bombing to the al-Qaeda network. Given that bin Laden is from Saudi Arabia, and given his hatred of the United States for its policies in the Arab region, it would not be surprising. Nonetheless, there are other Islamic-based groups opposed to the Saudi regime and its relations with the United States.[85] These groups have committed acts of terror against Saudi and American targets. "Saudi leaders are being forced to admit that they face a growing challenge to their authority, one they have sought to deny since a 1995 car bombing in Riyadh in which seven foreigners, five of them Americans training the National Guard, were killed."[86]

On the one hand, the United States seeks to weaken Saudi Arabia by calling on it to reinvent itself to American specifications, and on the other hand, the United States is faced with having to prop up the Saudi government and pressure it to take more forceful action against opposition Islamic groups. The United States is also seeking to weaken OPEC,[87] in which Saudi Arabia plays a big role. US policy has contradictory and conflicting demands regarding Saudi Arabia. In a sense, the existence of NCUSAR and the Saudi Institute in the United States reflects this contradiction. Noted expert on Saudi-US relations, Professor F. Gregory Gause, notes the following:

> Those who contend that the Saudi-US relationship can continue as it has are misreading political realities in both countries. However, those in the United States who argue that the Saudis should be viewed not as a strategic partner, but as an enemy, do not offer a practical alternative for American policy. Their course means giving up the influence that a decades-long relationship provides with a government that controls 25 percent of the world's known oil reserves and that can play a central role—positive or negative—in political and ideological trends in the Muslim world. They can offer no guarantee that any successor regime in Arabia would be more amenable to American interests.
>
> The American agenda with Saudi Arabia should concentrate on those foreign policy issues where Riyadh's cooperation is essential for American interests ... Washington should not involve itself overtly in sensitive domestic political issues in Saudi Arabia, like women's rights or the role of the religious establishment.
>
> A key realization ... is that any reform program with a "made-in-America" stamp on it will lead to a backlash within Saudi Arabia. Efforts to broaden political participation need to come from Saudi leaders, not from Washington, in order to be credible and acceptable in Saudi society. *Washington must also realize that elections in Saudi Arabia will yield representative bodies more anti-American than the current regime, and complicate American-Saudi relations.*[88]

Coincidentally, the United States finds itself in a similar contradiction with regard to Pakistan, but for different reasons.

Saudi Arabia has declined financially ever since the first Gulf War and is faced with a somewhat stagnant economy. The government does not know what to expect from the United States after the Iraq war, but the neocons are certainly pushing to reduce Saudi Arabia and eliminate its alleged support for various Islamic movements and resistance organizations in Palestine. As Alain Gresh notes, "Conspiracy theories flourish," regarding US intentions in Saudi Arabia, and adds that "research institutes close to the neo-conservatives propose" dividing the kingdom.[89]

The neocons/Likudniks have a further goal, and that is to

portray the conflict between the United States and various Arab/Muslim states not as political fallout from American foreign policy, but as a "clash of civilizations." Saudi Arabia, especially after the bombings, is defined by neocons/Likudniks as a prime example of Arab/Muslim "evilness." Media outlets are fed by various right-wing think tanks working together to spew out anti-Muslim, anti-Arab, and pro-Israel propaganda. Among these think tanks is the Jewish Institute for National Security Affairs (JINSA) in Washington, DC, which, in addition to briefings, arranges free trips to Israel for journalists and public officials, and the Washington Institute for Near East Policy, providing "expert" speakers on Middle East terrorism, who can be counted on for media bites calling Saudi Arabia a "state facilitator" of terrorism. The latter institute is a spin-off of AIPAC. Daniel Pipes's Middle East Forum and Steve Emerson's Investigative Project also promote negative Muslim images.[90]

Aware of these problems, Saudi Arabia has sought to reform its society. "We need change not because of American pressure, but to be stable and to be able to be economically competitive."[91] Two reform documents have emerged in the past months. The first is from Prince Abdullah, the de facto head of state, a proposal for a new "Arab Charter." It calls for internal reform and enhanced political participation in the Arab countries. The second is a petition signed by 104 Saudi intellectuals and presented to Abdullah on January 22, 2003, entitled "Vision for the Present and Future of the Homeland."[92] It calls for a Saudi constitution and bill of rights, "carefully couched in the language and values of Islam."[93] It also calls for local and regional elections, an independent judiciary, and a royal guarantee of freedom of expression, association, assembly, the right to vote and participate, women's human rights, and investigation of corruption. Educational reform is an important component of the reform measures.

Gause notes that three Saudi domestic areas require attention: economic, political, and social. He says that US help in the economic arena is the least sensitive issue. Trying to encourage democratic political reform to increase participation could backfire on the United States—as he notes above—since pushing for early elections "would likely produce representative assemblies that would push the regime in anti-liberal directions."[94] Gause cautions, "It is in the area of social issues that American pressure would be most counterproductive."[95] He advocates continuing a good relationship with Saudi Arabia, recognizing that it remains an important country for American interests. He believes a "normal" relationship with Saudi Arabia is in the best interests of the United States, and this means not forcing comprehensive political and social change. He notes, "What the United States should be seeking from Saudi Arabia is neither the 'special relationship' of the recent past nor the open enmity that some ideologues [in government] seek."[96] Gause summarizes as follows:

> We do not have to coddle the Saudis. But we do have to recognize their role in the region, in the larger Muslim world, and in the world oil market, and to realize that it is far better for American interests to have a Saudi government with which we can work."[97]

Can Saudi Arabia liberalize on its own and develop a popularly supported foundation to its government in place of the Wahhabi clerics and structure, thereby providing it with broader domestic legitimacy and political strength? Some reforms may happen, but the religious conservatives will fight them, especially since they will be interpreted in any case as a result of American pressure.[98] In the foreseeable future, will Saudi Arabia be able to free itself from American preponderance in its affairs? Saudi Arabia is not in a good position now politically, economically, and socially, and it could become more unstable in the future. This could have severe ramifications for the whole Gulf area by providing an opening for various sorts of opposition movements, predominantly with an Islamic stripe.

Iran

The May 2003 agreement between the US military in Iraq and the anti–Iranian regime terrorist organization, the Mujahideen Khalq, located in the border area with Iran—previously on the US list of terrorist organizations—raised speculation about a role the United States may have for the group in a future conflict with Iran. Originally, the United States allowed the organization to keep its weapons, but later it collected most of those weapons upon complaints from Iran. Nonetheless, it appears that Pentagon officials moved in May 2003 toward making the Mujahideen Khalq a US client.[99]

Chief editor William Kristol of the ultraconservative *Weekly Standard* sounded the word of the next target of the neocons/Likudniks. He said, "The next great battle—not we hope a military battle—will be for Iran. We are already in a death struggle with Iran over the future of Iraq."[100] "The Islamic government in Tehran ... primarily due to its backing of Lebanon's Hizbollah, has been a particular target for neo-conservatives like Kristol, *who sees it as the greatest long term threat to Israel.*"[101] Kristol had early on after 9/11 called on Washington to deliver an ultimatum to Syria and Iran to halt their support for Hizbollah, and if they did not comply, he urged the administration to take appropriate measures of retaliation.

Again the neocons/Likudniks are linking Iran to terrorism and claiming that Iran will send in agents to encourage the Shia in Iraq to resist the United States and develop an Islamic state there. Kristol and his colleagues claim that a democracy in Iraq will doom Iran, which is why Iran supports the Shia for an Islamic state. The Iranian reformers led by Khatami are for liberalization for Iran's own sake, but they are not against their government. They seek to liberalize their society but within an Islamic framework. The hard-liners led by Ayatollah Ali Khamenei, whose religious position carries more power and authority than that of the elected president, was critical of Khatami's "cooperation" with the United States regarding Afghanistan. When Bush listed Iran as part of the axis of evil, the hard-liners felt vindicated in their criticism of Khatami. However, with the US military success in Iraq, all regional countries were put on notice that it could happen to them if their behavior did not change. As a result, Khatami's approach of showing solidarity with Syria and Lebanon, while cautioning them not to take any action that could provide "reason" for the United States and/or Israel to attack them, enhanced his position regionally. Nonetheless, the struggle between the powerful hard-liners and the reformers continues in Iran. Khatami authorized talks between Iranian officials and the United States in Geneva—since broken off by the United States—in an effort to calm the US military appetite, goaded on by Israel and US neocons/Likudniks. Khatami, like the reformists of Syria and Saudi Arabia, calls for greater freedom and democracy in Iran, which he feels will strengthen Iran in any confrontation with the United States. However, in June 2003,

> Conservative Muslim clerics [the hard-liners led by Khamenei] overturned a bill that would have allowed voters a bigger voice in deciding who holds political power [in Iran]. The bill, which had easily passed Iran's reformist parliament, was rejected by

the Guardian Council, one of several appointive bodies domi-
nated by the clerics [who have the real power and authority in
Iran as compared to the elected officials such as President
Khatami and the parliament] who have blocked efforts to bring
Iran's government in line with the popular appetite for social
and economic change.[102]

This action on the part of the clerical hard-liners was followed by popular protests calling for the death of Supreme
Leader Ayatollah Ali Khamenei, an action usually punishable by
imprisonment.[103]

It appears the Bush administration has abandoned the reformists. By pressuring them, it is assumed the hard-liners will become more adamant, and this will allow the United States to
foment instability, leading to a regime change. Bush and Rumsfeld
continue to claim that Iran is developing nuclear weapons. They
have called for immediate inspection of Iranian facilities by the
International Atomic Energy Agency (IAEA). By the end of summer 2003, the United States and Israel had intensified their threats
against and warnings to Iran, which first appeared in the previously noted 1996 neocon strategy report prepared for Netanyahu.
Presently, there are European representatives in Iran negotiating
surprise site inspections to begin by the October 30, 2003, deadline set by the IAEA.[104] It appears that there is an agreement on
this. The question remains, is Iran developing nuclear warheads?
In an interview with an Iranian daily, Defense Minister Ali
Shamkhani spelled out Iran's defense doctrine, which seems to indicate that Iran is strengthening its defense posture. He noted:

> Deterrent defense means that in no way will Iran take an offen-
> sive measure. We are basing our strategy on sustaining the
> enemy's first strike. The first strike will not lead to surrender,
> but it should be a warning. Under these conditions, if there is the
> [capability] to sustain a first strike, the success of an Iranian sec-
> ondary resistance against the threats is our goal.
>
> However, defense from surprise threats means adopting a
> means of deterrence that causes the enemy to relinquish the
> threats. Under such circumstances, any country must take into
> consideration the risk it runs if it takes offensive measures
> against Iran.[105]

Was this all bluster, or has Iran been developing nuclear capabilities? Does the agreement for site inspections checkmate its alleged efforts?

The measured efforts of the reformists are dismissed by Iran-

ian monarchist exiles. They are pursuing the same route as the
Iraqi National Congress and the Lebanese right-wingers to re-
place the existing Iranian regime. In a May 9, 2003, *Financial
Times* article, Guy Dinmore and Najmeh Bozorgmehr note:

> United by their desire for regime change in Iran and encouraged
> by the overthrow of the Iraqi regime, exiled Iranian monarchists
> are developing an alliance in Washington with influential neo-
> conservatives as well as Pentagon officials and Israeli lobby
> groups.
>
> Analysts say supporters of Reza Pahlavi, the Virginia-based
> son of the last Shah of Iran, see a role model in Ahmad Chalabi,
> head of the Iraqi National Congress who is backed by powerful
> figures in the Pentagon as a future leader in Baghdad committed
> to a secular pro-western democracy.[106]

In a May 16, 2003, article by Marc Perelman, Perelman
quotes Pooya Dayanim, president of the Iranian-Jewish Public
Affairs Committee in Los Angeles as saying, "There is a pact
emerging between hawks in the administration, Jewish groups
and Iranian supporters of Reza Pahlavi ... to push for regime
change."[107] Perelman continues,

> Like Chalabi, Pahlavi has good relations with several Jewish
> groups. He has addressed the board of the hawkish Jewish Insti-
> tute for National Security Affairs and gave a public speech at the
> Simon Wiesenthal Center's Museum of Tolerance in Los Ange-
> les, and met with Jewish communal leaders.
>
> Pahlavi also has had quiet contacts with top Israeli officials.
> During the last two years ... he has met privately with Prime Min-
> ister Sharon and former prime minister Benjamin Netanyahu, as
> well as Israel's Iranian-born president, Moshe Katsav.
>
> For now, President Bush's official stance is to encourage the
> Iranian people to push the mullah regime aside themselves, but
> observers believe that the policy is not yet firm, and that has cre-
> ated an opportunity for activists.
>
> Meanwhile, in Congress, Democrat Rep. Tom Lantos of Cali-
> fornia is sponsoring a resolution supporting the people of Iran
> against the regime. Republican Senator Sam Brownback of
> Kansas has introduced an amendment....
>
> Supporters of the Shah's son, Pahlavi, have been supporting
> Brownback's amendment, known as the Iran Democracy Act. So
> has the main pro-Israel lobby, the American Israel Public Affairs
> Committee.[108]

On May 6, 2003, Senator Sam Brownback was the keynote
speaker at an AEI conference on Iran entitled, "The Future of
Iran: Mullahcracy, Democracy, and the War on Terrorism." The

conference was cosponsored by the Hudson Institute and the Foundation for the Defense of Democracy. Brownback elaborated on his efforts to promote "democracy" in Iran:

> I am planning to put forward in the Senate Foreign Authorization bill as it moves to the Senate floor this week [an amendment which] is titled The Iran Democracy Act. It states that it is US policy to support democracy in Iran.
>
> Further, the amendment would call for using the new Radio Farda to host programming from Iranian Americans who are talking with their families and loved ones inside Iran about the desire for an internationally monitored referendum vote on what form of government Iran should have.
>
> This amendment would also provide grants for private radio and TV stations in the U.S. that broadcast pro-democracy news and information into Iran.[109]

Brownback originally introduced the Iran Democracy Act some weeks earlier to the Senate Foreign Relations Committee. His colleagues on the committee—Joseph Biden, Chuck Hagel, Richard Lugar, John Rockefeller, and Paul Sarbanes—criticized it, and Brownback pulled the bill back and reintroduced it as an amendment to the Fiscal Year 2004 Foreign Relations Authorization Act. Supporters of the Iran Democracy Act include AIPAC, JINSA, and Iranian-exile monarchist groups, as well as the CDI.[110]

Michael Ledeen, a key supporter of Reza Pahlavi and regime change in Iran, is a fellow at the AEI. Speaking at the forum of JINSA on April 30, 2003, he declared, "The time for diplomacy is at an end; it is time for a free Iran, free Syria and free Lebanon."[111] Ledeen founded CDI with Michael Amitay, a former director of AIPAC; James Woolsey, former CIA head and AVOT member; and Georgetown adjunct professor Sohrab "Rob" Sobhani. Among other "supporters" of the coalition are Frank Gaffney, president of the Center for Security Policy and a former associate of Richard Perle; Congressman Jack Kemp; Dr. Joshua Muravchik, resident scholar at the AEI and adjunct scholar at the Washington Institute for Near East Policy (WINEP); R. Bruce McColm, director of the Institute for Democratic Strategies, former director of the International Republican Institute, and former director of Freedom House; and Dr. Raymond Tanter, adjunct scholar at WINEP and a former associate of Richard Perle. The coalition is an action group focusing on facilitating regime change in Iran.

According to Brown University scholar William O. Beeman,

the person to watch is Rob Sobhani, an American of Iranian ethnic heritage.[112] He became an energy policy specialist and served as a consultant for construction of an oil and gas pipeline across Afghanistan. The topic of his 1987 doctorate was Iranian-Israeli relations from 1948–88. He is apparently well connected in Washington. The speculation is that Sobhani is being groomed to be the secular head of an Iranian government while Reza Pahlavi—with whom he has had a longtime friendship—would be a constitutional monarch. Two facts about Sobhani: (1) he has appeared regularly on major television news programs such as the *Jim Lehrer News Hour*; and (2) he, Pahlavi, and Ledeen are connected to Benador Associates, a media agency that manages their media access and placement. This same agency represents Richard Perle, James Woolsey, Charles Krauthammer, Israeli Martin Kramer, and other conservatives who serve in the Bush administration.[113] "Pictures of Eleana Benador and Reza Pahlavi with Israeli supporter and AIPAC member Bob Guzzardi, and Middle East Forum head Daniel Pipes appear on Bob Guzzardi's website, www.bobguzzardi.com."[114]

Ledeen and Sobhani feel strongly that the United States could facilitate an internal coup in Iran, after which the US-groomed leaders could take over. Should such an attempt be made, the consequences would be difficult to forecast, but clearly, the multiethnic and multisectarian population of Iran could present problems. An Iranian reformer academic observed:

> If anybody took a look at Iranian history, the likelihood of fomenting a mass popular uprising in the midst of foreign interference is naïve ... Right now it would result in the opposite, emboldening a sense of collective resentment against a superior outside power ... You would have strong resentments and a closing together of reformers and conservatives.[115]

Cameron Kamran, an Iranian American commentator on the Middle East, cautions the Bush administration against regime change in Iran, especially one involving Reza Pahlavi. Kamran argues that the United States would be repeating mistakes of the past. "Many Iranians still bitterly remember the CIA coup in 1953 that replaced the elected government of Mohammed Mossadeq with the dictatorship of Shah Mohammed Reza Pahlavi. The Shah never recovered from the perception among Iranians that his power and legitimacy were manufactured and imported from abroad, and he was eventually overthrown."[116]

The direction that Iraqi and other local Shia take could figure into the Iranian equation. The unstable situation in Afghanistan could become a factor. Repercussions could possibly also be felt in Pakistan, ticking off Indian mobilization. Whether regional consequences from an attempted regime change in Iran produce new and pragmatic regional alliances to counter American strategic goals in the Middle East and Central Asia remains to be seen. In the meantime, an Israeli threat to execute a set of pre-emptive air strikes on Iran's nuclear facilities has appeared in the news media, but has been called a bluff. The appearance of the story was said to put Iran on notice and keep Iran's nuclear sites on the international agenda.[117] Nonetheless, Iran remains high on Israel's list of regional concerns.

Conclusion

First, the United States expects to create an arc of control around the Middle East and Central Asia to provide itself with great leverage in the region and world. Israel and India are key actors in this effort. The conquest of Iraq is supposed to make this possible and also to alter the behavior of regional states hostile to the United States and Israel, as well as India. Such a structure of control and occupation against the will of the people has already generated resistance in violent form. Still regional reformers, secular and Islamic, struggle to set a course for their countries that will checkmate American intentions, and hopefully without recourse to violence. Second, the United States expects to establish its strategic partner Israel as the dominant regional force, to force Arab and Muslim states to recognize and normalize political and economic relations with it, and all this without real concessions to Palestinian national claims. To paraphrase political analyst Professor Zia Mian on US intentions in the world from a talk he presented in Philadelphia on May 19, 2003: The US reserves the right to expand its sovereignty beyond its borders, and to limit or deny the sovereignty of states that fail to conform to its specifications.

It should be clear that the aggressive, unilateral US policies and actions in the Middle East and Central Asia, a predominantly Arab and Muslim area, ipso facto draw their support from the American public by constantly generating fear of Arabs and Muslims as whole communities. The political actors in the United States interested in emasculating the region and its people employ a whole range of created institutions, client exiles, the Zionist lobby, and the lobby's connections with the neocons in the Pentagon. Christian Evangelicals offer bedrock support for those actors. Condemnation of anti-Arab, anti-Muslim messages and messages supporting the protection of Arab and Muslim civil rights expressed by President Bush, Attorney General John Ashcroft, and members of Congress belie the reality of the official and "unofficial" forces arrayed against Arab and Muslim communities both here and abroad.

Epilogue

Several developments have come to light since completing this chapter, which further impact Arabs and Muslims negatively.

First, the pro-Likudists in the United States launched a campaign to deny Title VI (of the Higher Education Act) funding for Middle East Studies (and other area studies) that tend, in their view, to present one-sided critical analyses of American foreign policy and, by extension, of Israel's. Testifying before the Subcommittee on Select Education and the Workforce in the US House of Representatives on June 19, 2003, Stanley Kurtz of the Hoover Institute of Stanford University put forth the case. He particularly attacked what he alleged was the ruling intellectual paradigm in area studies—especially, he notes, in Middle Eastern Studies—i.e., postcolonial theory, which he attributed to the late Professor Edward Said of Columbia University. He took particular aim at Said's major publication, *Orientalism*. He claims that he and others are not against airing these views, but that they are not balanced by opposing views. His ideological colleague, Daniel Pipes, not only supported Kurtz's testimony, but also was instrumental in pushing for the campaign. Neither Kurtz nor Pipes have a tradition or reputation for allowing other points of view in their public forums and on Web sites. It is not balance they seek. Rather their efforts are aimed at having a chilling effect on valid assessment of US and Israeli policies, as well as de facto promoting negative images of Arabs and Muslims.

Second, President Bush betrayed his declared respect for Arabs and Muslims when he gave in to the pro-Likudists in his administration, supported by lobbyists on behalf of Israel, by appointing Daniel Pipes to the US Institute of Peace board, albeit for a shorter period than a congressional appointment would have allowed, while Congress was out of session. Pipes's candidacy had been severely criticized by US senators, including Senator Kennedy, as well as the various Arab American and Muslim American organizations. Given his history of racist remarks and unsubstantiated claims about Arab/Muslim culture and Muslims' alleged penchant for terrorism, his appointment by Bush sent a clear message to Arabs and Muslims everywhere.

Third, a Saudi Arabia Accountability Act was introduced in the US Senate on November 18, 2003, by known pro-Israeli senators, and supported by some of the same individuals and organizations that pushed through the Syria Accountability Act. Both bills allege that the target states support terrorism as one of the main reasons for the bills. Although each bill allows the president certain flexibility in applying the sanctions, their existence inspires fear and hatred of Arabs and Muslims. The original foundation for these bills comes not from the allegations of terrorism, but from a rethinking of American foreign policy strategy that began before and after the first Gulf War when it was clear that the United States would be the uncontested unipolar superpower in the world. The reports and documents produced by the pro-Likud neocons under the tutelage of then-Secretary of Defense Dick Cheney focused on reordering and re-mapping the world, beginning with the Middle East to suit American and Israeli interests. Their strategy called for regime change, beginning with Iraq, and then going on to Syria, Iran, and Saudi Arabia, among others. Preventive war, isolating the states, and installing compliant regimes or forcing existing regimes to be compliant with American/Israeli interests were the means. The use of legislative bills to pressure the states and weaken them internally intended to complement these efforts. The new book by Richard Perle and David Frum, *An End to Evil: How to Win the War on Terror,* reiterates and confirms in cold-blooded terms the neocon 1990s strategy and goals for reordering the world.

Fourth, the visual image of Saddam Hussein in American custody was purposely humiliating for Arabs and Muslims. This was not because Arabs admired or supported Hussein, but because he was used as a symbol to impress on the Arab/Muslim public America's might and superiority.

Fifth, the continuing chaos in Iraq, and the US media portrayal of Iraqi resistance as exclusively terrorism, generates and broadens fear and hatred of Arabs and Muslims in the West. The climbing death toll of US soldiers and high casualty figures may ultimately affect Bush's popularity, but they also reinforce frightening images of Arabs and Muslims. The conflict between the US-led coalition authority and Ayatollah Sistani regarding elections for an interim government demonstrates further that the United States is interested only in an Iraqi government that will be subservient to US interests and will invite US troops to remain in Iraq for an indefinite period. The Bush administration wants to create the facade that the United States will be out of Iraq by summer 2004, in time to claim before the presidential elections that it has brought democracy to Iraq and has completed its mission. Now seeking a UN fig leaf, the Bush administration aims to try to use the "legitimacy" of that institution to block Sistani's insistence on direct elections, not US handpicked caucuses.

Sixth, and finally, the introduction of Israeli military strategy and products and economic corporate penetration through proxies do not sit well with the highly Arab nationalist Iraqis. The latter factors, combined with the known commitment of a number of Iraqi Governing Council members to normalize relations with Israel without extracting a viable Israeli commitment to Palestinian legal, national, and individual rights, intensify Iraqi anger and resistance. To counter Iraqi and Palestinian resistance to American and Israeli occupation and to the US/Israeli partnership in the Middle East, a massive Israeli public relations campaign to portray Arabs as bloodthirsty and anti-Semitic has been joined with the attack on Title VI–funded Middle East Studies.

In summary, the linkage of domestic and international events sustains the American public's fear of Arabs and Muslims. This contributes to public support for the violations of the civil and human rights of Arabs and Muslims, as well as the abridgment of those same civil rights for all Americans.

Elaine C. Hagopian
February 5, 2004

NOTES

Chapter 1. Race and Civil Rights Pre-September 11, 2001: The Targeting of Arabs and Muslims. By Susan M. Akram and Kevin R. Johnson.

1. See Kevin R. Johnson, "The Antiterrorism Act, the Immigration Reform Act, and Ideological Regulation in the Immigration Laws: Important Lessons for Citizens and Noncitizens," *St Mary's Law Journal* 28 (1997): 841–69. See generally James Morton Smith, *Freedom's Fetters: The Alien and Sedition Laws and American Civil Liberties* (Ithaca, NY: Cornell University Press, 1956); see also James X. Dempsey and David Cole, *Terrorism and the Constitution: Sacrificing Civil Liberties in the Name of National Security* (Los Angeles: First Amendment Foundation, 1999).

2. Richard Delgado and Jean Stefancic, "Images of the Outsider in American Law and Culture: Can Free Expression Remedy Systemic Social Ills?" *Cornell Law Review* 77, no. 6 (1992): 1258; Cynthia Kwei Yung Lee, "Race and Self-Defense: Toward a Normative Conception of Reasonableness," *Minnesota Law Review* 81 (1996): 402–52; Margaret M. Russell, "Race and the Dominant Gaze: Narratives of Law and Inequality in Popular Film," *Legal Studies Forum* 15 (1991): 243; see also Jody Armour,

"Stereotypes and Prejudice: Helping Legal Decisionmakers Break the Prejudice Habit," *California Law Review* 83, no. 3 (May 1995): 733.

3. Natsu Taylor Saito, "Symbolism Under Siege: Japanese American Redress and the 'Racing' of Arab Americans as 'Terrorists,'" *Asian Law Journal* 8, no. 1 (May 2001): 11–26.

4. See Susan M. Akram, "Scheherezade Meets Kafka: Two Dozen Sordid Tales of Ideological Exclusion," *Georgetown Immigration Law Journal* 14 (1999): 54.

5. Edward W. Said, "A Devil Theory of Islam," *The Nation*, August 12, 1996, 28; see also Ahmed Yousef and Caroline F. Keeble, *The Agent: The Truth Behind the Anti-Muslim Campaign in America* (UASR Publishing Group, 1999).

6. See Nabeel Abraham, "Anti-Arab Racism and Violence in the United States," in *The Development of Arab-American Identity*, ed. Ernest McCarus (Ann Arbor, MI: University of Michigan Press, 1994); Jack G. Shaheen, *Reel Bad Arabs: How Hollywood Vilifies a People* (New York: Olive Branch Press, 2001); see also the archived reports of the American-Arab Anti-Discrimination Committee on anti-Arab hate crimes, http://www.adc.org.

7. See Nabeel Abraham, "The Gulf Crisis and Anti-Arab Racism in America," in *Collateral Damage: The New World Order at Home and Abroad*, ed. Cynthia Peters (Boston: South End Press, 1991), 255–78; see also Michael J. Whidden, "Unequal Justice: Arabs in America and United States Antiterrorism Legislation," *Fordham Law Review* 69, no. 6 (May 2001): 2825, and Suad Joseph, "Against the Grain of the Nation—The Arab," in *Arabs in America: Building a New Future*, ed. Michael W. Suleiman (Philadelphia: Temple University Press, 1999).

8. Alfred M. Lilienthal, "The Changing Role of B'nai B'rith's Anti-Defamation League," *Washington Report on Middle East Affairs*, June 1993, 18; Anti-Defamation League of B'nai B'rith, *Pro-Arab Propaganda in America: Vehicles and Voices: A Handbook* (New York: Anti-Defamation League of B'nai B'rith, 1983). The Middle East Studies Association (MESA) has passed two resolutions criticizing the

ADL for defaming students, teachers, and researchers as "pro-Arab propagandists." See Betsy Barlow, "Middle East Studies Association Condemns ADL Philadelphia Office," *Washington Report*, January–February 1997, 72; Phebe Marr, "MESA Condemns Blacklisting," *Washington Report*, December 17, 1984, 8.

9. See Ian F. Haney López, "Institutional Racism: Judicial Conduct and a New Theory of Racial Discrimination," *Yale Law Journal* 109, no. 8 (June 2000); see also Akram, "Scheherezade Meets Kafka," which traces the contemporary targeting of Arabs and Muslims in immigration enforcement (see n. 4).

10. For analysis of the balancing of necessary security measures and democratic values in response to terrorism, see Symposium, "Law and the War on Terrorism," *Harvard Journal of Law and Public Policy* 25 (Spring 2002); "Responding to Terrorism: Crime, Punishment, and War," *Harvard Law Review* 115 (2002): 1217–38; Peter Margulies, "Uncertain Arrivals: Immigration, Terror, and Democracy after September 11," *Utah Law Review* (2002): 481.

11. Ian F. Haney López, "The Social Construction of Race: Some Observations on Illusion, Fabrication, and Choice," *Harvard Civil Rights-Civil Liberties Law Review* 29, no. 1 (Winter 1994).

12. Michael Omi and Howard Winant, *Racial Formation in the United States: From the 1960s to the 1980s* (New York: Routledge and Kegan Paul, 1986).

13. Ibid., 68–69.

14. See Saito, "Symbolism Under Siege" (see n. 3).

15. *St. Francis Coll. v. Al-Khazraji*, 481 US 604, 610n4 (1987).

16. See Abraham, "Anti-Arab Racism and Violence" (see n. 6).

17. López, "Institutional Racism" (see n. 9); M. Cherif Bassiouni, introduction to *The Civil Rights of Arab-Americans*, ed. M. Cherif Bassiouni (Washington, DC: Association of Arab-American University Graduates, 1974). For analysis of the negative impacts of Operation Boulder (code name for Nixon's 1972 policy) on the civil rights of Arab Americans, see Abdeen M. Jabara, "Operation Arab:

The Nixon Administration's Measures in the United States After Munich," in Bassiouni, *Civil Rights of Arab-Americans,* 1–14.

18. Bruce Hoffman, *Terrorism in the United States and the Potential Threat to Nuclear Facilities* (Santa Monica, CA: Rand Corporation, 1986), 11, 15.

19. Ibid., 16.

20. Ibid., 12–15.

21. "Domestic Terrorism in the 1980s," *FBI Law Enforcement Bulletin,* October 1987, 13.

22. Chris Lutz, ed., *They Don't All Wear Sheets: A Chronology of Racist and Far Right Violence, 1980–1986* (Atlanta, GA: Center for Democratic Renewal, 1987); Anti-Defamation League of B'nai B'rith, *Extremism on the Right: A Handbook* (New York: Anti-Defamation League of B'nai B'rith, 1988).

23. Abraham, "Anti-Arab Racism and Violence," 157 (see n. 6).

24. Lilienthal, 18 (see n. 8).

25. Anti-Defamation League, *Pro-Arab Propaganda* (see n. 8).

26. Lilienthal, 18 (see n. 8).

27. Amy Kaufman Goott and Steven J. Rosen, *The Campaign to Discredit Israel* (Washington, DC: American Israel Public Affairs Committee, 1983); Jonathan S. Kessler and Jeff Schwaber, *The AIPAC College Guide: Exposing the Anti-Israel Campaign on Campus* (Washington, DC: American Israel Public Affairs Committee, 1984).

28. Paul Findley, *They Dare to Speak Out: People and Institutions Confront Israel's Lobby* (Westport, CT: Lawrence Hill, 1985); Naseer Aruri, "The Middle East on the U.S. Campus," *The Link* 18, no. 2 (May–June 1985); Edward Tivnan, *The Lobby: Jewish Political Power and American Foreign Policy* (New York: Simon and Schuster, 1987); Rachelle Marshall, "PACmen," *The Nation,* June 6, 1987; Rachelle Marshall, "The Decline of B'nai B'rith: From Protector to Persecutor," *Washington Report on Middle East Affairs,* April 1989, 19.

29. Delinda C. Hanley, "ADL and AJC Demand Muslim Pan-

elists Be Excluded," *Washington Report on Middle East Affairs,* January–February 2002, 83.

30. Ibid.

31. Ibid.

32. Rick Paddock, "A Spy for the Anti-Defamation League: Did a Liberal Civil Rights Group Get Caught with Its Binoculars Up?" *Cal. J.,* June 1, 1993, 2.

33. Abdeen Jabara, "The Anti-Defamation League: Civil Rights and Wrongs," *Covert Action,* no. 45 (Summer 1993): 28–29; see also San Francisco District Attorney's Office, "Organizational Victims of ADL Espionage" (1993), reprinted in *ADC Times,* May–June 1993, 21 (on file with Susan M. Akram).

34. Jabara, "The Anti-Defamation League," 30–31 (see n. 33).

35. Ibid., 31.

36. Ibid.; Jim McGee, "Jewish Group's Tactics Investigated," *Washington Post,* October 19, 1993.

37. Dennis Opatrny and Scott Winokur, "Israeli Man Held by Israel Linked to Spy Case," *San Francisco Examiner,* February 12, 1993; Jabara, "The Anti-Defamation League," 29 (see n. 33).

38. Bob Egelko, "Jewish Defense Group Settles S.F. Spying Suit," *San Francisco Chronicle,* February 23, 2002; Dennis King and Chip Berlet, "ADLgate," *Tikkun* 8 (July–August 1993): 31; Dennis Opatrny and Scott Winokur, "Police Said to Help Spy on Political Groups," *San Francisco Examiner,* March 9, 1993.

39. Final Settlement, *American-Arab Anti-Discrimination Committee v. Anti-Defamation League,* Civil Action No. 93-6358 RAP (C.D. Cal. 1999).

40. See McGee, n. 36.

41. Jabara, "The Anti-Defamation League," 37 (see n. 33).

42. Michael Gillespie, "Los Angeles Court Hands Down Final Judgment in Anti-Defamation League Illegal Surveillance Case," *Washington Report on Middle East Affairs,* December 1999, 43.

43. An ADL advertisement in the *New York Times,* May 11, 1997, entitled "We Hate Keeping Files on Hate," claims:

"For 83 years, ADL has considered it our duty to collect and process information on racists, anti-Semites and extremists by monitoring and analyzing publications of all kinds and to share our findings to help focus American public opinion on the dangers of bigotry and hatred" (copy on file with Susan M. Akram).

44. Abraham, "Anti-Arab Racism and Violence," 187 (see n. 6).

45. Ibid.

46. Shaheen, *Reel Bad Arabs,* 9 (see n. 6).

47. Ibid., 11.

48. Ibid., 15.

49. Ibid., 31–33.

50. Abraham, "Anti-Arab Racism and Violence," 188–92 (see n. 6).

51. Michael Guido, "Let's Talk About City Parks and the Arab Problem," cited in Abraham, "Anti-Arab Racism and Violence," 191 (see n. 6).

52. Governor Milliken quoted in Abraham, "Anti-Arab Racism and Violence," 196 (see n. 6).

53. *New York Times,* "Mondale Camp Returns Funds to U.S. Arabs," August 25, 1984.

54. Stephen Franklin, "Arab-Americans Fall Victim to Mideast: Kuwaiti Ship Flagging Sparks Fears," *Chicago Tribune,* July 12, 1987.

55. Editorial, "The Untouchables," *The Nation,* March 21, 1987.

56. Dean E. Murphy, "Mrs. Clinton Says She Will Return Money Raised by a Muslim Group," *New York Times,* October 26, 2000.

57. Neil MacFarquhar, "Saudi Sheik Regrets Giuliani Turning Down His Donation," *New York Times,* October 13, 2001.

58. Laurie Goodstein and Tamar Lewin, "Victims of Mistaken Identity, Sikhs Pay a Price for Turbans," *New York Times,* September 19, 2001; Tamar Lewin and Gustav Niebuhr, "Attacks and Harassment Continue on Middle Eastern People and Mosques," *New York Times,* September 18, 2001.

59. Lynne Duke, "Islam Is Growing in U.S. Despite an Uneasy Image," *Washington Post,* October 24, 1993.

60. Michael W. Suleiman, "The Arab Immigrant Experience," introduction to *Arabs in America,* 18 (see n. 7).

61. Editorial, "Don't Judge Islam by Verdicts," *Orlando Sentinel,* March 8, 1994.

62. Bernard Weinraub, "39 American Hostages Free After 17 Days," *New York Times,* July 1, 1985.

63. House Committee on the Judiciary, Subcommittee on Criminal Justice, *Ethnically motivated violence against Arab-Americans : Hearing before the Subcommittee on Criminal Justice of the Committee on the Judiciary,* 99th Cong., 1986, 57, 64.

64. *New York Times,* "Bomb Kills Leader of U.S. Arab Group," October 12, 1985.

65. Abraham, "Anti-Arab Racism and Violence," 171 (see n. 6).

66. Ibid., 172.

67. American-Arab Anti-Discrimination Committee, *1991 Report on Anti-Arab Hate Crimes: Political and Hate Violence Against Arab Americans* (Washington, DC: American-Arab Anti-Discrimination Committee Research Institute, 1992), 6.

68. Abraham, "Anti-Arab Racism and Violence," 204 (see n. 6).

69. Jim McGee, "Ex-FBI Officials Criticize Tactics on Terrorism," *Washington Post,* November 28, 2001.

70. Bassiouni, *Civil Rights of Arab-Americans* (see n. 17).

71. Elaine Hagopian, "Minority Rights in a Nation-State: The Nixon Administration's Campaign against Arab-Americans," *Journal of Palestine Studies* 5, nos. 1 and 2 (Autumn–Winter, 1975–76): 97–114.

72. Ibid., 102.

73. Noam Chomsky, *Pirates & Emperors: International Terrorism in the Real World* (Montreal: Black Rose Books, 1987), 117–30.

74. Ibid., 123.

75. Ibid., 118.

76. Emily Sachar, "FBI Grills NY Arab-Americans," *Newsday*, January 29, 1991.

77. Lisa Belkin, "For Many Arab-Americans, FBI Scrutiny Renews Fears," *New York Times*, January 12, 1991.

78. On March 1, 2003, the INS was reorganized into the US Immigration and Customs Enforcement (ICE) and the US Citizenship and and Immigration Services (CIS) agencies. For ease of reference this article will continue to refer to "INS" or "immigration services," because all events referred to occurred prior to the agency reorganization.

79. David Cole, "Guilt by Association: It's Alive and Well at INS," *The Nation*, February 15, 1993, 198–99.

80. *United States v. Palestine Liberation Organization*, 695 F. Supp. 1456 (S.D.N.Y. 1988), rejecting the US government's efforts to close the PLO office used in connection with its role as Permanent Observer to the United Nations; see also *Palestine Information Office v. Shultz*, 853 F.2nd 932 (D.C. Cir. 1988), and *Mendelsohn v. Meese*, 695 F. Supp. 1474 (S.D.N.Y. 1988), challenging the constitutionality of law requiring closure of the Palestine Information Office in Washington, DC.

81. House Committee on the Judiciary, Subcommittee on Administrative Law and Governmental Relations, *Legislation to Implement the Recommendations of the Commission on Wartime Relocation and Internment of Civilians: Hearing on HR 442 Before the Subcommittee on Administrative Law and Governmental Relations*, 100th Cong., 1987, 67 (submission of Investigations Division of the Immigration and Naturalization Service, emphasis added).

82. Memorandum from Investigations Division, Immigration and Naturalization Service, Alien Border Control (ABC) Group IV–Contingency Plans 16 (November 18, 1986), with attachments including INS, "Alien Terrorists and Undesirables: A Contingency Plan" (1986) (on file with Susan Akram).

83. John A. Scanlan, "American-Arab—Getting the Balance Wrong—Again!" *Administrative Law Review* 52, no. 1 (Winter 2000): 363–68.

84. Sharon LaFraniere and George Lardner, "U.S. Set to Photograph, Fingerprint all New Iraqi and Kuwaiti Visitors," *Washington Post,* January 11, 1991.

85. Immigration and Nationality Act (INA) Sec. 212(a) (27)–(29), 8 U.S.C. Sec. 1182(a) (27)–(29) (1952) (repealed 1990).

86. 22 U.S.C. Sec. 2691 (1988) (denying waiver to noncitizens connected with the Palestine Liberation Organization as well as representatives of organizations advocating totalitarian government).

87. The "PLO exception" is codified as INA Sec. 212(a), 8 U.S.C. Sec. 1182(a).

88. For the Supreme Court decision in the lengthy litigation, see *Reno v. American-Arab Anti-Discrimination Committee,* 525 US 471 (1999), citing other published federal court decisions in the case. For an example of the commentators on the implications of the case, see Hiroshi Motomura, "Judicial Review in Immigration Cases after AADC: Lessons from Civil Procedure," *Georgetown Immigration Law Journal* 14 (2000).

89. Dempsey and Cole, *Terrorism and the Constitution,* 33–34, discussing LA Eight case (see n. 1).

90. Senate Select Committee on Intelligence, *Nomination of William H. Webster: Hearings before the Select Committee on Intelligence of the United States Senate,* 100th Cong., 1st sess., 1987, 95 (emphasis added).

91. *American-Arab Anti-Discrimination Committee v. Reno,* 119 F. 3rd 1367, 1370 (9th Cir. 1997).

92. *American-Arab Anti-Discrimination Committee v. Meese,* 714 F. Supp. 1060 (C.D. Cal. 1989).

93. INA Sec. 212(a) (3) (B) (iii), 8 U.S.C. Sec. 1182(a) (3) (B) (iii) (emphasis added). After September 11, Congress further expanded the definition of "terrorist activity."

94. Gerald L. Neuman, "Terrorism, Selective Deportation and the First Amendment after *Reno v. AADC,*" *Georgetown Immigration Law Journal* 14 (2000): 322–27.

95. *Reno v. American-Arab Anti-Discrimination Committee,* 525 US 471–72 (1999). In reaching that conclusion, the Court relied on INA Sec. 242(g), 8 U.S.C. Sec. 1252(g):

"Except as provided in this section and notwithstanding any other provision of law, no court shall have jurisdiction to hear any cause or claim by or on behalf of any alien arising from the decision or action by the Attorney General to commence proceedings, adjudicate cases, or execute removal orders against any alien under this Act."

96. Stephen H. Legomsky, *Immigration and Refugee Law and Policy*, 3rd ed. (New York: Foundation Press, 2002), 86.

97. See Akram, "Scheherezade Meets Kafka," 52n4 (see n. 4).

98. *Rafeedie v. INS*, 688 F. Supp. 729 (D.D.C. 1988), *aff'd in part, rev'd in part, remanded*, 880 F.2nd 506 (D.C. Cir. 1989).

99. *Rafeedie v. INS*, 688 F. Supp., 734–35.

100. *Rafeedie v. INS*, 880 F.2nd, 516.

101. Antiterrorism and Effective Death Penalty Act of 1996, Public Law 104-132, *U.S. Statutes at Large* 110 (1996): 1213; see Whidden, "Unequal Justice," 2841–83, for summary of the genesis of AEDPA and analysis of its impact on Arabs and Muslims (see n. 7).

102. Illegal Immigration Reform and Immigrant Responsibility Act of 1996, Public Law 104-208, *U.S. Statutes at Large* 110 (1996): 3009.

103. Akram, "Scheherezade Meets Kafka," 52, 52n4, listing post-1996 secret evidence cases (see n. 4).

104. See *National Security Considerations Involved in Asylum Applications: Hearings Before the Senate Judiciary Committee on Technology, Terrorism, and Government Information*, 105th Cong., 1998, FDCH Political Transcripts, 5–14 (testimony of INS General Counsel Paul Virtue).

105. AEDPA at Sec. 303 (f) (2) (B) and at Sec. 504 (e) (3) (C).

106. For a general summary of the Iraqi Seven cases by the lead counsel, see Niels W. Frenzen, "National Security and Procedural Fairness: Secret Evidence and the Immigration Laws," *Interpreter Releases* 76 (1999): 1681n31.

107. *National Security Considerations Involved in Asylum Applications: Hearings Before the Senate Judiciary Committee on Technology, Terrorism, and Government Information*, 105th Cong., 1998, FDCH Political Transcripts, 23–27 (statement

of R. James Woolsey).

108. ACLU of Florida, "Palestinian Professor Challenges His Detention by INS as Illegal," May 14, 2002, http://www.aclufl.org/alnajjarhabeasrelease051402.html.

109. *In re Anwar Haddam,* 2000 BIA LEXIS 20, 1 (BIA December 1, 2000).

110. *Al-Najjar v. Reno,* 97 F. Supp. 2nd 1329, 1333–34 (S.D. Fla. 2000).

111. *Al-Najjar v. Ashcroft,* 257 F.3rd 1330, 1336–68 (2001) (stating that the attorney general had the authority to detain al-Najjar indefinitely).

112. *Al-Najjar v. Ashcroft,* 257 F.3rd 1262, 1274 (11th Cir. 2001).

113. For discussion of the facts and legal decisions in the Haddam case, see *In re Haddam,* No. A22-751-813 (BIA September 10, 1998), *aff'd; In re Anwar Haddam,* 2000 BIA LEXIS 20, 1 (BIA December 1, 2000); Akram, "Scheherezade Meets Kafka," 79–81, analyzing the INS proceedings against Haddam (see n. 4).

114. *Matter of Nasser Ahmed,* No. A90-674-238 (Immigration Court, June 24, 1999) (decision following remand); see also Dempsey and Cole, *Terrorism and the Constitution,* 128–31, discussing case (see n. 1).

115. *United States v. Rahman,* 189 F.3rd 88, 103 (2nd Cir. 1999).

116. Philip G. Schrag, *A Well-Founded Fear: The Congressional Battle to Save Political Asylum in America* (New York: Routledge, 2000), 42–44, 134, 137, 148, 162, 164, 217.

117. "How Did He Get Here?" *60 Minutes,* CBS, March 14, 1993.

118. Thomas Alexander Aleinikoff, David A. Martin, and Hiroshi Motomura, *Immigration and Citizenship: Process and Policy,* 4th ed. (St. Paul, MN: West Group, 1998), 863–71, 1028–29 (discussing summary exclusion provisions of 1996 immigration reforms).

Chapter 2. Profiled: Arabs, Muslims, and the Post–9/11 Hunt for the "Enemy Within." By Nancy Murray.

1.   "Excerpts from Attorney General's Testimony Before Sen-

ate Judiciary Committee," *New York Times*, December 7, 2001.

2.   Supreme Court rulings affirming that noncitizens have rights under the Constitution go back to the 1896 case of *Wong Wing v. US*. Recent Supreme Court rulings affirming this interpretation include the 1976 decision in *Mathews v. Diaz* (426 US 67) and the 2001 ruling in *Zadvydas v. Davis* (121 S. Ct. 2491), which cites a 1953 ruling that "aliens who have once passed through our gates, even illegally, may be expelled only after proceedings conforming to traditional standards of fairness encompassed in due process of law."

3.   An estimated 80 percent opposed racial profiling before the attacks of 9/11, and 70 percent believed some form of profiling was necessary after the attacks, according to Nicole Davis in "The Slippery Slope of Racial Profiling," *Color-Lines*, December 2001.

4.   See the comprehensive *Report on Hate Crimes and Discrimination Against Arab Americans: The Post–September 11 Backlash; September 11, 2001–October 11, 2002*, Hussein Ibish, ed. (Washington, DC: American-Arab Anti-Discrimination Committee Research Institute, 2003), available at http://www.adc.org/hatecrimes/.

5.   Sacrificing the rights of immigrants for "security" is the central theme of David Cole's book, *Enemy Aliens: Double Standards and Constitutional Freedoms in the War on Terrorism* (New York: New Press, 2003), which was published soon after this chapter was drafted. Cole maintains that "trading foreign nationals' liberties for citizens' security should be resisted for four reasons. The double standard is (1) illusory in the long run; (2) likely to prove counterproductive as a security matter; (3) a critical factor in the oft-regretted pattern of government overreaction in times of crisis; and (4) most importantly, constitutionally and morally wrong," (7).

6.   Mark Fazlollah, "Reports of Terror Crimes Inflated," *Philadelphia Inquirer*, May 15, 2003.

7.   If Congress passes the CLEAR (Clear Law Enforcement for Criminal Alien Removal) Act (HR 2671) or similar legisla-

tion, federal funds could be withheld from state and law enforcement agencies that do not agree to enforce immigration laws. State and local police who help round up illegal immigrants would be rewarded with a share of fines, forfeited property, and personal and agency immunity from any claim arising out of the enforcement of immigration law.

8. Uniting and Strengthening America by Providing Appropriate Tools Required to Intercept and Obstruct Terrorism Act, Public Law 107-56, *U.S. Statutes at Large* 115 (2001): 272. It was passed with only one senator and sixty-six members of the House of Representatives in opposition. The draft law was transmitted to Congress one week after the attack.

9. See David Cole, "The New McCarthyism: Repeating History in the War on Terrorism," *Harvard Civil Rights–Civil Liberties Law Review* 38, no. 1 (Winter 2003): 1–30.

10. The Department of Justice later told Congress that counting mosques and Muslims was a way of helping the FBI "reach out to the overwhelmingly law-abiding and patriotic members of these communities" so they can assist in locating "terrorists and their supporters who may reside among them in an effort to avoid detection. The demographic survey has facilitated the FBI's efforts in knowing where these communities are concentrated and where to turn for assistance." Jamie E. Brown, Acting Assistant Attorney General, US Department of Justice, Response to House Judiciary Committee chair F. James Sensenbrenner and ranking minority member John Conyers to "several questions to the Department on USA PATRIOT Act implementation and related matters" (cover letters dated May 13, 2003), 56. The full report is available at http://www.house.gov/judiciary/patriotlet051303.pdf.

11. Michael Isikoff, "The FBI Says, Count the Mosques," *Newsweek,* February 3, 2003.

12. US Department of Justice, *Justice Department Issues Policy Guidance to Ban Racial Profiling,* and *Fact Sheet: Racial Profiling,* June 17, 2003, http://www.usdoj.gov:80/opa/pr/2003/June/03_crt_355.htm. The Department of Justice states that in national security matters, race and ethnicity may only be used "to the extent permitted by the nation's

laws and the Constitution."

13. John Ashcroft, speech, US Mayors Conference, October 25, 2001.

14. See n. 1.

15. The Directorate of Border and Transportation Security in the Department of Homeland Security (DHS) now contains the Bureau of Customs and Border Protection, focused on the movement of goods and people across the borders, and the Bureau of Immigration and Customs Enforcement, which deals with immigration and customs investigations, detention, and deportation. A separate bureau in the DHS is the Bureau of Citizenship and Immigration Services, which handles refugee and asylum cases and the processing of visas and citizen documents. The National Network for Immigrant and Refugee Rights in a September 2003 report, *Human Rights and Human Security at Risk: The Consequences of Placing Immigration Enforcement and Services in the Department of Homeland Security,* argues, "Since placing immigration enforcement and services within the DHS just six months ago, abusive and discriminatory immigration enforcement has become even more entrenched, seriously jeopardizing community safety and compromising access to services. Immigration policies and practices that have been prone to abuse and human rights violations may now be even more difficult to reform or establish government accountability within a structure that cements immigration policies to a war against terrorism." See http://www.nnirr.org.

16. The *San Diego Union-Tribune* on July 27, 2002, reported that the INS had failed to process more than 200,000 old change of address forms. It had deposited them in an underground records facility in an abandoned mine near Kansas City (Marcus Stern, "Mishandled Address-Change Cards a Major Failure for INS").

17. The rule had not been enforced because it led to such an avalanche of forms that it was seen to be unworkable, according to the *Boston Globe,* July 23, 2002. Alex Gourevitch, in "Alien Nation" (*American Prospect,* January 13, 2003), states, "Within six weeks of announcing the change, the understaffed INS was swamped with 870,000 registra-

tion forms, and many more arrive each day. The information
was such a burden that the INS had to outsource some of the
processing to a private company. Many forms were simply
sent to a warehouse, leaving immigrants in fear that they
might be deported even though they had followed the law."

18. Two of the ninety-three whose names were listed in the
New York Times on November 28, 2001, were charged
with "failure of immigrant to register change of address."

19. Mark Bixler, "Minor Immigration Slip Becomes Costly,"
Atlanta Journal-Constitution, July 10, 2002.

20. The so-called twentieth hijacker, Zacarias Moussaoui, who
is the only person to face 9/11 charges in a federal court,
was arrested on August 16, 2001, after arousing suspicion
at a flight school in Minnesota. He was charged with overstaying his visa. An admitted member of al-Qaeda, Moussaoui has denied involvement in the 9/11 conspiracy. After
the Justice Department refused to allow him to interview
an al-Qaeda member by videoconference, a *New York
Times* editorial stated that "the Bush administration has
repeatedly tried to dodge the Constitution while prosecuting the war on terror. In the trial of Zacarias Moussaoui ...
the Justice Department is once again attempting to trample
the Bill of Rights." The editorial urged US District Judge
Leonie Brinkema to ensure that the Constitution "applies
fully in Mr. Moussaoui's case" ("The Trial of Zacarias
Moussaoui," July 28, 2003). On October 2, 2003, Judge
Brinkema, who had access to classified intelligence information about Moussaoui's background, called him "a re-
mote or minor participant in Al-Qaeda's war against the
United States" and ruled that he could not face capital
charges without "substantial proof" of his involvement in
or knowledge of the attacks. The government immediately
appealed her ruling to the conservative US Court of
Appeals for the Fourth Circuit.

21. A senior official in the Department of Justice Office of Public Affairs told the Office of the Inspector General that her
office "stopped reporting the cumulative totals after the
number reached approximately 1,200, because the statistics became confusing." Office of the Inspector General, US
Department of Justice, *The September 11 Detainees: A Re-*

view of the Treatment of Aliens Held on Immigration Charges in Connection with the Investigation of the September 11 Attacks, April 2003, 1. The full report is available at http://www.usdoj.gov/oig/igspecr1.htm.

22. Office of the Inspector General, 2 (see n. 21).

23. David Cole states that of more than five thousand persons who were detained under various operations aimed at the preventive detention of terrorist suspects who were not under criminal investigation, only five had been charged with any terrorist-related crime as of May 2003. Of that number, "one has been convicted of conspiracy to support terrorism; two were acquitted on all terrorism charges; the government dropped all terrorism charges against a fourth when he pleaded guilty to a minor infraction; and the fifth is awaiting trial." Cole, *Enemy Aliens,* 26 (see n. 5).

24. Danny Hakim, "Two Arabs Convicted and 2 Cleared of Terrorist Plot Against the US," *New York Times,* June 4, 2003.

25. "Value of Witness against Four Arabs Is Challenged," *New York Times,* May 8, 2003.

26. Danny Hakim, "Trial Set to Begin for Four Men Accused of Being in Terror Cell," *New York Times,* March 17, 2003.

27. Ibid.

28. *Code of Federal Regulations,* title 8, parts 236 and 241 (INS no. 2203-02).

29. See Amnesty International, *Amnesty International's Concerns Regarding Post September 11 Detentions in the USA,* report (March 14, 2002); Human Rights Watch, *Presumption of Guilt: Human Rights Abuses of Post–September 11 Detainees,* report (August 2002); Human Rights Watch, *In the Name of Counter-Terrorism: Human Rights Abuses Worldwide,* briefing paper for the 59th Session of the UN Commission on Human Rights (March 25, 2003); Lawyers Committee for Human Rights, *A Year of Loss: Reexamining Civil Liberties since September 11,* report (September 2002); Lawyers Committee for Human Rights, *Imbalance of Powers: How Changes to US Law and Policy Since 9/11 Erode Human Rights and Civil Liberties; September 2002–*

March 2003, report (March 2003); Blue Triangle Network, *Stop the Repression against Muslim, Arab, and South Asian Immigrants* (Dearborn, MI; January 2003); American Civil Liberties Union, *Insatiable Appetite: The Government's Demand for New and Unnecessary Powers After September 11* (April 2002; updated October 2002).

30. The "mosaic" theory appears to dominate the thinking of many of the programs based at the Defense Advanced Research Projects Agency (DARPA) in the Pentagon. One such program was retired admiral John Poindexter's Total Information Awareness, renamed "Terrorist Information Awareness" (TIA) to reassure a public worried about privacy rights. This system would gather electronic information on everyone in the country to look for hidden patterns of terrorist activity. After it became public that DARPA had used taxpayers' money over a period of two years to develop an online futures market that would enable anonymous traders to bet on the probability of terrorist attacks, assassinations, and future economic and political developments in the Middle East through a program called FutureMAP (Futures Markets Applied to Prediction), Poindexter was forced to resign, the terrorism futures market was scrapped, and TIA was defunded by Congress through 2004. Eight research programs associated with TIA in DARPA are being funded.

31. Office of the Inspector General, *September 11 Detainees* (see n. 21). The inspector general's report does not examine such aspects of the terrorism investigations as the use of material witness warrants, the refusal of the Department of Justice (DOJ) to release information about the detainees, and the closure of immigration hearings. On September 8, 2003, Inspector General Glenn Fine issued a follow-up report stating that the DOJ has taken some positive steps but has not gone far enough to end the abuses made public in his earlier report.

32. Five detainees have filed a class-action lawsuit alleging physical and verbal abuse and claiming that they were held long after receiving final removal orders. *Turkman v. Ashcroft*, 02-civ-2307 (E.D.N.Y., filed April 17, 2002).

33. Office of the Inspector General, 12 (see n. 21).

34. Ibid., 16.

35. Ibid., 64.

36. Brown, 35 (see n. 10). The report states that the USA PATRIOT Act was not used to hold the detainees "because traditional administrative bond proceedings have been sufficient to detain these individuals without bond." The USA PATRIOT Act required some kind of charge to be brought within seven days, which the government found an unnecessary restraint.

37. *Code of Federal Regulations,* title 8, part 287 (INS no. 2171-01).

38. See David Firestone, "US Makes It Easier to Detain Foreigners," *New York Times,* November 28, 2001.

39. Office of the Inspector General, 46 (see n. 21).

40. Christopher Drew with Judith Miller, "Though Not Linked to Terrorism Many Detainees Cannot Go Home," *New York Times,* February 18, 2002.

41. Brown, 49 (see n. 10). The report states that "as of January 2003, the total number of material witnesses detained in the course of the September 11 investigations was fewer than 50."

42. William McCall, "Friends Say FBI Holding Software Contractor," *Boston Globe,* April 4, 2003.

43. Anser Mehmood, a 42-year-old father of four living in Bayonne, New Jersey, never was asked questions by either the INS or FBI during his four months in solitary confinement. See David Rohde, "U.S.-Deported Pakistanis: Outcasts in 2 Lands," *New York Times,* January 20, 2003. We may learn more about the government's pursuit of "special interest" detainees from the case of Mohamed Kamel Bellahouel, an Algeria-born South Florida waiter. Bellahouel was detained in the immediate aftermath of 9/11 and held in custody for five months before his release on a ten thousand dollar immigration bond. In September 2003, Bellahouel appealed to the US Supreme Court to decide whether a district judge and the US Court of Appeals for the Eleventh Circuit acted unconstitutionally by sealing his case without explanation and hiding it from public view. At the time of writing, his

heavily censored appeal petition has not been accepted by the Supreme Court. Bellahouel was not charged with involvement in terrorism. An FBI agent told a federal immigration court that it was "likely" that he had waited on two of the 9/11 hijackers in the week before the attack (*Miami Business Review*, September 25, 2003). Bellahouel is now seeking to adjust his legal status and fight government efforts to deport him for overstaying his student visa.

44. Michael Janofsky, "Middle East Detainee Conducts Hunger Strike," *New York Times*, December 6, 2001.

45. *Federal Register* 66, no. 211 (October 31, 2001): 55062.

46. Sheik Rahman was convicted of heading the conspiracy to blow up the World Trade Center in 1993, and sentenced to sixty-five years in prison. The charges against Stewart and her two codefendants, her translator Mohammed Yousry and New York resident Ahmed Abdel Sattar, arise from the monitoring of her discussions with Sheik Rahman during prison visits that was already taking place under previous special administrative measures. Their case will be heard in Manhattan's federal district court.

47. Deborah L. Rhode, "Terrorists and Their Lawyers," *New York Times*, April 16, 2002.

48. Brown, 60 (see n. 10). The report states that as of February 2003, 1,141 absconders had been apprehended; 545 had been removed from the country; 391 were awaiting removal; and 44 were under criminal prosecution.

49. An estimated 8.7 million people are in the country illegally, approximately half from Mexico. Those from Middle Eastern countries make up about 1 percent of this total. Christopher Marquis, "Census Bureau Estimates 115,000 Middle Eastern Immigrants Are in the U.S. Illegally," *New York Times*, January 23, 2002.

50. In mid-2003, mass deportations were taking place in virtual secrecy, as planes carried Palestinians from Buffalo, New York, to Jordan and other Middle Eastern countries. Munir Lami had called his daughter Rose from York County Prison in Pennsylvania and asked her to come and sign release papers so he would be free. The next thing she heard was that the penniless, blind diabetic had been

moved to Buffalo for deportation. "Detainee Abruptly Deported," *York Dispatch*, August 20, 2003.

51. Office of the Inspector General, 68 (see n. 21).

52. Ann Davis, "FBI's Post-Sept. 11 'Watch List' Mutates, Acquires Life of its Own," *Wall Street Journal*, November 19, 2002.

53. Dan Eggen, "Plan for Counterterror Database Unveiled: Law Enforcement, Airlines Would Use FBI Watch List," *Washington Post*, September 17, 2003.

54. Eric Lichtblau, "Wanted: A Short List of 100,000 Terrorists," *New York Times*, September 21, 2003. There have been unconfirmed reports that the combined watch list that is being consolidated at the Terrorist Screening Center in Crystal City, Virginia, could contain as many as fourteen million names.

55. See Fox Butterfield, "Police are Split on Questioning of Mideast Men," *New York Times*, November 22, 2001.

56. John Wilke, "Justice Department Ends Interviews with Muslim Aliens," *Wall Street Journal*, March 20, 2002.

57. US General Accounting Office (GAO), *Homeland Security: Justice Department's Project to Interview Aliens after September 11, 2001* (GAO-03-459), April 2003, 5. The full report is available at http://www.gao.gov/cgi-bin/getrpt ?GAO-03-459.

58. Ibid., 16.

59. Ibid., Appendix I.

60. Rachel L. Swarns, "Report Raises Questions on Success of Immigrant Interviews," *New York Times*, May 10, 2003.

61. Download PDF version of brochure at http://www .ustreas.gov/rewards/pdfs/Green_Quest_Brochure.pdf.

62. Eric Lichtblau, "Agency to Expand Units Tracing Terrorist Finances," *New York Times,* January 10, 2003.

63. On December 4, 2003, the Ninth Circuit Court of Appeals ruled unconstitutional the material support provision of the 1996 Antiterrorism and Effective Death Penalty Act.

64. Associated Press, "Muslim Groups Criticize U.S. Raids," March 21, 2002.

65. Marwa El-Naggar, "'Operation Green Quest' Singles Out Muslims," *IslamOnline.net*, March 21, 2002, http://www .islamonline.net/english/news/2002-03/21/article10.shtml.

66. "FBI Sweeps Jewellers for 'Terror Link,'" *BBC News*, July 9, 2002, http://news.bbc.co.uk/1/hi/world/americas/ 2118256.stm.

67. John Mintz and Douglas Farah, "Muslim, Arab Stores Monitored as Part of Post-Sept. 11 Inquiry," *Washington Post*, August 12, 2002.

68. Issued on September 23, 2003, this executive order blocks assets of organizations and individuals linked to terrorism. By January 9, 2002, the list contained 168 groups and individuals.

69. See http://www.bice.immigration.gov/graphics/news/ newsrel/articles/icegqmar.htm.

70. The legal criteria for the designation of a Foreign Terrorist Organization under section 219 of the Immigration and Naturalization Act, as amended by the USA PATRIOT Act, includes terrorist activity that threatens "the security of US nationals or the national security (national defense, foreign relations, or the economic interests) of the United States." Office of Counterterrorism, *US Department of State Fact Sheet*, January 30, 2003. As of January 30, 2003, there were 36 organizations on the list.

71. David Cole, *Enemy Aliens*, 61 (see n. 5).

72. The Boston-area software firm Ptech is one of those that has been left "twisting in the wind" by what started out as a sensationalized media account of a supposed FBI "raid" on the company's office on December 6, 2002. In fact, Ptech, which had several Muslim employees, had itself contacted the FBI and arranged for government agents to visit. Its CEO, Oussama Ziade, wanted to clear the company of any suspicion of wrongdoing after Yasin al-Qadi, a Saudi venture capitalist who provided start-up money in 1995 but had not been directly involved with the company since 1999, was put on the US Treasury Department list of individuals suspected of financing terrorism.

73. Brown, 30 (see n. 10).

74. Ibid., 31. The *New York Times* reported that the Justice Department was using its expanded counterterrorism powers to seize millions of dollars from foreign banks that do business with the US, and that the Treasury had designated the Al Aksa International Foundation, based in Germany but with branches around Europe, the Middle East, and Africa, as a financial sponsor of terrorism. It was accused of sending funds to Hamas (Timothy L. O'Brien, "Muslim Charity Is Tied to Terror Group," May 30, 2003). In August 2003, Enaam Arnaout, head of the Benevolence International Foundation, was sentenced to eleven years and four months on a single count of "racketeering conspiracy." After spending more than a year in solitary confinement, Arnaout admitted providing humanitarian assistance to Afghan rebels in the 1990s and boots, tents, and uniforms to military groups in Bosnia and Chechnya.

75. Laurie Goodstein, "Muslims Hesitating on Gifts as U.S. Scrutinizes Charities," *New York Times,* April 17, 2003.

76. Matthew McCoy, "Three Others Taken into Custody in Syracuse," *Argonaut News,* February 28, 2003.

77. See Leif Thompson, "Lawyers Believe Agents May Have Violated Students' Rights,"*Argonaut News,* March 4, 2003. See Also Elizabeth "Brandt, "State Terror in Idaho," letter, CounterPunch Diary, March 10, 2003. Professor Brandt of the University of Idaho School of Law helped to organize legal support for the international students who had been threatened with deportation and/or perjury charges if they refused to talk. In a draft op-ed, she writes, "On the morning of 9/11 I comforted my children by saying 'don't worry, the terrorists don't know where Moscow, Idaho is!' Unfortunately, John Ashcroft does. It remains to be seen whether the government can prove its case against Al-Hussayyen. But the tranquility of Moscow, the civil liberties of the Muslim students at the University of Idaho, and the peace of mind of many members of this community are certainly casualties of our government's terror-instilling domestic war."

78. Matthew McCoy, "Al-Hussayyen Pleads Not Guilty to Charges," *Argonaut News,* February 28, 2003.

79. Roger Roy, "Giving to Charities Is Risky for Arabs," *Orlando Sentinel,* November 16, 2002.

80. "U.S. Defends Secret Evidence in Charity Case," *New York Times,* October 30, 2002. The Justice Department describes its success in these cases in Brown, 31 (see n. 10).

81. This Stanford University graduate had already registered with the INS in Newark on January 10, 2003, and again in Philadelphia on February 11, 2003, and had not been informed either time of this additional requirement. Sameer Ahmed, "INS Prevents Alum from U.S. Re-entry," *Stanford Daily,* April 15, 2003, http://daily.stanford.edu/tempo?page =content&id=10889&repository=0001_article.

82. Phyliss Boatwright, "Paperwork Snafu Prevents Local Doctor's Return to the US," *Roxboro-Courier,* May 24, 2003.

83. Secretary of State, Washington, DC, to All Diplomatic and Consular Posts Priority, P 100135Z May 10, 2003, SOP No. 15: Visas and Non-Compliance with National Security Entry Exit Registration System (NSEERS).

84. David Cole, "Blind Sweeps Return," *The Nation,* January 13, 2003.

85. Council on American-Islamic Relations, "Personal Accounts of INS Registration," report, January 7, 2003.

86. Brian Donohue, "Desperate Mideasterners Seek Asylum in Canada," *Newark Star-Ledger,* March 10, 2003.

87. Corey Kilgannon, "An American to His Friends, But Not to US: Teenager from Pakistan May Face Deportation," *New York Times,* April 19, 2003; Corey Kilgannon, "Pakistani Teenager Wins Battle Against US Deportation Order," *New York Times,* April 20, 2003.

88. See Rachel L. Swarns, "Fearful, Angry or Confused, Muslim Immigrants Register," *New York Times,* April 25, 2003. The number of illegal aliens caught in the special registration process was subsequently enlarged. According to the June 7, 2003, *New York Times,* more than thirteen thousand men who came forward for special registration now face deportation because of problems with their immigration status, and thousands are now leaving with their families for Canada, Europe, or Pakistan. "Some of those

facing deportation have waited months or years for officials to process applications to legalize their status ... Their
clients are only illegal, the lawyers say, because of the government's inefficiency." (Rachel L. Swarns, "Thousands of
Arabs and Muslims Could Be Deported, Officials Say.")

89. George Lardner Jr., "Congress Funds INS Registration Sys-
    tem But Demands Details," *Washington Post,* February 15,
    2003.

90. Thom Rose, "Immigrant Re-registration Abandoned,"
    United Press International, December 1, 2003.

91. "US to Target Student Visas," *Boston Metro,* May 30, 2003.

92. "Attorney General's Guidelines: Detecting and Preventing
    Terrorist Attacks," May 30, 2002. A Department of Justice
    fact sheet on the new guidelines is available at http://www
    .usdoj.gov/ag/speeches/2002/53002factsheet.htm.

93. Brown, 40 (see n. 10).

94. Jennifer Lee, "State Department Link Will Open Visa
    Database to Police Officers," *New York Times,* Jan-
    uary 31, 2003.

95. Brown, 47 (see n. 10).

96. Curt Anderson, "Ashcroft Expands FBI Arrest Powers,"
    Boston Globe, March 20, 2003.

97. The Department of Justice stated that the Mass Influx Rule
    [*Federal Register* 67, no. 142 (July 24, 2002): 48354], giv-
    ing authority to state and local police to enforce immigra-
    tion laws, was only operational at a time of "mass influx of
    aliens as declared by the Attorney General ... To date, there
    has been no declaration that a situation of a mass influx of
    aliens exists." Brown, 59 (see n. 10).

98. Jeffrey McMurray, "Alabama Troopers Begin Basic Train-
    ing in Immigration Law," Associated Press, May 20, 2003.

99. David Johnston and Don Van Natta Jr., "Agencies Monitor
    Iraqis in the U.S. for Terror Threat: Thousands Are
    Tracked," *New York Times,* November 17, 2002.

100. Eric Goldscheider and Jenna Russell, "Academic Alarm,"
     Boston Globe, November 24, 2002.

101. Department of Homeland Security, "Operation Liberty

Shield," press kit, http://www.dhs.gov/dhspublic/display
?theme=47&content=520 (emphasis in original).

102. Ann Davis, "Why a 'No Fly List' Aimed at Terrorists Often
Delays Others," *Wall Street Journal,* April 22, 2003.

103. Brown, 47 (see n. 10).

104. Ibid., 57.

105. Carl Takei, "Building a Nation of Snoops," *Boston Globe,*
May 14, 2003.

106. The piece that alarmed a member of the public was Ann
Withorn, "Almost Terrorists, 1970: Memories Recovered
in the War on Terrorism, 2002," *Sojourner,* April 2002.
Ann Withorn writes about the TIPS visit in "A Threshold
Inquiry: Consequences of Contemplating Terrorism in
2002," *Sojourner,* September 2002.

107. Ray Henry, "Evacuation Due to Muslim Prayers Sparks
Debate," *Boston Globe,* May 16, 2002.

108. Anand Vaishnav, "Schools Step Up Security after Visits,"
Boston Globe, May 22, 2002.

109. "Judge Says Cheney Can Keep Energy Papers Secret,"
Boston Herald, December 10, 2002.

110. For a good summary of PATRIOT II, see Anita Ramasas-
try, "PATRIOT II: The Sequel Why It's Even Scarier than
the First Patriot Act," *Findlaw's Writ,* February 17, 2003,
http://writ.findlaw.com/ramasastry/20030217.html.

111. By October 2003, some two hundred cities and towns
across the country and three state legislatures—representing more than twenty-five million people—had passed resolutions supporting civil liberties and opposing the USA
PATRIOT Act. See the Web sites of the American Civil Liberties Union (http://www.aclu.org) and the Bill of Rights
Defense Committee (http://www.bordc.org).

112. It presents a disturbing picture of intelligence agency blun-
ders, missed opportunities, turf wars, poor training, inepti-
tude, systemic weaknesses, and technological backward-
ness. The NSA, the CIA, and the FBI are all found gravely
wanting, but there is no effort to hold anyone in leadership
positions accountable. The report, *Joint Inquiry into Intelligence Community Activities before and after the Terrorist*

Attacks of September 11, 2001, is available at
http://www.gpoaccess.gov/serialset/creports/911.html.

113. The Senate voted for it 98–1; the House passed it 357–66.

114. FISA was passed in 1978 in response to the FBI's excesses
of the COINTELPRO era. The act established a wall between surveillance in criminal investigations, where a warrant could only be obtained on the showing of probable
cause, and surveillance for foreign intelligence-gathering
purposes, where an order could be obtained without probable cause from a FISA court. The USA PATRIOT Act dismantled the wall between intelligence gathering and
criminal investigations, allowing law enforcement to use
FISA court orders to spy on people without probable cause
of wrongdoing, and then more easily use the evidence gathered against them in criminal proceedings.

115. Section 326 calls for accounts to be screened against lists of
suspected terrorists and terrorist organizations. Banks can
voluntarily choose to close accounts that are "flagged" for
suspicious activity. In 2003, Fleet Bank closed twenty accounts belonging to Muslims in the Boston area.

116. Brown, 29 (see n. 10).

117. Ibid., 15.

118. Vice President Cheney decided not to attend the meeting
after the *Jerusalem Post* that morning had printed a front-
page article, "Cheney to Host Proterrorist Muslim Group,"
(see Janine Zacharia, "US Professor Accused of Funding
Islamic Jihad Visited White House," *Jerusalem Post,* February 23, 2003), which featured a picture of Sami al-Arian
campaigning with George and Laura Bush.

119. Eric Lichtblau and Judith Miller, "Officials Say Case
against Professor Had Been Hindered," *New York Times,*
February 22, 2003.

120. The Senate on May 8, 2003, passed the Kyl-Schumer
Amendment, making it even easier to get a warrant for surveillance of a noncitizen by removing the requirement of the
FISA Act that he or she must be acting on behalf of a foreign
power. Under the FISA Act, a "foreign power" is simply defined as "two people conspiring." By September 2003, there
were reports that the surveillance powers of the USA

PATRIOT Act were being used in a wide array of criminal investigations that had nothing to do with terrorism (see Editorial, "Patriot Act, Part II," *New York Times*, September 26, 2003, and *Security-Focus*, September 29, 2003). The *Washington Post* reported that the USA PATRIOT Act was being used to revive the 16-year-old deportation case against two Palestinian activists, Khader Hamide and Michel Shehadeh, who in 1987 were part of a group (the "LA Eight") arrested for distributing pro-Palestinian flyers. R. Jeffrey Smith, "PATRIOT Act Used in 16-Year-Old Deportation Case: Administration Revives 1987 Effort," *Washington Post*, September 23, 2003.

121. 215 F. Supp. 2nd 94 (D.D.C.), order stayed by 217 F. Supp. 2nd 94 (D.C. Cir., August 15, 2002).

122. *Center for National Security Studies, et al. v. U.S. Department of Justice*, nos. 02-5254 and 02-5300, 2003 WL 21382899 (D.C. Cir. June 17, 2003).

123. Neil A. Lewis, "Secrecy Is Backed on 9/11 Detainees," *New York Times*, June 18, 2003.

124. *American Civil Liberties Union of New Jersey, Inc. v. County of Hudson*, 352 N.J. Super. 44, 799 A.2nd 629, *cert. denied*, 803 A.2nd 1162 (N.J. 2002).

125. 195 F. Supp. 2nd 937 (E.D. Mich.), *aff'd*, 303 F.3rd 681 (6th Cir. 2002).

126. 303 F.3rd 681 (6th Cir. 2002).

127. 205 F. Supp. 2nd 288 (D.N.J. 2002), *rev'd* 308 F.3rd 198 (3rd Cir. 2002), *cert. denied*, no. 02-1289, 2003 WL 1191395 (U.S. 2003).

128. Lyle Denniston, "Justices Won't Review Secret Deportation Hearings," *Boston Globe*, May 28, 2003.

129. 202 F. Supp. 2nd 55 (S.D.N.Y. 2002).

130. Editorial, "Dishonesty in the Hunt for Terrorists," *New York Times*, August 26, 2002.

131. 316 F.3rd 450 (4th Cir. 2003), *aff'g* 294 F.3rd 598 (4th Cir. 2002).

132. Lyle Denniston, "Bush Administration Defends Detainee Policy," *Boston Globe*, December 4, 2003.

133. James Risen and Philip Shenon, "US Says It Halted Qaeda

Plot to Use Radioactive Bomb," *New York Times,* June 11, 2002.

134. Kevin Johnson and Toni Locy, "Threat of 'Dirty Bomb' Softened," *USA Today,* June 12, 2002.

135. Editorial, "Dirty Bombs and Civil Rights," *New York Times* June 12, 2002. Bush called the third American "enemy combatant"—white, upper-middle-class John Walker Lindh—"a poor fellow."

136. *Padilla ex rel. Newman v. Bush,* 233 F. Supp. 2nd 564 (S.D.N.Y. 2002), *aff'd on reh'g* by *Padilla ex rel. Newman v. Rumsfeld,* 243 F. Supp. 2nd 42 (S.D.N.Y. 2003). The government appealed the ruling to the Second Circuit Court of Appeals, which seemed unlikely to give the administration an easy ride. "As terrible as 9/11 was, it didn't repeal the Constitution," stated Judge Rosemary Pooler (*Boston Globe,* November 18, 2003).

137. The refusal of the Bush administration to observe international law and its own legal system in its treatment of the Guantánamo prisoners and its plans for military commissions to try them in secret if the presiding officer so rules have caused an outcry abroad. A three-judge panel of the US Court of Appeals for the District of Columbia Circuit ruled on March 11, 2003, that the detainees, who are termed "unlawful enemy combatants" by the administration, have no right to challenge their detention, since Cuba, not the US, has sovereignty over Guantánamo Bay. Even if they were innocent of committing hostile acts against the US, they would have no recourse to a US court, the judges ruled. On March 12, 2003, the *New York Times* editorialized about the Guantánamo prisoners: "Many were seized in the heat of battle, but others were turned over in exchange for rewards or bounties. Advocates for the prisoners maintain that one-third or more are being held on the basis of bad intelligence, or simply for being in the wrong place at the wrong time ... Those who were wrongly caught up in the military's net must have the opportunity to make their case ... The administration is trampling on their rights. It is also damaging America's reputation for fairness. The administration should rethink its policies, and the Supreme Court should reverse yesterday's unfortunate

decision" ("Forsaken at Guantánamo"). In early October, a senior official of the International Committee of the Red Cross publicly denounced the indefinite holding of more than six hundred detainees as "unacceptable." Neil A. Lewis, "Red Cross Criticizes Indefinite Detention in Guantánamo Bay," *New York Times*, October 10, 2003. On November 10, 2003, the US Supreme Court agreed to hear two appeals on behalf of sixteen Guantánamo prisoners and to decide whether they are entitled access to US civilian courts to challenge their indefinite detention.

138. Greg Miller, "Many Held at Guantanamo Not Likely Terrorists," *Los Angeles Times*, December 22, 2002.

139. Amber Mobley, "US Citizen Admits Planning Al Qaeda Attack," *Boston Globe*, June 20, 2003.

140. Faris initially pleaded guilty to conspiring to provide material support, including sleeping bags and cell phones, to al-Qaeda. He later told Federal District Court Judge Leonie Brinkema that he agreed to the plea because of harassment by federal agents and in the hopes of getting a book contract, and he denied working for al-Qaeda. His lawyer stated that prosecutors told Faris he could be declared an "enemy combatant" and sent indefinitely to Guantánamo Bay. On October 28, 2003, he was sentenced to twenty years in prison, the maximum he could get under the plea agreement. Eric Lichtblau, "Trucker Sentenced to 20 Years in Plot Against Brooklyn Bridge," *New York Times*, October 29, 2003.

141. "Al Qaeda in America: The Enemy Within," cover story, *Newsweek*, June 23, 2003.

142. Michael Isikoff and Mark Hosenball, "Terror Watch: America's Secret Prisoners," *Newsweek*, June 18, 2003.

143. Ibid.

144. Jimmy Breslin, "A Fate Sealed Under Secrecy," *Newsday*, June 22, 2003.

145. "Suspect Is Named Al Qaeda Soldier," *Boston Globe*, June 24, 2003.

146. Ibid.

147. See Nancy Murray and Sarah Wunsch, "Civil Liberties in Times of Crisis: Lessons from History," *Massachusetts*

Law Review 87, no. 2 (Fall 2002).

148. For example, on May 21, 2003, the host of *Matty in the Morning* on a major FM radio station in Boston said, "All Muslims should leave town ... Pack up in a caravan and leave ... Go back to wherever they came from ... I just mean, if they all leave town, it will make it easier for us to tell who the terrorists are."

149. See n. 4.

150. See David A. Harris, *Profiles in Injustice: Why Racial Profiling Cannot Work* (New York: New Press, 2002). In chapter 9, "Racial Profiling After September 11, 2001: New Reality, Same Problems," Harris writes: "Profiling is always overinclusive. Even a 'good' profile—one that is based on rigorously analyzed statistics that are culled from plentiful, systematically collected data—will cast suspicion over more innocent people than guilty ones. When we construct a profile using the wrong kind of characteristic—a racial or an ethnic one as opposed to markers of behavior—we spread our enforcement resources and efforts more thinly than we would otherwise. Even the FBI does not have unlimited man power; every person FBI agents must investigate because he 'looks like a terrorist' means that much less in the way of enforcement resources available to investigate individuals who actually behave suspiciously ... As with other forms of racial profiling, using ethnicity to try to identify terrorists has the added consequence of alienating the very community most able to help with effective law enforcement" (230–31).

151. His letter was circulated by MPACnews, http://www .mpacnews.org, an electronic mailing list of the Muslim Public Affairs Council, http://www.mpac.org.

152. See n. 6.

153. *Washington Post*, March 3, 2003. On December 8, 2003, the Transactional Records Access Clearinghouse (TRAC) of Syracuse University released a report documenting the fact that more than half of all 879 "terrorism" or "anti-terrorism-classified" convictions claimed by the government since 9/11 resulted in no jail time. Only twenty-three of those convicted of terrorism-related crimes

were sentenced to five or more years in prison. Of the 184 convictions that the government classified as "international terrorism," only three received sentences of more than five years. Eighty convictions resulted in no jail time. "Criminal Terrorism Enforcement Since the 9/11/01 Attacks: A TRAC Special Report" can be found online at http://trac .syr.edu/tracreports/terrorism/report031208.html.

154. Khalid Hasan, "US Court Frees Two Pakistanis Arrested on Terrorism Charges," *Daily Times,* April 10, 2003.

155. Robert E. Pierre, "FBI Apology Fails to Dissipate Cloud: 8 Terrorism Suspects Confined on Bogus Tip," *Washington Post,* May 24, 2003.

156. Matthew Purdy and Lowell Bergman, "Unclear Danger: Inside the Lackawanna Terror Case," *New York Times,* October 12, 2003.

157. Tatsha Robertson, "Some Doubt Strength of US Terrorism Cases," *Boston Globe,* May 27, 2003.

158. Brown, 21 (see n. 10).

159. *Boston Globe,* May 1, 2003.

160. Katrina Vanden Heuvel, ed., *The Nation, 1865–1990: Selections from the Independent Magazine of Politics and Culture* (New York: Thunder's Mouth Press, 1990), 33–36.

PART II: SUSTAINING AND REINFORCING DEMONIZATION OF ARABS AND MUSLIMS: MANUFACTURING RACIST IMAGES OF ARABS AND MUSLIMS

Chapter 3. "Our Enemies Among Us!": The Portrayal of Arab- and Muslim Americans in Post–9/11 American Media. By Robert Morlino.

1. The views and opinions expressed in this chapter are solely those of the author on behalf of the Trans-Arab Research Institute and are neither shared nor endorsed by any of his employers or educational institutions past, present, or future. The spelling of proper names in excerpts is presented as it appeared in publication or broadcast transcript. Additionally, italicization as emphasis is added in all excerpts

unless otherwise noted.

2. Steve Dunleavy, "Simply Kill These Bastards," *New York Post,* September 12, 2001.

3. Ann Coulter, "This Is War," *National Review Online,* September 13, 2001, http://www.nationalreview.com/coulter/coulter091301.shtml.

4. Howard Kurtz, "Commentators Are Quick to Beat Their Pens into Swords," *Washington Post,* September 13, 2001.

5. Bill O'Reilly, *The O'Reilly Factor,* Fox News Channel, September 13, 2001.

6. American-Arab Anti-Discrimination Committee, *Report on Hate Crimes and Discrimination Against Arab Americans: The Post–September 11 Backlash; September 11, 2001–October 11, 2002,* Hussein Ibish, ed. (Washington, DC: American-Arab Anti-Discrimination Committee Research Institute, 2003), available at http://www.adc.org/hatecrimes/.

7. Daniel Pipes, "Fighting Militant Islam, Without Bias," *City Journal,* Autumn 2001.

8. Associated Press, "N.Y. Judge Asks Arab-Born Woman Fighting Parking Ticket if She's a Terrorist," May 22, 2003.

9. Edward W. Said, *Covering Islam: How the Media and the Experts Determine How We See the Rest of the World,* 1st ed. (New York: Pantheon Books, 1981; rev. ed., 1st Vintage Books ed., New York: Vintage Books, 1997).

10. Keith Regan, "Ahead of the Curve: Quincy-Based Ptech Helps Big Business Stay Agile," *Patriot Ledger,* December 27, 2001.

11. Diane Sawyer, Charles Gibson, and Brian Ross, *Good Morning America,* ABC, December 6, 2002.

12. Dan Verton, "Ptech Workers Tell the Story Behind the Search," *Computerworld,* January 17, 2003. See also by Dan Verton, "Terrorist Probe Hobbles Ptech," *Computerworld,* January 17, 2003.

13. United Press International, "Agents Look for Tech Firm Terror-Link," December 6, 2002.

14 Associated Press, "Customs Agents Raid U.S. Software

Company," *Deseret News,* December 6, 2002.

15. *EWeek* staff, "Feds Raid Software Firm," *PC Magazine* (online), December 6, 2002, http://www.pcmag.com/ article2/0,4149,751361,00.asp.

16. "U.S. Raids Software Firm with Saudi Connections," Deutsche Press-Agentur, December 6, 2002; "US Agents Raid Software Firm with Alleged Al-Qaeda Links," Agence France Presse, December 7, 2002.

17. Rebecca Carr and Elliot Jaspin, "Suspected Terror Financier Target of Search," Cox News Service, December 6, 2002.

18. Mark Hosenball, "High-Tech Terror Ties?" *Newsweek,* December 6, 2002, available online at http://www .unansweredquestions.net/timeline/2002/ newsweek120602.html.

19. Steve Emerson, interview by Bill Press, *Buchanan and Press,* MSNBC, December 6, 2002.

20. Gregg Jarrett reporting on *The Big Story with John Gibson,* FOX News Network, December 6, 2002.

21. Bill Delaney, *TalkBack Live,* CNN, December 6, 2002.

22. Ibid.

23. Ibid.

24. Ibid.

25. See n. 20.

26. Ibid.

27. Niles Lathem, Lauren Black, and Marsha Kranes, "Anti-Terror Raid At Mass.-Based Software Firm," *New York Post,* December 7, 2002.

28. Pam Belluck and Eric Lichtblau, "Threats and Responses: The Money Trail," *New York Times,* December 7, 2002.

29. Ibid.

30. Paul Edward Parker, "Software Firm Investigated for Terrorism Ties," *Providence Journal-Bulletin,* December 7, 2002.

31. Ralph Ranalli, "Federal Investigation / Agency Questions," *Boston Globe,* December 8, 2002.

32. Karen Eschbacher and Julie Jette, "Negative Press Creates

Havoc for Ptech: Official Says $1M Account in Jeopardy," *Patriot Ledger*, December 7, 2002.

33. See n. 10.

34. *Patriot Ledger* staff, "Terrorism Raid Targets Quincy Firm," *Patriot Ledger*, December 6, 2002.

35. Christopher Walker and Karen Eschbacher, "Raided Company Denies Terror Ties: Ptech Says It May Have Had Money Ties to Saudi Financier Long Time Ago," *Patriot Ledger*, December 7, 2002.

36. Ibid.

37. See n. 32.

38. Julie Jette, "Expert Doubts Software Poses Danger," *Patriot Ledger*, December 7, 2002.

39. Jeffrey White, "Associates Say Ziade Gentle, Hard-Working," *Patriot Ledger*, December 7, 2002.

40. Editorial, "Our View: Quincy and Al Qaida," *Patriot Ledger*, December 10, 2002.

41. Julie Jette, "Ptech Fallout: Finger-Pointing, Wage Claims, Unpaid Taxes," *Patriot Ledger*, January 22, 2003.

42. "Senator Calls on FBI to Scrutinize Ptech Software," *Patriot Ledger*, January 23, 2003.

43. Casey Ross, "National Security or Invasion of Privacy?" *Patriot Ledger*, May 2, 2003.

44. Howard Kurtz, "Out of the Scoop Loop: Feds Fail to Deliver on Promised Tip," *Washington Post*, December 7, 2002.

45. Manuel Roig-Franzia, "Suspected Threat Shakes S. Florida," *Washington Post*, September 14, 2002.

46. Ibid.

47. Ann Coulter, "So Three Arabs Walk into a Bar," *WorldNetDaily*, September 18, 2002, http://www.worldnetdaily.com/news/article.asp?ARTICLE_ID=28986.

48. Jonathan Freedland, "An Appalling Magic," *Guardian*, May 17, 2003.

49. See n. 47.

50. Crown Publishing Group, "Crown Forum Imprint for Conservative Nonfiction Debuts in June From Crown Pub-

lishing Group," press release, April 21, 2003.

51. Sam Husseini, "Islam: Fundamental Misunderstandings about a Growing Faith," Fairness and Accuracy in Reporting, July–August 1995.

52. Bill O'Reilly, *The O'Reilly Factor,* Fox News, July 10, 2002.

53. Editorial, "A Victory for Knowledge," *Buffalo News,* August 22, 2002.

54. Wendy Kaminer, "Losing Our Religion," *American Prospect,* September 23, 2002.

55. Editorial, "Worthy Reading," *Lancaster Intelligencer Journal,* August 27, 2002.

56. Editorial, "Book Value," *Philadelphia Inquirer,* August 8, 2002.

57. Editorial, "Education in Context," *Bergen County (NJ) Record*, August 22, 2002.

58. Bill O'Reilly, *The O'Reilly Factor,* Fox News, August 26, 2002.

59. Paul Steinberger and Ryan Tuck, interview by Bill O'Reilly, *The O'Reilly Factor,* Fox News, September 25, 2002.

60. Eric Boehlert's coverage of the case, including "The Prime-Time Smearing of Sami Al-Arian" (January 19, 2002) and "Is Sami Al-Arian Guilty of Terrorist Plots?" (February 21, 2001), can be found in the archives on the *Salon* Web site, http://www.salon.com, as well as in the book *Afterwords: Stories and Reports From 9/11 and Beyond,* compiled by the editors of *Salon.com* (New York: Washington Square Press, 2002).

61. Robert McKee appeared on *The O'Reilly Factor* on March 21, 2002, and December 12, 2002.

62. Mary Jo Melone, "With Quiet Resolve, She Fights for Father," *St. Petersburg Times,* June 19, 2003.

63. James Zogby, interview with Joe Scarborough, *Scarborough Country,* MSNBC, May 19, 2003.

64. Lisa M. Collins, "Arab Advocate," *Detroit Metro Times,* March 19, 2003.

65. Keith Naughton, "The Blame Game," *Newsweek,* September 11, 2001.

66. See Jeffrey Gettleman, "Ambivalence in the Besieged Town of 'Run, Rudolph, Run,'" *New York Times*, May 31, 2003, and "Sympathy for Bombing Suspect May Cloud Search for Evidence," *New York Times*, June 2, 2002.

67. "Terrorism Stories: Three Cases, Two Standards," Fairness and Accuracy in Reporting, February 2000.

68. Tom Tomorrow, "A Lott Left," *This Modern World*, February 25, 2003.

69. See n. 51. Also see, "Terrorists Attack Ski Lodges, Not Doctors," Fairness and Accuracy in Reporting, December 1998.

Chapter 4. The New Cold Warriors. By Will Youmans.

1. Paul Wolfowitz, quoted in Lamis Andoni, "Bernard Lewis: In the Service of Empire," *Al-Ahram Weekly On-line*, December 12–18, 2002, http://weekly.ahram.org.eg/2002/616/re4.

2. Ibid.

3. Daniel Pipes, "From a Distance: Influencing Foreign Policy from Philadelphia" (Heritage Lecture, Heritage Foundation, June 5, 1991).

4. Steven Emerson, "How a Terrorist Enterprise Was Created, Maintained, Financed, and Coordinated from the Safety of the United States," *Jewish World Review*, February 25, 2003, http://www.jewishworldreview.com/0203/al_arian.asp.

5. For example, see Patrick Clawson and Daniel Pipes, "Turn Up the Pressure on Iran," *Jerusalem Post*, May 21, 2002.

6. See Martin Kramer's *Middle East Quarterly* bio at http://www.meforum.org/meq/editors.php.

7. John Mintz, "The Man Who Gives Terrorism a Name," *Washington Post*, November 14, 2001.

8. Louis Jacobson, Peter H. Stone, and Shawn Zeller, "Lobbying: K Street for December 1, 2001: A Little PR Help Never Hurts," *National Journal*, December 1, 2001.

9. See the USCFL Web site at www.freelebanon.org.

10. See the AIPAC Web site at www.aipac.org.

11. Richard Perle, "State Sponsors of Terrorism Should Be Wiped Out, Too," September 2001, http://freelebanon

.org/articles/a164.htm.

12. Dr. Wurmer's bio is available on the Hudson Institute Web site at https://www.hudson.org/learn/index.cfm ?fuseaction=staff_bio&eid=Wurmser.

13. Mark Perelman, "No Longer Obscure, Memri Translates the Arab World," *Forward,* December 7, 2001.

14. Statement of Steven Emerson Before the Senate Judiciary Committee, "An Investigation into the Modus Operandi of Terrorist Networks in the United States: The Structure of Osama Bin Laden, Al-Qaeda, Hamas and Other Jihadist Organizations in the United States," *DOJ Oversight: Preserving Our Freedoms While Defending Against Terrorism,* December 4, 2001.

15. Judith Rubin, "Islamic Terror Stalks America," *Jerusalem Post,* August 4, 1995.

16. Ibid.

17. Eric Boehlert, "Terrorists Under the Bed," review of *American Jihad: The Terrorists Living Among Us,* by Steven Emerson, *Salon,* March 5, 2002, www.salon.com/books/feature/2002/03/05/emerson/print.html.

18. Emerson on *Rivera Live,* CNBC, July 23, 1996.

19. Emerson's comments on the Smith incident are covered in Boehlert, "Terrorists Under the Bed" (see n. 17).

20. See n. 7.

21. Jeff Jacoby, "Steven Emerson and the NPR Blacklist," *Boston Globe,* February 7, 2002.

22. See n. 14.

23. See n. 7.

24. Kenneth Cooper, "2 in House Attacked for Use of 'Jihad' Video," *Washington Post,* June 27, 1995.

25. See n. 7.

26. "Biographical Sketch of Daniel Pipes," http://www .danielpipes.org/bios.

27. Pipes, "My Media Year," *National Review,* September 11, 2002.

28. Project for the New American Century to the Honor-

able George W. Bush, April 3, 2002, http://www
.newamericancentury.org/Bushletter-040302.htm.

29. Pipes, quoted in Johanna Neuman, "Peace Institute Suddenly
at Center of Controversy," *Los Angeles Times*, May 9, 2003.

30. John Hawkins, "An Interview with Daniel Pipes," *Right
Wing News,* August 29, 2002, http://rightwingnews.com/
interviews/pipes.php.

31. Pipes and Khalid Duran, "Muslims in the West: Can Conflict Be Averted?" *United States Institute of Peace,* August
1993.

32. Pipes, "Preventing War: Israel's Options," *Jerusalem Post,*
July 18, 2001.

33. See n. 26.

34. Holly J. Burkhalter, quoted in Neuman, "Peace Institute
Suddenly at Center of Controversy" (see n. 29).

35. See n. 3.

36. Robert Blitzer, quoted in Mintz, "Man Who Gives Terrorism a Name" (see n. 7).

37. Ibid. Emerson "says he does swap data with the Israelis—
as well as with intelligence officials from other nations, including Germany, England and Arab countries he declines
to name."

38. See Campus Watch at http://www.campus-watch.org, and
NoIndoctrination.org at http://www.noindoctrination.org.

39. Stanley Hoffman, "America Goes Backward," *New York
Review of Books*, June 12, 2003.

40. See n. 4.

41. Emerson, "The Terror Masters," *Wall Street Journal,*
April 18, 2003.

42. See n. 14.

43. See n. 17.

44. Elizabeth Drew, "The Neocons in Power," *New York
Review of Books*, June 12, 2003.

45. See Grayson Levy's Web site at http://www.grayson.org.il/,
and YeshaNews at http://www.yeshanews.org/. Cited in
CAIR, "Daniel Pipes' Web Site Maintained by Israeli Settler,"

http://www.cair-net.org/misc/people/daniel_pipes.html.

46. "Protocols of the Consultants of Zion," *Harper's Magazine,* July 2003, 14.

47. See n. 13.

48. Ibid.

49. Stephen Barr and Guy Gugliotta, "Preemption of Terrorists Is Urged," *Washington Post,* April 21, 1995.

50. Judith Miller, "Some Charities Suspected of Terrorist Role," *New York Times,* February 20, 2000; Richard Cole, "Fraud, Drug Trafficking and Charities in U.S. Help Finance Terrorists," Associated Press, May 26, 1997. Holy Land was closed again by the Palestinian Authority several months later (see Margot Dudkevitch, Steve Rodan, and Mohammed Najib, "PA Rounds Up Hamas Activists," *Jerusalem Post,* September 28, 1997).

51. "Seventeen Palestinians Injured in Eighth Day of Clashes in Hebron," Agence France Presse, June 21, 1997.

52. Nicolas Tatro, "Israel Urges Europeans to Block Hamas Fund Raising," Associated Press, August 6, 1997.

53. Neil Lewis, "Terror in Oklahoma: In Congress," *New York Times,* April 21, 1995.

54. Anti-Defamation League, "ADL Welcomes Improved Antiterrorism Bill," press release, April 15, 1996, http://www.adl.org/presrele/Teror_92/2712_92.asp.

55. Miller, "Some Charities Suspected of Terrorist Role" (see n. 50).

56. William Branigin, "Secret U.S. Evidence Entangles Immigrants," *Washington Post,* October 19, 1997.

57. See n. 4.

58. See n. 14.

59. Pipes, interview by Lou Dobbs, "War against Radical Islamists," *Lou Dobbs Moneyline,* CNN, June 13, 2002.

60. "Fueling a Culture Clash," *Washington Post,* April 19, 2003.

61. Duran and Pipes, "Faces of American Islam," *Policy Review,* August–September 2002.

62. Pipes, "A Muslim Swimming Pool in Lille, France," Web

log, www.danielpipes.org, June 15, 2003.

63. Neuman, "Peace Institute Suddenly at Center of Controversy" (see n. 29).

64. "PBS, Recruiting for Islam," *New York Post,* December 17, 2002. To download a transcript of the documentary, go to http://www.pbs.org/muhammad/transcripts /muhammad_script.pdf.

65. For a transcript of "From Jesus to Christ: The First Christians," see http://www.pbs.org/wgbh/pages/frontline/ shows/religion/etc/script1.html.

66. See n. 15.

67. Ibid.

68. Emerson, interviewed by Pipes, "Get Ready for Twenty World Trade Center Bombings," *Middle East Quarterly* 4, no. 2 (June 1997), http://www.meforum.org/article/353.

69. Lou Gelfand, "Reader Says Use of 'Fundamentalist' Hurting Muslims," *Minneapolis Star Tribune,* April 4, 1993.

70. Pipes to Ahmad Yusuf, letter in response to "Correspondence: 'The Reputation of Your Journal Has Been Damaged,'" *Middle East Quarterly* 4, no. 4 (December 1997), http://www.meforum.org/article/380.

71. Ibid.

72. See n. 61.

73. See n. 4.

74. See n. 15.

75. Pipes, "Naming the Enemy," *Jewish World Review,* November 19, 2002.

76. Pipes, "The Snipers: Crazy or Jihadis?" *New York Post,* October 29, 2002.

77. Pipes, quoted in "Fueling a Culture Clash" (see n. 60).

78. See n. 76.

79. Pipes and Jonathon Schanzer, "On to Baghdad?: Yes—The Risks Are Overrated," *New York Post,* December 3, 2001.

80. See n. 76.

81. Pipes, quoted in H.D.S Greenway, "The Real 'Danger Within' is Religious Hatred," *Boston Globe,* December 24,

2001 (emphasis added).

82. Pipes, "Bin Laden Is a Fundamentalist," *National Review Online*, October 22, 2001, http://www.nationalreview.com/comment/comment-pipes102201.shtml.

83. Ibid.

84. Lars Hedegaard and Daniel Pipes, "Something Rotten in Denmark?" *New York Post*, August 27, 2002.

85. Elisabeth Arnold and Elsebeth Gerner Nielsen, letter to the editor, *National Post*, September 6, 2002, available at http://www.meforum.org/article/pipes/450.

86. Pipes and Hedegaard, letter to the editor, *National Post*, September 10, 2002, available at http://www.meforum.org/article/pipes/450.

87. See n. 75.

88. "American Muslims and Politics," *Religion and Ethics Newsweekly*, PBS, November 2, 2001, http://www.pbs.org/wnet/religionandethics/week509/cover.html.

89. John Sugg, "Thought Crime on Campus," *Creative Loafing*, October 2, 2002, http://atlanta.creativeloafing.com/2002-10-02/fishwrapper.html.

90. See n. 59.

91. Fawaz Gerges and Pipes, interview by Lou Dobbs, "War against Radical Islamists" (see n. 59).

92. See n. 75.

93. See n. 14.

94. "FBI Charges Florida Professor with Terrorist Activities," CNN, February 20, 2003, http://www.cnn.com/2003/US/South/02/20/professor.arrest/.

95. Sugg, "What You Aren't Supposed to Know about the Arrest of Sami Al-Arian," *Washington Report on Middle East Affairs*, April 2003, 54, 92.

96. Ibid.

97. Marla Braverman, "The Arabist Predicament," review of *Ivory Towers on Sand: The Failure of Middle Eastern Studies in America*, by Martin Kramer, *Azure* 15 (Summer 2003).

98. Pipes and Schanzer, "Extremists on Campus," *New York Post,* June 25, 2002.

99. Campus Watch, http://www.campus-watch.org.

100. Campus Watch Web site quoted in Ali Abunimah and Nigel Parry, "Campus Watch: Middle East McCarthyism?" *Electronic Intifada,* September 25, 2002, http://electronicintifada.net/v2/article714.shtml.

101. Elizabeth Crawford, "Area-Studies Programs Come Under Fire at House Hearing," *Chronicle of Higher Education,* June 20, 2003; this attack is being considered as bill 3099 in the Senate.

102. Also, a LexisNexis search revealed no articles or statements indicating that Pipes has mentioned the JDL.

103. Reference to 2002 list. View list at http://usinfo.state .gov/topical/pol/terror/designated.htm.

104. For an incomplete but thorough profile of the JDL's record of violence, see Anti-Defamation League, "Backgrounder: The Jewish Defense League," http://www.adl.org/ extremism/jdl%5Fchron.asp.

105. Pipes, interviewed by Ahmad Yusuf, "Zionism, Islamism, and Jewish Politics in America: Dialogue between Daniel Pipes and Ahmad Yusuf," *Middle East Affairs Journal* (Winter–Spring 1999).

106. See n. 61.

107. Pipes, "American Muslims vs. American Jews," *Commentary,* May 1999.

108. See n. 31.

109. See n. 104.

110. Tom Tugend, "Never Say Never Again," *Jerusalem Post,* December 21, 2001.

111. Tugend, "JDL's Krugel Pleads Guilty to Bombing Plot Charges," *Jerusalem Post,* February 6, 2003.

112. See n. 15.

113. Emerson, "The Other Fundamentalists," *New Republic,* June 12, 1995, 21.

114. From excerpted portions of *American Jihad,* chap. 1, on WorldNetDaily, March 21, 2002, at http://www

.worldnetdaily.com/news/article.asp?ARTICLE_ID=26904.

115. Walter Goodman, "Television Review: An Impassioned Debate on Terror Restraints," *New York Times*, August 24, 1995.

116. Prepared Statement of Steven Emerson Before the Senate Judiciary Subcommittee on Terrorism, Technology and Government Information, "Terrorists in America: Five Years After the World Trade Center Bombing," *Federal News Service*, February 24, 1998.

117. Pipes, quoted in Clifford Geertz, "Which Way to Mecca? Part II," *New York Review of Books*, July 3, 2003.

118. Pipes, "Conspiracy: How the Paranoid Style Flourishes and Where It Comes From," *Booknotes*, C-SPAN, January 25, 1998. See transcript at http://www.booknotes.org/Transcript/?ProgramID=1397.

PART III: THE CONVERGENCE OF US DOMESTIC SHIFT TO THE FAR RIGHT AND THE PURSUIT OF GLOBAL EXPANSION: THE CRIMINALIZATION OF ARAB AND MUSLIM COMMUNITIES

Chapter 5. Roots of the American Antiterrorism Crusade. By Samih Farsoun.

1. See Noam Chomsky, *9-11* (New York: Seven Stories Press, 2001); Rahul Mahajan, *New Crusade, America's War on Terrorism* (New York: Monthly Review Press, 2002); Howard Zinn, *Terrorism and War* (New York: Seven Stories Press, 2002).

2. Chomsky, *9-11*, 11 (see n. 1).

3. Nicholas Lemann, "The Next World Order: The Bush Administration May Have a Brand-new Doctrine of Power," *New Yorker*, April 1, 2003, 44.

4. See George Bush and Brent Scowcroft, *A World Transformed* (New York: Random House, 1998).

5. See Francis Fukuyama, *The End of History and the Last Man* (New York: Avon Books, 1993).

6. Cf. John C. Cooley, *Unholy Wars, Afghanistan, America*

and International Terrorism (London: Pluto Press, 1999).

7.   See Noam Chomsky, *The New Military Humanism* (Monroe, ME: Common Courage Press, 1999).

8.   Chomsky, *9/11*, 14–17 (see n. 1).

9.   Lance Selfa, "A New Colonial 'Age of Empire'?" *International Socialist Review,* May–June 2002, 50.

10.   Immanuel Wallerstein, "The Eagle Has Crash Landed," *Foreign Policy,* July–August 2002, 5, http://www.foreignpolicy.com/issue_julyaug_2002/wallerstein.html.

11.   Cf. Marwan Bishara, "The Israelization of America's War," *Al-Ahram Weekly,* April 25–May 1, 2002.

12.   Martin Khor, "'Failed States' Theory Can Cause Global Anarchy," *Bangkok Post*, March 31, 2002 (as of November 2003, article could be read on *Financial Times* Web site, http://www.ft.com). Cf. Selfa, 53 (see n. 9).

13.   Paul Johnson, "Colonialism's Back—and Not a Moment Too Soon," *New York Times Magazine*, April 18, 1993.

14.   Sebastian Mallaby, "The Reluctant Imperialist," *Foreign Affairs* 81, no. 2 (March–April 2001): 19.

15   Max Boot, "The Case for An American Empire," *Weekly Standard*, October 15, 2001.

16.   See Samih Farsoun and Christina Zacharia, "Class, Economic Change and Liberalization in the Arab World," in Rex Brynen, et al., eds., *Political Liberalization and Democratization in the Arab World*, vol. 1 (Boulder, CO: Lynne Reinner, 1995).

17.   Samuel Huntington, *The Clash of Civilizations and the Remaking of the World* (New York: Simon and Schuster, 1998), 125.

18.   Ibid., 258.

19.   Council on American-Islamic Relations, 2002, http://www.cair-net.org/civilrights2002/.

20.   Nicholas Christof, "Bigotry in Islam—and Here," *New York Times*, July 9, 2002.

21.   "[An] act of terrorism, means any activity that (A) involves a violent act or an act dangerous to human life that is a violation of the criminal laws of the United States or any

State, or that would be a criminal violation if committed within the jurisdiction of the United States or of any State; and (B) appears to be intended (i) to intimidate or coerce a civilian population, (ii) to influence the policy of a government by intimidation or coercion or (iii) to affect the conduct of a government by assassination or kidnapping." United States Code Congressional and Administrative News, 98th Congress, Second Session, 1984, Oct. 19, volume 2; par 3077, 98 STAT. 2707 (West Publishing Co., 1984), cited in Chomsky, *9-11,* 16 (see n.1).

22. Lemann, 45–46 (see n. 3).

23. Ibid., 45.

24. Peter Kuznick, talk at American University, Washington, DC (May 2, 2002).

25. Joseph Cirincione, quoted in Kuznick (see n. 24).

26. See Richard Falk, "The New Bush Doctrine," *Nation,* July 15, 2002, 9–11.

27. Thomas E. Ricks and Vernon Loeb, "Bush Developing Military Policy of Striking First, New Doctrine Addresses Terrorism," *Washington Post,* June 10, 2002.

28. Jim Hoagland, "No Time to Think Small," *Washington Post,* June 30, 2002.

29. Ibid.

30. Lemann, 43 (see n. 3).

31. Glenn Kessler and Peter Slevin, "Preemptive Strikes Must be Decisive, Powell Says," *Washington Post,* June 15, 2002.

32. Wiliam A. Galston, "Why First Strike Will Surely Backfire," *Washington Post,* June 16, 2002.

33. See Matthew Moen, *The Christian Right and Congress* (Tuscaloosa, AL: University of Alabama Press, 1989), and Moen, "The Evolving Politics of the Christian Right," *PS: Political Science and Politics,* September 1996, http:// www.apsanet.org/PS/sept96/moen.cfm.

34. David Shribman in Ethics and Public Policy Center (EPPC), "The New Christian Right in Historical Context: A Conversation with Leo Ribuffo and David Shribman," *Center Conversations,* no. 2 (June 2001): 7, 8, http://www.eppc

.org/publications/pubID.1540/pub_detail.asp (emphasis in original).

35. Leo Ribuffo in EPPC, 1 (see n. 34).

36. Ibid., 2 (emphasis in original).

37. Ibid. (emphasis in original).

38. Rod Dreher, "Evangelicals and Jews Together: An Unlikely Alliance," *National Review Online*, April 5, 2002, http://www.nationalreview.com/dreher/dreher040502.asp.

39. Ribuffo, 3 (see n. 34).

40. Ibid., 4.

41. Ibid.

42. See Moen, "The Evolving Politics of the Christian Right" (see n. 33), and James L. Guth and John C. Green, eds., *The Bible and the Ballot Box* (San Francisco: Westview Press, 1991).

43. Leon Howell, "Ups and Downs of the Religious Right," posted at Religion Online, http://www.religion-online.org. (Posting notes, "This article appeared in *The Christian Century*, April 19–26, 2000, pp. 462–466.")

44. Sara Diamond, "The Threat of the Christian Right," Z *Magazine,* July–August 1995, 2, accessible online at http://www.zmag.org.

45. Ibid.

46. Jo-Ann Mort, "An Unholy Alliance in Support of Israel," *Los Angeles Times*, May 19, 2002.

47. Abraham McLaughlin and Gail Russell Chaddock, "Christian Right Steps in on Mideast," *Christian Science Monitor,* April 16, 2002, http://www.csmonitor.com/2002/0416/p01s01-uspo.html.

48. Allan C. Brownfeld, "Strange Bedfellows: The Jewish Establishment and the Christian Right," *Washington Report on Middle East Affairs,* August 2002, 71–72.

49. Romesh Ratnesar, "The Right's New Crusade: Lobbying For Israel," *Time*, April 29, 2002, available on CNN Web site, http://www.cnn.com/ALLPOLITICS/time/2002/05/06/crusade.html.

50. Bill Berkowitz, "Revving Up the Christian Movement for

Bush," *Z Magazine,* June 2000, http://www.zmag.org/
zmag/articles/berkowitzjune2000.htm.

51. Moen, "Evolving Politics of the Christian Right," 1
(see n. 33).

52. Lyman Kellstedt, cited in Moen, "Evolving Politics of the
Christian Right," 3 (see n. 33).

53. Mark J. Rozell and Clyde Wilcox, cited in Moen, "Evolving Politics of the Christian Right" (see n. 33).

54. Jonathan Steele, "New York Is Starting to Feel Like Brezh-
nev's Moscow: Public Debate in America Has Now
Become a Question of Loyalty," *Guardian,* May 16, 2002,
http://www.guardian.co.uk/comment/story/0,3604,716257
,00.html.

55. Michael Massing, "The Israel Lobby," *Nation,* June 10,
2002, http://www.thenation.com/docPrint.mhtm?I
=20020610&s=massing.

56. Richard Perle and Douglas J. Feith, *A Clean Break: A New
Strategy for Securing the Realm,* Institute for Advanced
Strategic and Political Studies report, June 1996,
http://www.israeleconomy.org/strat1.htm.

57. See n. 38.

58. *The Religion Report,* Radio National, Australian Broadcasting Corporation, January 5, 2002, www.abc.net.au/
rn/talks/8.30/relrpt/stories/s544092.htm.

59. Benjamin Netanyahu, *Terrorism: How the West Can Win*
(New York: Avon Books, 1987).

60. See n. 58.

61. Michael Lind, "The Israel Lobby," *Prospect Magazine,*
April 2002, 3.

62. Massing, 3 (see n. 55).

63. James Abourezk, former senator from South Dakota,
speech, American-Arab Anti-Discrimination Committee
annual convention (Washington, DC, June 2002).

64. George Sunderland, "Our Vichy Congress," *CounterPunch
Special Report,* May 10, 2002, http://www.counterpunch
.org/sunderland0510.html. "Sunderland" is a pseudonym
of a congressional staffer.

65. See n. 55.

66. Manar El-Shorbagy, "Hawks Have It Their Way," *Al-Ahram Weekly*, April 25–May 1, 2002, http://weekly.ahram.org.eg/2002/583/op11.htm.

67. Wallerstein, 6 (see n. 10).

68. Jim Lobe and Tom Barry, "Flying with The Hawks, President Bush Ignores CIA, State Department Experts," *TomPaine.com*, April 30, 2002, http://www.tompaine.com/feature.cfm/ID/5545.

69. Ali Abunimah, "Bush's Speech—A Vision of Permanent War," *Electronic Intifada*, June 24, 2002, http://electronicIntifada.net/v2/article403.shtml.

70. Aluf Benn, "Ariel Sharon Agrees to His Own Ideas," *Ha'aretz*, http://www.haaretzdaily.com, item No=183743.

71. James Bennet, "Speech Stuns Palestinians and Thrills Israelis," *New York Times*, June 25, 2002.

72. See n. 63.

73. David Ignatius, "Winning Friends in the Arab World," *Washington Post*, July 5, 2002.

Chapter 6. American Global Reach and the Anti-terrorist Crusade of George W. Bush. By Naseer Aruri.

1. The containment policy was first articulated by George F. Kennan (under the pseudonym "X"), "The Sources of Soviet Conduct," *Foreign Affairs*, July 1947.

2. See Naseer Aruri, "Globalization or Global Hegemony: The United States Versus the World," *Mideast Mirror (London)*, March 12, 1998.

3. Ibid.

4. Bernard Weinraub, "U.S. Says Libya May Have Plans to New Terror," *New York Times*, August 26, 1986; see also Naseer H. Aruri and John J. Carroll, "The Anti-Terrorist Crusade," *Arab Studies Quarterly*, vol. 9, no. 2 (Spring 1987): 186.

5. See Nicholas Lemann, "The Next World Order: The Bush Administration May Have a Brand New Doctrine of Power," *New Yorker*, April 1, 2002. Responding to George

W. Bush's threat to treat the "people who mistreat prisoners" as "war criminals," Paul Knox of the *Toronto Globe and Mail* wrote the following: "But nothing George Bush says on the subject of Geneva Conventions and international legal standards is likely to convince anyone. He has unleashed the greatest onslaught against international law of any U.S. president in living memory. He has torn up arms-control agreements and worked to sabotage the International Criminal Court. In his campaign against terrorism, he has not only flouted the venerable Geneva accords but sought to deny suspects the benefits of the law he is sworn to uphold." Knox, "How Bush kicked the [expletive] out of the Geneva Conventions," *Toronto Globe and Mail*, March 26, 2003, http://www.globeandmail.com/backgrounder/iraqcrisis/pages/c_geneva.html.

6. Marc Cooper, "An Interview with Gore Vidal: The Last Defender of the American Republic," *LA Weekly*, July 5–11, 2002; see also an editorial that appeared almost one year later (July 11, 2003) in the *Berkshire Eagle* (Pittsfield, Massachusetts), titled "Why Does 9/11 Inquiry Scare Bush?" It begins thus: "The Bush administration has never wanted an inquiry into the intelligence and law-enforcement failures that led up to the terrorist attacks of September 11, 2001, and it is doing its best to make sure we never get one. Even the tame commission of Washington insiders, led by men of the president's own party, is now complaining that its work is being hampered by foot-dragging from the Pentagon and Justice Department in producing documents and witnesses, in an effort to run the clock out on it before it can complete its work. The commission's leaders have taken the extraordinary step of accusing the White House of witness 'intimidation,' insisting that sensitive witnesses testify only in the presence of a 'monitor' from their agency."

7. See Chalmers Johnson, *Blowback: The Costs and Consequences of American Empire* (Boston: Little, Brown & Co., 2000).

8. Arundati Roy, "Mesopotamia. Babylon. The Tigris and Euphrates," *Guardian (London)*, April 2, 2003.

9. See Walter Laqueur, "We Can't Define 'Terrorism' But We Can Fight It," *Wall Street Journal*, July 16, 2002.

10. Jill Nelson, "America Creates Its Own Terrors," *USA Today*, July 5, 2002.

11. Seymour M. Hersh, "Who Lied to Whom? Why Did the Administration Endorse a Forgery about Iraq's Nuclear Program?" *New Yorker*, March 31, 2003.

12. John Hulsman, quoted in Robert Schlesinger, "We'll Strike First," *Boston Globe*, June 30, 2002.

13. George W. Bush, taken from "Complete Text of Bush's West Point Address," NewsMax, June 3, 2002, http://www
.newsmax.com/archives/articles/2002/6/2/81354.shtml.

14. Patrick J. Buchanan, "Bellicose Foreign Policy Irks Friends, Incites Foes," *USA Today*, June 24, 2002.

15. See n. 13.

16. George W. Bush, State of the Union address, January 2002. Transcript of speech available at http://www.whitehouse
.gov/news/releases/2002/01/20020129-11.html.

17. George W. Bush, address to the nation, September 7, 2003. Transcript of speech available at http://www.whitehouse
.gov/news/releases/2003/09/20030907-1.html.

18. Ibid.

19. Ibid.

20. Associated Press, "Bush: No Saddam Links to 9/11," September 17, 2003.

21. George W. Bush to the Speaker of the House of Representatives and the President Pro Tempore of the Senate, March 18, 2003. Full text of letter is available at http://usinfo
.state.gov/topical/pol/terror/03031906.htm.

22. According to CorpWatch, as the bombs began falling on Iraq on March 19, 2003, "thousands of employees of Halliburton, Vice President Dick Cheney's former company, are working alongside US troops in Kuwait and Turkey under a package deal worth close to a billion dollars. According to US Army sources, they are building tent cities and providing logistical support for the war in Iraq in addition to other hot spots in the 'war on terrorism.'" Pratap Chatterjee, "Halliburton Makes a Killing on Iraq War: Cheney's Former Company Profits from Supporting Troops," CorpWatch, March 20, 2003, http://www

.corpwatch.org/issues/PID.jsp?articleid=6008.

According to BBC News, "A US company has won a $4.8m (£3m) contract to manage Umm Qasr port in southern Iraq. The contract is the second awarded under US Government plans for reconstruction in Iraq. Stevedoring Services of America will be responsible for operating Iraq's only deep-water port, with the aim of allowing food and other humanitarian and reconstruction materials and supplies to be delivered efficiently.... *UK firms were said to be incensed by the solicitation of bids from US companies to rebuild Iraqi infrastructure....* US engineering firm Kellogg Brown & Root—part of Halliburton, the company once headed by US vice-president Dick Cheney—picked up a contract to put out oil well fires and repair oil facilities." "US Firm Wins Umm Qasr Deal," BBC News, March 25, 2003, http://news.bbc.co.uk/1/hi/business/2884701.stm (emphasis in original).

In an article titled "Cheney's Conflict with the Truth," Derrick Jackson writes: "On 'Meet the Press' last Sunday, Vice President Dick Cheney said, 'Since I left Halliburton to become George Bush's vice president, I've severed all my ties with the company, gotten rid of all my financial interests. I have no financial interest in Halliburton of any kind and haven't had now, for over three years.' That is the latest White House lie." Jackson goes on to quote a release by Senator Frank Lautenberg (D-NJ) showing that Cheney received $205,298 in deferred salary from Halliburton in 2001; $162,392 in 2002; and will continue to receive about $150,000 a year in 2003 and 2004. Cheney is also still holding 433,333 stock options. His salary from Halliburton exceeds his vice presidential salary of $198,600. Derrick Jackson, "Cheney's Conflict with the Truth," *Boston Globe*, September 19, 2003.

Maureen Dowd wrote the following in the *New York Times*: "Now Mr. Perle, who urged America to war with moral certitude, finds himself subject to questions about his own standards of right and wrong. Stephen Labaton wrote in The Times on Friday that Mr. Perle was advising the Pentagon on war even as he was retained by Global Crossing, the bankrupt telecommunications company, to help overcome Pentagon resistance to its proposed sale to a joint

venture involving a Hong Kong billionaire. The confidant
of Rummy and Wolfy serves as the chairman of the
Defense Policy Board, an influential Pentagon advisory
panel. That's why Global Crossing agreed to pay Mr. Perle
a fat fee: $725,000. The fee structure is especially smelly
because $600,000 of the windfall is contingent on govern-
ment approval of the sale. (In his original agreement, Mr.
Perle also asked the company to shell out for 'working
meals,' which could add up, given his status as a gourmand
from the Potomac to Provence, where he keeps a vacation
home among the feckless French.) Although his position on
the Defense Policy Board is not paid, Mr. Perle is still
bound by government ethics rules that forbid officials from
reaping financial benefit from their government positions.
He and his lawyer told Mr. Labaton that his work for
Global Crossing did not violate the rules because he did
not lobby for the company and was serving in an advisory
capacity to its lawyers." Maureen Dowd, "Perle's Plunder
Blunder," *New York Times*, March 23, 2003. For more on
Perle's dealings, see Seymour Hersh, "Lunch with the
Chairman: Why Was Richard Perle Meeting with Adnan
Khashoggi?" *New Yorker*, March 17, 2003, http://
www.newyorker.com/fact/content/?030317fa_fact.

23. Peter Vernezze, "Absolutism Not a Quality Americans
Ought to Seek in Presidents," *Standard-Examiner (Ogden,
UT)*, June 12, 2003.

24. See n. 13.

25. "Thousands of marines have been given a pamphlet called
'A Christian's Duty,' a mini prayer book which includes a
tear-out section to be mailed to the White House pledging
the soldier who sends it in has been praying for Bush. 'I
have committed to pray for you, your family, your staff
and our troops during this time of uncertainty and tumult.
May God's peace be your guide,' says the pledge, according
to a journalist embedded with coalition forces. The pamphlet, produced by a group called In Touch Ministries, offers a daily prayer to be made for the US president, a
born-again Christian who likes to invoke his God in
speeches. Sunday's is 'Pray that the President and his advisers will seek God and his wisdom daily and not rely on

their own understanding'. Monday's reads 'Pray that the President and his advisers will be strong and courageous to do what is right regardless of critics'." "US Soldiers in Iraq Asked to Pray for Bush," *ABC News Online,* Australian Broadcasting Corporation, March 30, 2003, http://www.abc.net.au/news/newsitems/s819685.htm.

26. George McGovern, "The Reason Why," *The Nation,* April 21, 2003, http://www.thenation.com/doc.mhtml?i= 20030421&s=mcgovern.

27. When the first Iraqi suicide bomber slammed his car into a US checkpoint in occupied Iraq, killing four soldiers, Robert Fisk wrote the following: "In a strange way, therefore, 11 September at last finds a symbolic connection with Iraq. While the attempts to link President Saddam's regime with Osama bin Laden turned out to be fraudulent, the anger that the US has unleashed is real, and has met the weapon the Americans fear most." Robert Fisk, "Sergeant's Suicidal Act of War Has Struck Fear into Allied Hearts," *Independent (UK),* March 31, 2003.

28. Praful Bidwai, "Machinehead," *Hindustan Times,* March 22, 2003, http://www.hindustantimes.com/news/ 181_218617,00120001.htm; Seymour Hersh wrote about the Niger affair: "On March 14th, Senator Jay Rockefeller, of West Virginia, the senior Democrat on the Senate Intelligence Committee, formally asked Robert Mueller, the F.B.I. director, to investigate the forged documents. Rockefeller had voted for the resolution authorizing force last fall. Now he wrote to Mueller, 'There is a possibility that the fabrication of these documents may be part of a larger deception campaign aimed at manipulating public opinion and foreign policy regarding Iraq.' He urged the F.B.I. to ascertain the source of the documents, the skill-level of the forgery, the motives of those responsible, and 'why the intelligence community did not recognize the documents were fabricated.' A Rockefeller aide told me that the F.B.I. had promised to look into it." (See n. 11.)

29. Roger Hardy, "US Options on Iran," BBC News, September, 2, 2003, http://news.bbc.co.uk/1/hi/world/middle_east/ 3115973.stm.

30. Steven Mufson, "The Way Bush Sees the World," *Washington Post*, February 17, 2002.

31. Ibid.

32. Ibid.

33. The text of the letter proposing a shift from a policy of containment to a policy of regime change in Iraq, bypassing the UN Security Council, and list of signatories follows. The signatories on this letter are the same people who form the neoconservative cabal now shaping American foreign policy. In response to this letter, Clinton proposed and Congress enacted a law for regime change in Iraq.

January 26, 1998
The Honorable William J. Clinton
President of the United States
Washington, DC

Dear Mr. President:

We are writing you because we are convinced that current American policy toward Iraq is not succeeding, and that we may soon face a threat in the Middle East more serious than any we have known since the end of the Cold War. In your upcoming State of the Union Address, you have an opportunity to chart a clear and determined course for meeting this threat. We urge you to seize that opportunity, and to enunciate a new strategy that would secure the interests of the U.S. and our friends and allies around the world. That strategy should aim, above all, at the removal of Saddam Hussein's regime from power. We stand ready to offer our full support in this difficult but necessary endeavor.

The policy of "containment" of Saddam Hussein has been steadily eroding over the past several months. As recent events have demonstrated, we can no longer depend on our partners in the Gulf War coalition to continue to uphold the sanctions or to punish Saddam when he blocks or evades UN inspections. Our ability to ensure that Saddam Hussein is not producing weapons of mass destruction, therefore, has substantially diminished. Even if full inspections were eventually to resume, which now seems highly unlikely, experience has shown that it is difficult if not impossible to monitor Iraq's chemical and biological weapons production. The lengthy period during which the inspectors will have been unable to enter many Iraqi facilities has made it even less likely that they will be able to uncover all of Saddam's secrets. As a result, in the not-too-distant future we will be unable to determine with any reasonable level of confidence whether Iraq does or does not possess such weapons.

Such uncertainty will, by itself, have a seriously destabilizing effect on the entire Middle East. It hardly needs to be added that if Saddam does acquire the capability to deliver weapons of mass destruction, as he is almost certain to do if we continue along the present course, the safety of American troops in the region, of our friends and allies like Israel and the moderate Arab states, and a significant portion of the world's supply of oil will all be put at hazard. As you have rightly declared, Mr. President, the security of the world in the first part of the 21st century will be determined largely by how we handle this threat.

Given the magnitude of the threat, the current policy, which depends for its success upon the steadfastness of our coalition partners and upon the cooperation of Saddam Hussein, is dangerously inadequate. The only acceptable strategy is one that eliminates the possibility that Iraq will be able to use or threaten to use weapons of mass destruction. In the near term, this means a willingness to undertake military action as diplomacy is clearly failing. In the long term, it means removing Saddam Hussein and his regime from power. That now needs to become the aim of American foreign policy.

We urge you to articulate this aim, and to turn your Administration's attention to implementing a strategy for removing Saddam's regime from power. This will require a full complement of diplomatic, political and military efforts. Although we are fully aware of the dangers and difficulties in implementing this policy, we believe the dangers of failing to do so are far greater. We believe the U.S. has the authority under existing UN resolutions to take the necessary steps, including military steps, to protect our vital interests in the Gulf. In any case, American policy cannot continue to be crippled by a misguided insistence on unanimity in the UN Security Council.

We urge you to act decisively. If you act now to end the threat of weapons of mass destruction against the U.S. or its allies, you will be acting in the most fundamental national security interests of the country. If we accept a course of weakness and drift, we put our interests and our future at risk.

Sincerely,

Elliott Abrams, Richard L. Armitage, William J. Bennett, Jeffrey Bergner, John Bolton, Paula Dobriansky, Francis Fukuyama, Robert Kagan, Zalmay Khalilzad, William Kristol, Richard Perle, Peter W. Rodman, Donald Rumsfeld, William Schneider Jr., Vin Weber, Paul Wolfowitz, R. James Woolsey, Robert B. Zoellick

As for Wolfowitz's advocacy of a war against Iraq since 1979, consider the following: "General Eric K. Shinseki, the Army chief of staff, points out that as a young Pentagon analyst Wolfowitz directed a secret assessment of Persian Gulf threats that marked Iraq as a menace to its neighbors and to American interests. This, Shinseki informs them with everything but a drumroll, was in 1979, a dozen years before Desert Storm." Bill Keller, "The Sunshine Warrior," *New York Times Magazine*, September 22, 2002.

34. Keller, "The Sunshine Warrior" (see n. 33).

35. Michael Lind, "The Weird Men Behind George W. Bush's War," *New Statesman*, April 7, 2003.

36. Ralph Nader, "Pre-emptive War on a Defenseless Country: Bush Is Acting Like a Judicially-Selected Dictator," *Counter-Punch,* March 25, 2003, http://www.counterpunch.org/nader03252003.html.

37. Richard Perle, "Thank God for the Death of the UN: Its Abject Failure Gave Us Only Anarchy; The World Needs Order," *Guardian (London),* March 21, 2003.

38. Guy Dinmore, "Ideologues Reshape World Over Breakfast," *Financial Times,* March 22, 2003.

39. Ari Shavit, "White Man's Burden," *Ha'aretz,* April 4, 2003.

40. For an insightful analysis of the war against Iraq, see Patrick Seale, "The United States and Britain Are Heading for Disaster," Mafhoum Press Review, March 28, 2003, http://www.mafhoum.com/press5/138seale.htm.

41. See Naseer Aruri, "Remapping the Middle East: Whose War Is It This Time?" *CounterPunch*, October 28, 2002, http://www.counterpunch.org/aruri1028.html. For a discussion of Israel's use of Oslo as a strategy, see Naseer H. Aruri, *Dishonest Broker: The U.S. Role in Israel and Palestine* (Cambridge, MA: South End Press, 2003), 167–92.

42. According to the American Arab Institute (http://www.aaiusa.org), pro-Israel retired US Lieutenant General Jay Garner will most likely lead the civil authority of Iraq after the fall of Saddam Hussein's regime. Garner was tapped in January by Defense Secretary Donald Rumsfeld to head the Office of Reconstruction and Humanitarian Assistance, which has been charged with devising a plan to rebuild Iraq after the current conflict. While many laud Garner for his compassion and humanitarianism, some are questioning the general's politics. *Forward* reports that Garner "maintains

ties with the Jewish Institute for National Security Affairs,"
a nonprofit organization committed to "strengthening the
strategic cooperation relationship between these two [Israel
and the United States] great democracies." In October
2000, in reaction to the second Intifada, Garner, along with
more than forty other US military officers, signed on to the
"JINSA Flag and General Officers Statement on Palestinian
Violence," a diatribe that places blame for the violence
squarely with the Palestinians. "The Palestinian-initiated
violence in Israel now strongly tells us that the necessary
good faith is sorely lacking on the Palestinian side. America's responsibility as a friend to Israel, the only country in
the Middle East that shares our democratic and humanitarian values, should never yield to America's role as facilitator
in this process. Friends don't leave friends on the battlefield."
The full text is available on the JINSA Web site at
http://www.jinsa.org/articles/print.html/documentid/1043.

43. "US Civilian Head for Iraq Took Paid Trip to Israel,"
Reuters, March 25, 2003. Following is an excerpt from the
Reuters story: "The retired U.S. general named as civilian
governor of occupied Iraq has visited Israel at the expense
of a lobbying group which says the United States needs Israel to project U.S. force in the Middle East. The coordinator for civilian administration in Iraq, Lt. Gen. Jay Garner,
put his name to an October 2000 statement blaming Palestinians for the outbreak of Israeli-Palestinian violence and
saying that a strong Israel is an important security asset to
the United States.

The statement was sponsored by the Jewish Institute for
National Security Affairs (JINSA), which pays for senior
retired U.S. military officers to visit Israel for security briefings by Israeli officials and politicians. Richard Perle, one
of the architects of the U.S. invasion of Iraq, is a member
of the institute's board of advisers ... In the 2000 statement,
Garner and 42 other senior retired officers said: 'We are
appalled by the Palestinian political and military leadership
that teaches children the mechanics of war while filling
their heads with hate. The security of the State of Israel is a
matter of great importance to U.S. policy in the Middle
East and eastern Mediterranean, as well as around the

world. A strong Israel is an asset that American military planners and political leaders can rely on,' the statement added. JINSA's mission statement, on its Web site, says the United States should maintain a presence in the Middle East because of its energy resources, governments 'amassing weapons of mass destruction' and 'the inherent instability in the region caused primarily by inter-Arab rivalries.'"

44. See n. 38.

45. Ibid. See also William O. Beeman, "Military Might: The Man behind 'Total War' in the Mideast," *San Francisco Chronicle*, May 14, 2003. Professor Beeman begins his article thus: "Most Americans have never heard of Michael Ledeen, but if the United States ends up in an extended shooting war throughout the Middle East, it will be largely due to his inspiration." He reports that Ledeen told JINSA on April 30, 2003, "The time for diplomacy is at an end; it is time for a free Iran, free Syria and free Lebanon."

46. Terrell E. Arnold, "Iran—The Next Israeli Domino," September 3, 2003, *Rense.com,* http://rense.com/general41/iran.htm.

47. Richard Sale, "Rice Blocked Plan for Raids on Syria," United Press International, May 2, 2003.

48. Lou Marano, "Voices of Dissent: Eric Margolis," United Press International, March 25, 2003, http://www.upi.com/view.cfm?StoryID=20030325-015143-7876r.

49. Tanya Reinhart interviewed by Jon Elmer, "A Slow, Steady Genocide," ZNet, September 11, 2003, http://www.zmag.org/content/showarticle.cfm?SectionID=22&ItemID=4180. For a discussion of "transfer" in Zionist history, see Nur Masalha, *Imperial Israel and the Palestinians: The Politics of Expansion* (London: Pluto Press, 2000).

50. Meron Benvenisti, "Preemptive Warnings of Fantastic Scenarios," *Ha'aretz,* August 15, 2002.

51. Jason Keyser, "Israel Urges U.S. to Attack Iraq," Associated Press, August 16, 2002.

52. Gideon Levy, "Smart Bombs, Obtuse Commentators," *Ha'aretz*, March 25, 2003. Levy continues thus:
    "A smile akin to that of a child describing his new

toys spreads on their face as they describe the magical allure of the American power of destruction. Former air force commanders, who apparently find it difficult to give up their posts, describe horrific bombing runs or flying extermination machines as if they were works of art.

"Brigadier General (res.) Aryeh Mizrahi outdid himself in one of these countless discussions when he pulled from his pocket a small model cluster bomb—apparently manufactured by Israel Military Industries (of which he is the chairman)—and with glittering eyes told viewers that the Americans were using that very weapon. He explained how it breaks up into a vast number of 'bomblets' and how it 'wreaked havoc' in the Lebanon War, 'pulverizing' whole armored battalions, and that 'everyone who saw the results in Lebanon was appalled'—it was positively 'raining steel,' he said.

"The small, smart bomb that Mizrahi brought was passed from hand to hand in the studio and the elderly generals fondled it reverently. It was an unforgettable spectacle. Of course, none of them bothered to point out the killing and destruction that a bomb like this can cause among innocent civilians, nor did anyone wonder what happens to a society whose spokesmen get so pathologically excited by weapons and killing."

53. Michael Kinsley, "What Bush Isn't Saying About Iraq," *Slate*, October 24, 2003, http://slate.msn.com/id/2073093/.

54. Steven Zak, "Matter of Honor," *Jewish World Review,* May 1, 2003. In this excerpt, the author first cites an article in *USA Today,* then one from *Ma'ariv* detailing support provided by Israel to the US during the war.

55. Richard Perle is also director of Israel's daily, the *Jerusalem Post,* and happens also to be chairman and CEO of Hollinger Digital Inc. Hollinger International (the parent group of Hollinger Digital) is the owner of both the *Sunday Telegraph* and the *Jerusalem Post*. See Inayat Bunglawala, "We Won't Forget the Terrible Things Done in Our Name," *Times (London),* March 25, 2003. Perle resigned as chair on March 27, 2003, after a senior Democrat called for an investigation for possible conflicts of interest in his roles as corporate adviser and Pentagon con-

sultant. See Reuters, "Invasion Architect in Hot Water over Conflicts of Another Kind," *Sydney Morning Herald,* March 27, 2003, http://www.smh.com.au/articles/ 2003/03/26/1048653750458.html.

56. See Brian Whitaker, "Selective MEMRI," *Guardian (London),* August 12, 2002.

57. Patrick J. Buchanan, "Whose War? A Neoconservative Clique Seeks to Ensnare Our Country in a Series of Wars that Are Not in America's Interest," *American Conservative,* March 24, 2003.

58. Stanley Hoffman, quoted in Buchanan, "Whose War?" (see n. 57).

59. Ian Traynor, "How American Power Girds the Globe with a Ring of Steel," *Guardian (London),* April 21, 2003.

60. See n. 39.

61. Norman Podhoretz, "In Praise of the Bush Doctrine," *Commentary* 114, no. 2, September 2002.

62. Lloyd Richardson to the *Financial Times,* quoted in Conn Hallinan, "U.S. and India—A Dangerous Alliance," Foreign Policy in Focus, May 6, 2003, http://www.fpif.org/ commentary/2003/0305india.html.

63. Department of Defense document, quoted in Hallinan, "U.S. and India" (see n. 62). See also Erica Strecker Downs, *China's Quest for Energy Security* (Santa Monica, CA: Rand Corporation, 2000), http://www.rand.org/ publications/MR/MR1244/.

64. See Aruri and Carroll, "The Anti-Terrorist Crusade" (see n. 4).

65. Justin Huggler, "Israelis Trained US Troops in Jenin-style Urban Warfare," *Independent,* March 29, 2003.

66. John Donnelly, "Nation Set to Push Sharon on Agreement," *Boston Globe*, October 10, 2001.

67. See Naseer H. Aruri, *Dishonest Broker: The U.S. Role in Israel and Palestine* (Cambridge, MA: South End Press, 2003), 201–04.

68. For analysis of the road map, see Naseer H. Aruri, "The Road Map: A Peace Plan or Another Palliative?" *Al*

Mubadara, May 17, 2003, http://www.almubadara.org/en/; Danny Rubinstein, "Fantasy Land," *Ha'aretz*, May 26, 2003; Michael A. Hoffman II, "The 'Road Map' for Peace Is a Swindle," May 29, 2003, *The Hoffman Wire*, http://www.hoffman-info.com/wire6.html; and Mouin Rabbani, "The Road from Aqaba," *Middle East Report Online*, June 13, 2003, http://www.merip.org/mero/mero061303.html.

69. See, for example, James Rubin, "Stumbling into War," *Foreign Affairs*, September–October 2003.

70. Steve LeBlanc, "Kennedy Says Case for Iraq War Was Fraud," Associated Press, September 18, 2003.

71. H.D.S. Greenway, "The Radical Hand behind Bush's War Moves," *Boston Globe*, September 19, 2003.

72. Ibid.

73. Immanuel Wallerstein, "Bush in Big Trouble at Home," Fernand Braudel Center Commentary, no. 121, September 15, 2003, http://fbc.binghamton.edu/121en.htm.

74. Mark Egan, "NY Times Columnist Sees Gloom in America's Future," Reuters, September 16, 2003.

75. Michael Peel, "Europe Must Not Buy Bush's Line," *Financial Times*, September 18, 2003.

76. James Harding, "Weakness in the White House: As Costs and Casualties Mount in Iraq, the Finger-Pointing Begins in Washington," *Financial Times*, September 15, 2003.

77. Evelyn Leopold, "Anan Challenges U.S. Doctrine of Preventive Action," Reuters, September 23, 2003.

78. It has been argued that the war on Iraq is an oil currency war aiming to arrest an OPEC momentum toward the euro as an oil transaction currency standard. Thus, in order to preempt OPEC, Washington needs to gain geostrategic control of Iraq along with its second-largest proven oil reserves. See W. Clark, "The Real Reasons for the Upcoming War with Iraq: A Macroeconomic and Geostrategic Analysis of the Unspoken Truth," Independent Media Center, January 2003, http://www.indymedia.org. This argument is supported by Immanuel Wallerstein's thesis about the war: "He [Bush] did this in order to demonstrate the overwhelm-

ing military superiority of the United States and to accomplish two primary objectives: (1) intimidate all potential nuclear proliferators into abandoning their projects; (2) squash all European ideas of an autonomous political role in the world-system." Immanuel Wallerstein, "Bush Bets All He Has," March 15, 2003, Fernand Braudel Center Commentary, no. 109, http://fbc.binghamton.edu/109en.htm. See also Amir Butler, "The Euro and the War on Iraq," *A True Word,* March 29, 2003, http://www.atrueword.com/index.php/article/view/49; Duncan Du Bois, "Defending the Dollar," *Natal Witness,* April 4, 2003. Du Bois sums up the four objectives in the war against Iraq, as outlined by Australian analyst Geoffrey Heard: "Return Iraq's oil reserves to the dollar circle; send a clear message to other oil producers as to what will happen to them if they try to leave the dollar zone; deal a setback to the EU and its euro; use the war as a cover to get Venezuela's oil back into the dollar circle by means of covert CIA action."

79. Karen Armstrong, "Our Role in the Terror," *Guardian (London),* September 18, 2003, http://www.guardian.co.uk/comment/story/0,3604,1044413,00.html.

80. Anthony Westell, "Who's Winning the War on Terror? Sorry, George," *Globe and Mail (Canada),* September 9, 2003.

Chapter 7. The Interlocking of Right-Wing Politics and US Middle East Policy: Solidifying Arab/Muslim Demonization. By Elaine C. Hagopian.

1. Thomas A. Dine, "The Revolution in U.S.-Israel Relations," *Journal of Palestine Studies* 15, no. 4 (Summer 1986), 134, 138–39.

2. Alain Gresh, "As for What the Young People Want, No One Is Sure," *Le Monde Diplomatique,* June 2003.

3. Kesher Talk is a part of Howard Fienberg's Web site at http://www.hfienberg.com/kesher/. The Saudi Institute's Web site is http://www.saudiinstitute.org.

4. Eli J. Lake, "The Search for Syrian Liberals: Few Good Men," *New Republic,* May 26, 2003.

5. Ibid.

6. Zaki Chehab, "Inside the Resistance: Popular Anger Is Forging an Alliance Between Diverse Strands of Iraq's Guerrilla Movement," *Guardian*, October 13, 2003; and Egyptian Popular Campaign to Confront US Aggression, "Cairo Declaration against U.S. Hegemony and War on Iraq and in Solidarity with Palestine," December 2002.

7. Murhaf Jouejati, "Recent Political Developments in Syria" (Middle East Seminar, Harvard University, May 8, 2003).

8. "US Military Leases Land in Kyrgyzstan," *Zaman (Istanbul)*, May 4, 2003, http://www.zaman.org.

9. Erica Strecker Downs, *China's Quest for Energy Security* (Santa Monica, CA: Rand Corporation, 2000), xi–xii, http://www.rand.org/publications/MR/MR1244/. This study was directed by US point man in Afghanistan and Iraq, Dr. Zalmay Khalildad—now the US ambassador to Afghanistan—and a former protégé of Paul Wolfowitz and Richard Perle. China's "dependence on energy imports is expected to increase significantly over the next 20 years. It is projected that China will need to import some 60 percent of its oil and at least 30 percent of its natural gas by 2020.... This report examines the measures that China is taking to achieve energy security and the motivations behind them. The study concludes that China's energy security activities can be explained in terms of China's long-standing fear of dependency on foreign energy. The Chinese government regards oil imports as a strategic vulnerability that could be exploited by foreign powers seeking to influence China. The United States is currently the most powerful country in the world and is perceived by many in China as uncomfortable with China's rising power. As a result, the Chinese government views the United States as the primary threat to China's energy security, and China's energy security activities, which are largely defensive in nature, reflect this concern." Also see Ross Munro, "China: The Challenge of a Rising Power," and Peter Rodman, "Russia: The Challenge of a Failing Power," in Robert Kagan and William Kristol, eds., *Present Dangers: Crisis and Opportunity in American Foreign and Defense Policy* (San Francisco: Encounter Books, 2000), 47–95.

10. Ed Blanche, "Israel Steps Up Military Aid to India, Consolidates Strategic Relationship," *Daily Star (Beirut)*,

June 26, 2003.

11. Larry Ramer, "Pro-Israel Activists Seeking Allies Among
     Immigrants from India: AIPAC, Others Stress Threat of
     Muslim Extremism in Outreach Bid to America's 1.6 Mil-
     lion South Asian Hindus," *Forward*, October 21, 2002.

12. Conn Hallinan, "U.S. and India—A Dangerous Alliance,"
     Foreign Policy in Focus, May 6, 2003, http://www.fpif
     .org/commentary/2003/0305india.html.

13. Martin Walker, "U.S., India Discuss 'Asian NATO,'"
     United Press International, May 29, 2003.

14. "India Signs Israeli Radar Deal," BBC News, October 12,
     2003, http://news.bbc.co.uk/go/pr/fr/-/2/hi/south_asia/
     3180114.stm.

15. See n. 13.

16. Peter Beaumont and Conal Urquhart, "Israel Deploys Nu-
     clear Arms in Submarines," *Observer*, October 12, 2003.

17. Abraham Rabinovich, "Iran Air-Strike Plan Seen as Bluff,"
     Washington Times, October 13, 2003.

18. Parsa Venkateshwar Rao Jr., "India's Right-wingers Woo
     Jewish Lobby," *Daily Star (Beirut)*, May 20, 2003. India's
     national security adviser Brajesh Mishra "acknowledged in
     his speech [at the annual dinner of the American Jewish
     Committee (AJC), May 8, 2003] the role played by Israel
     and the Jewish organization in improving India-US
     relations. He said 'We also value your (AJC) contribution to
     promoting India-US relations and India-Israel relations.'"

19. William Booth, "Shiite Leader Makes Bold Return to Iraq
     Holy City," *Washington Post*, May 13, 2003.

20. Eli J. Lake, "The Post-Saddam Danger from Iran, Persian
     Gulf," *New Republic*, October 7, 2002.

21. Dan Murphy, "Iraqi Shiite Split Widens," *Christian Science
     Monitor*, October 16, 2003.

22. Ian Fisher, "An Anti-American Iraqi Cleric Declares His
     Own Government," *New York Times*, October 12, 2003.

23. See n. 20.

24. Juan Cole, "The Iraqi Shiites: On the History of
     America's Would-be Allies," *Boston Review*, October—

November 2003.

25. Brian Knowlton, "Protesters in Iraq Assail U.S. Occupation," *International Herald Tribune*, May 20, 2003.

26. Murtaza Razvi, "Understanding the Iraqi Shia," *Dawn (Pakistan)*, May 17, 2003 (emphasis added).

27. Edmund Ghareeb, *The Kurdish Question in Iraq* (Syracuse, NY: Syracuse University Press, 1981), 138–42.

28. Michael Howard, "Kurds' Faith in New Iraq Fading Fast," *Guardian*, October 21, 2003.

29. "Turks' Troop Offer Could Be Dropped," Associated Press, October 22, 2003.

30. Karen Armstrong, "Faith and Freedom," *Guardian*, May 8, 2003.

31. William O. Beeman, "A Formidable Muslim Bloc Emerges," *Los Angeles Times*, June 1, 2003.

32. Jim Lobe, "Neo-con Fingerprints on Syria Raid," *Asia Times*, October 9, 2003, http://www.atimes.com; and Warren P. Strobel, "Policy Change Taking Shape in U.S. over Syria," Knight Ridder Newspapers, October 6, 2003.

33. Zaki Yahya, writing from Najaf, "Iraqis Call for Self-Rule," *Institute of War and Peace Reporting* Online, July 2, 2003, http://www.iwpr.net/index.pl?archive/irq/irq_25_1_eng.txt.

34. Ibid.

35. Ibid.

36. Robert G. Kaiser, "Bush and Sharon Nearly Identical on Mideast Policy," *Washington Post*, February 9, 2003.

37. US Department of State, *A Performance-Based Road Map to a Permanent Two-State Solution to the Israeli-Palestinian Conflict*, December 20, 2002 (released April 30, 2003), http://www.state.gov/r/pa/prs/ps/2003/20062.htm.

38. George W. Bush, speech, June 24, 2002, http://www.whitehouse.gov/news/releases/2002/06/20020624-3.html. Bush said, "The United States will not support the establishment of a Palestinian state until its leaders engage in a sustained fight against the terrorists and dismantle their infrastructure."

39. The most recent effort was reported by Leonard Doyle, "The Sacrifice: Palestine's Coveted Right to Return," *Independent,* October 14, 2003.

40. James Bennet, "Sharon Sets Hard Line on Settlements Policy," *New York Times*, May 13, 2003.

41. John Whitbeck, "The Road Map," *Daily Star (Beirut),* May 4, 2003.

42. Dan Ephron, "Sharon Statement Brings Storm of Criticism," *Boston Globe*, May 28, 2003.

43. Both quotes are in Ali Abunimah, "Who's Afraid of the Road Map?" *Daily Star (Beirut),* May 2, 2003.

44. Statement from Prime Minister's Bureau, as released by Israel's Government Press Office, "Israel Accepts 'Steps' of 'Road Map,' Qualified by 'Remarks,'" *Israel Insider*, May 25, 2003, http://www.israelinsider.com.

45. Daniel Ben Simon, *Ha'aretz,* May 2, 2003, available online at http://www.comeandsee.co.il/print.php?sid=450.

46. "Police Crack Down on Israeli Islamic Group," *Jordan Times*, May 14, 2003.

47. Palestinian Centre for Human Rights, "In a continuation of the policy of collective punishment against relatives of alleged Palestinian activists, Israeli occupying forces transfer a Palestinian from the West Bank to the Gaza Strip," press release (Ref. 72/3003), May 20, 2003.

48. BADIL, "The Occupation Continues: 16 Deported to Gaza; New Category of Refugees Created," press release (E42/03), October 17, 2003.

49. Chris McGreal in Jerusalem, *Guardian*, May 9, 2003.

50. Glenn Kessler, "White House Backs Latest Israeli Attacks," *Washington Post*, June 13, 2003.

51. Patrick Seale, "Sharon, Bush and the Race for 'Greater Israel,'" *Daily Star (Beirut),* October 17, 2003.

52. H.D.S. Greenway, "The War Inside Bush's Cabinet," *Boston Globe*, May 2, 2003.

53. See n. 39.

54. Richard Perle and Douglas J. Feith, *A Clean Break: A New Strategy for Securing the Realm,* Institute for Advanced

Strategic and Political Studies report, June 1996, 2. The full report is available at http://www.israeleconomy.org/strat1.htm.

55. Tabitha Petran, *Syria* (New York: Praeger Publishers, 1972).

56. Patrick Seale, *ASAD: The Struggle for the Middle East* (Berkeley: University of California Press, 1988).

57. Richard Sale, "Rice Blocked Plan for Raids on Syria," United Press International, May 2, 2003.

58. Patrick Seale, "Why Are the U.S. and Israel Threatening Syria?" *Al Hayat,* April 18, 2003.

59. See n. 7.

60. *Ha'aretz* and *Forward* staff, "Shifting Gears, Syria Offers to Reopen Negotiations with Israel," *Forward,* May 2, 2003. Also see, Tony Haddad, "Over 100 Congressmen Have Co-Sponsored the Syria Accountability and Lebanese Sovereignty Restoration Act of 2003," Lebanese American Council for Democracy, May 20, 2003.

61. Information in a memo by Tony Haddad of the Lebanese American Council for Democracy (Washington, DC), dated July 1, 2003, with subject heading "House Hearing," which was posted to the phoenicia list (copy on file with Elaine Hagopian). Haddad also announced a dinner and fundraiser for Congressman Eliot Engel, who is credited with "starting it all."

62. Alia Ibrahim, "Khatami Addresses Crowd of 50,000 at Cite Sportive," *Daily Star (Beirut),* May 14, 2003.

63. Sabine Darrous, "Khatami Addresses Parliament at End of 3-Day Visit," *Daily Star (Beirut),* May 15, 2003.

64. Patrick Seale, "What Must Syria do to Defend Itself?" *Daily Star (Beirut),* May 2, 2003.

65. Ibid.

66. Marc Sirois, http://www.yellowtimes.org, Lebanon, May 7, 2003.

67. See n. 4.

68. "Brief Biography of Farid N. Ghadry," which appears on the Reform Party of Syria's Web Site: http://www.reformsyria.com/bio_of_farid_n_ghadry.htm. Also see

Lake, "The Search for Syrian Liberals" (see n. 4).

69. See n. 4.

70. Farid N. Ghadry, "If Not Military Action, the Mistrust for the Baath Party in Syria dictates a New Solution," April 16, 2003, on his Web Site: http://www.reformsyria.com/.

71. Ibid.

72. Ghadry, "Brief Biography" (see n. 68).

73. David Ignatius, "A Road Map for Syria Too," *Washington Post*, June 3, 2003.

74. Mona Ziade, "Damascus Inks Major Oil Deal with American Firms: Agreement Dims Fears of Syrian Isolation," *Daily Star*, June 2, 2003.

75. Elaine C. Hagopian, "Redrawing the Map in the Middle East: Phalangist Lebanon and Zionist Israel," *Arab Studies Quarterly* 5, no. 4, 321–36. Also see, Livia Rokach, *Israel's Sacred Terrorism: A Study Based on Moshe Sharett's Personal Diary and Other Documents* (Belmont: AAUG Press, 1980), 17–27.

76. The author taught at AUB in 1973–74, and heard Professor Malik on more than one occasion express this feeling.

77. See the Middle East Forum Web site, http://www.meforum.org/experts.php.

78. See the USCFL Web site, http://freelebanon.org, and the LCCC Web site, http://www.104521ccc.com/.

79. The statement is posted on the Lebanese Information Center Web site, http://www.licus.org.

80. General Aoun's Web site is http://www.tayyar.org.

81. Lebanese American Council for Democracy, "Syria Is Responsible for Today's Attempted Attack on U.S. Embassy in Lebanon," May 15, 2003, http://www.LA-CD.org.

82. Ibid.

83. Fred Halliday, *Arabia without Sultans: A Survey of Political Instability in the Arab World* (New York: Vintage Books, 1974).

84. Thomas E. Ricks, "Briefing Depicted Saudis as Enemies," *Washington Post*, August 6, 2002.

85. Mamoun Fandy, *Saudi Arabia and the Politics of Dissent* (New York: Palgrave, 2001).

86. Ed Blanche, "Carnage in Saudi Arabia: A Disaster Waiting to Happen," *Daily Star (Beirut),* May 14, 2003.

87. Ed Blanche, "US Control of Baghdad and Its Crude May Signal New Assault on OPEC," *Daily Star (Beirut),* June 6, 2003.

88. F. Gregory Gause III, "The Approaching Turning Point: The Future of U.S. Relations with the Gulf States; Executive Summary," originally published by the Brookings Institution, Saban Center for Middle East Policy, May 14, 2003 (emphasis added). Available online on the Saudi American Forum Web site, http://www.saudi-american-forum.org/.

89. See n. 2.

90. Delinda C. Hanley, "Saudi Bashing: Who's Behind It and Why?" *Arab News,* April 26, 2003.

91. Robert Collier, "Saudis Take Small Step Toward Political Reform: Conservative Monarch Opens Ears to Criticism," *San Francisco Chronicle,* January 28, 2003.

92. Ibid.

93. Ibid.

94. F. Gregory Gause III, "Creating a 'Normal' U.S.-Saudi Relationship," p. 3, originally published by the Brookings Institution, Saban Center for Middle East Policy, June 4, 2003, and reproduced only by the Saudi-American Forum, http://www.saudi-american-forum.org/.

95. Ibid.

96. Ibid., 4.

97. Ibid.

98. For further discussion of dissent in Saudi Arabia, see Fandy, *Politics of Dissent* (n. 85).

99. Karl Vick, "Iranian Apathy May Hinder U.S. Bid to Foment Unrest: Reformists Warn Against Destabilization Campaign," *Washington Post,* May 29, 2003.

100. Quoted in Jim Lobe, "From Baghdad to Tehran," Foreign Policy in Focus, May 8, 2003, http://www.fpif.org/.

101. Ibid. (emphasis added).

102. Karl Vick, "Iranian Hard-Liners Block Reform Bill: Measure's Defeat Could be Turning Point in President's Struggle Against Clerics," *Washington Post*, June 4, 2003.

103. Ali Akbar Dareini, "Tehran Streets the Scene of More Violence by Militants," *Boston Globe*, June 14, 2003.

104. Bryan Bender, "Pressed, Iran Offers Nuclear Concessions," *Boston Globe*, October 22, 2003.

105. *Siasat-e-Rouz*, February 20, 2003.

106. Najmeh Bozorgmehr and Guy Dinmore, "Iranian Monarchist Exiles Seek Pact with US," *Financial Times*, May 9, 2003.

107. Marc Perelman, "New Front Sets Sights on Toppling Iran Regime," *Forward*, May 16, 2003.

108. Ibid.

109. Senator Brownback's full speech can be found on the Web site of the American Enterprise Institute, http://www.aei.org/newsID.17134/news_detail.asp.

110. National Iranian American Council, "Senator Brownback Announces Iran Democracy Act with Iranian Exiles," May 20, 2003, http://www.niacouncil.org/pressreleases/press087.asp. See also, Coalition for Democracy in Iran, "CDI Hails Introduction of Iran Democracy Act and Urges Swift Passage," May 20, 2003, http://www.c-d-i.org/pr/2003-05-20.shtml.

111. William O. Beeman, "The Man Behind 'Total War' in the Mideast," *San Francisco Chronicle*, May 14, 2003.

112. William O. Beeman, "Washington's Likely Plans to Restore the Iranian Monarch Are Foolhardy," *Daily Star (Beirut)*, June 2, 2003.

113. The information above on Sobhani is drawn primarily from Beeman (see n. 112).

114. Ibid.

115. See n. 99.

116. Cameron Kamran, "Iranians Don't Need American Kingmakers," *International Herald Tribune*, June 6, 2003.

117. Abraham Rabinovich, "Iran Air-Strike Plan Seen as Bluff," *Washington Times*, October 13, 2003.

INDEX

CONTRIBUTORS

Susan M. Akram is a clinical associate professor at the Boston University School of Law and a supervising attorney in the Boston University Civil Litigation Program. She holds an AB from the University of Michigan, a JD from Georgetown University, and the Diplome in Human Rights from the Institut International des Droits de l'Homme in Strasbourg, France. She was a Fulbright Scholar in Palestine in 1999–2000. Professor Akram served as lead counsel for the appeal to the Board of Immigration Appeals and co-counsel in the federal court litigation of the secret evidence case of Anwar Haddam. She is a member of a national network of attorneys representing noncitizens in secret evidence cases. Professor Akram has published extensively in the fields of US immigration, refugee, and human rights law.

Naseer Aruri is Chancellor Professor Emeritus of Political Science at the University of Massachusetts, Dartmouth. His latest books are *Dishonest Broker: The US Role in Israel and Palestine* (2003) and *The Obstruction of Peace: The U.S., Israel and the Palestinians* (1995). He is editor of *Palestinian Refugees: The Right of Return* (2001) and *Occupation: Israel over Palestine* (1989) and coeditor of *Revising Culture, Reinventing Peace: The Influence of Edward W. Said* (2001). He is a former member of the boards of Amnesty International USA and Human Rights Watch Middle East. He is currently president of the Trans-Arab Research Institute.

M. Cherif Bassiouni is a professor of law and president of the International Human Rights Law Institute at DePaul University.

Samih Farsoun is a professor of sociology at American University in Washington, DC. He is the secretary of the Board of Directors of the Trans-Arab Research Institute and of the Palestine Center in Washington, DC. He has published extensively in English and Arabic. His latest publications are *Palestine and the Palestinians* (1998) and a vastly expanded and updated edition of that book in Arabic (2003).

Elaine C. Hagopian is Professor Emerita of Sociology at Simmons College in Boston, a founder of the Trans-Arab Research Institute, and one of the organizers of the Right of Return Conference (2000). She was awarded two Fulbright-Hayes Faculty Research Grants for research in the Middle East and France (1971, 1983), served as Visiting Professor of Sociology and Anthropology at the American University of Beirut (1973–74), and was Distinguished Lecturer at the American University in Cairo (1974). She held appointments with UNICEF (United Arab Emirates) and UNESCO (Lebanon, Syria, Jordan, and Kuwait). Her publications include studies of Arab Americans; third world development; political sociology of the Middle East; and race, class, and gender.

Kevin R. Johnson is Associate Dean for Academic Affairs and a professor of law and Chicana/o studies at the University of California, Davis. He was the director of the Chicana/o Studies Program in 2000–01. He earned an AB from the University of California, Berkeley, and a JD from Harvard University.

Robert Morlino graduated from Columbia University's School of Journalism in 2002, where he served on the executive board of the Society of Professional Journalists chapter. He earned a BFA from New York University, where he was an editor and columnist at the *Washington Square News*. He has interned at the *Village Voice* newspaper in New York, covering city and state politics, and the cable news network MSNBC, covering the Middle East. He is currently a public policy researcher in Washington, D.C.

Nancy Murray is the director of the American Civil Liberties Union of Massachusetts' Bill of Rights Education Project, a program that she founded in 1987. Holding a BA from Harvard University and a PhB and PhD in Modern History from Oxford University, she has worked as a scholar, organizer, and human rights activist in the United Kingdom, Kenya, the United States, and the Middle East. She has written extensively on civil liberties, civil rights, and human rights issues and serves on the editorial committee of the journal *Race and Class*.

Will Youmans is a recent graduate of the Boalt Hall School of Law at the University of California, Berkeley. He received his BA in political science from the University of Michigan, Ann Arbor, where he won awards for outstanding student leadership as well as academic honors. His letters and writings have been published in the *Chronicle of Higher Education*, the *Philadelphia Inquirer*, the *San Francisco Chronicle*, and numerous university newspapers.

ABOUT PLUTO PRESS

Pluto Press specializes in challenging and innovative books that explore the most pressing political and social issues of our times. With a distinguished range of authors that includes Noam Chomsky, bell hooks, Ariel Dorfman, Howard Zinn, Frantz Fanon, Susan George, Greg Palast and William Rivers Pitt, our books offer radical insights into world affairs and provide an important critical counterpoint to the mainstream.

SEEDS OF HATE:
How America's Flawed Lebanon Policy Ignited the Jihad
Lawrence Pintak   0 7453 2043 0   September 2003
   "One of the most perceptive accounts of the nightmare in Lebanon."—*Washington Post*
   Former CBS journalist Lawrence Pintak traces the roots of the current "terror" crisis to America's involvement in Lebanon in the 1980s.

A WAR ON TERROR: Afghanistan and After
Paul Rogers   0 7453 2086 4   February 2004
   Moving from the war in Afghanistan and its aftermath to the Israeli/Palestinian conflict, the continuing development of al-Qaeda through to the war on Iraq, Rogers presents a uniquely cogent analysis of these rapid and traumatic events.

MODERN JIHAD: Tracing the Dollars Behind the Terror Networks
Loretta Napoleoni 0 7453 2117 8   September 2003
   "No punches are pulled in this alarming study of a $1.5 trillion terrorist economy that is as integral part of the Western economy as banking or big oil."—*Publishers Weekly*
   Presenting an astonishing array of evidence, taken from extensive research and interviews, the book is a fascinating account of the economic dynamics that lie at the heart of many of today's international problems.

THE ROAD TO AL-QAEDA: The Story of Bin Laden's Right-Hand Man
Montasser al-Zayyat   0 7453 2175 5   January 2004
   "[This] goes a long way towards explaining how complex things are...with an excellent introduction by Ibrahim M. Abu-Rabi describing the genesis of modern Islamist movements."—*Guardian*
   This controversial biography of al-Qaeda mastermind Ayman al-Zawahiri is already a bestseller across the Arab world. Written by an Egyptian human rights lawyer, it is the first explorations of the tensions between violent and non-violent factions in radical Islamist movements, from the perspective of an insider.

ABOUT HAYMARKET BOOKS

Haymarket Books is a non-profit, progressive book distributor and publisher, a project of the Center for Economic Research and Social Change.

We take inspiration and courage from our namesakes, the Haymarket Martyrs, who gave their lives fighting for a better world. Their struggle for the eight-hour day in 1886, which gave us May Day, the international workers' holiday, reminds workers around the world that ordinary people can organize and struggle for their own liberation. These struggles continue today in every corner of the globe—struggles against oppression, exploitation, hunger and poverty.

Visit our online bookstore at www.haymarketbooks.org.

THE STRUGGLE FOR PALESTINE
Lance Selfa, ed.   1 931859 00 0   2002
    In this important collection of essays, leading international solidarity activists offer insight into the ongoing struggle for Palestinian freedom and for justice in the Middle East.

THE FORGING OF THE AMERICAN EMPIRE
Sidney Lens   0 745321 00 3   2002
    This is the story of a nation—the United States—that has conducted more than 160 wars and other military ventures while insisting that it loves peace. In the process, the U.S. has forged a world empire while maintaining its innocence of imperialistic designs.

THE AMERICAN SOCIALIST MOVEMENT: 1897–1912
Ira Kipnis   1 931859 12 4   2004
    The American Socialist Party, at the height of its power, had more than a 150,000 members and won almost a million votes for its presidential candidate. Few books have more to offer to the student of the movement than this one.

THE CASE FOR SOCIALISM
Alan Maass   1 931859 09 4   2004
    "[Maass'] book charts a game plan for realistic radicals, who haven't given up hope for making revolutionary changes in a society that finds itself in the grip of a remorseless political entropy. Take cheer: History isn't over. In fact, it's hardly even begun for us. Read Maass. Then go out and make some." —Jeffrey St. Clair, coeditor of *CounterPunch*